Praise for

"There's so much alive and kicking in *Moving Targets* that most readers will find something in which to take delight. . . . *Moving Targets* is a surprise box. You don't know what you're going to get until you open it. But what you can count on from any Atwoodian performance is that you get humour . . . you get bite . . . you get lines of perfect pitch and tone."

— *Globe and Mail*

"Of all the books I have devoured over the past year, Margaret Atwood's *Moving Targets* is the most likely to tempt me into a second read. . . . Those who fear the Atwood arrow (with good reason), should regard *Moving Targets* as a warning that more, much more, is sure to come. . . . *Moving Targets* is a full and nourishing read, a multi-course meal of widely varied dishes from a brilliant literary chef, who, had she chosen the profession of law would have been a terror in the courtroom."

— *Gazette* (Montreal)

"The straightforward, clear writing makes reading even the pieces you don't completely agree with a pleasure, albeit in these cases a slightly guilty one. . . . I highly recommend this collection to anyone interested in books, reading, speculative fiction, hardboiled mysteries or the state of CanLit over the last 40-odd years. *Moving Targets* has something for almost every palate."

— *Hamilton Spectator*

"*Moving Targets* is a true gift; one that pays tribute to great contemporary authors, serves as a piece of nostalgia for the baby-boom generation, and is unabashedly Canadian in every sense of the word — humble, intelligent, and reflective."

— *Metro* (Toronto)

". . . the range of [Atwood's] interests and depth of her knowledge are truly impressive. She seems incapable of writing a thoughtless phrase or a purposeless sentence."

— *Georgia Straight* (Vancouver)

"Atwood is luminous in her own right, shedding so much light on the literary age and culture in which she lives. . . . Her style in these reviews is enough to make another review weep. She cuts incisively to the bones of the matter, drawing on a wealth of previous acquaintance not only with the works of the author at hand, but also with related books. . . . Reviewing this book, full of its own masterly executed critiques, is rather like instructing Wayne Gretzky in stick handling. . . . I can only imagine how delighted her long-time fans will be with this further glimpse into the writer as craftsman, evaluator, and champion."

— *New Brunswick Reader*

"What makes this book so easy and enjoyable to read . . . is the overall tone of casual intimacy. [Atwood] spills a few beans, plunges in with opinions that she feels no need to justify, adopts a tone that is both world-weary and unguarded, and assumes that if you don't like what she has to say, too bad. . . . Atwood is a genuinely enthusiastic, professionally trained reader, and a journeyman writer who can tackle anything from a book on recycling to a collection of anecdotes on mortification. . . . The result is refreshingly honest."

— *Telegram* (St. John's)

"Her accounts of the genesis of some of her best loved novels will give devotees of her work a fascinating glimpse behind the scenes of the museum."

— *Sunday Tribune* (UK)

"Atwood is an incisive critic. . . . her writing remains a model of clarity and lucidity, which more literary scholars would do well to emulate."

— *The Record* (Kitchener-Waterloo)

". . . her voice rings out clear and true. . . . heartfelt, passionate and personal pleas for a different way of looking at the world."

— *Guardian Weekly* (UK)

"Atwood's mind is defined by curiosity and acuteness. Her interests are many and varied and her take on events of the day, even if one is not always in agreement, is as interesting as it is provoking. Her intelligent feistiness makes *Moving Targets* a must-have sequel to *Second Words*."

— *London Free Press*

"It should go without saying that a collection of Margaret Atwood's essays is a must-read for her fans. It should also go without saying that it is a must-read for anyone with a serious interest in Canadian letters. But it's being said anyhow . . . Atwood demonstrates not only her skill as a writer, but also her skill as a reader. To be a good novelist one need only write well; to be a good essayist, one must read well too. . . . At her best, Atwood is wry, dry and understated. . . . As I read [*Moving Targets*], I found myself berating it sometimes, nodding gravely at other times, and scribbling furiously the whole time. It is an engaging book of essays — and that's the very best kind."

— *Fast Forward Weekly* (Calgary)

"This collection of essays, journalism and writerly bric-a-brac from Canada's pre-eminent novelist is a literary garage-saler's delight. When Atwood sets pen to paper, you never know what you might find. . . . These pieces display her formidable erudition and her wide experience in many forms, from poetry and literary criticism to political commentary and travel writing. . . . There's a reason garage sales never go out of business."

— *Winnipeg Free Press*

MOVING TARGETS

Also by Margaret Atwood

FICTION

The Edible Woman (1969)
Surfacing (1972)
Lady Oracle (1976)
Dancing Girls (1977)
Life Before Man (1979)
Bodily Harm (1981)
Murder in the Dark (1983)
Bluebeard's Egg (1983)
The Handmaid's Tale (1985)
Cat's Eye (1988)
Wilderness Tips (1991)
Good Bones (1992)
The Robber Bride (1993)
Alias Grace (1996)
The Blind Assassin (2000)
Good Bones and Simple Murders (2001)
Oryx and Crake (2003)

POETRY

Double Persephone (1961)
The Circle Game (1966)
The Animals in That Country (1968)
The Journals of Susanna Moodie (1970)
Procedures for Underground (1970)
Power Politics (1971)
You Are Happy (1974)
Selected Poems (1976)
Two-Headed Poems (1978)
True Stories (1981)
Interlunar (1984)
*Selected Poems II: Poems Selected
and New, 1976–1986* (1986)
Morning in the Burned House (1995)

NONFICTION

*Survival: A Thematic Guide to
Canadian Literature* (1972)
Days of the Rebels 1815–1840 (1977)
*Second Words: Selected Critical Prose
1960–1982* (1982)
*Strange Things: The Malevolent North
in Canadian Literature* (1996)
Two Solicitudes: Conversations
[with Victor-Lévy Beaulieu] (1998)
*Negotiating with the Dead:
A Writer on Writing* (2002)

FOR CHILDREN

Up in the Tree (1978)
Anna's Pet
[with Joyce Barkhouse] (1980)
For the Birds (1990)
*Princess Prunella and the
Purple Peanut* (1995)
*Rude Ramsay and the
Roaring Radishes* (2003)
*Bashful Bob and
Doleful Dorinda* (2004)

MOVING TARGETS

WRITING WITH INTENT
1982–2004

MARGARET ATWOOD

ANANSI

First published in hardcover in 2004 by House of Anansi Press Inc.

This edition published in 2005 by
House of Anansi Press Inc.
110 Spadina Avenue, Suite 801
Toronto, ON, M5V 2K4
Tel. 416-363-4343
Fax 416-363-1017
www.anansi.ca

Distributed in Canada by
HarperCollins Canada Ltd.
1995 Markham Road
Scarborough, ON, M1B 5M8
Toll free tel. 1-800-387-0117

House of Anansi Press is committed to protecting our natural environment. As part
of our efforts, this book is printed on New Leaf EcoBook 100 paper: it contains
100% post-consumer recycled fibres, is acid-free, and is processed chlorine-free.

09 08 07 06 05   1 2 3 4 5

LIBRARY AND ARCHIVES CANADA CATALOGUING IN PUBLICATION DATA

Atwood, Margaret, 1939–
Moving targets : writing with intent, 1982–2004 / Margaret Atwood.

Includes index.
ISBN 0-88784-177-5 (bound). — ISBN 0-88784-735-8 (pbk.)

1. Canadian literature — History and criticism. 2. Literature — History and criticism.
I. Title.

PS8501.T86A16 2004   C810.9'971   C2004-903096-5

Cover and text design: Bill Douglas at The Bang
Cover photograph: Getty Images/Taxi
Typesetting: Brian Panhuyzen

Canada Council
for the Arts

Conseil des Arts
du Canada

ONTARIO ARTS COUNCIL
CONSEIL DES ARTS DE L'ONTARIO

We acknowledge for their financial support of our publishing program
the Canada Council for the Arts, the Ontario Arts Council, and the Government of Canada
through the Book Publishing Industry Development Program (BPIDP).

Printed and bound in Canada

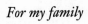

For my family

CONTENTS

Introduction   *1*

PART I: 1982–1989

1982–1989   *9*

1   Dennis Revisited   *13*

2   Wondering What It's Like to Be a Woman: *The Witches of Eastwick*, by John Updike   *17*

3   The Sorcerer as Apprentice: *Difficult Loves*, by Italo Calvino   *23*

4   Margaret Atwood Remembers Marian Engel   *26*

5   Introduction to *Roughing It in the Bush*, by Susanna Moodie   *34*

6   True North   *43*

7   Haunted by Their Nightmares: *Beloved*, by Toni Morrison   *59*

8   Afterword to *A Jest of God*, by Margaret Laurence   *65*

9   Preface to *The Canadian Green Consumer Guide*   *70*

10   Great Aunts   *72*

11   Introduction: Reading Blind, *The Best American Short Stories*   *85*

12   The Public Woman as Honorary Man: *The Warrior Queens*, by Antonia Fraser   *99*

13   Writing Utopia   *102*

PART II: 1990–2000

1990–2000   *115*

14 A Double-Bladed Knife: Subversive Laughter in Two Stories
    by Thomas King   *119*

15 Nine Beginnings   *130*

16 A Slave to His Own Liberation: *The General in His Labyrinth*,
    by Gabriel García Márquez   *137*

17 Afterword to *Anne of Green Gables*,
    by Lucy Maud Montgomery   *141*

18 Introduction: The Early Years, *The Poetry of Gwendolyn
    MacEwen*   *147*

19 Why I Love *The Night of the Hunter*   *152*

20 Spotty-Handed Villainesses: Problems of Female Bad
    Behaviour in the Creation of Literature   *157*

21 The Grunge Look   *173*

22 Not So Grimm: The Staying Power of Fairy Tales:
    From the Beast to the Blonde: On Fairy Tales and Their Tellers,
    by Marina Warner   *183*

23 A Rich Dessert from a Saucy Carter: *Burning Your Boats:
    The Collected Short Stories*, by Angela Carter   *188*

24 *An Experiment in Love*, by Hilary Mantel   *191*

25 In Search of *Alias Grace*: On Writing Canadian Historical
    Fiction   *196*

26 Masterpiece Theatre: *Trickster Makes This World: Mischief,
    Myth and Art* and *The Gift: Imagination and the Erotic Life
    of Property*, by Lewis Hyde   *218*

27 The Awkward Sublime   *224*

PART III: 2001–2004

2001–2004   *229*

28   Mordecai Richler: 1931–2001: Diogenes of Montreal   *232*

29   Introduction to *She*, by H. Rider Haggard   *234*

30   When Afghanistan Was at Peace   *242*

31   Mystery Man: Some Clues to Dashiell Hammett   *245*

32   Of Myths and Men: *Atanarjuat: The Fast Runner*   *259*

33   Cops and Robbers: *Tishomingo Blues*,
     by Elmore Leonard   *263*

34   Tiff and the Animals   *275*

35   The Indelible Woman: *To the Lighthouse*,
     by Virginia Woolf   *278*

36   The Queen of Quinkdom: *The Birthday of the World
     and Other Stories*, by Ursula K. Le Guin   *281*

37   Introduction to *Ground Works*, edited by Christian Bök   *293*

38   The Wrong Box: Matt Cohen, Fabulism,
     and Critical Taxonomy   *300*

39   Introduction to *Doctor Glas*, by Hjalmar Söderberg   *315*

40   Napoleon's Two Biggest Mistakes   *320*

41   Letter to America   *324*

42   Writing *Oryx and Crake*   *328*

43   George Orwell: Some Personal Connections   *331*

44   Arguing Against Ice Cream: *Enough: Staying Human in an
     Engineered Age*, by Bill McKibben   *339*

45   Foreword: Victory Gardens, *A Breath of Fresh Air*,
     by Elise Houghton   *351*

46 Carol Shields, Who Died Last Week, Wrote Books
   That Were Full of Delights *360*

47 Resisting the Veil: Reports from a Revolution *364*

48 Introduction to *The Complete Stories*, Volume 4,
   by Morley Callaghan *372*

49 He Springs Eternal: *Hope Dies Last: Keeping the Faith in
   Difficult Times*, by Studs Terkel *382*

50 To Beechy Island *395*

51 Mortification *406*

Acknowledgements *411*

Index *415*

INTRODUCTION

MOVING TARGETS is a companion volume to *Second Words*, the selection of my essays and forays into journalism published in 1982. In 1982 I was forty-two; I thought of myself as quite elderly. It's now twenty-two years later and I still think that, though — paradoxically — less frequently. The big difference between past and present is that I now know more of the plot. I suspect how all this is going to turn out for me in the long run, but if time runs true to form there are still some surprises left.

Like *Second Words*, *Moving Targets* consists of occasional pieces; that is, pieces written for specific occasions. The occasions in *Second Words* ranged from the appearance of a book by someone else, germinating — on my part — a review, to a public gathering — thus giving rise to a speech — to an anthology or Festschrift, for which some sort of focused observation was requested. This pattern continues in *Moving Targets*. Occasionally these essays have been in-aid-of: they've been fundraisers, they've been worthy-cause bandages, they've been dragon-slayings or Blue Fairy wand-wavings. Having had my character ruined by the Brownies and the Girl Guides in my youth, I have a difficult time resisting such lend-a-hand appeals.

A Brownie always gives in to the older folk, a Brownie never gives in to herself; but inevitably there comes a day when you gaze into the magic mirror and realize that, *faute de mieux*, you *are* the older folk, since most of the legitimate claimants to that title have died off. It's no coincidence that there was only one obituary-like piece in *Second Words*, but there are — sadly — rather more of them in *Moving Targets*.

Being the older folks has its upside, however. You're no longer too anxious about ruining your reputation, because it's far too late for that. Nor do you worry much about antagonizing this or that reviewer: everything bad that can be said about you has already been said, more than once. You know that fame is a mixed blessing, because for every statue of a worthy notable such as you are said to have become, there are at least a hundred pigeons roosting on its head. You know, too, that from the point of view of the younger generations — and how many of these younger generations there seem to be! — you're sort of dead already, because isn't everyone whose work is studied in high school sort of dead?

But some latitude may be accorded you as well: the kind of thing that might have got you called a mean, dangerous, radical red-toothed bitch when you were thirty may now be treated as the scatterbrained utterance of a cute old biddy. I'm not quite there yet, but I can see the turnoff.

What else has changed? When I began reviewing, it was 1960, I was still at university, and I wrote for the college magazine. I moved on to small literary reviews — I wrote a lot about poetry then — and eventually I found myself appearing in larger places such as the *Globe and Mail*, the *New York Times*, and the *Washington Post*. This is where *Second Words* ended: it was 1982, the women's movement had run through its exciting but exhausting 1970s period and was taking a breather, Canadian cultural nationalism appeared to have achieved many of its goals, *post-modernism* and *deconstruction* were the critical catchphrases of the day, the era of dot-coms was almost upon us, few people as yet had either fax machines or personal computers, and there were no cellphones. I was the mother of a six-year-old, with the laundry to show for it. I'd published five novels and a number of books of poetry, but was not exactly world-famous. I was however what Mordecai Richler used to call "world-famous in Canada," and that status, dubious though it was, attracted a certain amount of heat and lightning.

What hasn't changed? Looking back over this gathering of pages, I see that my interests have remained fairly constant, although I like to pretend their scope has broadened somewhat. Some of my earlier concerns — my environmental fretting, for example — were considered lunatic-fringe when I first voiced them, but have since moved to the centre of the stage. I dislike advocacy writing — it's not fun, because the issues that generate it are not fun — but I feel compelled to do a certain amount of it anyway. The effects are not always pleasant, since what may be common sense to one person is annoying polemic to another.

I still find it hard to make speeches; I still leave the writing of them to the last minute; I still feel I'm doing a grade two show-and-tell. I'm haunted by a metaphor from Edith Wharton's story "The Pelican," in which a public lecturer's talk is compared to the trick by which a magician produces reams and reams of blank white paper out of his mouth. I still find book reviewing a problem: it's so much like homework, and it forces me to have opinions instead of the Negative Capability that is so much more soothing to the digestion. I do it anyway, because those who are reviewed must review in their turn or the principle of reciprocity fails.

There's another reason, however: reviewing the work of others forces you to examine your own ethical and aesthetic tastes. What do we mean by "good" in a book? What qualities do we consider "bad," and why? Aren't there in fact two kinds of reviews, derived from two different ancestries? There's the newspaper review, which descends from gossip around the village well (loved her, hated him, she

3

shouldn't wear red but what can you expect with a family like hers, and did you get a load of the shoes?). And then there's the "academic" review, which descends from Biblical exegesis and other traditions that went in for the minute examination of sacred texts. This sort of analysis still secretly believes that some texts are more sacred than others, and that the application of a magnifying glass or some lemon juice or flames will reveal hidden meanings. I've written both kinds.

I still won't review a book I don't like, although to do so would doubtless be amusing for the Ms. Hyde side of me and entertaining for the more malicious class of reader. But either the book is really bad, in which case no one should review it, or it's good but not my cup of tea, in which case someone else should review it. It's a great luxury not to be a professional full-time reviewer: I'm at liberty to close books that don't seize hold of me. Over the years, history — military history included — has become more interesting to me; so has biography. As for fiction, some of my less highfalutin' reading preferences (crime writing, science fiction) have come out of the closet.

Speaking of these, it's as well to mention a pattern that recurs in these pages. As one reader of this manuscript has pointed out, I have a habit of kicking off my discussion of a book or author or group of books by saying that I read it (or him, or her, or them) in the cellar when I was growing up; or that I came across them in the bookcase at home; or that I found them at the cottage; or that I took them out from the library. If these statements were metaphors, I'd excise all of them except one; but they are simply snippets of my reading history. My justification for mentioning where and when I first read a book is that I think the impression a book makes on you is often tied to your age and circumstances at the time you read it, and your fondness for books you loved when young continues on with you through life.

Second Words was divided into three sections, and I've kept to the same chronological plan in *Moving Targets*. Part One covers the 1980s, during which I wrote and published *The Handmaid's Tale*, the novel of mine that is most likely to turn up on freshman reading lists. This was the period during which I graduated from being world-famous in Canada to being world-famous, sort of, in the way that writers are. (We are not talking the Rolling Stones here.) It ends with 1989, the year the Berlin Wall came down. Part Two collects pieces from the 1990s, culminating in 2000, when the twenty-first century began. Part Three runs from 2001 — the year of the notorious 9/11 disaster — to the present time. Not surprisingly, I found myself writing more about political issues during this last period than I had done for some time.

Why *Moving Targets*? As a title, that is. There are two meanings in the word *moving*, and one of them has to do with emotion: a moving target is one that moves you. Language cannot be separated from feeling, because language is itself a record of how we as human beings have responded to the world, not only intellectually but with what used to be called the heart. I can't write about subjects for which I feel nothing. Thus *moving*.

The second meaning is the more obvious one: moving targets move. These occasional pieces take aim, but the targets they're aiming at are far from stationary. Instead they're like the mechanical ducks in the amusement park, visible to the naked eye but often hard to hit. They're embedded in time, they flow along with it, they're changed by it, and anything said about them — like anything said about the shape of an amoeba — can only be approximate. Looking back at some of these essays — *essay*, in the sense of *attempt* — I feel I might write them in another way if I were writing them today. But I would not of course be writing them today, because the targets now are different.

Think of the track in the air left by an arrow in flight. *Trajectory* is a word that might describe such a thing: "the path of any body moving under the action of given forces."

Here, then, is *Moving Targets*: a collection of trajectories.

— Margaret Atwood 2004

PART I
1982–1989

1982–1989

THE EIGHT YEARS between 1982 and 1989 were energetic ones for me, and proved to be momentous for the world. At their beginning, the Soviet Union seemed firmly in place, due to last for a long while yet. But it had already been sucked into a costly and debilitating war in Afghanistan, and in 1989 the Berlin Wall would come tumbling down. It's amazing how quickly certain kinds of power structures crumble once the cornerstone falls out. But in 1982, nobody foresaw this outcome.

I began the period quietly enough. I was trying, unsuccessfully and for the second time, to write the book that was — much later — to become *Cat's Eye*, and I was ruminating about *The Handmaid's Tale*, although I was avoiding this second book as much as possible: it seemed too hopeless a task, and too deeply weird a concept.

Our family was living in Toronto's Chinatown, in a row house that had been modernized by the removal of many of its inner doors. I couldn't write there because it was too noisy, so I would bicycle westward to the Portuguese district, where I wrote on the third floor of another row house. I'd just finished editing *The New Oxford Book of Canadian Verse in English*, which had been spread out all over the same third floor. That had been a retrospective activity, and so was the first piece in *Moving Targets*. It's a Festschrift tribute to Dennis Lee, whom I'd first met and collaborated with at the beginning of my writing life.

In the autumn of 1983 I went with my immediate family to England, where we rented a Norfolk manse said to be haunted by nuns in the parlour, a jolly cavalier in the dining room, and a headless woman in the kitchen. None of these was seen by us, though a jolly cavalier did stray in from the neighbouring pub, looking for the washroom. The phone was a pay phone outside the house, in a booth also used for storing potatoes, and I would clamber over and through them to deal with the editing of — for instance — the Updike review that appears here.

I wrote in a separate space — a fisherman's cottage turned vacation home — where I struggled with the Aga heater as well as with the novel I'd started. I got my first case of chilblains doing this, but had to give up on the novel when I found myself snarled up in the time sequence, with no way out.

Right after that we went to West Berlin, where, in 1984, I began *The Handmaid's Tale*. We made some side visits, to Poland, East Germany, and Czechoslovakia, which doubtless contributed to the atmosphere of the book: totalitarian dictatorships, however different the costumes, share the same climate of fear and silence.

I finished the book in the spring of 1985, where I was Visiting Chair at the University of Alabama in Tuscaloosa. It was the last book I wrote on an electric typewriter. I faxed the chapters as they were finished to my typist in Toronto, to be retyped properly, and I recall being amazed by the magic of instant transmission. The book came out in Canada in 1985 and in England and the United States in 1986, and was shortlisted for the Booker Prize, among other forms of uproar. I bought a black outfit for the dinner.

We spent part of 1987 in Australia, where I was finally able to come to grips with *Cat's Eye*. The snowiest scenes in the book were written during balmy spring days in Sydney, with cuckaburras yelling for hamburger on the back porch. The book was published in 1988 in Canada and the United States and in England in 1989, where it too was shortlisted for the Booker Prize. I had to buy another black outfit. Shortly afterwards, the fatwa was proclaimed against Salman Rushdie. Who knew that this was the first straw in what was to become not only a wind, but a hurricane?

All this time *The Handmaid's Tale* had been making its progress through the intestinal workings of the film industry. It finally emerged in finished form, scripted by Harold Pinter and directed by Volker Schlöndorff. The film premiered in the two Berlins in 1989, just as the Wall had fallen: you could buy pieces of it, with the coloured ones being more expensive. I attended the film festivities. There were the same kinds of East German border guards who had been so cold in 1984, but now they were grinning and exchanging cigars with tourists. The East Berlin audience was the more receptive to the film. "This was our life," one woman told me quietly.

How euphoric we felt, for a short time, in 1989. How dazed by the spectacle of the impossible made real. How wrong we were about the brave new world we were about to enter.

DENNIS REVISITED

WHEN I WAS ASKED to write a small piece on Dennis Lee, I began by counting up the number of years I've known him. It came as a slight shock to discover that it was over twenty. I first met him, ludicrously enough, at a Freshman Mixer at Victoria College, University of Toronto, in the fall of 1957. I was somewhat in awe of him, since, like everyone else, I knew he'd won the Prince of Wales Scholarship for the highest grade thirteen marks in the province of Ontario; but nevertheless there I was, shuffling around the floor with him, while he explained that he was going to be a United Church minister. I, on the other hand, was already doggedly set on being a writer, though I had scant ideas about how this was to be accomplished. At that time I thought, in my intolerant undergraduate way, that poetry and religion — especially the religion of the United Church — did not mix, which brought us to the end of the dance.

Then there was a gap, as Dennis was in mainstream English and I had digressed into Philosophy and English, foolishly thinking that my mind would thereby be broadened. But logic and poetry did not mix either, and in second year I switched back, having missed Bibliography forever. Some time later, Dennis and I became friends and collaborators. I suppose it was inevitable. Art of any kind, in the late 1950s, in

Toronto, at Victoria College, was not exactly a hot topic, and those of us who dared to risk incurring the pejorative label "arty" practised herding and defensive dressing. We worked on *Acta Victoriana*, the literary magazine; we wrote on, and acted in, the yearly satirical revue. At one point, Dennis and I invented a pseudonym for literary parodies, which combined both our names and which lingered on after our respective departures: Shakesbeat Latweed. "Shakesbeat," because the first thing we wrote was a poem called "Sprattire," variations on the first four lines of "Jack Spratt," as if by various luminaries, from Shakespeare to a Beat poet. According to my mother, we laughed a lot while writing it. Dennis, then as now, had a faintly outrageous sense of humour concealed beneath his habitually worried look.

Dennis took fourth year off and went to Germany, thus enabling me to get a Woodrow Wilson fellowship (if he'd been there, *he'd* have got it). After that I was away from Toronto for the next ten years. So it must have been by letter, or during one of my infrequent visits back (I seem to remember Hart House theatre, at intermission; but intermission of what?) that he contacted me about the House of Anansi Press. Some people were starting a publishing house, he said, and they wanted to reprint my book of poems, *The Circle Game*, which had won the Governor General's Award that year but was out of print. He said they wanted to do two thousand copies. I thought they were crazy. I also thought the idea of a publishing house was a little crazy too; it was still only 1967. But by this time both Dennis and I were cultural nationalists of a sort, though we'd come to it separately. We were both aware that the established publishing houses had been timorous about new writing, particularly in prose fiction, though also to a certain extent in poetry. The dreaded "colonial mentality" was not yet a catchphrase but it was on its way. The first four Anansi authors got small grants from the Canada Council, most of which we bumped back into the company. It amazes me now to realize how little money it took to start Anansi. But it took a lot more blood and guts, much of both Dennis's.

During the late 1960s — the period of Anansi's rapid growth and the establishment of Dennis's reputation as an editor — I was in Boston, then Montreal, then Edmonton, so was in touch only by letter. I worked in various ways on three Anansi books with Dennis: George Bowering's *The Gangs of Kosmos*, bill bissett's *nobody owns th earth*, and, less intensively, Michael Ondaatje's *The Collected Works of Billy the Kid*. When my own book, *Power Politics*, was ready to be seen, I felt it was an Anansi book and took it to Dennis. I returned from England in 1971, joined Anansi's board, and worked with various writers (sometimes with Dennis, sometimes alone), including Paulette Jiles, Eli Mandel, Terrence Heath, P. K. Page, John Thompson, and Patrick Lane; and Dennis himself, with whom I edited the second edition of *Civil Elegies*. Our most engrossing collaboration at that time, however, was his editing of my critical work *Survival*. Dennis was indispensable for the book, and in top editorial form: fast, incisive, full of helpful suggestions, and, by the end, just as exhausted as I was.

Small publishing is an energy drainer, as anyone who has done it will testify. By 1973 Dennis was withdrawing more and more from Anansi, and shortly thereafter so was I.

I think it was in the summer of 1974 that Dennis read the first draft of *Lady Oracle* for me, with the usual helpful results. The editorial conference took place on the top of a rail fence, which was typical of Dennis as an editor. The process was never what you would call formal. Given the choice of a dining-room table or a kitchen full of dirty dishes and chicken carcasses and cat litter boxes, Dennis would go for the kitchen every time.

This is as good a place as any to throw in my two cents' worth about Dennis-as-editor. The reputation is entirely deserved. When he's "on," he can give another writer not only generous moral support but also an insightful, clear view of where a given book is trying to go. This is usually conveyed not in conversation alone but in pages and pages of single-spaced, detailed, and amended notes. I have never worked with an editor who delivers so much in such a condensed mode. His willingness to enter so fully into a book's sources of energy make him more than usually vulnerable to invasion by the author's psyche and to the demands of the author's clamorous ego. At one stage of his life he was acting not only as surrogate midwife but as surrogate shrink and confessor to far too many people. It's no wonder that he's fled from the editing process from time to time. It's no wonder too that he's sometimes become bored or impatient with the Super-editor uniform. He is also a writer, and both his own time and the attention and acclaim of others has often gone to the editing when it could or should have gone to the writing. It's his writing that's of primary importance for Dennis. It's also, I think, the hardest thing to talk to him about and the hardest thing for him to do.

When I try to picture Dennis to myself, it's the anxious wrinkles on his forehead that appear first, like the Cheshire Cat's grin. Next comes the pipe, eternally puffing, or sometimes a cigar. Then the rest of him appears, on the run, rumpled, harassed by invisible demons, replete with subterranean energy, slightly abstracted, sometimes perplexed, in spite of it all well-meaning, kindly in an embarrassed and hesitant way; and, when he's talking to you about something important, working very hard not only at but towards saying exactly what he wants to say, which is usually complex. Sometimes Dennis is less complex when he's had a few drinks and is playing the piano, for instance, or when he's making a terrible pun. This maniacal side of Dennis is most visible in *Alligator Pie* and its sequels, and probably keeps him sane; but friendly old Uncle Dennis is of course not the whole story.

I don't have the whole story, and it's clear to me after twenty-odd years that I'm not likely ever to have it. Dennis isn't what you'd call an easily accessible person. In any case, the whole story isn't finished yet. There's more to come.

2

WONDERING WHAT IT'S LIKE
TO BE A WOMAN

THE WITCHES OF EASTWICK
BY JOHN UPDIKE

THE WITCHES OF EASTWICK is John Updike's first novel since the much-celebrated *Rabbit Is Rich*, and a strange and marvellous organism it proves to be. Like his third novel, *The Centaur*, it is a departure from baroque realism. This time, too, Mr. Updike transposes mythology into the minor keys of small-town America, but this time he pulls it off, possibly because, like Shakespeare and Robert Louis Stevenson before him, he finds wickedness and mischief more engrossing as subjects than goodness and wisdom.

Mr. Updike's titles are often quite literal, and *The Witches of Eastwick* is just what it says. It's indeed about witches, real ones, who can fly through the air, levitate, hex people, and make love charms that work, and they live in a town called Eastwick. It's Eastwick rather than Westwick, since, as we all know, it's the east wind that blows no good. Eastwick purports to be in Rhode Island because, as the book itself points out, Rhode Island was the place of exile for Anne Hutchinson, the Puritan foremother who was kicked out of the Massachusetts Bay colony by the forefathers for female insubordination, a quality these witches have in surplus.

These are not 1980s Womanpower witches. They aren't at all interested in healing the earth, communing with the Great Goddess, or gaining Power-within (as opposed to Power-over). These are *bad* witches, and Power-within, as far as they are concerned, is no good at all unless you can zap somebody with it. They are spiritual descendants of the seventeenth-century New England strain and go in for sabbats, sticking pins in wax images, kissing the Devil's backside, and phallus worship; this latter though — since it is Updike — is qualified worship. The Great Goddess is present only in the form of Nature itself, or, in this book, Nature herself, with which they, both as women and as witches, are supposed to have special affinities. Nature, however, is far from Wordsworth's big motherly breast. She, or it, is red in tooth, claw, and cancer cell, at best lovely and cruel, at worse merely cruel. "Nature kills constantly, and we call her beautiful."

How did these middle-class, small-town, otherwise ordinary women get their witchy powers? Simple. They became husbandless. All three are divorcées and embodiments of what American small-town society tends to think about divorcées. Whether you leave your husband or are left "doesn't make any difference," which will be news to many abandoned women stuck with full child support. Divorced then, and, with the images of their former husbands shrunk and dried and stored away in their minds and kitchens and cellars, they are free to be themselves, an activity Mr. Updike regards with some misgivings, as he regards most catchwords and psychofads.

Being yourself involves artistic activity, albeit of minor kinds. Lexa makes ceramic earthmothers, which are sold in the local crafts store, Jane plays the cello, and Sukie writes, badly, a gossip column for the weekly paper, her participles dangling like earrings. All three are dabblers, but their "creativity" is seen in the same light as that of other, more accomplished female artists. The townspeople of Eastwick, who act as a collective chorus, credit them with "a certain distinction, an inner boiling such as had in other cloistral towns produced Emily Dickinson's verses and Emily Brontë's inspired novel."

It's doubtful, however, that either of the Emilys went in for the sexual loop-the-loops indulged in by these three weird sisters. Sisters in more senses than one because the novel is cunningly set at a precise moment in America's recent history. The women's movement has been around just long enough for some of its phrases to have seeped from New York to the outer darkness of provincial towns like Eastwick, and the witches toss around words like "chauvinist" in light social repartee. In the public, male world, which is offstage, the Vietnam War goes on, watched by the witches' children on their television sets, and the antiwar activists are making bombs in cellars.

The witches don't busy themselves with "causes," however. At first, they are merely restless and bored; they amuse themselves with spiteful gossip, playing mischievous tricks and seducing unhappily married men, which Eastwick supplies in strength; for if the witches are bad, the wives are worse, and the men are eviscerated. "Marriage," one of the husbands thinks, "is like two people locked up with one lesson to read, over and over, until the words become madness."

But enter the Devil, the world's best remedy for women's boredom, in the form of the dark, not very handsome but definitely mysterious stranger Darryl Van Horne, who collects pop art and has an obvious name. Now mischief turns to *maleficio*, real evil occurs and people die, because Van Horne's horn becomes a bone of contention — nothing like not enough men to go around to get the witches' cauldrons bubbling. And when Van Horne is snatched into marriage by a newcomer witchlet, the eye of newt comes out in earnest.

This may sound like an unpromising framework for a serious novelist. Has Mr. Updike entered second childhood and reverted to Rosemary's babyland? I don't think so. For one thing, *The Witches of Eastwick* is too well done. Like Van Horne, Mr. Updike has always wondered what it would be like to be a woman, and his witches give him a lot of scope for this fantasy. Lexa in particular, who is the oldest, the plumpest, the kindest, and the closest to Nature, is a fitting vehicle for some of his most breathtaking similes. In line of descent, he is perhaps closer than any other living American writer to the Puritan view of Nature as a lexicon written by God, but in hieroglyphs, so that unending translation is needed. Mr. Updike's prose, here more than ever, is a welter of suggestive metaphors and cross-references, which constantly point toward a meaning constantly evasive.

His version of witchcraft is closely tied to both carnality and mortality. Magic is hope in the face of inevitable decay. The houses and the furniture moulder, and so do the people. The portrait of Felicia Gabriel, victim wife and degenerate after-image of the one-time "peppy" American cheerleading sweetheart, is gruesomely convincing. Bodies are described in loving detail, down to the last tuft, wart, wrinkle, and bit of food stuck in the teeth. No one is better than Mr. Updike at conveying the sadness of the sexual, the melancholy of motel affairs — "amiable human awkwardness," Lexa calls it. This is a book that redefines magic realism.

There's room too for bravura writing. The widdershins dance, portrayed as a tennis game in which the ball turns into a bat, followed by the sabbat as a hot-tub-and-pot session, is particularly fetching. Students of traditional Devil-lore will have as much fun with these transpositions as Mr. Updike had. Van Horne, for instance, is part Mephistopheles, offering Faustian pacts and lusting for souls, part alchemist-chemist, and part Miltonic Satan, hollow at the core; but he's also a shambling klutz whose favourite comic book is — what else? — *Captain Marvel.*

Much of *The Witches of Eastwick* is satire, some of it literary playfulness and some plain bitchery. It could be that any attempt to analyze further would be like taking an elephant gun to a puff pastry: An Updike should not mean but be. But again, I don't think so. What a culture has to say about witchcraft, whether in jest or in earnest, has a lot to do with its views of sexuality and power, and especially with the apportioning of powers between the sexes. The witches were burned not because they were pitied but because they were feared.

Cotton Mather and Nathaniel Hawthorne aside, the great American witchcraft classic is *The Wizard of Oz*, and Mr. Updike's book reads like a rewrite. In the original, a good little girl and her familiar, accompanied by three amputated males, one sans brain, one sans heart, and one sans guts, go seeking a wizard who turns out to be a charlatan. The witches in Oz really have superhuman powers, but the male figures do not. Mr. Updike's Land of Oz is the real America, but the men in it need a lot more than self-confidence; there's no Glinda the Good, and the Dorothy-like ingenue is a "wimp" who gets her comeuppance. It's the three witches of Eastwick who go back, in the end, to the equivalent of Kansas — marriage, flat and grey maybe, but at least known.

The Witches of Eastwick could be and probably will be interpreted as just another episode in the long-running American serial called "Blaming Mom." The Woman-as-Nature-as-magic-as-powerful-as-bad-Mom package has gone the rounds before, sometimes accompanied by the smell of burning. If prattle of witchcraft is heard in the land, can the hunt be far behind? Mr. Updike provides no blameless way of being female. Hackles will rise, the word "backlash" will be spoken; but anyone speaking it should look at the men in this book, who, while proclaiming their individual emptiness, are collectively, offstage, blowing up Vietnam. That's *male* magic. Men, say the witches, more than once, are full of rage because they can't make babies, and even male babies have at their centre "that aggressive vacuum." Shazam indeed!

A Martian might wonder at the American propensity for tossing the power football. Each sex hurls it at the other with amazing regularity, each crediting the other with more power than the other thinks it has, and the characters in this book join in the game with glee. The aim seems to be the avoidance of responsibility, the reversion to a childlike state of Huckleberry Finn-like "freedom." What the witches want from the Devil is to play without consequences. But all the

Devil can really offer is temptation; hot-tubbery has its price, and the Devil must have his due; with the act of creation comes irreversibility, and guilt.

Mr. Updike takes "sisterhood is powerful" at its word and imagines it literally. What if sisterhood really is powerful? What will the sisters use their "powers" for? And — given human nature, of which Mr. Updike takes not too bright a view — what then? Luckily these witches are only interested in the "personal," rather than the "political"; otherwise they might have done something unfrivolous, like inventing the hydrogen bomb.

The Witches of Eastwick is an excursion rather than a destination. Like its characters, it indulges in metamorphoses, reading at one moment like Kierkegaard, at the next like Swift's *A Modest Proposal*, and at the next like Archie comics, with some John Keats thrown in. This quirkiness is part of its charm, for, despite everything, charming it is. As for the witches themselves, there's a strong suggestion that they are products of Eastwick's — read America's — own fantasy life. If so, it's as well to know about it. That's the serious reason for reading this book.

The other reasons have to do with the skill and inventiveness of the writing, the accuracy of the detail, the sheer energy of the witches, and, above all, the practicality of the charms. The ones for getting suitable husbands are particularly useful. You want a rich one, for a change? First you sprinkle a tuxedo with your perfume and your precious bodily fluids, and then. . . .

3

THE SORCERER AS APPRENTICE

DIFFICULT LOVES
BY ITALO CALVINO

DIFFICULT LOVES is a beautifully translated collection of early stories by the highly regarded Italian writer, Italo Calvino. Mr. Calvino is perhaps best known in North America for his antinovel, *If on a Winter's Night a Traveler*, his pseudo-geography, *Invisible Cities*, and for *Italian Folk Tales*, which really are. What you think of the fictions of the mature Calvino will depend partly on whether you consider flirtation a delightful way of passing the time or a boring waste of it, and whether, after a magic show, you feel charmed or had. It's possible to get the sense you're being toyed with, that Mr. Calvino is fiddling with you and doesn't much care whether Rome is burning or not; that "reality" and "truth" are, for him, categories irrelevant to the hermetic world of art. There's something to be said for this stance: why should a rose, or Isak Dinesen for that matter, have to demonstrate social relevance? Still, if you go too far into the palace of artifice you can turn into a rococo clock, a fate Mr. Calvino has so far been adroit enough to avoid.

All the more interesting then to open *Difficult Loves*, expecting tricks with string, and to realize that instead you are watching a writer in the process of getting where he later got. These are very early stories indeed: the earliest were written in 1945, when Mr. Calvino was a damp-eared twenty-two, and the latest date from the 1950s, when he was in his early thirties.

Of the four sections in the book, the first, "Riviera Stories," is the most realistic in its inclinations. The stories are hardly stories at all but studies, carefully observed and detailed sketches of people in certain landscapes, social situations, and postures. Already Mr. Calvino is displaying a sensual delight in description, a painterliness if you like, but these pieces are for the most part fragmentary, like Leonardo's studies of hands. Among them, two — "A Goatherd at Luncheon" and "Man in the Wasteland" — are less embryonic, but it is not until the second section, "Wartime Stories," that the fingerprints of a major talent begin to be visible. From the subject matter — peasants and partisans versus German soldiers and Italian Fascists — you might expect shrapnel and gore, death and squalor, and some is in fact provided. But the surprise is the freshness, the sweetness even, that is present despite it. "Animal Woods," about a German soldier lost in a forest in which the peasants have hidden their animals, has the clear charm of a fairy tale, and "One of the Three Is Still Alive" manages to turn another German, a naked, harried one this time, into a sort of momentary Adam.

In the third section, "Postwar Stories," we find ourselves in an urban landscape reminiscent of early Fellini films and populated with waifs and strays, eccentrics, fat and/or distorted prostitutes, and men given to bizarre excesses. The baroque blends with the grotesque in the sensuous gluttony of "Theft in a Pastry Shop." And "Desire in November" is every fur fetishist's dream come true.

Finally, in the fourth section, "Stories of Love and Loneliness," Mr. Calvino hits what was to become increasingly his stride. Of the eight stories in this section, five explore the borderline that divides (or does it?) illusion from reality, the imagination from the outside world, art from its subject matter. The photographer who ends by being unable to photograph anything but other photographs and destroys his love affair in the process, the man who can't enjoy a real woman because he's too involved in reading about an imaginary one, the nearsighted man who must choose between seeing and being seen and the poet for whom woman, nature, silence, and serenity form one set, while men, civilization, words, and suffocation form another — these are early articulations of the illusionist's dilemma, of the complex relationship of the artist to a world he can't quite believe in as long as he views it as material for an art which is not quite believable either. It is the artist's love for the "real" world that drives him to transform it into an artifact, and, paradoxically — according to logic — to deny it. As the photographer says, "The minute you start saying of something, 'Ah, how beautiful! We must photograph it!' you are already close to the view of the person who thinks that everything that is not photographed is lost, as if it had never existed."

Difficult Loves has some of the fascination of a photo album (the author at twenty-two, the author at twenty-six, the author at thirty), but it has a lot more to offer than that. The quirkiness and grace of the writing, the originality of the imagination at work, the occasional incandescence of vision, and a certain lovable nuttiness make this collection well worth reading, and for more than archaeological reasons.

4

MARGARET ATWOOD REMEMBERS
MARIAN ENGEL

He speaks in his own voice. She sat up and said that out loud.
— Marian Engel, *Bear*

We're all wrecks when it comes to it, but some of us have written
books and I think we should be given credit for that.
— Marian Engel, in a letter

She understood that he would never be with her more
than at the present moment. The surprise to come was that
he wouldn't be with her less.
— Alice Munro, *Who Do You Think You Are?*

I first saw Marian on a book, hers. It was called *No Clouds of Glory*,
and on the front there was a coffee-cup ring you thought was real
until you tried to wipe it off. The back showed the author, a tomboy-
ish but pretty young woman with a gamine haircut, her top buttons
undone, holding a cigarette and caught in the act of inhaling, looking sideways at the viewer with a grin that was amused, mischievous,
even, you might say, provocative. Marian didn't like that picture, for
some reason. (Also she didn't like the title, which wasn't hers. As soon

as she got the chance, with the paperback, she put her own back on: *Sarah Bastard's Notebook*.)

I didn't know that at the time. I thought it was a good picture. I was a young author myself, and conscious of others, especially women. I read the book, looked at the picture, thought: *She'd be too much for me*. As it turned out, Marian thought the same thing about me; so after we'd gone through that, we could become friends.

The last picture I saw of her she did like. It's the one on *Room of One's Own*, Engel issue, summer of '84. There was some doubt as to whether she'd be alive to see it but she was. Those were the months when she waxed and waned. ("Very complimentary," she said. "Probably because of the state I'm in." She was pleased, but nothing escaped her. However, she did not say *dying*.)

In the picture, she's sitting in a chair in her living room, looking good enough. You can't tell she could hardly walk. She showed me the picture and then turned the magazine over. On the back was the rest of the picture: books piled up and spilling over, a table heaped with objects. "The usual chaos," she said. She liked having it in the picture, because it was true, not airbrushed, not artist-as-icon. None of her heroines are bodiless wisps, and several are downright sloppy, a condition she was, as a writer, excellent at describing.

Alice Munro, writer: "When I was young, in the 1950s, I used to sit around in kitchens with my married girlfriends; there would be exchanges, revelations, a kind of desperate honesty, a subversive wit. When I first read Marian's books — particularly *The Honeyman Festival* — I had the same sense of release and exhilaration. She'd caught something that was like the tone of those early conversations; it wasn't just an extension, it was a *vindication* of all that talk. It was the *way* she wrote. That sort of material wasn't commonly used; domestic material was either sentimentalized and sugared over, or it was turned back on itself, filled with irony and self-deprecation. She used it as straight literary material, and she made me see that it was possible to use it."

She thought she was untidier than that mythical beast, "other people." She had some ideal of perfection she felt others embodied but she fell short of. Maybe this came from her shattering early childhood, maybe it was part of that cleanliness-oriented, small-town, Ontario, Protestant upbringing provided by her adoptive parents. Whatever it was, it was always getting her into trouble with interviewers. She felt a need to be forthright with them, to show herself to them as fully human, dirty dishes, empty bottles, and all; or maybe she was in the grip of that modest self-disparagement small towns require. So she would tell stories on herself, times when she'd done things she regretted or made a fool of herself, and of course the interviewers would print these stories and present them as the whole truth and then she'd get mad, at herself as much as anyone. She was no saint, nor in her opinion was anybody — saintliness irritated her — but this other thing wasn't the real picture either, and she knew it. She had, among other things, a sense of decorum, and it was hard for her not to let that stifle her as a writer.

Timothy Findley, writer: "She used to pull her head in like a turtle when she laughed, because laughing out loud wasn't something one did, not according to her upbringing and mine as well. Once when I was chairman of the Writers' Union I was getting an ovation for something or other, and Marian was sitting in the front row. She pointed her finger at me and said, 'Look at you!' Because we both knew this was something that wasn't done.

"There was always that conflict — the 'lady' she'd been taught to be, and the bohemian thing. As a student she was defiant about which boys she'd go out with — she'd choose the offbeat ones on purpose; but the 'lady,' the inhibiting background, was never stamped out. Writing *Bear* nearly killed her; she was astonished by her own daring. 'I put that *word* on the page,' she'd say to me."

She knew why the dishes were dirty: she was a professional writer, not a professional housekeeper, and few can afford to be both. She thought of writing as an honourable profession. But she felt that Canada didn't really have a language for that yet. During her years in France, she met a man who asked her what she did. She told him. "*C'est un bon métier*," he said. It was one of the stories from her past that she liked, especially the word *métier*. Such a word released the writer from the ranks of jugglers and personalities, those who made faces for a living, and instead took writing seriously.

Along with this professionalism (for although the dishes may have been undone the deadlines were met) went her obsession with supporting herself, difficult though this habitually was.

"Don't tell anyone I've got cancer," she said to me early on.

"Why not?" I said. She was nearly broke, as often; I could see some advantages, and anyway it was the truth.

"I might not be able to get another job."

She didn't want perks, special treatment. Also she didn't want deathbed condolences. A dying person can be thought of as dying or as living. Marian thought of herself as living.

She did not deny what was happening to her. She just didn't want it to interfere with her enjoyment of life, which, at its height, was vast. So when we did talk about her illness, we talked practical arrangements: reclining beds, tilting tables you could screw a type-writer onto. Damned if she'd give up writing. Nor did she.

Two months before she did die, she planned to go to Paris, with her two teenaged children and a wheelchair. By that time she could no longer walk and was living on painkillers, but she wanted to revisit the city where she'd made so many important discoveries for herself, twenty-five years or so before. All her friends cheered her on, aware that she might not make it there, let alone back. But her own stance was jaunty, "full of courage and comedy," as George Woodcock has put it. Or it appeared to be.

"Even towards the end," says Jane Rule, the writer, "there was that larkiness and hilarity. She wrote me from Paris: 'You haven't lived until you've gone over the cobblestones of Paris in a wheelchair.' She sent me a postcard. It was a view of a Paris street, taken from inside a basement, looking up through bars. She wrote on it: 'The Engel view — always looking up.'"

Which was not always entirely true. For us she brought back a more prophetic gift: a scented candle in a glass container that said on the outside: FOIN COUPÉ (CUT HAY).

There are a lot of stories that epitomize her, because she had a lot of friends. One comes from Bob Weaver, the former producer of the CBC radio program *Anthology*, and patron uncle of many writers. When she could still walk, although on a cane, she met him for lunch. Halfway through lunch, she said, "Oh my God."

"What?" said Bob, fearing a medical crisis.

"I've come here with my dress on inside out."

"Oh," said Bob, seeing that it was so.

"Usually my daughter checks me over. But she was out. What'll I do?"

"You have three choices," said Bob. "You can change it here, you can go to the washroom, or we can brazen it out."

"We'll brazen it out," said Marian.

When they'd said goodbye on the street, she called after him. He looked back and saw her leaning on her cane, waving.

"You can use this in your memoirs," she shouted.

She didn't always give such permission. "Copyright, eh?" she'd say, when telling something from her life that she wanted to save up and use herself. She knew the hazards of having other writers for friends.

Byrna Barclay, writer: "When Marian Engel began publishing I was up to my armpits in diaper pails and the other domestic symbols she wrote about. When I read *The Honeyman Festival* — in the bathtub, my favourite escape then — I almost drowned myself in the artistic statement she created about all our lives. Years later, after she won the Governor General's Award and I dared to fulfill my own writing dream, I met Marian at a conference on regional literature in Banff. At the banquet she told me — and the other people at our table — a story about winning the coveted GG. She had fifteen invitations to pass out, but no one to take to the official ceremony. She had bought a red evening gown. On the day of the awards, she was told it was an afternoon garden party, and she had nothing else to wear. She wore the red dress anyway and, flanked by her mother and her analyst, went to the garden party. No one else would talk to her. Except Joe Fafard, the sculptor, who arrived in a blue jean suit. It seems to me that red evening dress should hang in a writers' hall of fame."

We often talked about writing. Not the content of it, nor the craft, but about how one managed to do it at all. For her, given the circumstances of her life, which even before her illness were often prohibitively painful and difficult, this was a major subject. I was often astonished that she was able to write as well, as much, and as uncomplainingly as she did. She made me feel lazy, and somewhat spoiled.

Once, during a fragmented period in my own life, she gave me two pieces of advice. "Don't let other people take advantage of you." And: "Steal time."

David Young, writer: "It was difficult for her to take gifts from people or to allow herself things. She was a real string saver, she had a tremendous sense of thrift. But in the last few years that eased up — she made a garden out of what used to be a junk heap, in her backyard. It was a scaled-down version of something quite grand; she got infinite pleasure out of it. If you were over visiting her she'd make you pull out the weeds, at the back, where she couldn't get to them herself.

"She was stubborn and she had a temper, she'd give you both barrels if necessary. She could be abrasive and undiplomatic, in her official dealings, but she was idealistic and persistent too — in cultural politics, for instance. She served as first chairman of the Writers' Union of Canada, and she decided that Payment for Public Use — of writers' books, in libraries — was what she'd go for, and she never gave up on it.

"She phoned me at midnight two weeks before she died. 'This pain isn't going to get better,' she said. And that was it. She'd decided."

Graeme Gibson, writer: "The time before, in July, when she almost died, I'd just come back from England. I went see her in the hospital; she looked terrible. 'I wanted so much to be well for your return,' she said. I sat with her and after a while she apologized for not being entertaining, and I realized I'd better leave, because as long as I was there she was going to exert herself, for me."

Once, during a bad spell, I was visiting her in hospital, and a medical crisis really did strike. Buzzers were sounded, nurses hurried in, and I had to leave. As I did — as she was being lifted, stuck with needles — in the midst of all that, she winked at me.

This wink demolished me. It was so typical of her, but also so gallant and doomed, bagpipers going into battle, the Polish cavalry charging the tanks on horseback. It was meant, I knew, to cheer me up, but it said other things too: that no matter how gruesome things were, they had a funny side; that there was a conspiracy going on, between us, behind the doctors' backs. The doctors and her body were engaged in some solemn business or other that was of concern to her, but it wasn't the whole story.

Despite the alterations made in her by illness and drugs, here was the same expression I'd first caught her at, on that book cover: mischief, fun. *Relish* was a word she liked; "I've been naughty," she would say, with some pleasure. So there was something to be had, savoured, seen, understood, even at such a moment.

She would not have found this wink of hers courageous. Unless somebody else had done it, of course.

5

INTRODUCTION

ROUGHING IT IN THE BUSH
BY SUSANNA MOODIE

THE READER WILL, I hope, forgive me beginning this introduction with my own involvement with Susanna Moodie. I am not a scholar or historian, but a writer of fiction and poetry, and such people are notoriously subjective in their reading.

While I was growing up in the 1940s and early 1950s, Susanna Moodie's *Roughing It in the Bush* sat in our bookcase, which it was my job to dust. It was with the grown-up books, but I always noticed it anyway because of the two interlocking *O*s of the author's last name, which were featured in the rounded typographical style of 1913 on the cover. I recall opening the book and looking at the frontispiece — a snow-covered log cabin — but I did not read this book at the time. For one thing, it was not a novel, and I was not interested in books that were not novels. For another, my father told me that it was a "classic" and that I would "find it interesting to read some day." I tended to shy away from books that were so described. For yet another, it was about people living in a log cabin in the bush. I myself had spent a large part of my childhood in cabins, log and otherwise, in the bush, and did not find anything exotic about the notion. I was more interested in medieval castles, or, on the other hand, ray guns. *Roughing It in the Bush*, I thought, would be tame stuff.

My second encounter with this book was in grade six, when part of it appeared in our reader. It was the section in which the Moodies' chimney catches fire and the house does too. This rang true: chimney fires caused by overstuffing were one of the bugbears of my childhood. Still, every author in the grade six reader came to us clothed in the dull grey mantle of required reading, and I forgot about Susanna Moodie and went on to other matters, such as Jane Austen.

My third experience with Susanna Moodie was of an altogether different order. When I was a graduate student at the Harvard Department of English Literature, at that time a sort of Jungian hothouse, I had a particularly vivid dream. I had written an opera about Susanna Moodie, and there she was, all by herself on a completely white stage, singing like Lucia di Lammermoor. I could barely read music, but I was not one to ignore portents: I rushed off to the library, where the Canadiana was kept in the bowels of the stacks beneath Witchcraft and Demonology, got out both *Roughing It in the Bush* and Mrs. Moodie's later work, *Life in the Clearings versus the Bush*, and read them at full speed.

At first I thought my unconscious had given me a bad tip. Despite the drama of many of the incidents described, the prose was Victorian in a quasi-Dickensian semi-jocular way, veering into Wordsworthian rhapsody when it came to sunsets, and there was a patina of gentility that offended my young soul, as did the asides on the servant question and the lower-classness of many of the emigrants already in place.

However, the Shadow will not be mocked, and Susanna Moodie began to haunt me. About a year and a half later I began a series of poems that became a book, *The Journals of Susanna Moodie*, which by now has doubtless been thrust down many an adolescent throat. What kept bringing me back to the subject — and to Susanna Moodie's own work — were the hints, the gaps between what was said and what hovered, just unsaid, between the lines, and the conflict between what

Mrs. Moodie felt she ought to think and feel and what she actually did think and feel. Probably my poems were about these tensions. So are her books.

Some years later, I wrote a television play based on a notable murder in *Life in the Clearings*, and later still a short book of social history of the period from 1815 to 1840; and both of these experiences forced me to grapple a little with the background and climate of Susanna Moodie's books. They also made me consider Moodie herself in a newer light. Life in a log cabin in the bush had been normal and pleasant for me, but it was obvious that it was, and had to be, quite otherwise for her. I got culture shook from flush toilets, she got it from mosquitoes, swamps, trackless wildernesses, and the thought of bears. In some ways, we were each other's obverse.

The forces that combined to waft Susanna Moodie to Upper Canada in 1832 were wafting many others as well. In 1760, with the capture of Quebec, Britain had acquired the Canadas, Upper and Lower (so called because, though Upper Canada was "lower" than Lower Canada, travel to both was via the St. Lawrence River, and Upper Canada was further upstream). Then came the American Revolution and an influx of immigrant United Empire Loyalists to Upper Canada. Then came the War of 1812 in North America and the Napoleonic Wars in Europe. The end of these wars sent many soldiers back into the potential labour force in Britain, with widespread unemployment as a result. The effects of the Highland Clearances and the Irish potato famine were still being felt. Many of the poor in Britain looked toward emigration to the colonies as a solution that offered them at least the hope of bettering their condition, a belief that was encouraged both by the ruling classes in England and by the ship owners, merchants, and land speculators lying in wait for them along the way. Pamphlets, settlers' guides, and other forms of propaganda poured forth, depicting Upper Canada as a bucolic wonderland with a climate much like Britain's, where industry and virtue would inevitably be rewarded.

Rising to these lures or impelled by the pinch of necessity, seven and a half million people crossed the ocean from Britain between 1800 and 1875. In 1832, fifty thousand emigrants entered Upper and Lower Canada. The population of Upper Canada became seven times larger during the first third of the century. "In 1830," as Moodie says, "Canada became the great landmark for the rich in hope and poor in purse."

Susanna Moodie was not from a poor family, but from the genteel middle-to-upper middle class: however, many from families like hers also chose to emigrate at this time. There was a surplus of younger sons in Britain, of which Mr. Moodie was one, and many among the gentry or near-gentry saw a chance, in the Colonies, of becoming more nearly what they thought they already were: landed gentry. Susanna Moodie, her sister Catharine Parr Traill, later to become the author of *The Canadian Settler's Guide*, and her brother Samuel Strickland were three who made the choice.

What they may have been expecting beforehand can be gathered from *The Young Emigrants; or, Pictures of Canada*, a children's book written by Catharine Parr Traill in 1826, six years before she and Susanna actually went to Canada. In it, the ideal immigrant family, who are middle class like the Moodies, speedily acquire a prosperous farm, which they tend with the aid of friendly servants and a little discreet poultry feeding and gardening by the women. They whip up a comfortable and spacious four-bedroom dwelling where they spend the day supervising things and the evenings in practising their musical accomplishments and in "social chat or innocent gaiety" with their equally genteel neighbours.

The reality, when Susanna Moodie and Catharine Parr Traill actually encountered it, was far otherwise. The most "English" land in Upper Canada, the fertile and relatively warm Niagara Peninsula, was already taken. After a pleasant-enough first-class crossing, far above the horrors of the steerage where the poor travelled in stench-filled, overcrowded semidarkness, they got their first taste of the

Canadas when they landed at Grosse Isle and discovered that to many of the steerage travellers the New World meant a deplorable levelling of social classes. "Whurrah! my boys! . . . Shure we'll all be jintlemen," Susanna Moodie heard one Irish labourer shouting. She was to encounter this spirit in many forms later on: saucy servants who wanted to eat at the same table, earlier settlers who looked upon her with contempt, "Late Loyalists" from the United States who cheated her and borrowed, without returning, anything she was fool enough to lend them. Gentlefolk like here were the target of considerable malice, she found: when the family moved into one dwelling, they found the floor flooded, the fruit trees girdled, and a dead skunk stuffed up the chimney. Later, when she'd had time to mull it over, she came to understand what these people might have had against her: yes, the British class system could be repressive. But at the time this was just one of many obstacles that were set in her path.

There were others. Nature, which Wordsworth had declared, "never did betray / The heart that loved her," looked quite different in the thickly treed wilds of Canada from the way it looked in even the craggiest parts of England. Susanna Moodie did her best with vistas and panoramas and picturesque scenery, but she much preferred Canadian Nature from a distance; the deck of a moving boat, for instance. Up close, there were likely to be mosquitoes, mud, ruts, swamps, and stumps. Also, there was winter, which was not like anything she'd encountered before. And there was the nightmare of clearing the land, without the aid of tractors, and of wrenching a few vegetables from the apparently grudging soil.

Above all, there was her own inexperience, her own unfitness for the kind of hardship and labour she found herself compelled to do. Her first home, near Coburg, was rented sight unseen on the understanding that it was "a delightful summer residence," but it turned out to be a doorless one-room shack that Mrs. Moodie took at first sight to be a pigsty. Her second home was even farther out in the backwoods. After seven years in the bush, Mrs. Moodie had acquired some of the skills necessary for a settler's wife — she could make coffee from dandelion roots and bake bread that didn't resemble a cinder, for instance — but, despite her *post facto* sentimentality about her woodland home, she was happy to profit by Mr. Moodie's elevation to the position of Sheriff of Belleville and to kiss the wilderness "adieu."

We should remember too that the years she spent in the bush were child-bearing ones for her; in those days before modern medicine, when a doctor, even if there had been one available, wouldn't have been much help, not all the children eventually survived. Mrs. Moodie is reticent on the subject, but she says at one point, rather chillingly, that she never felt really at home in Canada until she had buried some of her children in it. She may have come to "love" her rustic house and her new country somewhat, but to get to that point she'd had to pass through "a hatred so intense that I longed to die, that death might effectually separate us forever." The point of her book, she more than once reminds us, is to discourage other English gentlefolk from doing what she herself had done. The Canadian frontier, she claims, is for the working classes, who are strong enough to put up with it. Drunkenness, debt, decline, and "hopeless ruin" are more likely to be the lot of the transplanted gentleman.

Now that such warnings are no longer needed, what does *Roughing It in the Bush* have to offer the modern reader? Quite a lot, as it turns out. Although it isn't a novel, but one of those books that purports to tell the plain truth — as, indeed, early novels did too — it's structured like a novel. It has a plot, which combines the journey with the ordeal, as the emigrant-travellers encounter a new land, cope with the strange inhabitants and customs they find there, overcome hardships that range from cholera to starvation. Looked at in this light, *Roughing It in the Bush* can be seen as belonging to a distinct tradition of travel writing — a tradition that perhaps culminates in Eric

Newby's *A Short Walk in the Hindu Kush* — in which the horribleness of the journey, the filthiness and squalor of the accommodations, and the awfulness of the food are outdone only by the traveller's self-perceived lunacy in having undertaken the trip at all. It also has a meticulously described setting: the confrontation with a harsh and vast geography was, and was to become, a dominant motif in Canadian writing. It also has characters; "character sketches," with dialogue included, are something Mrs. Moodie is particularly good at, and "Brian, the Still Hunter" has frequently been anthologized as a short story. But the most complex and ambiguous character in her book is herself.

If Catharine Parr Traill with her imperturbable practicality is what we like to think we would be under the circumstances, Susanna Moodie is what we secretly suspect we would have been instead. Time and again she rises above the prejudices of her own age and position, but time and again she sinks back into them. She doesn't know how to do things right, she makes mistakes, she's afraid of cows, she gets caught out on the lake in thunderstorms. But (surely like us!) she is not a total ninny; she can keep her head in emergencies, she has an innate decency and a respect for natural virtue and courtesy, and she has a sense of humour and can laugh at her own ineptness.

There is another way of reading Moodie, and that is to place her with three other women writers who were among the first to produce much of anything resembling literature in Upper Canada. One was of course Susanna Moodie's sister, Mrs. Traill. Another was Anne Langton, who settled near Sturgeon Lake and wrote *A Gentlewoman in Upper Canada*. The fourth did not settle but passed through quite thoroughly: Anna Jameson, the author of *Winter Studies and Summer Rambles in Canada*. All were gentlewomen, all looked at the growing colony with a critical though not entirely harsh eye, and all demonstrate that gender is not the only thing to be taken into account when accomplishments of one sort or another are being evaluated: their class gave these women a literary edge over those of their less well-educated fellow citizens who happened to be male.

In fact, when you place the early literature of the Canadas beside that of the United States, a curious thing emerges. It's possible to cover American literature from, say, 1625 to 1900, without spending much time at all on women writers, with the exception of Ann Bradstreet and Emily Dickinson. Attention focuses on the "great" and overwhelmingly male American writers of the period: Melville, Poe, Hawthorne, Whitman, Thoreau. English Canada produced no such classics at this time — it was settled later — but if you study the literature at all, you can't ignore the women. Possibly the reason for the relative preponderance of women writers in Canada can be found in the different ages in which the two were initially settled: America in the Puritan seventeenth century, English Canada in the nineteenth, the age of the letter and the journal, at a time when many women were already literate. In any case, it's a situation that has persisted until today: the percentage of prominent and admittedly accomplished women writers, in both prose and poetry, is higher in Canada than it is in any of the other English-speaking countries. The same is true of Quebec, in which some of the first writing was done by nuns who had come to convert the Indians (and where, incidentally, the first English-language novel in Canada was written, also by a woman).

Susanna Moodie did not intend to write a Canadian classic, nor would she have anticipated or relished being claimed as an ancestress by the modern women's movement; she was a creature of her own society, and would have disapproved of many feminist principles. But, as others, including T. S. Eliot, have pointed out, a work of literature gains meaning not only from its own context but from those later contexts it may find itself placed within. Susanna Moodie's account of her struggles, failures, and survival have resonance for us now partly because we have produced our own literature of struggles, failures, and survival. She was not Superwoman, but she coped some-how, and lived to write about it, and even managed to squeeze a kind of wisdom from her ordeal.

6
TRUE NORTH

Land of the silver birch,
Home of the beaver,
Where still the mighty moose
Wanders at will,
Blue lake and rocky shore,
I will return once more;
Boom-diddy-boom-boom
Boom-biddy-boom-boom
Boo-OO-oo-oo-oom.
— Archaic Song

WE SANG THIS ONCE, squatting around the papier-mâché Magic Mushroom in the Brownie pack, or while pretending to be wolves in Cub Scouts, or while watching our marshmallows turn to melted Styrofoam on the ends of our sticks at some well-run, fairly safe summer camp in the wilds of Muskoka, Haliburton, or Algonquin Park. Then we grew up and found it corny. By that time we were into Jean-Paul Sartre and the lure of the nauseous. Finally, having reached the age of nostalgia, we rediscovered it on a cassette in The Children's Book Store, in a haunting version that invested it with all the emotional resonance we once thought it possessed, and bought it, under the pretence of giving our children a little ethnic musical background.

It brought tears to our eyes, not for simple reasons. Whales get to us that way too, and whooping cranes, and other things hovering on the verge of extinction but still maintaining a tenuous foothold in the world of the actual. The beavers are doing all right — we know this because they just decimated our poplars — but the mighty moose is having a slimmer time of it. As for the blueness of the lakes, we worry about it: too blue and you've got acid rain.

Will we return once more, or will we go to Portugal instead? It depends, we have to admit, partly on the exchange rate, and this makes us feel disloyal. I am, rather quixotically, in Alabama, teaching, even more quixotically, a course in Canadian literature. Right now we're considering Marian Engel's novel *Bear.* Since everything in Canada, outside Toronto, begins with geography, I've unfolded a large map of Ontario and traced the heroine's route north; I've located the mythical house of the book somewhere on the actual shore of Georgian Bay, northern edge. I've superimposed a same-scale map of Alabama on this scheme, to give the students an idea of the distances. In the north, space is larger than you think, because the points of reference are farther apart.

"Are there any words you came across that puzzled you?" I ask.

Blackfly comes up. A large black fly is proposed. I explain black-flies, their smallness, their multitude, their evil habits. It gives me a certain kick to do this: I'm competing with the local water moccasins.

Mackinaw. A raincoat? Not quite. *Loon. Tamarack. Reindeer moss. Portage. Moose. Wendigo.*

"Why does she make Lucy the old Indian woman talk so funny?" they ask. Lucy, I point out, is not merely Indian but a *French-speaking* Indian. This, to them, is a weird concept.

The north is another country. It's also another language. Or languages.

Where is the north, exactly? It's not only a place but a direction, and as such its location is relative: to the Mexicans, the United States is the north, to Americans Toronto is, even though it's on roughly the same latitude as Boston.

Wherever it is for us, there's a lot of it. You stand in Windsor and imagine a line going north, all the way to the pole. The same line going south would end up in South America. That's the sort of map we grew up with, at the front of the classroom in Mercator projection, which made it look even bigger than it was, all that pink stretching on forever, with a few cities sprinkled along the bottom edge. It's not only geographical space, it's space related to body image. When we face south, as we often do, our conscious mind may be directed down there, toward crowds, bright lights, some Hollywood version of fame and fortune, but the north is at the back of our minds, always. There's something, not someone, looking over our shoulders; there's a chill at the nape of the neck.

The north focuses our anxieties. Turning to face north, face the north, we enter our own unconscious. Always, in retrospect, the journey north has the quality of dream.

Where does the north begin?

Every province, every city, has its own road north. From Toronto you go up the 400. Where you cross the border, from here to there, is a matter of opinion. Is it the Severn River, where the Shield granite appears suddenly out of the earth? Is it the sign announcing that you're halfway between the equator and the North Pole? Is it the first gift shop shaped like a wigwam, the first town — there are several — that proclaims itself The Gateway to the North?

As we proceed, the farms become fewer, rockier, more desperate-looking, the trees change their ratios, coniferous moving in on deciduous. More lakes appear, their shorelines scraggier. Our eyes narrow and we look at the clouds: the weather is important again.

One of us used to spend summers in a cottage in Muskoka, before the road went in, when you took the train, when there were big cruise ships there, and matronly motor launches, and tea dances at the hotels, and men in white flannels on the lawns, which there may still be. This was not just a cottage but a Muskoka cottage, with boat-house and maid's quarters. Rich people went north in the summers then, away from cities and crowds; that was before the cure for polio, which has made a difference. In this sort of north, they tried to dupli-cate the south, or perhaps some dream of country life in England. In the living room there were armchairs, glass-fronted bookcases, fam-ily photos in silver frames, stuffed birds under glass bells. The north, as I said, is relative.

For me, the north used to be completely in force by the Trout Creek planing mill. Those stacks of fresh-cut lumber were the true gateway to the north, and north of that was North Bay, which used to be, to be blunt, a bit of an armpit. It was beef-sandwich-on-white-bread-with-gravy-and-canned-peas country. But no more. North Bay now has shopping malls, and baskets of flowers hanging from lampposts above paving-stone sidewalks, downtown. It has a Granite Club. It has the new, swish, carpeted buildings of Laurentian University. It has gourmet restaurants. And in the airport, where southbound DC-9s dock side by side with northbound Twin Otters, there's a book rack in the coffee shop that features Graham Greene and Kierkegaard, hardly standard airport fare.

The south is moving north.

We bypass North Bay, which now has a bypass, creeping southerli-ness, and do not go, this time, to the Dionne Quints Museum, where five little silhouettes in black play forever beside an old log cabin, complete with the basket where they were packed in cotton wool, the oven where they were warmed, the five prams, the five Communion dresses.

Beyond North Bay there is a brief flurry of eccentricity — lawns populated with whole flocks of wooden-goose windmills — and then we go for miles and miles past nothing but trees, meeting nothing but the occasional truck loaded with lumber. This area didn't used to be called anything. Now it's the Near North Travel Area. You can see signs telling you that. Near what, we wonder uneasily? We don't want to be near. We want to be far.

At last we see the Ottawa River, which is the border. There's a dam across it, two dams, and an island between them. If there were a customs house it would be here. A sign faces us saying *Bienvenue*; out the back window there's one saying *Welcome*. This was my first lesson in points of view.

And there, across the border in Quebec, in Témiscaming, is an image straight from my childhood: a huge mountain made of sawdust. I always wanted to slide down this sawdust mountain until I finally did, and discovered it was not like sand, dry and slippery, but damp and sticky and hard to get out of your clothes. This was my first lesson in the nature of illusion.

Continue past the sawdust mountain, past the baseball diamond, up the hill, and you're in the centre of town, which is remarkable for at least three things: a blocks-long public rock garden, still flourishing after more than forty-five years; a pair of statues, one a fountain, that look as if they've come straight from Europe, which I think they did; and the excellent, amazingly low-priced hamburgers you can get at the Boulevard Restaurant, where the décor, featuring last year's cardboard Santa Claus and a stuffed twenty-three-pound pike, is decidedly northern. Ask the owner about the pike and he'll tell you about one twice as big, forty-five pounds in fact, that a fellow showed him strapped to the tailgate of his van, and that long too.

You can have this conversation in either French or English: Témiscaming is a border town and a northern one, and the distinctions made here are as likely to be north-south as French-English. Up in these parts you'll hear as much grumbling, or more, about

Quebec City as you will about Ottawa, which is, after all, closer. Spit in the river and it gets to Ottawa, eh?

For the north, Témiscaming is old, settled, tidy, even a little prosperous-looking. But it's had its crises. Témiscaming is the resource economy personified. Not long ago it was a company town, and when the company shut down the mill, which would have shut down the town too, the workers took the unprecedented step of trying to buy it. With some help they succeeded, and the result was Tembec, still going strong. But Témiscaming is still a one-industry town, like many northern towns, and its existence is thus precarious.

Not so long ago, logging was a different sort of business. The men went into the woods in winter, across the ice, using horse-drawn sledges, and set up camp. (You still come across these logging camps now and then in your travels through the lakes, abandoned, already looking as ancient as Roman aqueducts; more ancient, since there's been no upkeep.) They'd cut selectively, tree by tree, using axes and saws and the skills that were necessary to avoid being squashed or hacked. They'd skid the trees to the ice; in the spring, after the ice went out, there would be a run down the nearest fast river to the nearest sawmill.

Now it's done with bulldozers and trucks, and the result is too often a blitzed shambles; cut everything, leave a wreck of dead and, incidentally, easily flammable branches behind. Time is money. Don't touch the shoreline though, we need that for tourists. In some places, the forest is merely a scrim along the water. In behind it's been hollowed out.

Those who look on the positive side say it's good for the blueberries.

Sometimes we went the other way, across to Sudbury, the trees getting smaller and smaller and finally disappearing as you approached. Sudbury was another magic place of my childhood. It was like interplanetary travel, which we liked to imagine, which was still just imagination in those days. With its heaps of slag and its barren shoulders of stone, it looked like the moon. Back then, we tell the children, before there were washer-dryers and you used something called a wringer washer and hung the sheets out on something called a clothesline, when there weren't even coloured sheets but all sheets were white, when Rinso white and its happy little washday song were an item, and Whiter than White was a catch phrase and female status really did have something to do with your laundry, Sudbury was a housewife's nightmare. We knew people there; the windowsills in their houses were always grey.

Now the trees are beginning to come back because they built higher smokestacks. But where is all that stuff going now?

The Acid Rain Dinner, in Toronto's Sheraton Centre, in 1985. The first of these fundraising events was fairly small. But the movement has grown, and this dinner is huge. The leaders of all three provincial parties are here. So is the minister of the environment from the federal government. So are several labour leaders, and several high-ranking capitalists, and representatives of numerous northerly chambers of commerce, summer residents' associations, tourist-camp runners, outfitters. Wishy-washy urban professionals who say "frankly" a lot bend elbows with huntin', shootin', fishin', and cussin' burnt-necks who wouldn't be caught dead saying "frankly." This is not a good place to be overheard saying that actually acid rain isn't such a bad thing because it gets rid of all that brown scum and leeches in the lake, or who cares because you can water-ski anyway. Teddy Kennedy, looking like a bulky sweater, is the guest speaker. Everyone wears a little gold pin in the shape of a raindrop. It looks like a tear.

Why has acid rain become the collective Canadian nightmare? Why is it — as a good cause — bigger than baby-seal bashing? The reasons aren't just economic, although there are lots of those, as the fishing-camp people and foresters will tell you. It's more than that, and cognate with the outrage aroused by the uninvited voyage of the American icebreaker *Polar Sea* through the Northwest Passage, where almost none of us ever goes. It's territorial, partly; partly a felt violation of some area in us that we hardly ever think about unless it's invaded or tampered with. It's the neighbours throwing guck into our yard. It's our childhood dying.

On location, in summer and far from the glass and brass of the Sheraton Centre, we nervously check our lakes. Leeches still in place? Have the crayfish, among the first to go, gone yet? (We think in terms of "yet.") Are the loons reproducing, have you seen any young? Any minnows? How about the lichen on the rocks? These inventories have now become routine, and that is why we're willing to fork out a hundred dollars a plate to support our acid-rain lobby-ists in Washington. A summer without loons is unthinkable, but how do you tell that to people who don't know it because they've never had any to begin with?

We're driving through Glencoe, in the Highlands of Scotland. It's imposing, as a landscape: bleak, large, bald, apparently empty. We can see why the Scots took so well to Canada. Yet we know that the glens and crags round about are crawling with at least a thousand campers, rock climbers, and other seekers after nature; we also know that, at one end of this glen, the Campbells butchered the MacDonalds in the seventeenth century, thus propelling both of them into memo-rable history. Go walking here and you'll find things human; outlines of stone fences now overgrown, shards of abandoned crofts.

In Europe, every scrap of land has been claimed, owned, re-owned, fought over, captured, bled on. The roads are the only no man's land. In northern Canada, the roads are civilization, owned by the collective human *we*. Off the road is *other*. Try walking in it, and you'll soon find out why all the early traffic here was by water. "Impenetrable wilderness" is not just verbal.

And suppose you get off the road. Suppose you get lost. Getting lost, elsewhere and closer to town, is not knowing exactly where you are. You can always ask, even in a foreign country. In the north, get-ting lost is not knowing how to get out.

You can get lost on a lake, of course, but getting lost in the forest is worse. It's tangly in there, and dim, and one tree does begin to look remarkably like another. The leaves and needles blot up sound, and you begin to feel watched: not by anyone, not by an animal even, or anything you can put a name to, just watched. You begin to feel judged. It's as if something is keeping an eye on you just to see what you will do.

What will you do? Which side of the tree does moss grow on, and here, where there are ferns and the earth is damp, or where it's dry as tinder, it seems that moss grows everywhere, or does not grow at all. Snippets of Boy Scout lore or truisms learned at summer camp come back to you, but scrambled. You tell yourself not to panic: you can always live off the land.

Easier said than done, you'd soon find. The Canadian Shield is a relatively foodless area, which is why even the Indians tended to pass through it, did not form large settlements except where there was arable land, and remained limited in numbers. This is not the Mekong Delta. If you had a gun you could shoot something, maybe, a red squirrel perhaps; but if you're lost you probably don't have a gun, or a fishing rod either. You could eat blueberries, or cattail stems, or crayfish, or other delicacies dimly remembered from stories about people who got lost in the woods and were found later in good health although somewhat thinner. You could cook some reindeer moss, if you had matches.

Thus you pass on to fantasies about how to start a fire with a magnifying glass — you don't have one — or by rubbing two bits of stick together, a feat at which you suspect you would prove remarkably inept.

The fact is that not very many of us know how to survive in the north. Rumour has it that only one German prisoner of war ever made it out, although many made it out of the actual prisoner-of-war camps. The best piece of northern survival advice is: *Don't get lost.*

One way of looking at a landscape is to consider the typical ways of dying in it. Given the worst, what's the worst it could do? Will it be delirium from drinking salty water on the high seas, shrivelling in the desert, snakebite in the jungle, tidal waves on a Pacific isle, volcanic fumes? In the north, there are several hazards. Although you're prob- ably a lot safer there than you are on the highway at rush hour, given the odds, you still have to be a little wary.

Like most lessons of this sort, those about the north are taught by precept and example, but also, more enjoyably, by cautionary nasty tale. There is death by blackfly, the one about the fellow who didn't have his shirt cuffs tight enough in the spring and undressed at night only to find he was running with blood, the ones about the lost trav- ellers who bloated up from too many bites and who, when found, were twice the size, unrecognizable, and dead. There is death from starva- tion, death by animal, death by forest fire; there is death from something called "exposure," which used to confuse me when I heard about men who exposed themselves: why would they intentionally do anything that fatal? There's death by thunderstorm, not to be sneered at: on the open lake, in one of the excessive northern midsummer thunderstorms, a canoe or a bush plane is a vulnerable target. The north is full of Struwwelpeter-like stories about people who didn't do as they were told and got struck by lightning. Above all, there are death by freezing and death by drowning. Your body's heat-loss rate in the water is twenty times that in air, and northern lakes are cold. Even in a life jacket, even holding on to the tipped canoe, you're at risk. Every summer the numbers pile up.

Every culture has its exemplary dead people, its hagiography of landscape martyrs, those unfortunates who, by their bad ends, seem to sum up in one grisly episode what may be lurking behind the next rock for all of us, all of us who enter the territory they once claimed as theirs. I'd say that two of the top northern landscape martyrs are Tom Thomson, the painter who was found mysteriously drowned near his overturned canoe with no provable cause in sight, and the

Mad Trapper of Rat River, also mysterious, who became so thoroughly bushed that he killed a Mountie and shot two others during an amazing wintertime chase before being finally mowed down. In our retelling of these stories, mystery is a key element. So, strangely enough, is a presumed oneness with the landscape in question. The Mad Trapper knew his landscape so well he survived in it for weeks, living off the land and his own bootlaces, eluding capture. One of the hidden motifs in these stories is a warning: maybe it's not so good to get *too* close to Nature.

I remember a documentary on Tom Thomson that ended, rather ominously, with the statement that the north had taken him to herself. This was, of course, pathetic fallacy gone to seed, but it was also a comment on our distrust of the natural world, a distrust that remains despite our protests, our studies in the ethics of ecology, our elevation of "the environment" to a numinous noun, our save-the-tree campaigns. The question is, would the trees save us, given the chance? Would the water, would the birds, would the rocks? In the north, we have our doubts.

A bunch of us are sitting around the table, at what is now a summer cottage in Georgian Bay. Once it was a house, built by a local man for his family, which finally totalled eleven children, after they'd outgrown this particular house and moved on to another. The original Findlay wood-burning cook stove is still in the house, but so also are some electric lights and a propane cooker, which have come since the end of the old days. In the old days, this man somehow managed to scrape a living from the land: a little of this, a little of that, some fishing here, some lumbering there, some hunting in the fall. That was back when you shot to eat. *Scrape* is an appropriate word: there's not much here between the topsoil and the rock.

We sit around the table and eat, fish among other things, caught by the children. Someone mentions the clams: there are still a lot of them, but who knows what's in them any more? Mercury, lead, things like that. We pick at the fish. Someone tells me not to drink the tap water. I already have. "What will happen?" I ask. "Probably nothing," they reply. "Probably nothing" is a relatively recent phrase around here. In the old days, you ate what looked edible.

We are talking about the old days, as people often do once they're outside the cities. When exactly did the old days end? Because we know they did. The old days ended when the youngest of us was ten, fifteen, or twenty; the old days ended when the oldest of us was five, or twelve, or thirty. Plastic-hulled super-boats are not old days, but ten-horsepower outboard motors, *circa* 1945, are. There's an icebox in the back porch, unused now, a simple utilitarian model from Eaton's, ice chamber in the top section, metal shelves in the bottom one. We all go and admire it. "I remember iceboxes," I say, and indeed I can dimly remember them, I must have been five. What bits of our daily junk — our toasters, our pocket computers — will soon become obsolete, and therefore poignant? Who will stand around, peering at them and admiring their design and the work that went into them, as we do with this icebox? "So this was a *toilet seat*," we think, rehearsing the future. "Ah! A *light bulb*," the ancient syllables thick in our mouths.

The kids have decided some time ago that all this chat is boring, and have asked if they can go swimming off the dock. They can, though they have to watch it, as this is a narrow place and speedboats tend to swoosh through, not always slowing down. Waste of gas, in the old days. Nobody then went anywhere just for pleasure, it was the war and gas was rationed.

"Oh, *that* old days," says someone.

There goes a speedboat now, towing a man strapped in a kneeling position to some kind of board, looking as if he's had a terrible accident, or is about to have one. This must be some newfangled variety of water-skiing.

"Remember Klim?" I say. The children come through, trailing towels. "What's Klim?" one asks, caught by the space-age sound of the word.

"Klim was 'milk' spelled backwards," I say. "It was powdered milk."

"Yuk," they say.

"Not the same as now," I say. "It was whole milk, not skim; it wasn't instant. You had to beat it with an eggbeater." And even then some of it wouldn't dissolve. One of the treats of childhood was the little nodules of pure dry Klim that floated on top of your milk.

"There was also Pream," says someone. How revolutionary it seemed.

The children go down to take their chances in the risky motorized water. Maybe, much later, they will remember us sitting around the table, eating fish they themselves had caught, back when you could still (what? Catch a fish? See a tree? What desolations lie in store, beyond the plasticized hulls and the knee-skiers?). By then we will be the old days, for them. Almost we are already.

A different part of the north. We're sitting around the table, by lamplight — it's still the old days here, no electricity — talking about bad hunters. Bad hunters, bad fishers, everyone has a story. You come upon a campsite, way in the back of beyond, no roads into the lake, they must have come in by float plane, and there it is, garbage all over the place, beer cans, blobs of human poop flagged by melting toilet paper, and twenty-two fine pickerel left rotting on a rock. Business executives who get themselves flown in during hunting season with their high-powered rifles, shoot a buck, cut off the head, fill their quota, see another one with a bigger spread of antlers, drop the first head, cut off the second. The woods are littered with discarded heads, and who cares about the bodies?

New way to shoot polar bear: you have the natives on the ground finding them for you, then they radio the location in to the base camp, the base camp phones New York, fellow gets on the plane, gets himself flown in, they've got the rifle and the clothing all ready for him, fly him to the bear, he pulls the trigger from the plane, doesn't even get out of the g.d. *plane*, they fly him back, cut off the head, skin it, send the lot down to New York.

These are the horror stories of the north, one brand. They've replaced the ones in which you got pounced upon by a wolverine or had your arm chewed off by a she-bear with cubs or got chased into the lake by a moose in rut, or even the ones in which your dog got porcupine quills or rolled in poison ivy and gave it to you. In the new stories, the enemies and the victims of old have done a switch. Nature is no longer implacable, dangerous, ready to jump you; it is on the run, pursued by a number of unfair bullies with the latest technology.

One of the key nouns in these stories is *float plane*. These outrages, this banditry, would not be possible without them, for the bad hunters are notoriously weak-muscled and are deemed incapable of portaging a canoe, much less paddling one. Among their other badnesses, they are sissies. Another key motif is money. What money buys these days, among other things, is the privilege of no-risk slaughter.

As for us, the ones telling the stories, tsk-tsking by lamplight, we are the good hunters, or so we think. We've given up saying we only kill to eat; Kraft Dinner and freeze-dried food have put paid to that one. Really there's no excuse for us. However, we do have some virtues left. We can still cast a fly. We don't cut off heads and hang them stuffed on the wall. We would never buy an ocelot coat. We paddle our own canoes.

We're sitting on the dock at night, shivering despite our sweaters, in mid-August, watching the sky. There are a few shooting stars, as there always are at this time in August, as the earth passes through the Perseids. We pride ourselves on knowing a few things like that, about the sky; we find the Dipper, the North Star, Cassiopeia's Chair, and talk about consulting a star chart, which we know we won't actually do. But this is the only place you can really *see* the stars, we tell each other. Cities are hopeless.

Suddenly, an odd light appears, going very fast. It spirals around like a newly dead firecracker, and then bursts, leaving a cloud of luminous dust, caught perhaps in the light from the sun, still up there somewhere. What could this be? Several days later, we hear that it was part of an extinct Soviet satellite, or that's what they say. That's what they would say, wouldn't they? It strikes us that we don't really know very much about the night sky at all any more. There's all kinds of junk up there: spy planes, old satellites, tin cans, man-made matter gone out of control. It also strikes us that we are totally dependent for knowledge of these things on a few people who don't tell us very much.

Once, we thought that if the balloon ever went up we'd head for the bush and hide out up there, living — we naively supposed — off the land. Now we know that if the two superpowers begin hurling things at each other through the sky, they're likely to do it across the Arctic, with big bangs and fallout all over the north. The wind blows everywhere. Survival gear and knowing which moss you can eat is not going to be a large help. The north is no longer a refuge.

Driving back toward Toronto from the Near North, a small reprise runs through my head:

> Land of the septic tank,
> Home of the speedboat,
> Where still the four-wheel-drive
> Wanders at will,
> Blue lake and tacky shore,
> I will return once more:
> Vroom-diddy-vroom-vroom
> Vroom-diddy-vroom-vroom
> Vroo-OO-oo-oom.

Somehow, just as the drive north inspires saga and tragedy, the drive south inspires parody. And here it comes: the gift shops shaped like teepees, the maple-syrup emporiums that get themselves up like olde-tyme sugaring-off huts; and, farther south, the restaurants that pretend to offer wholesome farm fare, the stores that pretend to be general stores, selling quilts, soap shaped like hearts, high-priced fancy conserves done up in frilly cloth caps, the way Grandma (whoever she might be) was fondly supposed to have made them.

And then come the housing developments, acres of prime farmland turning overnight into Quality All-Brick Family Homes; and then come the Industrial Parks; and there, in full antibloom, is the city itself, looming like a mirage or a chemical warfare zone on the horizon. A browny-grey scuzz hovers above it, and we think, as we always do when facing re-entry, we're going into *that*? We're going to breathe *that*?

But we go forward, as we always do, into what is now to us the unknown. And once inside, we breathe the air, not much bad happens to us, we hardly notice. It's as if we've never been anywhere else. But that's what we think, too, when we're in the north.

7

HAUNTED BY THEIR NIGHTMARES

BELOVED

BY TONI MORRISON

BELOVED IS Toni Morrison's fifth novel, and another triumph. Indeed, Ms. Morrison's versatility and technical and emotional range appear to know no bounds. If there were any doubts about her stature as a pre-eminent American novelist, of her own or any other generation, *Beloved* will put them to rest. In three words or less, it's a hair-raiser.

In *Beloved*, Ms. Morrison turns away from the contemporary scene that has been her concern of late. This new novel is set after the end of the Civil War, during the period of so-called Reconstruction, when a great deal of random violence was let loose upon blacks, both the slaves freed by Emancipation and others who had been given or had bought their freedom earlier. But there are flashbacks to a more distant period, when slavery was still a going concern in the South and the seeds for the bizarre and calamitous events of the novel were sown. The setting is similarly divided: the countryside near Cincinnati, where the central characters have ended up, and a slave-holding plantation in Kentucky, ironically named Sweet Home, from which they fled eighteen years before the novel opens.

There are many stories and voices in this novel, but the central one belongs to Sethe, a woman in her mid-thirties who is living in an

Ohio farmhouse, with her daughter, Denver, and her mother-in-law Baby Suggs. *Beloved* is such a unified novel that it's difficult to discuss it without giving away the plot, but it must be said at the outset that it is, among other things, a ghost story, for the farmhouse is also home to a sad, malicious, and angry ghost, the spirit of Sethe's baby daughter, who had her throat cut under appalling circumstances eighteen years before, when she was two. We never know this child's full name, but we — and Sethe — think of her as Beloved, because that is what is on her tombstone. Sethe wanted "Dearly Beloved," from the funeral service, but had only enough strength to pay for one word. Payment was ten minutes of sex with the tombstone engraver. This act, which is recounted early in the novel, is a keynote for the whole book: in the world of slavery and poverty, where human beings are merchandise, everything has its price, and price is tyrannical.

"Who would have thought that a little old baby could harbor so much rage?" Sethe thinks, but it does; breaking mirrors, making tiny handprints in cake icing, smashing dishes, and manifesting itself in pools of blood-red light. As the novel opens, the ghost is in full possession of the house, having driven away Sethe's two young sons. Old Baby Suggs, after a lifetime of slavery and a brief respite of freedom — purchased for her by the Sunday labour of her son Halle, Sethe's husband — has given up and died. Sethe lives with her memories, almost all of them bad. Denver, her teenage daughter, courts the baby ghost because, since her family has been ostracized by the neighbours, she doesn't have anyone else to play with.

The supernatural element is treated, not in an *Amityville Horror*, watch-me-make-your-flesh-creep mode, but with magnificent practicality, like the ghost of Catherine Earnshaw in *Wuthering Heights*. All the main characters in the book believe in ghosts, so it's merely natural for this one to be there. As Baby Suggs says, "Not a house in the country ain't packed to its rafters with some dead Negro's grief. We lucky this ghost is a baby. My husband's spirit was to come back in here? or yours? Don't talk to me. You lucky." In fact, Sethe would rather have the ghost there than not there. It is, after all, her adored child, and any sign of it is better, for her, than nothing.

This grotesque domestic equilibrium is disturbed by the arrival of Paul D., one of the "Sweet Home men" from Sethe's past. The Sweet Home men were the male slaves of the establishment. Their owner, Mr. Garner, is no Simon Legree; instead he's a best-case slave-holder, treating his "property" well, trusting them, allowing them choice in the running of his small plantation, and calling them "men" in defiance of the neighbours, who want all male blacks to be called "boys." But Mr. Garner dies, and weak, sickly Mrs. Garner brings in her handiest male relative, who is known as "the schoolteacher." This Goebbels-like paragon combines viciousness with intellectual pre-tensions; he's a sort of master-race proponent who measures the heads of the slaves and tabulates the results to demonstrate that they are more like animals than people. Accompanying him are his two sadistic and repulsive nephews. From there it's all downhill at Sweet Home, as the slaves try to escape, go crazy, or are murdered. Sethe, in a trek that makes the ice-floe scene in *Uncle Tom's Cabin* look like a stroll around the block, gets out, just barely; her husband, Halle, doesn't. Paul D. does, but has some very unpleasant adventures along the way, including a literally nauseating sojourn in a nineteenth-century Georgia chain gang.

Through the different voices and memories of the book, including that of Sethe's mother, a survivor of the infamous slave-ship crossing, we experience American slavery as it was lived by those who were its objects of exchange, both at its best — which wasn't very good — and at its worst, which was as bad as can be imagined. Above all, it is seen as one of the most viciously antifamily institutions human beings have ever devised. The slaves are motherless, fatherless, deprived of their mates, their children, their kin. It is a world in which people suddenly vanish and are never seen again, not through accident or covert oper-ation or terrorism, but as a matter of everyday legal policy.

Slavery is also presented to us as a paradigm of how most people behave when they are given absolute power over other people. The first effect, of course, is that they start believing in their own superiority and justifying their actions by it. The second effect is that they make a cult of the inferiority of those they subjugate. It's no coincidence that the first of the deadly sins, from which all the others were supposed to stem, is Pride, a sin of which Sethe is, incidentally, also accused.

In a novel that abounds in black bodies — headless, hanging from trees, frying to a crisp, locked in woodsheds for purposes of rape, or floating downstream drowned — it isn't surprising that the "whitepeople," especially the men, don't come off too well. Horrified black children see whites as men "without skin." Sethe thinks of them as having "mossy teeth" and is ready, if necessary, to bite off their faces, and worse, to avoid further mossy-toothed outrages. There are a few whites who behave with something approaching decency. There's Amy, the young runaway indentured servant who helps Sethe in childbirth during her flight to freedom, and incidentally reminds the reader that the nineteenth century, with its child labour, wage slavery, and widespread and accepted domestic violence, wasn't tough only for blacks but for all but the most privileged whites as well. There are also the abolitionists who help Baby Suggs find a house and a job after she is freed. But even the decency of these "good" whitepeople has a grudging side to it, and even they have trouble seeing the people they are helping as full-fledged people, though to show them as totally free of their xenophobia and sense of superiority might well have been anachronistic.

Toni Morrison is careful not to make all the whites awful and all the blacks wonderful. Sethe's black neighbours, for instance, have their own envy and scapegoating tendencies to answer for, and Paul D., though much kinder than, for instance, the woman-bashers of Alice Walker's novel *The Color Purple*, has his own limitations and flaws. But then, considering what he's been through, it's a wonder he isn't a mass murderer. If anything, he's a little too huggable, under the circumstances.

Back in the present tense, in chapter one, Paul D. and Sethe make an attempt to establish a "real" family, whereupon the baby ghost, feeling excluded, goes berserk, but is driven out by Paul D.'s stronger will. So it appears. But then, along comes a strange, beautiful, real flesh-and-blood young woman, about twenty years old, who can't seem to remember where she comes from, who talks like a young child, who has an odd, raspy voice and no lines on her hands, who takes an intense, devouring interest in Sethe, and who says her name is Beloved.

Students of the supernatural will admire the way this twist is handled. Ms. Morrison blends a knowledge of folklore — for instance, in many traditions, the dead cannot return from the grave unless called, and it's the passions of the living that keep them alive — with a highly original treatment. The reader is kept guessing; there's a lot more to Beloved than any one character can see, and she manages to be many things to several people. She is a catalyst for revelations as well as self-revelations; through her we come to know not only how, but why, the original child Beloved was killed. And through her also Sethe achieves, finally, her own form of self-exorcism, her own self-accepting peace.

Beloved is written in an antiminimalist prose that is by turns rich, graceful, eccentric, rough, lyrical, sinuous, colloquial, and very much to the point. Here, for instance, is Sethe remembering Sweet Home:

> . . . suddenly there was Sweet Home rolling, rolling, rolling out before her eyes, and although there was not a leaf on that farm that did not want to make her scream, it rolled itself out before her in shameless beauty. It never looked as terrible as it was and it made her wonder if hell was a pretty place too. Fire and brimstone all right, but hidden in lacy groves. Boys hanging from the most beautiful sycamores in the world. It shamed her — remembering the

wonderful soughing trees rather than the boys. Try as she might to make it otherwise, the sycamores beat out the children every time and she could not forgive her memory for that.

In this book, the other world exists and magic works, and the prose is up to it. If you can believe page one — and Ms. Morrison's verbal authority compels belief — you're hooked on the rest of the book.

The epigraph to *Beloved* is from the Bible, Romans 9:25: "I will call them my people, which were not my people; and her beloved, which was not beloved." Taken by itself, this might seem to favour doubt about, for instance, the extent to which Beloved was really loved, or the extent to which Sethe herself was rejected by her own community. But there is more to it than that. The passage is from a chapter in which the Apostle Paul ponders, Job-like, the ways of God toward humanity, in particular the evils and inequities visible everywhere on the earth. Paul goes on to talk about the fact that the Gentiles, hitherto despised and outcast, have now been redefined as acceptable. The passage proclaims, not rejection, but reconciliation and hope. It continues: "And it shall come to pass, that in the place where it was said unto them, Ye are not my people; there shall they be called the children of the living God."

Toni Morrison is too smart, and too much of a writer, not to have intended this context. Here, if anywhere, is her own comment on the goings-on in her novel, her final response to the measuring and dividing and excluding "schoolteachers" of this world. An epigraph to a book is like a key signature in music, and *Beloved* is written in major.

AFTERWORD

A JEST OF GOD
BY MARGARET LAURENCE

I STILL HAVE my first copy of *A Jest of God*. It is, in fact, the first edition, with a medium-sized format, not very good quality paper, an unprepossessing jacket, maroon background, formal green border, no illustration. I got it for Christmas in 1966, from my parents, who had learned with some apprehension that I wanted to be a writer, and had done their best by giving me a book by one of the few Canadian writers they (or anyone else) knew about at the time. I was a graduate student in English Literature at Harvard University. I read it in one sitting.

I had already read one other novel by Margaret Laurence, *The Stone Angel*, dropped into my hands by Jane Rule when I was living in Vancouver. It knocked me out, to put it mildly. So when I seized with eagerness on *A Jest of God*, it was in part to see if a hard act could be followed.

It could. But more of that shortly.

Four months later, I was notified by phone that I had won the Governor General's Award for Poetry for my first book, *The Circle Game*, which had been published in the fall. At first I thought this announcement was an error, or a joke. When it turned out to be true, delight set in — I was very broke, and the money would go a long way — and then panic. My wardrobe at the time consisted of tweed skirts, dark-hued cardigans with woolly balls on them, and grey Hush Puppies, all appropriate for female graduate students but hardly suitable for the proposed formal dinner. What would I wear?

Worse, what would I say to Margaret Laurence, who had won the Governor General's Award for Fiction that year for *A Jest of God*? I had studied the handsome, austere photograph of her on the inside jacket flap, and had decided that nobody except Simone de Beauvoir would have such power to reduce me to a quaking jelly. I was in awe of her talent, but also I was afraid of her hairdo. This was a serious person, who would make judgements: unfavourable ones, about me. One zap from that intellect and I would be squashed like a bug.

My two Harvard roommates took me in hand. They did not know what the Governor General's Award was, but they did not want me to disgrace them. They went at me with big rollers and some hairset and lent me a dress. I'd been adjusting to new contact lenses, and they were adamant about these: into my eyes they must go on the gala evening, no tortoise-shell horn-rims allowed.

The ceremony and then the dinner went on longer than I had expected, and at the end of the first course I began to weep. It was the lenses: I had not yet developed the knack of removing them without a mirror. The two gentlemen from Quebec who flanked me thought I was overcome with emotion, and were solicitous. I sat there in a frenzy of embarrassment, with the tears trickling from my eyes, wondering how soon I could decently make my escape. As soon as the presentation was concluded, I rushed to the washroom like Cinderella fleeing the ball.

Who should be in there but Margaret Laurence? She was in black and gold, but otherwise not at all as anticipated. Instead she was warm, friendly, and sympathetic. Also, she was more of a dithering nervous wreck than I was.

It was a moment worthy of Rachel Cameron, that avatar of social awkwardness and self-conscious embarrassment. Like Rachel,

I had made an idiot of myself; like Rachel, too, I got my share of kindness from an unexpected source.

Much as I admire other books by Margaret Laurence, *A Jest of God* holds a special place for me. Possibly because, when I read it, I was at the right age to appreciate the craft that lay behind its apparent artlessness. A few years earlier and I might have preferred the more obviously artistic, the more overtly experimental. I might have rejected its simplicity of an apple in favour of something more baroque, or — let's face it — more existential and French.

As it was, I found it an almost perfect book, in that it did what it set out to do, with no gaps and no excesses. Like a pool or a well, it covers a small area but goes down deep. I once heard a Norwegian writer describe the work of another author as "an egg of a book." *A Jest of God*, too, is an egg of a book — plain, self-contained, elegant in form, holding within it the essentials of a life.

That life is Rachel Cameron's, who shares with several of Laurence's protagonists a Scottish last name and a biblical first name. Her namesake, however, is not the Rachel of the Jacob and Leah saga in Genesis, but that of Jeremiah 31:15: "Rachel weeping for her children refused to be comforted for her children, because they were not." Like several of Margaret Laurence's fictions, especially those concerned with the inhabitants of the town of Manawaka, Rachel's story is told as first-person narration, and is the story of a woman trapped in a prison partly of her own making. But the prison here is smaller and more tightly locked than any of the others. Hagar of *The Stone Angel* gets to Vancouver, as does Stacey of *The Fire-Dwellers*; Morag Gunn of *The Diviners* travels even farther afield, to Toronto and also England. But apart from her trip to the hospital, we never see Rachel anywhere but in her hometown: her break for freedom at the end of the book exists mostly in the future tense. Rachel's prison is so hard for her to get out of because it is made mostly from virtues gone sour: filial devotion, self-sacrifice, the concern for appearances advocated by St. Paul, a sense of duty, the desire to avoid hurting others, and the wish to be loved. It may be hard for us to remember, now, that Rachel is not some sort of aberration but merely the epitome of what nice girls were once educated to be. To go against such overwhelming social assumptions, to assert instead one's self, as Rachel finally does, takes more than a little courage and a good deal of desperation. Desperation and courage are the two magnetic poles of this book, which begins with the first and arrives at the second.

The desperation is conveyed by the texture of the prose, the accuracy of the physical details. Rachel's inner monologue is a little masterpiece in itself, rendered in a language by turns colloquial and flat as prairie speech, terse and ironic as jokes, self-mocking, charged with nervous irritability, and eloquent as psalms. Then there are the entirely believable, entirely minor, entirely horrifying domestic snippets from Rachel's claustrophobic life with her sweetly nagging hypochondriac of a mother, who plays guilt like a violin: the awfulness of the bridge-night asparagus sandwiches, the rotting, monstrous rubber douche bag Rachel unearths during her feverish brush with sex. Any novelist writing this kind of realism has to get such details right or the whole illusion falls apart. In *A Jest of God*, Laurence does not put a foot wrong.

Oddly, for a novel about what used to be called a spinster, *A Jest of God* is structured almost entirely around children, and the flow of time and emotion in and around them; and thus around mothers and mothering, fathers and fathering, and the relationships, often interchangeable, between those who mother and are mothered, those who give and receive nurturing and comfort. Rachel's false pregnancy is an ambiguous indication of the lesson she comes to learn: how to be a mother, to herself first of all, since true mothering has been denied her.

Rachel Cameron begins as a child, still stuck in the time of the little girls' skipping chant she hears through her open classroom window, still playing dutiful daughter to a mother who treats her as if she is only half grown. At the age of thirty-four, she arrives at gawky adolescence, agonizing over her appearance and sexuality, going through a painful and unrequited crush. But she ends as an adult, having real-ized the childishness of her own mother and thus her inability to offer emotional safety, having accepted the risks inherent in being alive, having taken her true place in time: "Beside me sleeps my eld-erly child. . . . What will happen? What will happen. It may be that my children will always be temporary, never to be held. But so are everyone's."

Rereading *A Jest of God* yet again, I was cheered by how little it has dated. Some of the social customs and sexual constraints may have vanished, but the kinds of expectations placed on women, although in different costume, are still around — perfect physical beauty, total self-confidence, angelic and selfless nurturing of one variety or another. What Rachel can offer us now as readers is something we still need to know: how to acknowledge our own human and necessary limitations, our own foolishness. How to say both No, and Yes.

9

PREFACE

THE CANADIAN GREEN CONSUMER GUIDE

By now, most people know we're in danger.

We've heard about the thinning ozone layer, the greenhouse effect, acid rain, the destruction of the world's forests, arable lands, and drinkable water. The danger we're in is enormous: if we don't do something about it, its results could be as devastating as those of a worldwide nuclear catastrophe. We have finally realized that we cannot continue to dump toxic chemicals and garbage into the water, air, and earth of this planet without eventually killing both it and ourselves — because everything we eat, drink, and grow has its ultimate source in the natural world.

However, most people don't know what to do. In the face of such an enormous global problem, they feel helpless. But although the problem is global, the solutions must be local. Unless we begin somewhere, we will never begin at all. An absence of small beginnings will spell the end.

During the Depression and the war, conservation was a way of life. It wasn't called that. It was called saving, or salvaging, or rationing. People saved things and reused them because materials were expensive or scarce. They saved string, rubber bands, bacon fat, newspapers, tin cans and glass bottles, old clothes. They made new things out of old things; they darned socks, turned shirt collars. They grew Victory Gardens. "Waste not, want not" was their motto.

Then came the end of the war, a new affluence, and the Disposable Society. We were encouraged to spend and waste; it was supposed to be good for the economy. Throwing things out became a luxury. We indulged.

We can no longer afford our wasteful habits. It's Back to the Basics, time for a return to the Three Rs: *Reduce. Reuse. Recycle. Refuse*, too, to buy polluting products, and *rethink* your behaviour. For instance, use less energy: cut your overhead and increase profits, and stave off a tax hike. Dry your clothes on a rack: humidify your home and lower your hydro bill. Leave excess packaging at the store: let *them* dispose of it. Manufacturers will get the message pretty quick, not just from you but from disgruntled retailers. Start a compost heap. Vote for politicians with the best environmental platforms. Choose non-disposables: razors with real blades instead of the plastic chuck-it-out kind, fountain pens rather than toss-outs. Shop for organic veggies; do it using a shopping basket so you won't have to cart home all those annoying plastic bags that pile up under the sink. Lobby for country-of-origin labels on all food, so you know you aren't eating destroyed Amazonian rainforest with every hamburger bite.

Pollution control, like charity, must begin at home. It's true that industries are major polluters, but industries, in the final analysis, are market- and therefore consumer-driven. If enough of us refuse to buy polluting products, the manufacturers will go out of business. Even a small percentage swing in buying patterns can mean the difference between profit and loss.

This is wartime. Right now we're losing, but it's a war we can still win, with some good luck, a lot of good will, and a great many intelligent choices. This book is a guide to some of those choices. Although they are about familiar, harmless-looking, everyday objects, they are, in the final analysis, life-or-death choices.

And the choice is yours.

10

GREAT AUNTS

Aunt J., who was my third and youngest aunt, took me to my first writers' conference. That was in Montreal, in 1958, when I was eighteen. I had already produced several impressive poems; at least I was impressed by them. They had decaying leaves, garbage cans, cigarette butts, and cups of coffee in them. I had been ambushed by T. S. Eliot several months previously, and had wrestled him to a standstill. I did not yet know that it was the done thing, by now, to refer to him as T. S. Idiot.

I didn't show my seedy poems to my mother, who was the oldest of the three sisters and therefore pragmatic, since it was she who had had to tend the others. She was the athlete of the family and was fond of horses and ice-skating and any other form of rapid motion that offered escapes from domestic duties. My mother had only written one poem in her life, when she was eight or nine; it began, "I had some wings, They were lovely things," and went on, typically for her, to describe the speed of the subsequent flight. I knew that if I forced her to read my butt-and-coffee-ground free verses, she would say they were very nice, this being her standard response to other puzzlements, such as my increasingly dour experiments with wardrobe. Clothing was not a priority of hers either.

But Aunt J. had written reams, according to my mother. She was a romantic figure, as she had once had pleurisy and had been in a san, where she had made flowery shellwork brooches; I had received several of these treasures for Christmas, as a child, in tiny magical boxes with cotton wool in them. Tiny boxes, cotton wool: these were not my mother's style. Aunt J. had to be careful of her health, an infirmity that seemed to go along with writing, from what I knew. She cried at the sad places in movies, as I did, and had flights of fantasy as a child in the Annapolis Valley of Nova Scotia, which was where they had all grown up. Her middle name was Carmen, and to punish what they thought to be her inordinate pride over this her two older sisters had named the pig Carmen.

Aunt J. was rounded in outline, myopic (as I was), and depicted herself as a sentimental pushover, though this was merely a useful fiction, part of the self-deprecating camouflage adopted by women then, for various useful purposes. Underneath her facade of lavender-coloured flutter she was tough-minded, like all three of those sisters. It was this blend of soft and hard that appealed to me.

So I showed my poems to Aunt J. She read them and did not laugh, or not in my presence; though knowing her I doubt that she laughed at all. She knew what it was to have ambitions as a writer, though hers had been delayed by Uncle M., who was a bank manager, and by their two children. Much later, she herself would be speaking at conferences, sitting on panels, appearing nervously on talk shows, having authored five books of her own. Meanwhile she wrote children's stories for the weekly Sunday school papers and bided her time.

She sent my gloomy poems to Second Cousin Lindsay, who was an English professor at Dalhousie University. He said I had promise. Aunt J. showed me his letter, beaming with pleasure. This was my first official encouragement.

The writers' conference Aunt J. took me to was put on by the Canadian Authors Association, which at that time was the only writers' organization in Canada. I knew its reputation — it was the same tea-party outfit about which F. R. Scott had written, "Expansive puppets percolate self-unction / Beneath a portrait of the Prince of Wales." It was rumoured to be full of elderly amateurs; I was unlikely to see anyone there sprouting a three-day beard or clad in a black turtleneck pullover, or looking anything like Samuel Beckett or Eugene Ionesco, who were more or less my idea of real writers. But Aunt J. and I were both so desperate for contact with anything that smacked of the world of letters that we were willing to take our chances with the CAA.

Once at the conference, we opted for a paper to be given by an expert on Fanny Burney. I goggled around the room: there were a lot of what I thought were middle-aged women, in flowered dresses — not unlike Aunt J.'s own dress — and little suits, though there was no one who looked like my idea of a writer: pallid, unkempt, red-eyed. But this was Canada and not France, so what could I expect?

Up to this time I had seen only one Canadian writer in the flesh. His name was Wilson MacDonald and he'd turned up in our high-school auditorium, old and wispy and white-haired, where he'd recited several healthy-minded poems about skiing, from memory, and had imitated a crow. I had a fair idea what Jean-Paul Sartre would have thought of him, and was worried that I might end up that way myself: wheeled out for a bunch of spitball-throwing teenaged thugs, doing birdcalls. You could not be a real writer and a Canadian too, that much was clear. As soon as I could, I was going to hit Paris and become incomprehensible.

Meanwhile, there I was in Montreal, waiting for the Fanny Burney expert with Aunt J. We were both nervous. We felt like spies of a sort, infiltrators; and so like infiltrators we began to eavesdrop. Right behind us was sitting a woman whose name we recognized because she frequently had poems about snow-covered spruce trees published in the daily Montreal newspaper. She was not discussing spruce trees now, but a hanging that had taken place the day before, at the prison. "It was so dreadful for him," she was saying. "He was so upset."

Our ears were flapping: had she known the condemned man personally? If so, how creepy. But as we listened on, we gathered that the upset man was not the hanged one; it was her husband, who was the prison chaplain.

Several gaps opened at my feet: the gap between the sentimentality of this woman's poems and the realities of her life, between the realities of her life and her perceptions of them; between the hangers and the hanged, and the consolers of the hanged, and the consolers of the hangers. This was one of my first intimations that, beneath its facade of teacups and outdoor pursuits and various kinds of trees, Canada — even this literary, genteel segment of Canada, for which I had such youthful contempt — was a good deal more problematic than I had thought.

But I should have known that already.

In the early part of my childhood, I had not known any of my relatives, because they lived in Nova Scotia, two thousand miles away. My parents had left Nova Scotia during the Depression because there were no jobs there. By the time I was born, the Second World War had begun, and nobody travelled great distances without official reasons and gas coupons. But although my aunts were not present in the flesh, they were very much present in the spirit. The three sisters wrote one another every week, and my mother read these letters out loud, to my father but by extension to myself and my brother, after dinner. They were called "letters from home." *Home*, for my mother, was always Nova Scotia, never wherever we might be living at the time, which gave me the vague idea that I was misplaced. Wherever I actually was living myself, *home* was not there.

So I was kept up on the doings of my aunts, and also of my cousins, my second cousins, and many other people who fitted in somewhere but were more distantly related. In Nova Scotia, it's not what you do or even who you know that is the most important thing about you. It's which town you're from and who you're related to. Any conversation between two Maritimers who've never met before will begin this way, and go on until both parties discover that they are in fact related to each other. I grew up in a huge extended family of invisible people.

It was not my invisible aunts in their present-day incarnation who made the most impression on me. It was my aunts in the past. There they were as children, in the impossible starched and frilled dresses and the floppy satin hair bows of the first decades of the century, or as teenagers, in black and white in the photograph album, wearing strange clothing — cloche hats, flapper coats up over the knee, standing beside antique motor cars, or posed in front of rocks or the sea in striped bathing suits that came halfway down their legs. Sometimes their arms would be around one another. They had been given captions, by my mother: "We Three," "Bathing Belles." Aunt J. was thin as a child, dark-eyed, intense. Aunt K., the middle sister, looked tailored and brisk. My mother, with huge Pre-Raphaelite eyes and wavy hair and model's cheekbones, was the beauty, a notion she made light of: she was, and remained, notorious for her bad taste in clothes, a notion she cultivated so she wouldn't have to go shopping for them alone. But all three sisters had the same high-bridged noses; Roman noses, my mother said. I pored over these pictures, intrigued by the idea of the triplicate, identical noses. I did not have a sister myself then, and the mystique of sisterhood was potent for me.

The photo album was one mode of existence for my invisible aunts. They were even more alive in my mother's stories, for, although she was no poet, my mother was a raconteur and deadly mimic. The characters in her stories about "home" became as familiar to me as characters in books; and, since we lived in isolated places and moved a lot, they were more familiar than most of the people I actually encountered.

The cast was constant. First came my strict, awe-inspiring grand-father, a country doctor who drove around the dirt roads in a horse and sleigh, through blizzards, delivering babies in the dead of night and threatening to horsewhip his daughters — especially my mother — for real or imagined transgressions. I did not know what a horsewhip was, so this punishment had the added attraction of the bizarre.

Then came my distracted, fun-loving grandmother, and my Aunt K., a year younger than my mother but much more intellectual and firm of will, according to my mother. Then Aunt J., sentimental and apt to be left out. These three were "the girls." Then, somewhat later, "the boys," my two uncles, one of whom blew the stove lids off the country schoolhouse with some homemade explosive hidden in a log, the other who was sickly but frequently had everyone "in stitches." And the peripheral figures: hired girls who were driven away by the machinations of my mother and Aunt K., who did not like hav-ing them around, hired men who squirted them while milking the cows; the cows themselves; the pig; the horses. The horses were not really peripheral characters; although they had no lines, they had names and personalities and histories, and they were my mother's partners in escapades. Dick and Nell were their names. Dick was my favourite; he had been given to my mother as a broken-down, ill-treated hack, and she had restored him to health and glossy beauty. This was the kind of happy ending I found satisfactory.

The stories about these people had everything that could be asked for: plot, action, suspense — although I knew how they would turn out, having heard them before — and fear, because there was always the danger of my grandfather's finding out and resorting to the horsewhip threat, although I don't believe he actually horse-whipped anyone.

What would he find out? Almost anything. There were many things he was not supposed to know, many things the girls were not supposed to know, but did. And what if he were to find out that they knew? A great deal turned, in these stories and in that family, on concealment; on what you did or did not tell; on what was said as distinct from what was meant. "If you can't say anything good, don't say anything at all," said my mother, saying a great deal. My mother's stories were my first lesson in reading between the lines.

My mother featured in these stories as physically brave, a walker of fences and also of barn ridgepoles, a sin of horsewhipping proportions — but shy. She was so shy that she would hide from visitors behind the barn, and she could not go to school until Aunt K. was old enough to take her. In addition to the bravery and the shyness, however, she had a violent temper. "Like Father's," she said. This was improbable to me, since I could not remember any examples. My mother losing her temper would have been a sight to behold, like the Queen standing on her head. But I accepted the idea on faith, along with the rest of her mythology.

Aunt K. was not shy. Although she was younger than my mother, you would never know it: "We were more like twins." She was a child of steely nerves, according to my mother. She was a ringleader, and thought up plots and plans, which she carried out with ruthless efficiency. My mother would be drawn into these, willy-nilly: she claimed she was too weak of will to resist.

"The girls" had to do household chores, more of them after they had driven away the hired girls, and Aunt K. was a hard worker and an exacting critic of the housework of others. Later on in the story, Aunt K. and my mother had a double wedding; the night before this event they read their adolescent diaries out loud to one another and then burnt them. "We cleaned the kitchen," said Aunt K.'s diary. "The others did not do an A-I job." My mother and Aunt J. would always laugh when repeating this. It was, as Matthew Arnold would have had it, a touchstone line for them, about Aunt K.

But there was even more to Aunt K. She was a brilliant student, and had her MA in History from the University of Toronto. My grandfather thought my mother was a flighty, pleasure-bent flibbertigibbet until she saved her own money from schoolteaching and sent herself to college; but he was all set to finance Aunt K. for an advanced degree at Oxford. However, she turned this down in favour of marrying a local Annapolis Valley doctor and having six children. The reason, my mother implied, had something to do with Great-Aunt Winnie, who also had an MA, the first woman to receive one from Dalhousie, but who had never married. Aunt Winnie was condemned — it was thought of as a condemnation — to teach school forever, and who turned up at family Christmases looking wistful. In those days, said my mother, if you did not get married by a certain age, it was unlikely that you ever would. "You didn't think about not marrying," said Aunt J. to me, much later. "There wasn't any *choice* about it. It was just what you did."

Meanwhile, there was my Aunt K. in the album, in a satin wedding gown and a veil identical to my mother's, and later, with all six children, dressed up as the Old Woman Who Lived in a Shoe in the Apple Blossom Festival Parade. Unlike the stories in books, my mother's stories did not have clear morals, and the moral of this one was less clear than most. Which was better? To be brilliant and go to Oxford, or to have six children? Why couldn't it be both?

When I was six or seven and my brother was eight or nine and the war was over, we began to visit Nova Scotia, every summer or every second summer. We had to: my grandfather had had something called a coronary, more than one of them in fact, and he could die at any moment. Despite his strictness and what seemed, to me, to be acts of gross unfairness, he was loved and respected. Everyone agreed on that.

These visits were a strain. We reached Nova Scotia from Ontario by driving at breakneck speed and for a great many hours at a time over the postwar highways of Quebec and Vermont and New Brunswick, so that we would arrive cranky and frazzled, usually in the middle of the night. During the visits we would have to be on whispering good behaviour in my grandfather's large white house, and meet and be met by a great many relatives we hardly knew.

But the worst strain of all was fitting these real people — so much smaller and older and less vivid than they ought to have been — into the mythology in my possession. My grandfather was not galloping around the countryside, roaring threats and saving babies. Instead he carved little wooden figures and had to have a nap every afternoon, and his greatest exertion was a stroll around the orchard or a game of chess with my brother. My grandmother was not the harried although comical mother of five, but the caretaker of my grandfather. There were no cows any more, and where were the beautiful horses, Dick and Nell?

I felt defrauded. I did not want Aunt J. and Aunt K. to be the grown-up mothers of my cousins, snapping beans in the kitchen. I wanted them back the way they were supposed to be, in the bobbed haircuts and short skirts of the photo album, playing tricks on the hired girls, being squirted by the hired man, living under the threat of horse-whipping, failing to do an A-1 job.

Once, I went on a literary outing with both my aunts.

It was in the early 1970s, when I was over thirty and had published several books. Aunt J.'s husband had died, and she'd moved from Montreal back to Nova Scotia to take care of my ageing grandmother. I was visiting, and the aunts and I decided to drive over to nearby Bridgetown, to pay a call on a writer named Ernest Buckler. Ernest Buckler had written a novel called *The Mountain and the Valley*, the mountain being the North Mountain, the valley being the Annapolis Valley. He'd had some success with it in the States — at that time, in Canada, a surefire ticket to hatred and envy — but because he was an eccentric recluse, the hatred and envy quotient was modified. But his success in the States had not been duplicated in Canada, because his Toronto publishers were United Church teetotallers, known for throwing launch parties at which they served fruit juice. (Modernization came finally, with the addition of sherry, doled out in a separate room, into which those who craved it could slink furtively.) These publishers had discovered that there were what my mother referred to as "goings-on" in Buckler's book, and had hidden it in the stock room. If you wanted to actually buy one, it was like getting porn out of the Vatican.

I had read this book as a young adolescent because somebody had given it to my parents under the impression that they would like it because it was about Nova Scotia. My mother's comment was that it was not what things were like when she was growing up. I snuck this book up onto the garage roof, which was flat, where I swiftly located the goings-on and then read the rest of the book. It was probably the first novel for adults that I ever did read, with the exception of *Moby Dick*.

So I remembered Ernest Buckler's book with fondness; and by the 1970s I'd become involved in a correspondence with him. So over we went to see him in the flesh. My Aunt J. was all agog, because Ernest Buckler was a real writer. My Aunt K. drove. (My Aunt J. never drove, having scraped the doorhandles off the car on one of her few attempts, according to her.)

Aunt K. knew the vicinity well, and pointed out the places of interest as we went by. She had a good memory. It was she who had told me something everyone else had forgotten, including myself: that I had announced, at the age of five, that I was going to be a writer.

During this drive, however, her mind was on other historical matters. "That's the tree where the man who lived in the white house hanged himself," she said. "That's where the barn got burned down. They know who did it but they can't prove a thing. The man in there blew his head off with a shotgun." These events may have taken place years, decades before, but they were still current in the area. It appeared that the Valley was more like *The Mountain and the Valley* than I had suspected.

Ernest Buckler lived in a house that could not have been changed for fifty years. It still had a horsehair sofa, antimacassars, a wood stove in the living room. Ernest himself was enormously likeable and highly nervous, and anxious that we be pleased. He hopped around a lot, talking a mile a minute, and kept popping out to the kitchen, then popping in again. We talked mostly about books, and about his plans to scandalize the neighbourhood by phoning me up at my grandmother's house, on the party line, and pretending we were having an affair. "That would give the old biddies something to talk about," he said. Everyone listened in, of course, whenever he had a call, but not just because he was a local celebrity. They listened in on everyone.

After we left, my Aunt J. said, "That was something! He said you had a teeming brain!" (He had said this.) My Aunt K.'s comment was, "That man was oiled." Of the three of us, she was the only one who had figured out why Mr. Buckler had made such frequent trips to the kitchen. But it was understandable that he should have been secretive about it: in the Valley, there were those who drank, and then there were decent people.

Also: there were those who wrote, and then there were decent people. A certain amount of writing was tolerated, but only within limits. Newspaper columns about children and the changing seasons were fine. Sex, swearing, and drinking were beyond the pale.

I myself, in certain Valley circles, was increasingly beyond the pale. As I became better known, I also became more widely read there, not because my writing was thought of as having any particular merit but because I was Related. Aunt J. told me, with relish, how she'd hidden behind the parlour door during a neighbour's scandalized visit with my grandmother. The scandal was one of my own books: how, asked the outraged neighbour, could my grandmother have permitted her granddaughter to publish such immoral trash?

But blood is thicker than water in the Valley. My grandmother gazed serenely out the window and commented on the beautiful fall weather they were having, while my Aunt J. gasped behind the door. My aunts and mother always found the spectacle of my grandmother preserving her dignity irresistible, probably because there was so much dignity to be preserved.

This was the neighbour, the very same one, who as a child had led my aunts astray, sometime during the First World War, inducing them to slide down a red clay bank in their little white lace-edged pantaloons. She had then pressed her nose up against the glass of the window to watch them getting spanked, not just for sliding but for lying about it. My grandmother had gone over and yanked the blind down then, and she was doing it now. Whatever her own thoughts about the goings-on in my fiction, she was keeping them to herself. Nor did she ever mention them to me.

For that I silently thanked her. I suppose any person, but especially any woman, who takes up writing has felt, especially at first, that she was doing it against a huge largely unspoken pressure, the pressure of expectation and decorum. This pressure is most strongly felt, by women, from within the family, and more so when the family is a strong unit. There are things that should not be said. Don't tell. If you can't say anything nice, don't say anything at all. Was that counterbalanced adequately by that other saying of my mother's: "Do what you think is right, no matter what other people think"? And did those other people whose opinion did not matter include the members of one's family?

With the publication of my first real book, I was dreading disapproval. I didn't worry much about my father and mother, who had gracefully survived several other eccentricities of mine — the skirts hand-printed with trilobites and newts, the experiments with beer parlours, the beatnik boyfriends — although they had probably bitten their tongues a few times in the process. Anyway, they lived in Toronto, where goings-on of various kinds had now become more common; not in Nova Scotia, where, it was not quite said, things might be a bit more narrow. Instead, I worried about my aunts. I thought they might be scandalized, even Aunt J. Although she had been subjected to some of my early poems, coffee cups and rotting leaves were one thing, there was more than dirty crockery and mulch in this book. As for Aunt K., so critical of the shoddy housework and drinking habits of others, what would she think?

To my surprise, my aunts came through with flying colours. Aunt J. thought it was wonderful — a real book! She said she was bursting with pride. Aunt K. said that there were certain things that were not done in her generation, but they could be done by mine, and more power to me for doing them.

· This kind of acceptance meant more to me than it should have, to my single-minded all-for-art twenty-six-year-old self. (Surely I ought to be impervious to aunts.) However, like the morals of my mother's stories, what exactly it meant is far from clear to me. Perhaps it was a laying-on of hands, a passing of something from one generation to another. What was being passed on was the story itself: what was known, and what could be told. What was between the lines. The permission to tell the story, wherever that might lead.

Or perhaps it meant that I too was being allowed into the magical static but ever-continuing saga of the photo album. Instead of three different-looking young women with archaic clothes and identical Roman noses, standing with their arms around each other, there would now be four. I was being allowed into *home*.

INTRODUCTION: READING BLIND

THE BEST AMERICAN SHORT STORIES

WHENEVER I'M ASKED to talk about what constitutes a "good" story, or what makes one well-written story "better" than another, I begin to feel very uncomfortable. Once you start making lists or devising rules for stories, or for any other kind of writing, some writer will be sure to happen along and casually break every abstract rule you or anyone else has ever thought up, and take your breath away in the process. The word *should* is a dangerous one to use when speaking of writing. It's a kind of challenge to the deviousness and inventiveness and audacity and perversity of the creative spirit. Sooner or later, anyone who has been too free with it will be liable to end up wearing it like a dunce's cap. We don't judge good stories by the application to them of some set of external measurements, as we judge giant pumpkins at the Fall Fair. We judge them by the way they strike us. And that will depend on a great many subjective imponderables, which we lump together under the general heading of taste.

All of which may explain why, when I sat down to read through the large heap of stories from which I was to select for this collection, I did so with misgiving. There were so many stories to choose from, and all of them, as they say, publishable. I knew this because they had already been published. Over the course of the previous year, the indefatigable and devoted series editor, Shannon Ravenel, had read every short story in every known magazine, large or small, famous or obscure, in both the United States and Canada — a total of more than two thousand stories. Of these she had chosen a hundred and twenty, from which I was to pick twenty. But how was I to do this? What would be my criteria, if any? How would I be able to tell the best from the merely better? How would I *know*?

I had elected to read these stories "blind," which meant that Shannon Ravenel had inked out the names of the authors. I had no idea, in advance, how these small black oblongs would transform the act of editing from a judicious task to a gleeful pleasure. Reading through these authorless manuscripts was like playing hooky: with a hundred strokes of a black marker, I had been freed from the weight of authorial reputation. I didn't have to pay any attention to who ought to be in because of his or her general worthiness or previous critical hosannas. I didn't have to worry about who might feel slighted if not included. That weighing, measuring, calculating side of me — and even the most scrupulously disinterested editor has one — had been safely locked away, leaving me to wallow among the ownerless pages unencumbered. Picking up each new story was like a child's game of Fish. You never knew what you would get: it might be a piece of plastic or it might be something wonderful, a gift, a treasure.

In addition to remaining ignorant about authorial worth, I could disregard any considerations about territory. I had no way of knowing, for instance, whether a story with a female narrator was by a female author, whether one with a male narrator was by a man; whether a story about a Chinese immigrant was by a writer with a Chinese background, whether one about a nineteenth-century Canadian poet was by a Canadian. I've recently heard it argued that writers should tell stories only from a point of view that is their own, or that of a group to which they themselves belong. Writing from the point of view of someone "other" is a form of poaching, the appropriation of material you haven't earned and to which you have no right. Men, for instance, should not write as women; although it's less frequently said that women should not write as men.

This view is understandable but, in the end, self-defeating. Not only does it condemn as thieves and imposters such writers as George Eliot, James Joyce, Emily Brontë, and William Faulkner, and, incidentally, a number of the writers in this book; it is also inhibiting to the imagination in a fundamental way. It's only a short step from saying we can't write from the point of view of an "other" to saying we can't read that way either, and from there to the position that no one can really understand anyone else, so we might as well stop trying. Follow this line of reasoning to its logical conclusion, and we would all be stuck with reading nothing but our own work, over and over; which would be my personal idea of hell. Surely the delight and the wonder come not from who tells the story but from what the story tells, and how.

Reading blind is an intriguing metaphor. When you read blind, you see everything but the author. He or she may be visible intermittently, as a trick of style, a locale about which nobody else is likely to write, a characteristic twist of the plot; but apart from such clues he is incognito. You're stranded with the voice of the story.

The Voice of the Story, the Story as Voice

> In the houses of the people who knew us we were asked to come in and sit, given cold water or lemonade; and while we sat there being refreshed, the people continued their conversations or went about their chores. Little by little we began to piece a story together, a secret, terrible, awful story.
> — Toni Morrison, *The Bluest Eye*

> It is only the story that can continue beyond the war and the warrior. . . . It is only the story . . . that saves our progeny from blundering like blind beggars into the spikes of the cactus fence.

> The story is our escort; without it, we are blind. Does the blind
> man own his escort? No, neither do we the story; rather it is the
> story that owns us.
>
> — Chinua Achebe, *Anthills of the Savannah*

How do we learn our notions of what a story is? What sets "a
story" apart from mere background noise, the wash of syllables that
surrounds us and flows through us and is forgotten every day? What
makes a good story a unified whole, something complete and satisfying in itself? What makes it significant speech? In other words,
what qualities was I searching for, perhaps without knowing it, as I
read diligently through my pile of tear sheets?

I've spoken of "the voice of the story," which has become a sort
of catch-all phrase; but by it I intend something more specific: a
speaking voice, like the singing voice in music, that moves not across
space, across the page, but through time. Surely every written story
is, in the final analysis, a score for voice. Those little black marks on
the page mean nothing without their retranslation into sound. Even
when we read silently, we read with the ear, unless we are reading
bank statements.

Perhaps, by abolishing the Victorian practice of family reading
and by removing from our school curricula those old standbys, the set
memory piece and the recitation, we've deprived both writers and
readers of something essential to stories. We've led them to believe
that prose comes in visual blocks, not in rhythms and cadences; that
its texture should be flat because a page is flat; that written emotion
should not be immediate, like a drumbeat, but more remote, like a
painted landscape: something to be contemplated. But understatement can be overdone, plainsong can get too plain. When I asked a
group of young writers, earlier this year, how many of them ever read
their own work aloud, not one of them said she did.

I'm not arguing for the abolition of the eye, merely for the rein-
statement of the voice, and for an appreciation of the way it carries

the listener along with it at the pace of the story. (Incidentally, reading aloud disallows cheating; when you're reading aloud, you can't skip ahead.)

Our first stories come to us through the air. We hear voices.

Children in oral societies grow up within a web of stories; but so do all children. We listen before we can read. Some of our listening is more like listening in, to the calamitous or seductive voices of the adult world, on the radio or the television or in our daily lives. Often it's an overhearing of things we aren't supposed to hear, eavesdropping on scandalous gossip or family secrets. From all these scraps of voices, from the whispers and shouts that surround us, even from the ominous silences, the unfilled gaps in meaning, we patch together for ourselves an order of events, a plot or plots; these, then, are the things that happen, these are the people they happen to, this is the forbidden knowledge.

We have all been little pitchers with big ears, shooed out of the kitchen when the unspoken is being spoken, and we have probably all been tale bearers, blurters at the dinner table, unwitting violators of adult rules of censorship. Perhaps this is what writers are: those who never kicked the habit. We remained tale bearers. We learned to keep our eyes open, but not to keep our mouths shut.

If we're lucky, we may also be given stories meant for our ears, stories intended for us. These may be children's Bible stories, tidied up and simplified and with the vicious bits left out. They may be fairy tales, similarly sugared, although if we are very lucky it will be the straight stuff in both instances, with the slaughters, thunderbolts, and red-hot shoes left in. In any case, these tales will have deliberate, moulded shapes, unlike the stories we have patched together for ourselves. They will contain mountains, deserts, talking donkeys, dragons; and, unlike the kitchen stories, they will have definite endings. We are likely to accept these stories as being on the same level of reality as the kitchen stories. It's only when we are older that we are taught to regard one kind of story as real and the other kind as mere invention. This is about the same time we're taught to believe that dentists are useful, and writers are not.

Traditionally, both the kitchen gossips and the readers-out-loud have been mothers or grandmothers, native languages have been mother tongues, and the kinds of stories that are told to children have been called nursery tales or old wives' tales. It struck me as no great coincidence when I learned recently that, when a great number of prominent writers were asked to write about the family member who had had the greatest influence on their literary careers, almost all of them, male as well as female, had picked their mothers. Perhaps this reflects the extent to which North American children have been deprived of their grandfathers, those other great repositories of story; perhaps it will come to change if men come to share in early child care, and we will have old husbands' tales. But as things are, language, including the language of our earliest-learned stories, is a verbal matrix, not a verbal patrix.

I used to wonder why — as seems to be the case — so many more male writers chose to write from a female point of view than the other way around. (In this collection, for instance, male authors with female narrators outnumber the reverse four to one.) But possibly the prevailing gender of the earliest storytelling voice has something to do with it.

Two kinds of stories we first encounter — the shaped tale, the overheard impromptu narrative we piece together — form our idea of what a story is and colour the expectations we bring to stories later. Perhaps it's from the collisions between these two kinds of stories — what is often called "real life" (and which writers greedily think of as their "material") and what is sometimes dismissed as "mere litera-ture" or "the kinds of things that happen only in stories" — that original and living writing is generated. A writer with nothing but a formal sense will produce dead work, but so will one whose only excuse for what is on the page is that it really happened. Anyone who has been trapped in a bus beside a nonstop talker graced with no narrative skill or sense of timing can testify to that. Or, as Raymond Chandler says in *The Simple Art of Murder*:

> All language begins with speech, and the speech of common men at that, but when it develops to the point of becoming a literary medium it only looks like speech.

Expressing yourself is not nearly enough. You must express the story.

The Uncertainty Principle

All of which gets me no closer to an explanation of why I chose one story over another, twenty stories over the remaining hundred. The uncertainty principle, as it applies to writing, might be stated: *You can say why a story is bad, but it's much harder to say why it's good.* Determining quality in fiction may be as hard as determining the reason for the happiness in families, only in reverse. The old saying has it that happy families are all happy in the same way, but each unhappy family is unique. In fiction, however, excellence resides in divergence, or how else could we be surprised? Hence the trickiness of the formulations.

Here is what I did. I sat on the floor, spread out the stories, and read through them in no particular order. I put each completed story into a "yes" pile, a "no" pile, and a "maybe" pile. By the time I'd gone through them once, I had about twenty-five stories in "yes," an equal number in "no," and the rest in "maybe."

Here things got harder. The first fourteen yes stories were instant choices: I knew I wouldn't change my mind about them. After that there were gradations, yeses shading to maybes, maybes that could easily be on the low end of yes. To make the final choices, I was forced to be more conscious and deliberate. I went back over my fourteen instant yes stories and tried to figure out what, if anything, they had in common.

They were widely different in content, in tone, in setting, in narrative strategy. Some were funny, others melancholy, others contemplative, others downright sad, yet others violent. Some went over ground that, Lord knows, had been gone over before: the breakdown, the breakup, love and death. Collectively they did not represent any school of writing or propound any common philosophy. I was beginning to feel stupid and lacking in standards. Was I to be thrown back on that old crutch of the Creative Writing Seminar, *It worked for me*?

Perhaps, I thought, my criteria are very simple minded. Perhaps all I want from a good story is what children want when they listen to tales both told and overheard — which turns out to be a good deal.

They want their attention held, and so do I. I always read to the end, out of some puritanical, and adult, sense of duty owed; but if I start to fidget and skip pages, and wonder if conscience demands I go back and read the middle, it's a sign that the story has lost me, or I have lost it.

They want to feel they are in safe hands, that they can trust the teller. With children this may mean simply that they know the speaker will not betray them by closing the book in the middle, or mixing up the heroes and the villains. With adult readers it's more complicated than that, and involves many dimensions, but there's the same element of keeping faith. Faith must be kept with the language — even if the story is funny, its language must be taken seriously — with the concrete details of locale, mannerism, clothing; with the shape of the story itself. A good story may tease, as long as this activity is foreplay and not used as an end in itself. If there's a promise held out, it must be honoured. Whatever is hidden behind the curtain must be revealed at last, and it must be at one and the same time completely unexpected and inevitable. It's in this last respect that the story (as distinct from the novel) comes closest to resembling two of its oral predecessors, the riddle and the joke. Both, or all three, require the same mystifying buildup, the same surprising twist, the same impeccable sense of timing. If we guess the riddle at once, or if we can't guess it because the answer makes no sense — if we see the joke coming, or if the point is lost because the teller gets it muddled — there is failure. Stories can fail in the same way.

But anyone who has ever told, or tried to tell, a story to children will know that there is one thing without which none of the rest is any good. Young children have little sense of dutifulness or of delaying anticipation. They are longing to hear a story, but only if you are longing to tell one. They will not put up with your lassitude or boredom: if you want their full attention, you must give them yours. You must hold them with your glittering eye or suffer the pinches and whispering. You need the Ancient Mariner element, the Scheherazade element: a sense of urgency. *This is the story I must tell; this is the story you must hear.*

Urgency does not mean frenzy. The story can be a quiet story, a story about dismay or missed chances or a wordless revelation. But it must be urgently told. It must be told with as much intentness as if the teller's life depended on it. And, if you are a writer, so it does, because your life as the writer of each particular story is only as long, and as good, as the story itself. Most of those who hear it or read it will never know you, but they will know the story. Their act of listening is its reincarnation.

Is all this too much to ask? Not really; because many stories, many of these stories, do it superbly.

DOWN TO SPECIFICS

But they do it in a multiplicity of ways. When I was reading through the stories, someone asked me, "Is there a trend?" There is no trend. There are only twenty strong, exciting, and unique stories.

I didn't think anyone could ever write a story about taking drugs in the 1960s that would hold my attention for more than five minutes, but Michael Cunningham does it brilliantly in "White Angel" — because the narrator is a young boy, "the most criminally advanced nine-year-old in my fourth-grade class," who is being initiated into almost everything by his adored sixteen-year-old brother. The sensual richness of this story is impressive; so is the way it shifts from out-of-control feverishness and hilarity, as the two brothers scramble their brains with acid against a background of *Leave It to Beaver* Cleveland domesticity ("We slipped the tabs into our mouths at breakfast, while our mother paused over the bacon"), to the nearly unbearable poignancy of its tragic ending.

Another story that blindsided me by taking an unlikely subject and turning it inside out was "The Flowers of Boredom." Who could hope to write with any conviction or panache about working as a paper shuffler for a defence contractor? But Rick DeMarinis does. The visionary glimpse of cosmic horror at the end is come by honestly, step by step, through dailiness and small disgusts. This story is one of those truly original collisions between delicately handled form and banal but alarming content that leaves you aghast and slightly battered.

"Hell lay about them in their infancy," Graham Greene remarks in *The Lawless Roads*, and this is the tone of Barbara Gowdy's "Disneyland." If "The Flowers of Boredom" views the military enterprise as a giant, superhuman pattern, "Disneyland" squints at it through Groucho Marx glasses gone rotten. The controlling figure is a domineering father obsessed with his early-1960s fallout shelter. He and his mania would be ludicrous, almost a parody, viewed from a safe distance; but the distance is not safe. This man is seen from beneath by his children, who are forced to play platoon to his drill sergeant in the smelly, dark, tyrannical, and terrifying hell in which he has imprisoned them. The sense of claustrophobia and entrapment are intense.

There are several other fine stories that concern themselves with the terrors, and sometimes the delights, of childhood and with the powerlessness of children caught under the gigantic, heedless feet of the adult world. Mark Richard's "Strays," with its two poor, white boys abandoned by their runaway mother and rescued, after a fashion, by their rogue gambler of an uncle, is one fine example. Its deadpan delivery of the squalid and the grotesque reminds us that everything that happens to children is accepted as normal by them; or if not exactly normal, unalterable. For them, reality and enchantment are the same thing, and they are held in thrall.

Dale Ray Phillips's "What Men Love For" contains another child who is under a spell, that cast by his fragile, manic-depressive mother. Against the various rituals she uses to keep herself stuck together, and those the boy himself is in the process of inventing for his own preservation, there's the magic of his father — a magic of luck, risk, hope, and chance embodied in the motorcycle he drives too fast.

"The Boy on the Train," by Arthur Robinson, is a wonderful, warped memoir of sorts. Instead of being about one childhood, it's really about two. Two children grow up to be fathers, two fathers misunderstand their sons, and two sons bedevil their fathers in niggling, embarrassing, or nauseating ways designed to get right under their skin: "In prepubescence, Edward gazed at his face in the mirror a great deal and studied the effects he could get with it. Once he discovered that a strip of toothpaste artfully placed just below a nostril produced an effect that could easily turn his father's queasy stomach. The result was more than he could have hoped for." The beautiful way this story turns around on itself, loops back, plays variations on three generations, is a delight to follow.

Two of these stories have an almost fablelike simplicity and structure. One of them is M. T. Sharif's "The Letter Writer," whose hapless protagonist, Haji, is arrested during the Iranian revolution because he is suspected of being the brother of a supposed spy and can't prove he isn't. But the authorities can't prove he is, and since he won't confess and they can't convict him, he is given a make-work job: covering up the bare arms, legs, heads, and necks of women pictured in Western magazines by drawing clothes on them with pen and ink. Earlier, a passing dervish had prophesied that Haji would end up living in a palace, attended by concubines and servants. The manner in which this fate is actually fulfilled is reminiscent of both Kafka and the tradition of the ironic Eastern tale.

Harriet Doerr's "Edie: A Life" has the plain charm of a sampler. It violates almost every rule I have ever heard about the construction of short stories. It doesn't concentrate, for instance, on an in-depth study of character, or on a short period of time, a single incident that focuses a life. Instead it gives the entire life, in miniature as it were, complete and rounded and unexplained as an apple.

Other stories persuade us and move us in other ways. Larry Brown, in "Kubuku Rides (This Is It)," gives his sad story of an alcoholic wife its edge and drive through the immediacy and vigour of his language, as does Blanche McCrary Boyd in her uneasily uproarious "The Black Hand Girl." (The hand, which is a man's, gets black by being sprained in a panty girdle. Read on.) Douglas Glover, in "Why I Decide to Kill Myself and Other Jokes," also draws on the mordant, self-deprecating humour of women. There's a murder with a hammer, a rescue from the snow, an attempted rescue with a skillet. There's a Chinese woman, in David Wong Louie's "Displacement," who is trying to make the best of America, and a native Indian woman, in Linda Hogan's "Aunt Moon's Young Man," who is also trying to make the best of it. There's a left-wing mother whose son rebels by taking up religion. But these are just hints. To get the real story, you have to read the story, as always.

I must admit that, although I was reading blind, I did guess the identities of three of the authors. Bharati Mukherjee's "The Management of Grief" wasn't even a guess, as I had read it before and it had stayed with me. It's a finely tuned, acutely felt story about an Indian immigrant wife's reactions when the plane carrying her husband and sons is blown up over the Irish Sea by terrorists. The sleepwalking intensity with which she gropes her way through the emotional debris scattered by these senseless deaths and eventually makes a mystic sense out of them for herself is sparely but unsparingly rendered.

When I read "The Concert Party," I guessed that it was either by Mavis Gallant or by a male writer doing a very good imitation of her. Who else would, or could, write so convincingly and with such interest about a hopeless nerd from Saskatchewan bungling around loose in France in the early 1950s? The story did turn out to be by Mavis Gallant, leaving me to admire once again her deftness with a full canvas, her skill at interweaving the fates of her characters, her sharp eye for the details of small pomposities, and her camera work, if it may be called that. Watch the way she shifts, at the end, from closeup to long shot:

> Remembering Edie at the split second when she came to a decision, I can find it in me to envy them. The rest of us were born knowing better, which means we were stuck. When I finally looked away from her it was at another pool of candlelight, and the glowing, blooming children. I wonder now if there was anything about us for the children to remember, if they ever later on reminded one another: There was that long table of English-speaking people, still in bud.

I think I would recognize an Alice Munro story in Braille, even though I don't read Braille. The strength and distinctiveness of her voice will always give her away. "Meneseteung" is, for my money, one of Alice Munro's best and, in the manner of its telling, quirkiest stories yet. It purports to be about a minor sentimental "poetess" — the word, here, is appropriate — living in a small, raw, cowpat-strewn, treeless nineteenth-century town, which is a far cry from our idyllic notions of a golden past as the poet's sugary verses are from real life. Our sweet picture of bygone days is destroyed, and, in the process, our conceptions of how a story should proceed. Similarly, the poet herself disintegrates in the harsh and multiple presence of the vivid life that surrounds her and that finally proves too huge and real for her. Or does it? Does she disintegrate or integrate? Does crossing the borders of convention lead toward insanity or sanity? "She doesn't mistake that for reality, and neither does she mistake anything else for reality," we are told when the crocheted roses on the tablecloth began to float, "and that is how she knows that she is sane."

The last word is not the poet's, however, but the nameless narrator's, the "I" who has been searching for the poet, or scraps of her, through time. These last words could be an epigraph for this collection of stories, or for the act of writing itself:

> People are curious. A few people are. They will be driven to find things out, even trivial things. They will put things together, knowing all along that they may be mistaken. You see them going around with notebooks, scraping the dirt off gravestones, reading microfilm, just in the hope of seeing this trickle in time, making a connection, rescuing one thing from the rubbish.

I thank all the authors in this book for the pleasure their stories have given me, and for what they added to my own sense of what a story is, and can be.

From listening to the stories of others, we learn to tell our own.

THE PUBLIC WOMAN AS
HONORARY MAN

THE WARRIOR QUEENS
BY ANTONIA FRASER

THE WARRIOR QUEENS, Antonia Fraser's most recent historical essay, is lore-packed, quirky in its approach, and fascinating to read. If non-fiction books can be thought of as detailed answers to unvoiced questions, then the question answered by this one is: How have female political and military leaders gotten away with it? How have they managed to fob themselves off on those hardest to convince soldiers and other politicians, those quintessentially male devisers and players of boys' games — as worthy leaders of the charge or captains of the ship of state, although long of hair and bulgy of breast? Such women have been few enough in number so that the exceptions have very much proven the rule. But what about those exceptions? What was their strategy, their sleight of hand? What was their secret?

In pursuit of answers, Fraser has assembled a remarkable group of women for our contemplation. She begins with Boadicea herself, that famed but shadowy first-century British tribal queen who led a revolt against the occupying and oppressive Romans, massacred a lot of them, and was said to have committed suicide when her forces were massacred in return. Fraser provides as faithful an account of the events as is possible, given that information is scarce and reports vary. But she is just as interested in Boadicea's

metamorphoses in historical and literary accounts through the ages
— from pious patriot and martyr, mother of her people, to unwom-
anly, bloodthirsty shrew, to symbol of heroic British imperialism,
ironic in view of the fact that her own revolt was against an earlier
imperialism. The accounts of her have varied according to what men
considered proper womanly behaviour, and to what the British considered proper British behaviour; thus Boadicea has been both slut
and saint. Very early on, the myth detached itself from the real
woman in question, and has been floating around ever since, ready
to stick itself like a leech to any woman hardy enough to brandish a
spear or declare for office.

Fraser follows up with a varied assortment of women from many
centuries and civilizations who have held, however briefly, the reins of
power: Zenobia, the third-century Queen of Palmyra who also challenged Roman rule; Empress Maud, of the twelfth-century English
wars of succession; Queen Tamara of Georgia, "The Lion of the
Caucasus"; Elizabeth I, inspiring her troops to battle the Spanish
Armada; Isabella of Spain; the engaging Queen Jinga of Angola, who
successfully defied the Portuguese colonists; Catherine the Great of
Russia; the Vietnamese heroines, Trung Trac and Trung Nhi; the
amazing Rani of Jhansi, who fought the British in India; Indira
Gandhi; Golda Meir; and a good many more, concluding with that
handy bookend to Boadicea, Margaret Thatcher. Their childhoods,
their paths to leadership, and their styles vary enormously, but they
have one thing in common: All were instantly mythologized. Male
military leaders, taken for all in all, have been men, and that has been
enough; but female ones cannot be mere women. They are aberra-
tions, and as such are thought to partake of the supernatural or the
monstrous: angels or devils, paragons of chastity or demons of
lust, Whores of Babylon or Iron Maidens. Sometimes they have prof-
ited from the female saints or goddesses available to them through
their cultures, sometimes they have had to work against such images.
Their femininity has been both shackle and banner.

As leaders, they have had to be, like female doctors a decade ago, better than men. They have shamed their male followers by displaying superior courage; they have shamed their male adversaries by inflicting defeat on them at the hands of a mere woman. They have outmanoeuvred, outtalked, outblustered, and in some cases outshot and outridden the cream of the male crop. Altogether they are an impressive lot, and Fraser is to be congratulated for rescuing them from their own myths and for giving them their due as individuals, the lesser-known among them as well as the household words.

But although they have been trotted out like a roll call by many advocates for the equality of women, and presented in many guises — from turn-of-the-century pageants to Judy Chicago's *Dinner Party* — these women have seldom allied themselves with women in general, or with movements for the improvement of their lot. More typically, they have distanced themselves from women, like Elizabeth I, who was against female rule but saw herself as a divinely placed exception, or like Catherine the Great, who spoke of the "weak, frivolous, whining species of women." Many have preferred the status of honorary males. If you're playing boys' games, you need to be one of the boys.

This book should be required reading for any woman going into politics, truck driving, or the army; indeed, by any woman going into anything, unless her chosen field is uniquely feminine. Public women are put through different tests of nerve, attract different kinds of criticism, and are subject to different sorts of mythologizing than are men, and *The Warrior Queens* indicates what kinds.

Those of us for whom politics is a spectator sport will find it useful too. It goes a long way toward explaining the various media transformations of, for instance, Margaret Thatcher, from her Attila-the-Hen period through her Iron-Maiden–Falklands-War phase to her incarnation as an editorial-cartoon Boadicea, complete with whip and chariot, triumphant on election day and dragging a clutch of pygmy men in her wake. Women leaders, it seems, find it difficult to be life sized. For good or ill, they are gigantic.

13

WRITING UTOPIA

How DID *The Handmaid's Tale* get written? The answer could be, partly on a rented electric typewriter with a German keyboard in a walk-up flat in West Berlin, and partly in a small house in Tuscaloosa, Alabama — which, it was announced to me with a certain pride, is the per capita murder capital of the U.S. "Gosh," I said. "Maybe I shouldn't be here." "Aw, don't y'all worry," they replied. "They only shoots family." But although these two places provided, shall we say, a certain atmosphere, there is more to the story than that.

The Handmaid's Tale, I must explain for the benefit of the one person in the audience who may not have read it yet — out in paperback, and a bargain of creepy thrills for only $4.95 — is set in the future. This conned some people into believing it is science fiction, which, to my mind, it is not. I define science fiction as fiction in which things happen that are not possible today — that depend, for instance, on advanced space travel, time travel, the discovery of green monsters on other planets or galaxies, or which contain various technologies we have not yet developed. But in *The Handmaid's Tale*, nothing happens that the human race has not already done at some time in the past, or which it is not doing now, perhaps in other countries, or for which it has not yet developed the technology.

We've done it, or we're doing it, or we could start doing it tomorrow. Nothing inconceivable takes place, and the projected trends on which my future society is based are already in motion. So I think of *The Handmaid's Tale* not as science fiction, but as speculative fiction; and, more particularly, as that negative form of Utopian fiction which has come to be known as the Dystopia.

A Utopia is usually thought of as a fictional perfect society, but in fact the word does not mean "perfect society." It means "nowhere," and was used sardonically by Sir Thomas More as the title of his own sixteenth-century fictional discourse on government. Perhaps he meant to indicate that, although his Utopia made more rational sense than the England of his day, it was unlikely to be found anywhere outside a book.

Both the Utopia and the Dystopia concern themselves with the designing of societies; good societies for the Utopias, bad ones for the Dystopias. There is some of the same pleasure in this, for the writer, that we used to get as children when we built sand cities, or dinosaur jungles from Plasticine or drew entire wardrobes for paper dolls. But in a Utopia, you get to plan everything — the cities, the legal system, the customs, even facets of the language. The Dystopian bad design is the Utopian good design in reverse — that is, we the readers are supposed to deduce what a good society is by seeing, in detail, what it isn't.

The Utopia-Dystopia as a form tends to be produced only by cultures based on monotheism — or, like Plato's system, on a single idea of the Good — and which postulate also a single, goal-oriented timeline. Cultures based on polytheism and the circularity of time don't seem to produce them. Why bother to try to improve society, or even to visualize it improved, when you know it's all going to go around again, like clothes in the wash? And how can you define a "good" society as opposed to a "bad" one if you see good and bad as aspects of the same thing? But Judeo-Christianity, being a linear monotheism — one God and one plot line, from Genesis to

Revelation — has generated many fictional Utopias, and a good many attempts to create the real thing right here on earth, the venture of the Pilgrim Fathers being one of them — "We shall be as a city upon a hill, a light to all nations," — and Marxism being another. In Marxism, history replaces God as a determinant and the classless society replaces the New Jerusalem, but change-through-time, heading in the direction of perfection, is similarly postulated. In the background of every modern Utopia lurks Plato's Republic and the Book of Revelation, and modern Dystopias have not been *un*influenced by various literary versions of Hell, especially those of Dante and Milton, which in their turn go right back to the Bible, that indispensable sourcebook of Western literature.

Sir Thomas More's original *Utopia* has a long list of descendants, many of which I read as I hacked my way through high school, through college, and later through graduate school. This list includes Swift's *Gulliver's Travels*, and, in the nineteenth century, William Morris's *New From Nowhere*, in which the ideal society is a kind of artists' colony; H. G. Wells's *Time Machine*, in which the lower classes actually eat the upper; Butler's *Erewhon*, in which crime is a sickness and sickness is a crime; and W. H. Hudson's *A Crystal Age*. In our own century, the classics are Huxley's *Brave New World*, Bellamy's *Looking Backwards*, and, of course, *Nineteen Eighty-four*, to mention a few. Utopias by women are also of note, though not as numerous. There are, for instance, *Herland* by Charlotte Perkins Gilman, and *Woman on the Edge of Time* by Marge Piercey.

Utopias are often satirical, the satire being directed at whatever society the writer is currently living in; that is, the superior arrangements of the Utopians reflect badly on *us*. Dystopias are often more like dire warnings than satires, dark shadows cast by the present into the future. They are what will happen to us if we don't pull up our socks.

What aspects of this life interest such writers? To no one's surprise, their concerns turn out to be much the same as those of society.

There are, of course, the superficial matters of clothing and cuisine; partial nudity and vegetarianism making regular appearances. But the main problems are the distribution of wealth, labour relations, power structures, the protection of the powerless, if any, relations between the sexes, population control, urban planning, often in the form of an interest in drains and sewers, the rearing of children, illness and its ethics, insanity ditto, the censorship of artists and suchlike riff-raff and antisocial elements, individual privacy and its invasion, the redefinition of language, and the administration of justice. If, that is, any such administration is needed. It is a characteristic of the extreme Utopia, at one end, and the extreme Dystopia at the other, that neither contains any lawyers. Extreme Utopias are communities of spirit, in which there cannot be any real disagreements among members because all are of like and right mind; extreme Dystopias are absolute tyrannies, in which contention is not a possibility. In Utopia, then, no lawyers are needed; in Dystopia, no lawyers are allowed.

In between, however, is where most Utopia-Dystopias as well as most human societies fall, and here the composers of these fictions have shown remarkable fecundity. Relations between the sexes exhibit perhaps the widest range. Some Utopias go for a sort of healthy-minded communal sex; others, like W. H. Hudson's *A Crystal Age*, for an antlike arrangement in which most citizens are sexually neutral and only one pair per large country mansion actually breed, which is how they cut down on the birth rate. Still others, like Marge Piercey's, allow men to participate almost equally in child rearing by allowing them to breast-feed via hormone injections, an option that may not rejoice your hearts but at least has the virtue of novelty. Then there are Huxley's ritualistic group sex and bottle babies, Skinner's boxes, and various minor science fictions, written by men I hasten to add, in which women devour their mates or paralyze them and lay eggs on them, *à la* spiders. Sexual relations in extreme Dystopias usually exhibit some form of slavery or, as in Orwell, extreme sexual repression.

The details, then, vary; but the Utopia-Dystopia as a form is a way of trying things out on paper first to see whether or not we might like them, should we ever have the chance to put them into actual practice. In addition, it challenges us to re-examine what we understand by the word *human*, and above all what we intend by the word *freedom*. For neither the Utopia or the Dystopia is open-ended. Utopia is an extreme example of the impulse to order; it's the word *should* run rampant. Dystopia, its nightmare mirror image, is the desire to squash dissent taken to inhuman and lunatic lengths. Neither are what you'd call tolerant, but both are necessary to the imagination: if we can't visualize the good, the ideal, if we can't formulate what we want, we'll get what we don't want, in spades. It's a sad commentary on our age that we find Dystopias a lot easier to believe in than Utopias: Utopias we can only imagine, Dystopias we've already had. But should we try too hard to enforce Utopia, Dystopia rapidly follows; because if enough people disagree with us we'll have to eliminate or suppress or terrorize or manipulate them, and then we've got *Nineteen Eighty-four*. As a rule, Utopia is only safe when it remains true to its name and stays nowhere. It's a nice place to visit, but do we really want to live there? Which may be the ultimate moral of such stories.

All this was by way of background, to let you know that I'd done the required reading long before launching myself into *The Handmaid's Tale*. There are two other lots of required reading I would like to mention. The first had to do with the literature of the Second World War — I read Winston Churchill's memoirs when I was in high school, not to mention a biography of Rommel, the Desert Fox, and many another tomes of military history. I read these books partly because I was an omnivorous reader and they were there; my father was a history buff and these things were just lying around. By extension, I read various books on totalitarian regimes, of the present and the past; the one that sticks out was called *Darkness at Noon*, by Arthur Koestler. (This was not my only reading when I was in high school;

I was also reading Jane Austen and Emily Brontë and a particularly lurid book of sci-fi called *Donovan's Brain*. I would read anything, and still will; when all else is lacking, I read airline in-flight magazines, and I have to say, I am getting tired of those articles on billionaire businessmen. Don't you think it's time for some other kinds of fiction?)

This so-called "political" area of my reading was reinforced later by travel, to various countries where, to put it mildly, certain things we consider freedoms are not universally in force, and by conversations with many people; I remember in particular meeting a woman who had been in the French Resistance during the war, and a man who had escaped from Poland at the same time.

The other lot of required reading has to do with the history of the seventeenth-century Puritans, especially those who ended up in the United States. At the front of *The Handmaid's Tale*, there are two dedications. One is to Perry Miller, who was a professor of mine at the dreaded Harvard Graduate School, and who almost single-handedly was responsible for resurrecting the American Puritans as a field for literary investigation. I had to take a lot of this stuff, and I needed to "fill my gap" in order to pass my Comprehensives, and this was one area I had not studied as an undergraduate. Perry Miller pointed out that, contrary to what I had been taught earlier, the American Puritans did not come to North America in search of religious toleration, or not what we mean by it. They wanted the freedom to practise *their* religion, but they were not particularly keen on anyone else practising his. Among their noteworthy achievements were the banishing of so-called heretics, the hanging of Quakers, and the well-known witchcraft trials. I get to say these bad things about them because they were my ancestors — in a way, *The Handmaid's Tale* is my book about my ancestors — and the second dedication, to Mary Webster, is indeed to one of these very same ancestors. Mary was a well-known witch, or at least she was tried for witchcraft and hanged. But it was before they had invented the drop, which breaks your neck — they merely strung her up and let her dangle, and when they came to cut her down the next morning she was still alive. Under the law of double jeopardy, you couldn't execute a person twice for the same crime, so she lived for another fourteen years. I felt that if I was going to stick my neck out by writing this book, I'd better dedicate it to someone with a very tough neck.

Puritan New England was a theocracy, not a democracy; and the future society proposed in *The Handmaid's Tale* has the form of a theocracy too, on the principle that no society every strays completely far from its roots. Stalinist Russia would have been unthinkable without Czarist Russia to precede it, and so forth. Also, the most potent forms of dictatorship have always been those that have imposed tyranny in the name of religion; and even folk like the French Revolutionaries and Hitler have striven to give a religious force and sanction to their ideas. What is needed for a really good tyranny is an unquestionable idea or authority. Political disagreement is political disagreement; but political disagreement with a *theocracy* is heresy, and a good deal of gloating self-righteousness can be brought to be bear upon the extermination of heretics, as history has demonstrated, through the Crusades, the forcible conversions to Islam, the Spanish Inquisition, the burnings-at-the-stake under the English Queen Bloody Mary, and so on down through the years. It was in the light of history that the American constitutionalists in the eighteenth century separated Church from State. It is also in the light of history that my leaders in *The Handmaid's Tale* recombine them.

All fictions begin with the question *What if*. The *what if* varies from book to book — what if John loves Mary, what if John doesn't love Mary, what if Mary gets eaten by an enormous shark, what if the Martians invade, what if you find a treasure map, and so forth — but there is always a *what if*, to which the novel is the answer. The *what if* for *The Handmaid's Tale* could be formulated: what if it *can* happen here? What kind of *it* would it be? (I have never believed any fictions about the Russians taking over. If they can't get their refrigerators to work, they wouldn't quite frankly stand much of a chance. So that, for me, is not a plausible *it*.)

Or *what if* you wanted to take over the U.S. and set up a totalitarian government, the lust for power being what it is? How would you go about it? What conditions would favour you, and what slogan would you propose, what flag would you fly, that would attract the necessary 20 percent of the population, without which no totalitarianism can stay in power? If you proposed Communism, you'd be unlikely to get many takers. A dictatorship of liberal democrats would be seen even by the slightly dull-witted as a contradiction in terms. Although many dubious acts have been committed, let's face it, in the name of the great god democracy, they've usually been done in secret, or with a good deal of verbal embroidery covering them up. In this country, you'd be more likely to try some version of Puritan Fatherhood if you wanted a takeover. That would definitely be your best plan.

But true dictatorships do not come *in* in good times. They come in in bad times, when people are ready to give up some of their freedoms to someone — anyone — who can take control and promise them better times. The bad times that made Hitler and Mussolini possible were economic, with some extra frills such as a shortage of men in proportion to women, due to the high death rates during the First World War. To make my future society possible, I proposed something a little more complex. Bad economic times, yes, due to a shrinking area of global control, which would mean shrinking markets and fewer sources of cheap raw materials. But also a period of widespread environmental catastrophe, which has had several results: a higher infertility and sterility rate due to chemical and radiation damage (this, by the way, is happening already) and a higher birth-defect rate, which is also happening. The ability to conceive and bear a healthy child would become rare, and thus valued; and we all know who gets most — in any society — of the things that are rare and valued. Those at the top. Hence my proposed future society, which, like many human societies before it, assigns more than one woman to its

favoured male members. There are lots of precedents for this practice, but my society, being derived from Puritanism, would of course
need Biblical sanction. Luckily for them, Old Testament patriarchs
were notoriously polygamous; the text they chose as their cornerstone is the story of Rachel and Leah, the two wives of Jacob, and
their baby competition. When they themselves ran out of babies, they
pressed their handmaids into service and counted the babies as their
own, thus providing a Biblical justification for surrogate motherhood,
should anyone need one. Between these five people — not two — the
twelve tribes of Israel were produced.

Woman's place, in the Republic of Gilead — so named for the
mountain where Jacob promised to his father-in-law Laban that
he would protect his two daughters — woman's place is strictly in the
home. My problem as a writer was — given that my society has
stuffed all women back into their homes, how did they go about it?
How do you *get* women back into the home, now that they are running around *outside* the home, having jobs and generally flinging
themselves around? Simple. You just close your eyes and take several
giant steps back, into the not-so-very-distant past — the nineteenth
century, to be exact — deprive them of the right to vote, own property, or hold jobs, and prohibit public prostitution into the bargain,
to keep them from hanging out on street corners, and presto, there
they are, back in the home. To stop them from using their Amex gold
cards to make quick airplane escapes, I have their credit frozen
overnight; after all, if everyone is on computers and cash is obsolete
— which is where we're heading — how simple to single out any one
group — all those older than sixty, all those with green hair, all
women. Of the many scary features of my future society, this one
seems to have got to the most people. That their beloved, friendly,
well-trained credit cards could rise up against them! It is the stuff of
nightmares.

This then is part of the core of what I hope you will think is
relentless logic running like a spine through *The Handmaid's Tale*.

While I was writing it, and for some time after, I kept a scrapbook with clippings from newspapers referring to all sorts of material that fitted in with the premises on which the book was based — everything from articles on the high level of PCBs found in polar bears, to the biological mothers assigned to SS troops by Hitler, in addition to their legal wives, for purposes of child production, to conditions in prisons around the world, to computer technology, to underground polygamy in the state of Utah. There is, as I have said, nothing in the book without a precedent. But this material in itself would not constitute a novel. A novel is always the story of an individual, or several individuals, never the story of a generalized mass. So the real problems in the writing of *The Handmaid's Tale* were the same as the problems involved in the writing of any novel: how to make the story real at a human and individual level. The pitfalls that Utopian writing so frequently stumbles into are the pitfalls of disquisition. The author gets too enthusiastic about sewage systems or conveyor belts, and the story grinds to a halt while the beauties of these are explained. I wanted the factual and logical background to my tale to remain background; I did not want it usurping the foreground.

PART II

1990–2000

1990–2000

NINETEEN NINETY WAS supposed to be the first year of a brand-new era. The Soviet Union was changed utterly. Germany was reunifying, a thing we thought we'd never witness in this lifetime. The West and that body of practices and values attached to something called "capitalism" or "the free-market economy" seemed triumphant. It was not yet foreseen that, with the disappearance of its enemy, the Western moral balloon would lose helium: it's great to champion freedom in the absence of it, but hard to feel hand-on-heart noble about shopping malls and parking lots and the right to kill yourself through overeating.

We approached the last decade before that artificial times-change hinge, The Millennium, in a strange state of disorientation. But, as the Italian writer Roberto Calasso has pointed out, heroes have a need for monsters, though monsters can do very well without heroes; and the monster-producing energies were gathering themselves together throughout the decade.

Things were quieter on the writing front, mine at least. In 1991 I published *Wilderness Tips*, a collection of stories written during the late 1980s. In the same year we went to France in search of writing time. We could not rent one house for the whole period, so we rented three successive houses — one for fall, one for winter, one for spring — in and around the town of Lourmarin, in Provence. It was in these three houses that I began writing my novel *The Robber Bride*, the occasion for the essay in this volume called "Spotty-Handed Villainesses." I also put together a selection of very short fiction called *Good Bones*, a companion to the 1983 *Murder in the Dark*. It was published in 1992, with a cover design I'd pasted together out of issues of French *Vogue* magazine. (Both books were done for a small press, and author collage saves money.)

We returned to Canada in time for the summer of 1992. I completed *The Robber Bride* in January of 1993, on a train going across Canada. My father had died earlier that month, right after I myself had been seriously ill with scarlet fever, and it was an effort of will to finish.

A book of poetry, *Morning in the Burned House*, came out in 1995. Also in that year I published a series of four lectures I'd given at Oxford University on the subject of Canadian literature and the North. The title was *Strange Things*, after the first words in the Robert Service poem "The Cremation of Sam McGee." That poem goes on to talk about the men who moil for gold, and it was a moiling sort of decade.

I began the novel *Alias Grace* while I was on a book tour in Europe — in Switzerland, a suitably Freudian/Jungian locale. The process is described in the essay, "In Search of *Alias Grace*." What I didn't put in is that right after finishing the book we went to a small village in western Ireland, and I had to edit the book by FedEx — I did not yet have e-mail — which meant that I had to hang a tea towel on the hedge so the deliveryman would know where we were.

I wrote *The Blind Assassin* after several false starts, one of them in Canada, one of them in a curious rented-by-Internet flat in London. The breakthrough came, again, in France, where I was writing on the assemblage of end tables that served as a desk. I finished it in 1999, and did the editing partly in Madrid, where I was also finishing the six lectures I gave at Cambridge University that year, on the subject of writers and writing, which were published as *Negotiating with the Dead*. So during the early months of that year, it was bright blue skies and sunlight and the eating of churros, and then in the spring it was the wonderful Cambridge gardens, and bluebells in the woods, and mist.

The Blind Assassin came out in the fall. It became the fourth of my books to be shortlisted for the Booker Prize, and I had to put together another black outfit. To my surprise, the book committed what Oscar Wilde would have called an unpardonable solecism of style by actually winning. Many Canadians were pleased by this. Some weren't.

To backtrack: on New Year's Eve 2000, the millennium was ushered in. Our computers were all supposed to go into meltdown, but they didn't. My mother was by this time very old and nearly blind, but she could still see bright lights. We arranged some fireworks outside her picture window so she could participate, and my sister accidentally set fire to the backyard. That's my image of the grand event — my sister jumping up and down in the dry weeds, attempting to stamp out the conflagration.

On my journal page that began the year 2000, I scribbled: *The fireworks were very good on TV except for the fatuous commentary. Nothing leaked. The church bells rang. It was quite warm. There was a half moon, The angels did not arrive, or at least none visible to the naked eye. No bombs fell. No snow. No terrorists around here.*

Famous last words.

14

A DOUBLE-BLADED KNIFE

SUBVERSIVE LAUGHTER IN TWO STORIES
BY THOMAS KING

> When Brebeuf and His Brethren first came out, a friend
> of mine said that the thing to do now was to write
> the same story from the Iroquois point of view.
> — JAMES REANEY, "The Canadian Poet's Predicament"

ONCE UPON A TIME long ago, in 1972 to be exact, I wrote a book called *Survival*, which was about Canadian literature; an eccentric subject in those days, when many denied there was any. In this book, there was a chapter entitled *First People: Indians and Eskimos as Symbols*. What this chapter examined was the uses made by non-Native writers of Native characters and motifs, over the centuries and for their own purposes. This chapter did not examine poetry and fiction written by Native writers in English, for the simple reason that I could not at that time find any; although I was able to recommend a small list of nonfiction titles. The closest thing to "imaginative" writing by Natives were "translations" of Native myths and poetry, which might turn up at the beginnings of anthologies, or be offered as a species of indigenous fairy tale in grade-school readers. (Why did I overlook Pauline Johnson? Perhaps because, being half-white, she somehow didn't rate as the real thing, even among Natives; although she is undergoing reclamation today.)

The figures in the stories and poems I analyzed ran the gamut. There were Indians and Eskimos seen as closer to Nature and therefore more noble, as closer to Nature and therefore *less* noble, as savage victimizers of whites and as victims of savage whites. There was a strong tendency among younger writers to claim Natives as kin, or as their "true" ancestors (which may have something to it, since all people on earth are descended from hunter-gatherer societies). There were a lot of adjectives.

Lacking among them was *funny*. Savage irony and morbid humour did sometimes enter the picture as a kind of self-flagellation device for whites, but on the whole Natives were treated by almost everyone with the utmost gravity, as if they were either too awe-inspiring as blood-curdling savages or too sacrosanct in their status of holy victim to allow of any comic reactions either to them or by them. Furthermore, nobody ever seems to have asked them what, if anything, *they* found funny. The Native as presented in non-Native writing was singularly lacking in a sense of humour; sort of like the "good" woman of Victorian fiction, who acquired at the hands of male writers the same kind of tragic-eyed, long-suffering solemnity.

Things are changing. Natives are now writing fiction, poetry, and plays, and some of the literature being produced by them is both vulgar and hilarious. A good many stereotypes are hitting the dust, a few sensibilities are in the process of being outraged. The comfortable thing about a people who do not have a literary voice, or at least not one you can hear or understand, is that you never have to listen to what they are saying about *you*. Men found it very disconcerting when women started writing the truth about the kinds of things women say about them behind their backs. In particular, they did not appreciate having the more trivial of their human foibles revealed, nor did they appreciate being laughed at. Nobody does, really. But when I heard that the nickname given to a certain priest by the

Indians was "Father Crotchface," because of his beard, it caused me to reflect. For instance, *Father Crotchface and His Brethren* would have altogether a different ring to it, no?

Recently I read, in separate "little" magazines, two outstanding stories by the same author, Thomas King.[1] They seem to me to be "perfect" stories — by which I mean that as narrations they are exquisitely timed, that everything in them appears to be there by right, and that there is nothing you would want to change or edit out. Another way of saying this is that they are beautifully written. But apart from these aesthetic qualities, which they share with other stories, they impressed me in quite different ways.

They ambush the reader. They get the knife in, not by whacking you over the head with their own moral righteousness, but by being funny. Humour can be aggressive and oppressive, as in keep-'em-in-their-place sexist and racist jokes. But it can also be a subversive weapon, as it has often been for people who find themselves in a fairly tight spot without other, more physical, weapons.

As these two stories have not yet appeared in a collection (although they will soon), you'll forgive me for summarizing.

The first one I'd like to discuss is called "Joe the Painter and the Deer Island Massacre." It's set in a small coastal town north of San Francisco. The narrator is an Indian man; the subject of his narration is a white man called "Joe the Painter." Nobody in the town except the narrator really likes Joe. He's loud and overly friendly, and has the disconcerting habit of blowing his nose into the gutter, one nostril at a time: "Whenever he felt a clog in his 'breathing-trap,' as he called it, he'd step to the curb, lean over so as not to get his shoes dirty, hold one nostril shut with his thumb, snort, and blow out the other one." But the thing that really gets people about Joe is his honesty. He knows everyone's dirty-underwear business, and announces it at the top of his lungs in the form of questions, such as, "'Howdy, Mrs. Secord, how's the girls? Looks like you been living off pudding. Say, you pregnant again?'" or, "'Howdy, Connie, how's the boil doing?'"

The action gets going when Joe finds out that the town is planning to have a pageant contest in celebration of its own centennial, and that there's some grant money available to those who wish to get up a pageant. Joe is overflowing with civic spirit, and decides to enter the contest. His entry is to be about the town's founder, one Matthew Larson, and a long-ago incident called "The Deer Island Massacre," involving a local band of Indians. Joe describes the event as follows: "'Yes, a massacre. Larson's two brothers were killed, but Larson survived and built the town. That's how this place was started. Make a good pageant, huh?'"

At this point the narrator — whom we know only as "Chief," because that's what Joe calls him — assumes that the massacre is the usual movie kind, that is, instigated by treacherous Indians, with heavy losses but with eventual triumph for the whites. He's been asked by Joe to recruit the Indians for this affair, but he isn't so sure his friends and relations will like the idea. However, he's overwhelmed by Joe: "'What's to like? It's all history. You can't muck around with history. It ain't always the way we'd like it to be, but there it is. Can't change it.'"

Before the pageant, the Indians congregate on Deer Island — "'Just like the old days,'" as the narrator's father says — and begin rehearsing. Joe decides they don't look enough like Indians, and rounds up some wigs and some black yarn braids from the town. The day for the pageant arrives, and Joe introduces it in proper fashion. It is being presented, he says, by the Native Son Players. The narrator likes this. "'Damn, that Joe was creative! Sounded professional,' he thinks." (We, the readers, like it because it's a really vicious touch, and because it twists on a couple of levels. It's the kind of kitschy phrasing Joe would come up with; it plays on "Native"; and these *are* the Native Sons, although white Americans have often appropriated the designation for themselves alone.)

The first act recounts the arrival of Larson, played by Joe, who is greeted by Redbird, played by the narrator. The second act dramatizes the growing friction between Indians and whites as the latter encroach on Deer Island and want to build things on it. The third is the massacre itself, and here is where we all get a jolt, audience and readers alike — because the massacre is not perpetrated by the Indians. It's done by the whites, sneaking up in the dead of night and butchering the Indians as they lie asleep. The Indians playing the whites open fire, making *bang bang* noises. The Indians playing the Indians leap about, slapping little plastic restaurant ketchup packets on themselves for blood. "'Protect the women and children,'" cries Redbird — a line straight from the wagonside of many a Western movie Indian-and-wagon-train sequence.

The Indian actors thoroughly enjoy themselves. Soon they are all lying "dead," while flies buzz around the ketchup and Joe soliloquizes over their bodies: "'I abhor the taking of a human life, but civilization needs a strong arm to open the frontier. Farewell, Redman. Know that from your bones will spring a new and stronger community forever.'"

The audience is paralyzed by Joe's pageant. This is not what they had in mind at all! It seems, somehow, to be in the most outrageous bad taste. It has mentioned — as is Joe's habit — something that has been deemed unmentionable. And it does so with a childlike straightforwardness and honesty that is infuriating. (As the town bartender has said earlier, "'Honesty makes most people nervous.'") The town is scandalized. But, after all, what has Joe done? All he has done is to re-enact history, the part of it that is not usually celebrated; and this has called the notion of "history" itself into question.

Joe's pageant does not win. It is termed "inappropriate" by the mayor. The pageant that does win — about the founding of the first city council — is entirely "appropriate," and entirely boring. "History," the history we choose to recount, is what we find "appropriate." The Indians go home, saying that if Joe ever needs some Indians again just give them a call.

The story ends where it begins: the narrator is still the only person in town who likes Joe.

Well now, we say. What are we to make of this apparently artless but secretly designing story? And why are we left sitting, like the audience, with our mouths open? Why do we feel so *sandbagged*? And — because he's never told us — just why *does* the narrator like Joe?

I think the answers will be somewhat different, depending on — for instance — whether the reader is a white person or a Native person. But I assume that the narrator likes Joe for a couple of reasons. First, Joe is entirely although tactlessly honest, and for this reason he is the only white in the town who can look back at the town's founding, see that it was based on the ruthless massacre of the earlier incumbents, and say it out loud. Second, Joe is not sentimental over this. He does not romanticize the slaughtered Indians, or weep crocodile tears over them now that they are no longer the main competition. He deals with history in the same practical, unselfconscious way he blows his nose. He doesn't feel any sanctimonious guilt either. He lays the actions out and lets them speak for themselves.

Third, Joe has a high opinion of the narrator. The title "Chief" is not a joke for him. He knows the narrator is not a Chief, but he thinks of him as one anyway. Joe and the "Chief" each possess qualities that the other one values.

Read in the light of the long North American tradition of Indians-as-characters-in-white-fiction, this wonderfully satiric but deadpan story could be seen as a kind of parody-in-miniature of Fenimore Cooper's Leatherstocking tales, or of the Lone Ranger and Tonto — the fearless white leader with a penchant for straight speaking and for seeing justice done, the loyal Indian sidekick who comes up with the manpower and the sound effects. It would not work nearly so well as ambush if our minds had not already been lulled into somnolence by a great deal of storytelling in which things were seen far otherwise.

The second story gives us an even more radical departure from the expected. It's called "One Good Story, That One," and in it Thomas King invents not just a new slant on an old story but a new kind of narrative voice. The "Chief" in "Joe the Painter and the Deer Island Massacre" lived in a white-folks' town and was familiar with its vocabulary and ways. Not so the narrator of "One Good Story," an older Indian who appears to spend most of his time in the Canadian bush, although he has been to Yellowknife. It's clear from the outset that English is far from being either his mother tongue or his language of first choice. It's more like a language of last resort. However, as he uses it to tell his story, it becomes strangely eloquent. King employs this created, truncated voice to suggest, among other things, the pacing of a Native narrator. This storyteller will take his time, will repeat himself, sometimes for emphasis, sometimes for rhythm, sometimes as a delaying tactic, sometimes to get things straight.

His story is about telling a story, and about the kinds of stories that are expected of him, and about the kinds that have been told to him; it's also a story about refusing to tell a story, but we don't know that until the end of the story.

His is minding his own business at his "summer place" when his friend Napaio arrives with three white men:

> Three men come to my summer place, also my friend Napaio.
> Pretty loud talkers, those ones. One is big. I tell him maybe looks
> like Big Joe. Maybe not.
>
> Anyway.
>
> They come and Napaio too. Bring greetings, how are you,
> many nice things they bring to says. Three.
>
> All white.
>
> Too bad, those.

What do these three want? It turns out they are anthropologists, and they want a story. At first the narrator tries to put them off with stories about people he knows: Jimmy who runs the store, Billy Frank and the dead-river pig. But this will not do.

> Those ones like old story, says my friend, maybe how the world was put together. Good Indian story like that, Napaio says. Those ones have tape recorders, he says.
>
> Okay, I says.
>
> Have some tea.
>
> Stay awake.
>
> Once upon a time.
>
> Those stories start like that, pretty much, those ones, start on time.

The story he proceeds to relate is not what the anthropologists were looking for at all. Instead it is a hilarious version of the Book of Genesis, a white-folk story played back to them in an Indian key, with the narrator's own commentary.

"There was nothing," he begins. "Pretty hard to believe that, maybe." Enter the creator. "Only one person walk around. Call him god." God gets tired of walking around, so he begins to create. "Maybe that one says, we will get some stars. So he does. And then he says, maybe we should get a moon. So, they get one of them too. Someone writes all this down, I don't know. Lots of things left to get."

The narrator launches into a long list of things god now "gets," a list which he narrates both in his own language and in English, and which includes several animals, a flint, a television set, and a "grocery story." God then creates the Garden of "Evening," and two human beings, Evening herself — the garden is clearly hers — and a man, "Ah-damn." "Ah-damn and Evening real happy, those ones. No clothes, those, you know. Ha, Ha, Ha, Ha. But they pretty dumb, then. New, you know."

Evening discovers the famous tree, which has a lot of things growing on it, such as potatoes, pumpkins, and corn. It also has some "mee-so," apples. Evening has it in mind to eat some of them, but "that one, god" re-enters the picture. He has a bad temper and shouts, and is compared by the narrator to a man called Harley James who used to beat up his wife. "God" orders Evening to leave the apples alone. He is selfish, and will not share.

However, Evening eats an apple, and being a good woman, takes some to share with Ah-damn. The latter is busy writing down the names of the animals as they parade by. "Pretty boring that," says the narrator. Writing down does not interest him.

Again, we get a long list of the animals, in two languages. But now the story goes even further off the Biblical beaten track, because Coyote comes by a lot of times, in different disguises. "Gets dressed up, fool around."

And now the narrator shifts entirely into his own language, which we paleface readers can't follow at all. He even tells a joke, which is presumably about Coyote, but how are we to know? *What kind of a story is this anyway?* Well, it's changing into a story about the coyote. "Tricky one, that coyote. Walks in circles. Sneaky."

Evening recognizes immediately, from the tracks on the floor, that the coyote has been around more than once. But she feeds Ah-damn anyway, dumb bunny that he is, like "white man." She herself is pointedly identified as an Indian woman, which accounts for her intelligence.

God comes along and is cheesed off because the apples have been eaten. Evening tells him to "calm down, watch some television," but god wants to kick Evening and Ah-damn out of the garden, "go somewhere else. Just like Indian today."

Evening says that's fine with her, there's lots of other good places around, but Ah-damn lies about how many apples he ate, and whines as well. It avails him nothing and he gets thrown out, "'right on those rocks. Ouch, ouch, ouch, that one says.'" Evening has to come back and fix him up.

What about the snake? He's been forgotten by the narrator, but is stuck back in at the end. He's in the tree along with the apples, but there's not much to tell about him. The reason he hisses is that Evening stuck an apple in his mouth for trying to get too friendly.

The narrator's story ends with Ah-damn and Evening coming "out here" and having a bunch of kids. "That's all. It is ended."

But Thomas King's story ends another way. The white anthropologists pack up, none too pleased but putting a good face on it. "'All of those ones smile. Nod their head around. Look out window. Make happy noises. Say goodbyes, see you later. Leave pretty quick.'" The narrator's last gloss is, "'I clean up all the coyote tracks on the floor.'"

If the narrator has a "good Indian story" to tell, he's kept it to himself. He certainly isn't going to tell it to the white anthropologists, who are seen as sneaky coyotes, mischief makers, indulging in disguises and fooling around. Instead he's fed them one of their own stories back, but he's changed the moral. No secondary creation of Eve from a rib, no original sin, no temptation by Satan, no guilt, no "sweat of your brow" curse. The bad behaviour displayed is displayed by "god," who is greedy, selfish, loud-mouthed, and violent. Adam is stupid, and Eve, who is generous, level-headed, peace-loving, and nurturing, comes out the hero of the story. In the course of his tale, the Indian narrator is able to convey to the whites more or less what he thinks of white behaviour in general. Nor can they do anything about it, as this is a situation they themselves have sought out — for their own benefit, since, we assume, they wish to use the Indian's story as "material" — and the etiquette of storytelling prevents them from intervening in the story to protest either its form or its content.

"One Good Story" could be seen as a variant of the Wise Peasant motif, or "putting one over on the city slicker" by pretending to be a lot dumber than you really are; although, in this case, the city slicker category includes any white reader. We feel "taken" by the story, in several ways: we get taken in by it, because this narrative voice has considerable charm and straight-faced subtlety; but we also get taken for a ride, just as the three anthropologists are. Perhaps we have been taken for even more of a ride than we realize. How do we know what all those Indian words *really* mean? We don't, and that is very much one of the points. The narrator himself doesn't know what "Saint Merry" means. Tit for tat. Another tit for tat is that we are forced to experience first-hand how it must feel to have your own religious stories retold in a version that neither "understands" nor particularly reverences them. The Biblical Fall of Man has seldom been recounted with such insouciance.

At the same time, and in the midst of our cross-cultural nervousness, we sympathize with the narrator rather than the anthropologists, just as, in "Joe the Painter," we have taken the side of the odd men out, Joe and the "Chief," as against the conventional townspeople. Thomas King knows exactly what he's doing.

Both of these stories are about Indians who are expected to "play Indian," to enact some white man's version of themselves, to serve a symbolic agenda other than their own. Both narrators, in their own ways, refuse: the first by participating in a farcical pageant that undermines the whole "How the West Was Won" myth, the second by withholding his authentic "Indian" tales and hilariously subverting a central and sacrosanct "white" story.

What other inventive twists of narrative and alarming shifts of viewpoint are in store for us from this author? Time, which begins all stories, will tell.

1. Thomas King has published the following works: ed., with Cheryl Calver and Helen Hoy, *The Native in Literature* (Toronto: ECW, 1985); ed., Native Fiction issue of *Canadian Fiction Magazine* No. 60 (1987); *Medicine River* (novel) (Toronto: Penguin, 1990); ed., *"All My Relations": An Anthology of Contemporary Canadian Native Prose* (Toronto: McClelland & Stewart, 1990); *One Good Story, That One* (story cycle, in progress).

15

NINE BEGINNINGS

1. *Why do you write?*

I've begun this piece nine times. I've junked each beginning.

I hate writing about my writing. I almost never do it. Why am I doing it now? Because I said I would. I got a letter. I wrote back *no*. Then I was at a party and the same person was there. It's harder to refuse in person. Saying *yes* had something to do with being nice, as women are taught to be, and something to do with being helpful, which we are also taught. Being helpful to women, giving a pint of blood. With not claiming the sacred prerogatives, the touch-me-not self-protectiveness of the artist, with not being selfish. With conciliation, with doing your bit, with appeasement. I was well brought up. I have trouble ignoring social obligations. Saying you'll write about your writing is a social obligation. It's not an obligation to the writing.

2. *Why do you write?*

I've junked each of nine beginnings. They seemed beside the point. Too assertive, too pedagogical, too frivolous or belligerent, too falsely wise. As if I had some special self-revelation that would encourage others, or some special knowledge to impart, some pithy saying that would act like a talisman for the driven, the obsessed. But

I have no such talismans. If I did, I would not continue, myself, to be so driven and obsessed.

3. *Why do you write?*

I hate writing about my writing because I have nothing to say about it. I have nothing to say about it because I can't remember what goes on when I'm doing it. That time is like small pieces cut out of my brain. It's not time I myself have lived. I can remember the details of the rooms and places where I've written, the circumstances, the other things I did before and after, but not the process itself. Writing about writing requires self-consciousness; writing itself requires the abdication of it.

4. *Why do you write?*

There are a lot of things that can be said about what goes on around the edges of writing. Certain ideas you may have, certain motivations, grand designs that don't get carried out. I can talk about bad reviews, about sexist reactions to my writing, about making an idiot of myself on television shows. I can talk about books that failed, that never got finished, and about why they failed. The one that had too many characters, the one that had too many layers of time, red herrings that diverted me when what I really wanted to get at was something else, a certain corner of the visual world, a certain voice, an inarticulate landscape.

I can talk about the difficulties that women encounter as writers. For instance, if you're a woman writer, sometime, somewhere, you will be asked: *Do you think of yourself as a writer first, or as a woman first?* Look out. Whoever asks this hates and fears both writing and women.

Many of us, in my generation at least, ran into teachers or male writers or other defensive jerks who told us women could not really write because they couldn't be truck drivers or Marines and therefore didn't understand the seamier side of life, which included sex with women. We were told we wrote like housewives, or else we were treated like honorary men, as if to be a good writer was to suppress the female.

Such pronouncements used to be made as if they were the simple truth. Now they're questioned. Some things have changed for the better, but not all. There's a lack of self-confidence that gets instilled very early in many young girls, before writing is even seen as a possibility. You need a certain amount of nerve to be a writer, an almost physical nerve, the kind you need to walk a log across a river. The horse throws you and you get back on the horse. I learned to swim by being dropped into the water. You need to know you can sink, and survive it. Girls should be allowed to play in the mud. They should be released from the obligations of perfection. Some of your writing, at least, should be as evanescent as play.

A ratio of failures is built into the process of writing. The wastebasket has evolved for a reason. Think of it as the altar of the Muse Oblivion, to whom you sacrifice your botched first drafts, the tokens of your human imperfection. She is the tenth Muse, the one without whom none of the others can function. The gift she offers you is the freedom of the second chance. Or as many chances as you'll take.

5. Why do you write?

In the mid-1980s I began a sporadic journal. Today I went back through it, looking for something I could dig out and fob off as pertinent instead of writing this piece about writing. But it was useless. There was nothing in it about the actual composition of anything I've written over the past six years. Instead there are exhortations to myself — to get up earlier, to walk more, to resist lures and distractions. *Drink more water*, I find. *Go to bed earlier.* There were lists of how many pages I'd written per day, how many I'd retyped, how many yet to go. Other than that, there was nothing but descriptions of rooms, accounts of what we'd cooked and/or eaten and with whom, letters written and received, notable sayings of children, birds and animals seen, the weather. What came up in the garden. Illnesses, my own and those of others. Deaths, births. Nothing about writing.

January 1, 1984. Blakeny, England. As of today, I have about 130 pp. of the novel done and it's just beginning to take shape & reach the point at which I feel that it exists and can be finished and may be worth it. I work in the bedroom of the big house, and here, in the sitting room, with the wood fire in the fireplace and the coke fire in the dilapidated Roeburn in the kitchen. As usual I'm too cold, which is better than being too hot — today is grey, warm for the time of year, damp. If I got up earlier maybe I would work more, but I might just spend more time procrastinating — as now.

And so on.

6. *Why do you write?*

You learn to write by reading and writing, writing and reading. As a craft it's acquired through the apprentice system, but you choose your own teachers. Sometimes they're alive, sometimes dead.

As a vocation, it involves the laying on of hands. You receive your vocation and in your turn you must pass it on. Perhaps you will do this only through your work, perhaps in other ways. Either way, you're part of a community, the community of writers, the community of storytellers that stretches back through time to the beginning of human society.

As for the particular human society to which you yourself belong — sometimes you'll feel you're speaking for it, sometimes — when it's taken an unjust form — against it, or for that other community, the community of the oppressed, the exploited, the voiceless. Either way, the pressures on you will be intense; in other countries, perhaps fatal. But even here — speak "for women," or for any other group that is feeling the boot, and there will be many at hand, both for and against, to tell you to shut up, or to say what they want you to say, or to say it a different way. Or to save them. The billboard awaits you, but if you succumb to its temptations you'll end up two-dimensional.

Tell what is yours to tell. Let others tell what is theirs.

7. *Why do you write?*

Why are we so addicted to causality? *Why do* you *write?* (Treatise by child psychologist, mapping your formative traumas. Conversely: palm-reading, astrology, and genetic studies, pointing to the stars, fate, heredity.) *Why do you write?* (That is, why not do something useful instead?) If you were a doctor, you could tell some acceptable moral tale about how you put Band-Aids on your cats as a child, how you've always longed to cure suffering. No one can argue with that: But writing? What is it *for?*

Some possible answers: *Why does the sun shine? In the face of the absurdity of modern society, why do anything else? Because I'm a writer. Because I want to discover the patterns in the chaos of time. Because I must. Because someone has to bear witness. Why do you read?* (This last is tricky: maybe they don't.) *Because I wish to forge in the smithy of my soul the uncreated conscience of my race. Because I wish to make an axe to break the frozen sea within.* (These have been used, but they're good.)

If at a loss, perfect the shrug. Or say: *It's better than working in a bank.* Or say: *For fun.* If you say this, you won't be believed, or else you'll be dismissed as trivial. Either way, you'll have avoided the question.

8. *Why do you write?*

Not long ago, in the course of clearing some of the excess paper out of my workroom, I opened a filing cabinet drawer I hadn't looked into for years. In it was a bundle of loose sheets, folded, creased, and grubby, tied up with leftover string. It consisted of things I'd written in the late 1950s, in high school and the early years of university. There were scrawled, inky poems, about snow, despair, and the Hungarian Revolution. There were short stories dealing with girls who'd had to get married, and dispirited, mousy-haired high-school English teachers — to end up as either was at that time my vision of Hell — typed finger-by-finger on an ancient machine that made all the letters half-red.

There I am, then, back in grade twelve, going through the writers' magazines after I'd finished my French Composition homework, typing out my lugubrious poems and my grit-filled stories. (I was big on grit. I had an eye for lawn litter and dog turds on sidewalks. In these stories it was usually snowing damply, or raining; at the very least there was slush. If it was summer, the heat and humidity were always wiltingly high and my characters had sweat marks under their arms; if it was spring, wet clay stuck to their feet. Though some would say all this was just normal Toronto weather.)

In the top right-hand corners of some of these, my hopeful seventeen-year-old self had typed, "First North American Rights Only." I was not sure what "First North American Rights" were; I put it in because the writing magazines said you should. I was at that time an aficionado of writing magazines, having no one else to turn to for professional advice.

If I were an archaeologist, digging through the layers of old paper that mark the eras in my life as a writer, I'd have found, at the lowest or Stone Age level — say around ages five to seven — a few poems and stories, unremarkable precursors of all my frenetic later scribbling. (Many children write at that age, just as many children draw. The strange thing is that so few of them go on to become writers or painters.) After that there's a great blank. For eight years, I simply didn't write. Then, suddenly, and with no missing links in between, there's a wad of manuscripts. One week I wasn't a writer, the next I was.

Who did I think I was, to be able to get away with this? What did I think I was doing? How did I get that way? To these questions I still have no answers.

9. *Why do you write?*

There's the blank page, and the thing that obsesses you. There's the story that wants to take you over and there's your resistance to it. There's your longing to get out of this, this servitude, to play hooky, to do anything else: wash the laundry, see a movie. There are words and their inertias, their biases, their insufficiencies, their glories. There are the risks you take and your loss of nerve, and the help that comes when you're least expecting it. There's the laborious revision, the scrawled-over, crumpled-up pages that drift across the floor like spilled litter. There's the one sentence you know you will save.

Next day there's the blank page. You give yourself up to it like a sleepwalker. Something goes on that you can't remember afterwards. You look at what you've done. It's hopeless.

You begin again. It never gets any easier.

16

A SLAVE TO HIS OWN LIBERATION

THE GENERAL IN HIS LABYRINTH
BY GABRIEL GARCÍA MÁRQUEZ

THE GENERAL of the title of Gabriel García Márquez's new novel is Simón Bolívar, "The Liberator," who in the years 1811–24 led the revolutionary armies of South America in a brilliant and gruelling series of campaigns that swept the Spaniards from their former colonies. In the process many rich and long-established cities were devastated, vast wealth was captured and squandered, whole populations were laid waste through slaughter, famine, and disease, and, in the aftermath, the unified South America Bolívar so fervently desired — a country that would have balanced, and challenged, the United States — fell apart in a series of jealous bickerings, intrigues, assassinations, secessions, local feuds, and military coups.

Had Bolívar not existed, Mr. García Márquez would have had to invent him. Seldom has there been a more fitting match between author and subject. Mr. García Márquez wades into his flamboyant, often improbably and ultimately tragic material with enormous gusto, heaping detail upon sensuous detail, alternating grace with horror, perfume with the stench of corruption, the elegant language of public ceremony with the vulgarity of private moments, the rationalistic clarity of Bolívar's thought with the malarial intensity of his emotions, but tracing always the main compulsion that drives his protagonist:

the longing for an independent and unified South America. This, according to Bolívar himself, is the clue to all his contradictions.

Just now, when empires are disintegrating and the political map is being radically redrawn, the subject of *The General in His Labyrinth* is a most timely one. It is noteworthy that Mr. García Márquez has chosen to depict his hero not in the days of his astonishing triumphs but in his last months of bitterness and frustration. One feels that, for the author, the tale of Bolívar is exemplary not just for his own turbulent age but for ours as well. Revolutions have a long history of eating their progenitors.

Each book by Mr. García Márquez is a major literary event. Each has also been quite different from its predecessors, and the new novel, ably translated by Edith Grossman, is no exception. It is set in the past, but to call it a historical novel would be to do it an injustice. Nor is it one of those fictions — such as, for instance, "A Maggot" by John Fowles — in which a few real personages are mingled with the imagined ones. In this book the element of the real is front and centre: most of the people in it actually lived; all of the events and most of the incidents actually took place, and the rest have their foundation in voluminous research: if someone eats a guava, then guavas existed, in that place and at that season.

But Mr. García Márquez avoids a chronological narrative (although, very helpfully, the linear sequence of events is provided in a note at the end). Instead he begins his book at the point at which General Bolívar, an old man at the age of forty-six, literally shrunken by the unspecified illness that will soon kill him, is rejected as president of the new government he himself has helped to create. Cold-shouldered by the elite, jeered by the rabble, he leaves the Colombian city of Bogotá for a meandering journey by barge down the Magdalena River with the stated intention of sailing to Europe.

He never makes it. Thwarted by the oppressive and calamitous weather, by the machinations of his enemies — in particular his fellow revolutionary and archrival, Francisco de Paula Santander — by the political ambitions of his friends, by his illness, and above all by his own reluctance to leave the scene of his former glories, he wanders from city to city, house to house, refuge to refuge, dragging his increasingly baffled and restless entourage in his wake. In some places he is treated with scorn, in others with veneration; he endures endless celebrations in his honour, pleas for his intercession, fiestas and official receptions, punctuated by the brutal interventions of nature — floods, heat waves, epidemics — and by fresh episodes in the decay of his own body.

Always he is dogged by a question he refuses to answer: will he recapture the presidency in order to suppress the anarchy and civil war that are threatening to tear the continent apart? In other words, is he willing to purchase unity at the expense of a rudimentary democracy, and at the price of a dictatorship headed by himself? Possibly he is waiting for the right moment to make a comeback; but this moment never arrives. "The headlong race between his misfortunes and his dreams" is won by the misfortunes, and the monster at the centre of his "labyrinth" gets him in the end.

The structure of the book is itself labyrinthine, turning the narrative back on itself, twisting and confusing the thread of time until not only the general but the reader cannot tell exactly where or when he is. Woven into the present, as memory, reveries, dream, or feverish hallucination, are many scenes from the general's earlier life: near catastrophes in war, splendid triumphs, superhuman feats of endurance, nights of orgiastic celebration, portentous turns of fate, and romantic encounters with beautiful women, of which there seem to have been a large number. There is the deeply suppressed image of his young wife, dead after eight months of marriage; there is his devoted, cigar-smoking Amazonian mistress, Manuela Sáenz, who once saved him from assassination. But there were also — according to his faithful valet, José Palacios, who plays Leporello to Bolívar's Don Juan — thirty-five other serious affairs, "not counting the one-night birds, of course."

Of course: because Bolívar is not only a prime exponent of the well-known Latin American machismo but a true child of the Romantic age. His political imagination was formed by the French Revolution; his heroes were Napoleon and Rousseau. Like Byron, he was a romantic ironist, a skeptic in religion, a flouter of social norms, a philanderer — a man capable of great self-sacrifice in the pursuit of large and glorious goals, but otherwise a worshipper at the altar of his own ego. He approached each new woman as a challenge; "once satisfied, he [would] . . . send them extravagant gifts to protect himself from oblivion, but, with an emotion that resembled vanity more than love, he would not commit the least part of his life to them."

On the subject of politics, Mr. García Márquez's Bolívar is little short of prophetic. Just before his death, he proclaims that South America "is ungovernable, the man who serves a revolution plows the sea, this nation will fall inevitably into the hands of the unruly mob and then will pass into the hands of almost indistinguishable petty tyrants." He foresees the perils of debt: "I warned Santander that whatever good we had done for the nation would be worthless if we took on debt because we would go on paying interest till the end of time. Now it's clear: debt will destroy us in the end." He has something to say, as well, about the role of the United States in Latin American affairs: inviting the United States to the Congress of Panama is "like inviting the cat to the mice's fiesta." "Don't go . . . to the United States," he warns a colleague. "It's omnipotent and terrible, and its tale of liberty will end in a plague of miseries for us all." As Carlos Fuentes has remarked, the patterns of Latin American politics, and of United States intervention in them, have not changed much in 160 years.

In addition to being a fascinating literary tour de force and a moving tribute to an extraordinary man, *The General in His Labyrinth* is a sad commentary on the ruthlessness of the political process. Bolívar changed history, but not as much as he would have liked. There are statues of "The Liberator" all over Latin America, but in his own eyes he died defeated.

17

AFTERWORD

ANNE OF GREEN GABLES
BY LUCY MAUD MONTGOMERY

ANNE OF GREEN GABLES is one of those books you feel almost guilty liking, because so many other people seem to like it as well. If it's that popular, you feel, it can't possibly be good, or good for you.

Like many others, I read this book as a child, and absorbed it so thoroughly that I can't even remember when. I read it to my own daughter when she was eight, and she read it again to herself later, and acquired all the sequels — which she, like everyone else including the author, realized were not on quite the same level as the original. I saw the television series too, and, despite rewrites and excisions, the central story was as strong and as appealing as ever.

And several summers ago, when my family and I were spending some time on Prince Edward Island, I even saw the musical. The theatre gift store was offering *Anne* dolls, an *Anne* cookbook, and *Anne* paraphernalia of all kinds. The theatre itself was large but crowded; in front of us was a long row of Japanese tourists. During one especially culture-specific moment — a dance in which a horde of people leapt around holding eggs glued on to spoons clenched between their teeth — I wondered what the Japanese tourists could possibly be making of it. Then I took to wondering what they could be making of the whole phenomenon. What did they make of the *Anne* dolls, the

Anne knick-knacks, the *Anne* books themselves? Why was Anne Shirley, the talkative red-haired orphan, so astonishingly popular among them?

Possibly it was the red hair: that must be exotic, I thought. Or possibly Japanese women and girls found Anne encouraging: in danger of rejection because she is not the desired and valued boy, she manages to win over the hearts of her adoptive parents and to end the book with a great deal of social approval. But she triumphs without sacrificing her sense of herself: she will not tolerate insult, she defends herself, she even loses her temper and gets away with it. She breaks taboos. On a more conventional level, she studies hard at school and wins a scholarship, she respects her elders, or at least some of them, and she has a great love of Nature (although it is Nature in its more subdued aspect; hers is a pastoral world of gardens and blossoming trees, not mountains and hurricanes).

It was helpful for me to try looking at *Anne*'s virtues through other eyes, because for a Canadian woman — once a Canadian girl — *Anne* is a truism. Readers of my generation, and of several generations before and since, do not think of *Anne* as "written." It has simply always been there. It is difficult not to take the book for granted, and almost impossible to see it fresh, to realize what an impact it must have had when it first appeared.

It is tempting to think of *Anne* as just a very good "girls' book," about — and intended for — pre-adolescents. And on one level, it is just that. Anne's intense friendship with the ever-faithful Diana Barry, the hatefulness of Josie Pye, the schoolroom politics, the tempest-in-a-teapot "scrapes," Anne's overdone vanity, and her consciousness of fashion in clothes and bookmarks — all are familiar to us, both from our own observation and experience and from other "girls' books."

But *Anne* draws on a darker, and, some would say, a more respectable literary lineage. Anne Shirley is, after all, an orphan, and the opening chapters of *Jane Eyre* and *Oliver Twist* and *Great Expectations*, and, later and closer to Anne, the bad-tempered, unhappy, sallow-faced little Mary of *The Secret Garden*, have all contributed both to Anne Shirley's formation as orphan-heroine and to the reader's understanding of the perils of orphanhood in the nineteenth and early twentieth centuries. Unless she had been allowed to stay at Green Gables, Anne's fate would have been to be passed around as a cheap drudge from one set of uncaring adults to another. In the real world, as opposed to the literary one, she would have been in great danger of ending up pregnant and disgraced, raped — like many of the Barnardo Homes female orphans — by the men in the families in which they had been "placed." We have forgotten, by now, that orphans were once despised, exploited, and feared, considered to be the offspring of criminals or the products of immoral sex. Rachel Lynde, in her tales of orphans who have poisoned and set fire to the families who have taken them in, is merely voicing received opinion. No wonder Anne cries so much when she thinks she will be "returned," and no wonder Marilla and Matthew are considered "odd" for keeping her!

But Anne partakes of another "orphan" tradition as well: the folk-tale orphan who wins despite everything, the magic child who appears, as it seems, from nowhere — like King Arthur — and proves to have qualities far superior to anyone around her.

Such literary echoes may form the structural underpinnings of Anne's tale, but the texture is relentlessly local. L. M. Montgomery stays within the parameters of the conventions available to her: nobody goes to the bathroom in this book, and although we are in the country, no pigs are visibly slaughtered. But, that said, she remains faithful to her own aesthetic credo, as set forth by Anne's beloved schoolteacher Miss Stacy, who "won't let us write anything but what might happen in Avonlea in our own lives." Part of the current interest in "Avonlea" is that it appears to be a "jollier," more innocent world, long gone and very different from our own; but for Montgomery, "Avonlea" was simply reality edited. She was determined to write from what she knew: not the whole truth, perhaps, but not a total romanticization either. Rooms and clothes and malicious gossip are described much as they were, and people talk in the vernacular, minus the swear words — but then, the people we hear speaking are mostly "respectable" women, who would not have sworn anyway. This world was familiar to me through the stories told to me by my Maritime parents and aunts: the sense of community and "family," the horror of being "talked about," the smug rectitude, the distrust of outsiders, the sharp division between what was "respectable" and what was not, as well as the pride in hard work and the respect for achievement, all are faithfully depicted by Montgomery. Marilla's speech to Anne — "I believe in a girl being fitted to earn her own living whether ever she has to or not" — may sound like radical feminism to some, but in fact it is just a sample of Maritime self-reliance. My mother was brought up like that; consequently, so was I.

Montgomery wrote from her own experience in another and more profound way as well. Knowing what we now know about her life, we realize that Anne's story was a mirror image of her own, and gathers much of its force and poignancy from thwarted wish fulfillment. Montgomery, too, was virtually an orphan, abandoned by her father after her mother's death to a set of strict, judgemental grandparents, but she never gained the love she grants so lavishly to Anne. Anne's experience of exclusion was undoubtedly hers; the longing for acceptance must have been hers as well. So was the lyricism; so was the sense of injustice; so was the rebellious rage.

Children identify with Anne because she is what they often feel themselves to be — powerless and scorned and misunderstood. She revolts as they would like to revolt, she gets what they would like to have, and she is cherished as they themselves would like to be. When I was a child, I thought — as all children do — that Anne was the centre of the book. I cheered her on, and applauded her victories over the adults, her thwartings of their wills. But there is another perspective.

Although *Anne* is about childhood, it is also very much centred on the difficult and sometimes heartbreaking relationship between children and adults. Anne seems to have no power, but in reality she has the vast though unconscious power of a beloved child. Although she changes in the book — she grows up — her main transformation is physical. Like the Ugly Duckling, she becomes a swan; but the inner Anne — her moral essence — remains much what it has always been. Matthew, too, begins as he means to go on: he is one of those shy, childlike men who delight Montgomery's heart (like Cousin Jimmy in the *Emily* books), he loves Anne from the moment he sees her, and he takes her part in every way and on every occasion.

The only character who goes though any sort of essential transformation is Marilla. *Anne of Green Gables* is not about Anne becoming a good little girl: it is about Marilla Cuthbert becoming a good — and more complete — woman. At the book's beginning, she is hardly even alive; as Rachel Lynde, the common-sense voice of the community, puts it, Marilla is not *living*, just *staying*. Marilla takes Anne on, not out of love as Matthew does, but out of a cold sense of duty. It is only in the course of the book that we realize there is a strong family resemblance between the two. Matthew, as we have always known, is a "kindred spirit" for Anne, but the kinship with Marilla goes deeper: Marilla, too, has been "odd," ugly, unloved. She, too, has been the victim of fate and injustice.

Anne without Marilla would — admit it — be sadly one-dimensional, an overtalkative child whose precocious cuteness might very easily pall. Marilla adds the saving touch of lemon juice. On the other hand, Anne acts out a great many of Marilla's concealed wishes, thoughts, and desires, which is the key to their relationship. And, in her battles of will with Anne, Marilla is forced to confront herself, and to regain what she has lost or repressed: her capacity to love, the full range of her emotions. Underneath her painful cleanliness and practicality, she is a passionate woman, as her outpouring of grief at Matthew's death testifies. The most moving declaration of love in the book has nothing to do with Gilbert Blythe: it is Marilla's wrenching confession in the penultimate chapter:

> Oh, Anne, I know I've been kind of strict and harsh with you maybe — but you mustn't think I didn't love you as well as Matthew did, for all that. I want to tell you now when I can. It's never been easy for me to say things out of my heart, but at times like this it's easier. I love you as dear as if you were my own flesh and blood and you've been my joy and comfort ever since you came to Green Gables.

The Marilla we first meet could never have laid herself bare like this. Only when she has recovered — painfully enough, awkwardly enough — her capacity to feel and express, can she become what Anne herself has lost long ago, and truly wants: a mother. But to love is to become vulnerable. At the beginning of the book, Marilla is all-powerful, but by the end, the structure has been reversed, and Anne has much more to offer Marilla than the other way around.

It may be the ludicrous escapades of Anne that render the book so attractive to children, but it is the struggles of Marilla that give it resonance for adults. Anne may be the orphan in all of us, but then, so is Marilla. Anne is the fairy-tale, wish-fulfillment version, what Montgomery longed for. Marilla is, more likely, what she feared she might become: joyless, bereft, trapped, hopeless, unloved. Each of them saves the other. It is the neatness of their psychological fit — as well as the invention, humour, and fidelity of the writing — that makes *Anne* such a satisfying and enduring fable.

18

INTRODUCTION: THE EARLY YEARS

THE POETRY OF GWENDOLYN MACEWEN

For we are great statements in our days
And on the basis of that we can expect small audiences.

GWENDOLYN MACEWEN was born in Toronto in September 1941, during the darkest days of the Second World War. She died, unexpectedly and far too young, in 1987, at the age of forty-five.

Due to family disruptions — her mother was frequently hospitalized for mental illness, her father became an alcoholic — her childhood was stressful; but the conviction that she would be a poet came to her as a saving grace in early adolescence. She began publishing poetry in the well-respected journal *The Canadian Forum* when she was sixteen, and at the age of eighteen — although warned against such a rash step by more practical heads — she left high school to pursue her vocation.

The late 1950s was not the best time for such a move, especially if you were a woman. In the world of conventional North American popular culture, Doris Day and Betty Crocker ruled supreme and Mom-and-Dad domesticity was the norm; rebellion against the bourgeoisie was embodied by Marlon Brando and his all-boy *Wild Ones* motorbike gang. The music was rock 'n' roll or jazz, heavily male both. "Artist" meant male painter; any woman rash enough to take brush in hand was regarded as a dabbler. The Beat Generation writers had a place for women, true, but only as complaisant help-meets; they were expected to keep on cookin' and smilin' and payin' the rent, and to keep out of the hair of their genius men. Women artists of any kind, in that still heavily Freudian era, were assumed to have adjustment problems. *Man Does, Woman Is*, as Robert Graves so dauntingly put it; and if women insisted on doing rather than being, they were likely to end up with their heads in the oven.

For Gwendolyn MacEwen, all of this was compounded you would think by location. Toronto was not exactly a centre of cosmo-politan artistic energy at the time. Montreal was considered to be the cultural heartland, for both English-speaking and French-speaking artists alike, whereas Toronto was thought of as a puritanical provin-cial backwater, a boring, constipated place where you couldn't get wine with dinner. Persons of taste sneered at it, even and especially those who lived there. Colonialism lingered on, and it was assumed that first-rate cultural products were imported from abroad — from Europe if you were old-fashioned, from New York if you thought of yourself as the cutting edge.

But for young writers, even young female writers, there were compensations. Cultural trends are never as oppressively homoge-neous in the outbacks as they are in the centres, and in Canada there was a generation of woman poets just before MacEwen's who hadn't heard yet that they were supposed to just be: Phyllis Webb, Anne Wilkinson, Jay Macpherson, P. K. Page, Margaret Avison. And the writing community was so small, beleaguered, and desirous of rein-forcements that it was welcoming to any newcomer with talent, especially such an outstanding talent as MacEwen's. Oddly enough, this period — so forbidding and desertlike to the casual view — was, for writing, an age of youthful successes. In addition to Leonard Cohen it produced Daryl Hine, who published his first major col-lection when he was under twenty; James Reaney, the boy wonder from Stratford; Marie-Claire Blais, the girl wonder from Quebec; Jay Macpherson, who won the country's foremost literary award when she was twenty-seven; Michael Ondaatje, bpNichol, Joe Rosenblatt, bill bissett — all early publishers; and many others. So although Gwendolyn MacEwen started publishing very early, she wasn't alone.

Nor was it unusual for her to begin with poetry. Like many of her contemporaries, she eventually produced several novels and collections of short stories, and during the course of her career she also produced radio plays, translations for the theatre, and travel writing; but the poetry appeared first. Indeed, for most of the 1960s poetry was the predominant literary form in Canada: the few existing publishers were reluctant to take chances with new novelists, as novels were expensive to produce and were thought to have a severely limited audience inside Canada and none whatsoever outside it. But poems could be published as broadsheets, or in one of the five or six "little" magazines then extant, or by very small, frequently self-operated presses; or they could be broadcast on the radio — notably on the CBC's pivotal program *Anthology*. Or they could be read aloud.

I first met Gwendolyn MacEwen in the fall of 1960, at The Bohemian Embassy, a coffee house — it was, by then, the age of coffee houses — that featured jazz and folksinging, and, on Thursday nights, poetry readings. The Embassy had the décor of its period — the checked tablecloths, the candles in the Chianti bottles; it was also a smoke-filled firetrap. But it was mecca to the poetry community, and MacEwen, who must have been nineteen then, was already a regular reader there. She was a slight-figured, doe-eyed person with long dark hair, who read in an accomplished, sultry, caressing voice that owed, perhaps, a little to Lauren Bacall. The combination of the childlike appearance, the rich voice, and the poetic authority were compelling — you came away from a MacEwen reading feeling you'd been let in on a unique and delicious secret.

MacEwen's primary interest as a poet was in language and in its corollary, mythmaking. In this she was not alone: the late 1950s and the early 1960s comprised a sort of minor Age of Myth, though there were, of course, other influences around. Northrop Frye's *Anatomy of Criticism* held critical centre stage, with Marshall McLuhan and his structural analysis of popular culture moving up strongly. Leonard Cohen's first volume was called *Let Us Compare Mythologies*; James Reaney's magazine *Alphabet* was entirely devoted to the "mythopoeic" approach, or to correspondences between "real life" and "story"; and Canadian poets were endlessly telling each other that what they really needed to do was to create an "indigenous mythology." In this context, MacEwen's interest in what we might call a mythic structuring of reality — or the structuring of a mythic reality, in opposition to the disappointing world of mundane experience she often refers to as "Kanada" — seems less bizarre. True, no one else settled on Ancient Egypt and the Middle East with quite the same intensity as she does, but her imaginative otherworld is not limited to one time or place. In general — and especially in her earlier poetry — she opposes the works of children, magicians, adventurers, escape artists, the hierarchical and splendid past, the divinely mad, the "barbaric," and poetry, to that of grown-ups, materialists, bureaucrats, the modern daily grind, stolid sanity, the "tame," and newspaper prose.

One of the paradoxes of MacEwen's work is that the protagonists she chooses — in Yeatsian terms, the *personae* — are almost invariably male. She speaks in a female voice when addressing, as the lyric "I," a male "You," but when she uses a more dramatic form, or writes a poem about a heroic figure, the central character is usually a man, such as the escape artist Manzini, or Sir John Franklin, or — in a later, major work — Lawrence of Arabia. When female figures from history or story do appear as speakers, they are likely to be exceptions to their sex; Egyptian princesses, not ordinary Egyptian women; H. Rider Haggard's *She*, with her supernatural powers.

But this is not really surprising. The roles available to women at the time lacked energy; and if what interested you was magic, risk, and exploration, rather than, say, quiet contemplation in the garden between meals, the choice of a male voice was almost inevitable. MacEwen wanted to be out on the sharp edge with the boys, not back in the kitchen with the girls; she was entranced with cosmic predicaments, and the time for female astronauts had not yet come. She might have analyzed the female condition and then tapped the resulting anger, like Sylvia Plath; but then she would have been a very different kind of poet. Power — including the dark side of power — was much more interesting to her than powerlessness. Even in the love poems, in which she repeatedly invokes and extols what appears to be a transcendent male figure — a kind of male muse — it's evident who is doing the invoking; and invoking is after all a kind of conjuring, with success dependent on the expertise and verbal skill of the conjuror. What engaged her was not complaint but exuberance, not descent but ascent: not the fire, but the *rising* fire.

The first volume of Gwendolyn MacEwen's selected poems covers the first fifteen years of her poetic career, from the late 1950s to the early 1970s. It traces the bright trajectory of her early verse, followed by the astonishingly rapid development and exfoliation of her talent. In these poems her range and craft, her poetic strength and intelligence, speak for themselves. Over these years she created, in a remarkably short time, a complete and diverse poetic universe and a powerful and unique voice, by turns playful, extravagant, melancholy, daring, and profound. To read her remains what it has always been: an exacting but delightful pleasure, though not one without its challenges and shadows.

Deal, infidel, the night is indeed difficult.

19

WHY I LOVE
THE NIGHT OF THE HUNTER

I'M INCAPABLE of choosing my single favourite anything, so I picked *The Night of the Hunter* for other reasons. First, it's among those films that made an indelible impression on me when it came out. That was in 1955, when I was a teenager and the theatres were blue with smoke: your boyfriend held his cigarette in one hand and attempted to sneak the other into your Peter Pan bra. What was on the screen was the secondary action, and it's a tribute to *The Night of the Hunter* that I can't remember which boyfriend I saw it with. So gripping was it that it warped my young brain, and several of its images have haunted me ever since. The underwater Shelley Winters, for instance, in her aspect of wrecked mermaid, has made several disguised appearances in my own writing.

My second reason was that The Word festival is an English event, and this film has an English connection. It was directed by Charles Laughton, who had a noteworthy stage career in London and made many English films before joining the European exiles who illuminated Hollywood from the 1930s to the 1950s. A bleak romantic trapped in an odd body, he often played monsters, which doubtless informed his direction of *The Night of the Hunter* — as did his interest in art and his wide literary and Biblical background. Surely it's his sympathy with the material that enabled him to extract such extraordinary performances from the cast — Robert Mitchum, Shelley Winters, and Lillian Gish in particular.

The film came out in the same year as *The Blackboard Jungle* and *Rebel Without a Cause*, so did not have the impact it deserved, although it has gathered a serious following since. European critics in particular have delved into its filmic influences, supplied Freudian analyses (frail mothers, sons and their torn loyalties to fathers, whether dead, fake, or ideal — *vide* the portrait of Abraham Lincoln tucked into the trial scene), and made Bettelheimian references to its fairy-tale depth-psychology, not to mention the depth-psychology of Laughton himself.

This film and its director appear made for each other — paradoxical, because *The Night of the Hunter* is such a profoundly American film. It is also a writers' film, another reason I chose it for a literary festival. For many films, the scenario serves only as a skeleton upon which the director hangs his own ideas and effects, but almost every image in this film — every rabbit, owl, and so forth — was thoroughly described in the scenario. A script like this probably wouldn't get to first base in Hollywood today: it would be considered too wordy.

The film was adapted from a novel by Davis Grubb, and was written by James Agee, the author of *Let Us Now Praise Famous Men* and *A Death in the Family*, and of the film *The African Queen*. Both Grubb and Agee grew up in the Ohio Valley during the Depression, which is where and when the film is set. Both were part of a general movement that turned away from the cosmopolitanism of the 1920s to focus on the dark, poverty-stricken heartland of America. But Agee and Grubb, although they remembered the 1930s, were not writing then. By their time, they would have had the benefit of a generation of literary scholars dedicated to the unravelling of the twisted, Gothic skeins of American Puritanism, through such earlier writers as Hawthorne, Poe, Melville, and Twain. It shows.

The film has a double framework. It opens with Rachel — an older woman whom we later meet as a rescuer of stray children — invoking the world of bedtime stories and dreams. (One might say that if this is her idea of a restful tale for kiddies she's a sadistic bitch, because this dream is a nightmare; but then, folk tales have always been nightmares. Her job as narrator is to render the nightmare at least partially safe.) The next framework is a social one: the Depression, cause of the desperation that drives the film's initial robbery.

Within this double frame is the folkloric tale itself, with its ogre (played by Mitchum). His name is Harry, as in "Old Harry," vernacular for the Devil. Cross Richard the Third with Milton's Satan and enclose him in a Southern psychopath posing as a preacher, and this character is what you'd get. He cannot be explained by the Depression — he is simply radical evil — but, in Laughton's hands, he's a complex figure as well, one of those fast-talking con men who recur throughout American art, embraced by society, then torn apart by it. He's a monster, but finally a sacrificial one.

On one level the plot is simplicity itself: Dad has done a stickup and, before being arrested, has stashed the money in a doll. This Mammonish idol, a Venus of Willendorf with its tummy stuffed with cash, becomes the desired treasure in the struggle between evil and innocence. The robber's two children — a girl and an older boy — have been sworn not to tell the doll's secret to anybody, especially not to their mother, the fleshly and therefore wilful Willa. Wolfish fellow-prisoner Harry knows about the money, but not where it's hidden; so after Dad is hanged he puts on his sheep's clothing and goes off to romance the widow, oozing sexual power from every pore but especially from his lower eyelids. Willa falls for it and marries him, but Harry's not interested in her body. He cuts her throat and sinks her in the river, then claims she's run off, as demonish women do.

Now he can get his hands on the kids. He forces the secret of the doll, but the children make their escape in a boat and go down the Ohio River, with the enraged preacher hunting them. It's a quintessential American image — the two floating innocents recall Huckleberry Finn and Jim, and, behind them, that favourite American Biblical image, the Ark riding the Deluge with its Saving Remnant — in this case, the deluge that has overwhelmed the children's mother. That this particular deluge is all mixed up with adult sexuality, and also with the repression of it, is quintessentially American as well — it being the nature of Puritanism to produce a world which repudiates sexuality but is also thoroughly sexualized.

The children are sheltered by Rachel (who's a good woman, since she's well past sex), and stalked by their pursuer. Finally there's a standoff, a capture and a trial, and the villain is neutralized. But we can't breathe easy: the metaphysics are too unsettling. The film is punctuated by images of hands: toward the beginning, the preacher makes a puppet show with his knuckles, which have LOVE and HATE tattooed on them. Will love win out over hate? If so, what kind of love? Does God himself love you or hate you, and if you place yourself in his hands, what is the nature of those hands?

The hands return at the end, when there's a duet sung by Harry the monster and Rachel the saviour — incidentally, perhaps the only time Jesus has appeared in the guise of a sweet little old lady with a gun. They sing the hymn "Leaning on the Everlasting Arms" — they both sing it, but each is referring to a different arm; and at the end of every arm there's a hand, and for every right hand there's also a left.

But for every Song of Experience there's a Song of Innocence, and it's the child's-eye view that gives this film its translucence and candour. Its crucial perspective is that of the young boy, John Harper, poised between innocence and experience. He alone distrusts the preacher from the beginning, he alone realizes what's become of his mother; but, tellingly, he refuses to testify against her murderer. Son of a hanged killer and a butchered mother, stepson of a maniac, he has strong reason to distrust the adult world, but Rachel's house can shelter him only while he remains a child. Perhaps he will grow up to become a robber. Or perhaps, as his name suggests, a singer of blood-spattered sagas and the author of apocalyptic revelations?

There's a happy ending complete with Christmas presents, but we don't credit it and neither should John. He knows too much. In other words, if it's the night of the hunter, what will it be the day of, once that morning sun comes up?

SPOTTY-HANDED VILLAINESSES

PROBLEMS OF FEMALE BAD BEHAVIOUR
IN THE CREATION OF LITERATURE

MY TITLE IS "Spotty-Handed Villainesses"; my subtitle is "Problems of Female Bad Behaviour in the Creation of Literature." I should probably have said, "in the creation of novels, plays, and epic poems." Female bad behaviour occurs in lyric poems, of course, but not at sufficient length.

I began to think about this subject at a very early age. There was a children's rhyme that went:

There was a little girl
Who had a little curl
Right in the middle of her forehead;
When she was good, she was very, very good,
And when she was bad, she was horrid!

No doubt this is a remnant of the Angel/Whore Split so popular among the Victorians, but at the age of five I did not know that. I took this to be a poem of personal significance — I did after all have curls — and it brought home to me the deeply Jungian possibilities of a Dr. Jekyll–Mr. Hyde double life for women. My older brother used this verse to tease me, or so he thought. He did manage to make "very, very good" sound almost worse than "horrid," which remains an accurate analysis for the novelist. Create a flawless character and you create an insufferable one, which may be why I am interested in spots.

Some of you may wonder whether the spotty-handedness in my title refers to age spots. Was my lecture perhaps going to centre on that once-forbidden but now red-hot topic, The Menopause, without which any collection of female-obilia would be incomplete? I hasten to point out that my title is not age related; it refers neither to age spots nor to youth spots. Instead it recalls that most famous of spots, the invisible but indelible one on the hand of wicked Lady Macbeth. Spot as in guilt, spot as in blood, spot as in "out, damned." Lady Macbeth was spotted, Ophelia unspotted; both came to sticky ends, but there's a world of difference.

But is it not, today — well, somehow *unfeminist* — to depict a woman behaving badly? Isn't bad behaviour supposed to be the monopoly of men? Isn't that what we are expected — in defiance of real life — to somehow believe, now? When bad women get into literature, what are they doing there, and are they permissible, and what, if anything, do we need them for?

We do need something like them; by which I mean something disruptive to static order. When my daughter was five, she and her friend Heather announced that they were putting on a play. We were conscripted as the audience. We took our seats, expecting to see something of note. The play opened with two characters having breakfast. This was promising — an Ibsenian play perhaps, or something by G. B. Shaw? Shakespeare is not big on breakfast openings, but other playwrights of talent have not disdained them.

The play progressed. The two characters had more breakfast. Then they had more. They passed each other the jam, the cornflakes, the toast. Each asked if the other would like a cup of tea. What was going on? Was this Pinter, perhaps, or Ionesco, or maybe Andy Warhol? The audience grew restless. "Are you going to do anything except have breakfast?" we said. "No," they said. "Then it isn't a play," we said. "Something else has to happen."

And there you have it, the difference between literature — at least literature as embodied in plays and novels — and life. *Something else has to happen.* In life we may ask for nothing more than a kind of eternal breakfast — it happens to be my favourite meal, and certainly it is the most hopeful one, since we don't yet know what atrocities the day may choose to visit upon us — but if we are going to sit still for two or three hours in a theatre, or wade through two or three hundred pages of a book, we certainly expect something more than breakfast.

What kind of something? It can be an earthquake, a tempest, an attack by Martians, the discovery that your spouse is having an affair; or, if the author is hyperactive, all of these at once. Or it can be the revelation of the spottiness of a spotty woman. I'll get around to these disreputable folks shortly, but first let me go over some essentials that may be insulting to your intelligence, but that are comforting to mine, because they help me to focus on what I'm doing as a creator of fictions. If you think I'm flogging a few dead horses — horses which have been put out of their pain long ago — let me assure you that this is because the horses are not in fact dead but are out there in the world, galloping around as vigorously as ever.

How do I know this? I read my mail. Also, I listen to the questions people ask me, both in interviews and after public readings. The kinds of questions I'm talking about have to do with how the characters in novels ought to behave. Unfortunately, there is a widespread tendency to judge such characters as if they were job applicants, or public servants, or prospective roommates, or somebody you're considering marrying. For instance, I sometimes get a question — almost always, these days, from women — that goes something like, "Why don't you make the men stronger?" I feel that this is a matter which should more properly be taken up with God. It was not, after all, I who created Adam so subject to temptation that he sacrificed eternal life for an apple; which leads me to believe that God — who is, among other things, an author — is just as enamoured of character flaws and dire plots as we human writers are. The characters in the average novel are not usually people you would want to get involved with at a personal or business level. How then should we go about responding to such creations? Or, from my side of the page, which is blank when I begin — how should I go about creating them?

What is a novel, anyway? Only a very foolish person would attempt to give a definitive answer to that, beyond stating the more or less obvious facts that it is a literary narrative of some length which purports, on the reverse of the title page, not to be true, but seeks nevertheless to convince its readers that it is. It's typical of the cynicism of our age that, if you write a novel, everyone assumes it's about real people, thinly disguised; but if you write an autobiography everyone assumes you're lying your head off. Part of this is right, because every artist is, among other things, a con artist.

We con artists do tell the truth, in a way; but, as Emily Dickinson said, we tell it slant. By indirection we find direction out — so here, for easy reference, is an elimination-dance list of what novels are not.

- Novels are not sociological textbooks, although they may contain social comment and criticism.
- Novels are not political tracts, although "politics" — in the sense of human power structures — is inevitably one of their subjects. But if the author's main design on us is to convert us to something — whether that something be Christianity, capitalism, a belief in marriage as the only answer to a maiden's prayer, or feminism, we are likely to sniff it out, and to rebel. As André Gide once remarked, "It is with noble sentiments that bad literature gets written."
- Novels are not how-to books; they will not show you *how to* conduct a successful life, although some of them may be read this way. Is *Pride and Prejudice* about how a sensible middle-class

nineteenth-century woman can snare an appropriate man with a good income, which is the best she can hope for out of life, given the limitations of her situation? Partly. But not completely.

- Novels are not, primarily, moral tracts. Their characters are not all models of good behaviour — or, if they are, we probably won't read them. But they *are* linked with notions of morality, because they are about human beings and human beings divide behaviour into good and bad. The characters judge each other, and the reader judges the characters. However, the success of a novel does not depend on a Not Guilty verdict from the reader. As Keats said, Shakespeare took as much delight in creating Iago — that archvillain — as he did in creating the virtuous Imogen. I would say probably more, and the proof of it is that I'd bet you're more likely to know which play Iago is in.

- But although a novel is not a political tract, a how-to book, a sociology textbook, or a pattern of correct morality, it is also not merely a piece of Art for Art's Sake, divorced from real life. It cannot do without a conception of form and a structure, true, but its roots are in the mud; its flowers, if any, come out of the rawness of its raw materials.

- In short, novels are ambiguous and multifaceted not because they're perverse but because they attempt to grapple with what was once referred to as the human condition, and they do so using a medium that is notoriously slippery — namely, language itself.

Now, let's get back to the notion that in a novel, something else has to happen — other than breakfast, that is. What will that "something else" be, and how does the novelist go about choosing it? Usually it's backwards to what you were taught in school, where you probably got the idea that the novelist had an overall scheme or idea and then went about colouring it in with characters and words, sort of like paint-by-numbers. But in reality the process is much more like wrestling a greased pig in the dark.

Literary critics start with a nice, clean, already-written text. They then address questions to this text, which they attempt to answer; "what does it mean" being both the most basic and the most difficult. Novelists, on the other hand, start with the blank page, to which they similarly address questions. But the questions are different. Instead of asking, first of all, "What does it mean," they work at the widget level; they ask, "Is this the right word?" "What does it mean" can only come when there is an "it" to mean something. Novelists have to get some actual words down before they can fiddle with the theology. Or, to put it another way: God started with chaos — dark, without form and void — and so does the novelist. Then God made one detail at a time. So does the novelist. On the seventh day, God took a break to consider what he'd done. So does the novelist. But the critic starts on Day 7.

The critic, looking at plot, asks, "What's happening here?" The novelist, creating plot, asks, "What happens next?" The critic asks, "Is this believable?" The novelist, "How can I get them to believe this?" The novelist, echoing Marshall McLuhan's famous dictum that art is what you can get away with, says, "How can I pull this off?" — as if the novel itself were a kind of bank robbery. Whereas the critic is liable to exclaim, in the mode of the policeman making the arrest, "Aha! You can't get away with that!"

In short, the novelist's concerns are more practical than those of the critic; more concerned with "how to," less concerned with metaphysics. Any novelist — whatever his or her theoretical interests — has to contend with the following how-to questions:

— What kind of story shall I choose to tell? Is it, for instance, comic or tragic or melodramatic, or all? How shall I tell it? Who will be at the centre of it, and will this person be a) admirable or b) not? And — more important than it may sound — will it have a happy ending, or not? No matter what you are writing — what genre and in what style, whether cheap formula or high-minded experiment — you will still have to answer — in the course of your writing — these essential questions. Any story you tell must have a conflict of some sort, and it must have suspense. In other words: something other than breakfast.

Let's put a woman at the centre of the something-other-than-breakfast, and see what happens. Now there is a whole new set of questions. Will the conflict be supplied by the natural world? Is our female protagonist lost in the jungle, caught in a hurricane, pursued by sharks? If so, the story will be an adventure story and her job is to run away, or else to combat the sharks, displaying courage and fortitude, or else cowardice and stupidity. If there is a man in the story as well, the plot will alter in other directions: he will be a rescuer, an enemy, a companion in struggle, a sex bomb, or someone rescued by the woman. Once upon a time, the first would have been more probable, that is, more believable to the reader; but times have changed and art is what you can get away with, and the other possibilities have now entered the picture.

Stories about space invasions are similar, in that the threat comes from outside and the goal for the character, whether achieved or not, is survival. War stories per se — ditto, in that the main threat is external. Vampire and werewolf stories are more complicated, as are ghost stories; in these, the threat is from outside, true, but the threatening thing may also conceal a split-off part of the character's own psyche. Henry James's *The Turn of the Screw* and Bram Stoker's *Dracula* are in large part animated by such hidden agendas; and both revolve around notions of female sexuality. Once all werewolves were male, and female vampires were usually mere sidekicks; but there are now female werewolves, and women are moving in on the star bloodsucking roles as well. Whether this is good or bad news I hesitate to say.

Detective and espionage stories may combine many elements, but would not be what they are without a crime, a criminal, a tracking-down, and a revelation at the end; again, all sleuths were once male, but sleuthesses are now prominent, for which I hope they lay a votive ball of wool from time to time upon the tomb of the sainted Miss Marple. We live in an age not only of gender crossover but of *genre* crossover, so you can throw all of the above into the cauldron and stir.

Then there are stories classed as "serious" literature, which centre not on external threats — although some of these may exist — but on relationships among the characters. To avoid the eternal breakfast, some of the characters must cause problems for some of the others. This is where the questions really get difficult. As I've said, the novel has its roots in the mud, and part of the mud is history; and part of the history we've had recently is the history of the women's movement, and the women's movement has influenced how people read, and therefore what you can get away with, in art.

Some of this influence has been beneficial. Whole areas of human life that were once considered nonliterary or subliterary — such as the problematical nature of homemaking, the hidden depths of motherhood, and of daughterhood as well, the once-forbidden realms of incest and child abuse — have been brought inside the circle that demarcates the writable from the nonwritable. Other things, such as the Cinderella happy ending — the Prince Charming one — have been called into question. (As one lesbian writer remarked to me, the only happy ending she found believable any more was the one in which girl meets girl and ends up with girl; but that was fifteen years ago, and the bloom is off even that romantic rose.)

To keep you from being too depressed, let me emphasize that none of this means that you, personally, cannot find happiness with a good man, a good woman, or a good pet canary; just as the creation of a bad female character doesn't mean that women should lose the vote. If bad male characters meant that, for men, all men would be disenfranchised immediately. We are talking about what you can get away with in art; that is, what you can make believable. When Shakespeare wrote his sonnets to his dark-haired mistress, he wasn't saying that blondes were ugly, he was merely pushing against the notion that only blondes were beautiful. The tendency of innovative literature is to include the hitherto excluded, which often has the effect of rendering ludicrous the conventions that have just preceded the innovation. So the form of the ending, whether happy or not, does not have to do with how people live their lives — there is a great deal of variety in that department (and, after all, in life every story ends with death, which is not true of novels). Instead it's connected with what literary conventions the writer is following or pulling apart at the moment. Happy endings of the Cinderella kind do exist in stories, of course, but they have been relegated largely to genre fiction, such as Harlequin romances.

To summarize some of the benefits to literature of the women's movement — the expansion of the territory available to writers, both in character and in language; a sharp-eyed examination of the way power works in gender relations, and the exposure of much of this as socially constructed; a vigorous exploration of many hitherto-concealed areas of experience. But as with any political movement that comes out of real oppression — and I do emphasize the *real* — there was also, in the first decade at least of the present movement, a tendency to cookie-cut: that is, to write to a pattern and to over-sugar on one side. Some writers tended to polarize morality by gender — that is, women were intrinsically good and men bad; to divide along allegiance lines — that is, women who slept with men were sleeping with the enemy; to judge by tribal markings — that is, women who wore high heels and makeup were instantly suspect, those in overalls were acceptable; and to make hopeful excuses: that is, defects in women were ascribable to the patriarchal system and would cure themselves once that system was abolished. Such over-simplifications may be necessary to some phases of political movements. But they are usually problematical for novelists, unless the novelist has a secret desire to be in billboard advertising.

If a novelist writing at that time was also a feminist, she felt her choices restricted. Were all heroines to be essentially spotless of soul — struggling against, fleeing from, or done in by male oppression? Was the only plot to be The Perils of Pauline, with a lot of moustache-twirling villains but minus the rescuing hero? Did suffering prove you were good? (If so — think hard about this — wasn't it all for the best that women did so much of it?) Did we face a situation in which women could do no wrong, but could only have wrong done to them? Were women being confined yet again to that alabaster pedestal so beloved of the Victorian age, when Woman as better-than-man gave men a licence to be gleefully and enjoyably worse than women, while all the while proclaiming that they couldn't help it because it was their nature? Were women to be condemned to virtue for life, slaves in the salt mines of goodness? How intolerable.

Of course, the feminist analysis made some kinds of behaviour available to female characters that, under the old dispensation — the prefeminist one — would have been considered bad, but under the new one were praiseworthy. A female character could rebel against social strictures without then having to throw herself in front of a train like Anna Karenina; she could think the unthinkable and say the unsayable; she could flout authority. She could do new bad-good things, such as leaving her husband and even deserting her children. Such activities and emotions, however, were — according to the new moral thermometer of the times — not really bad at all; they were good, and the women who did them were praiseworthy. I'm not against such plots. I just don't think they are the only ones.

And there were certain new no-no's. For instance: was it at all permissible, any more, to talk about women's will to power, because weren't women supposed by nature to be communal egalitarians? Could one depict the scurvy behaviour often practised by women against one another, or by little girls against other little girls? Could one examine the Seven Deadly Sins in their female versions — to remind you, Pride, Anger, Lust, Envy, Avarice, Gluttony, and Sloth — without being considered antifeminist? Or was a mere mention of such things tantamount to aiding and abetting the enemy, namely the male power structure? Were we to have a warning hand clapped over our mouths, yet once again, to prevent us from saying the unsayable

— though the unsayable had changed? Were we to listen to our mothers, yet once again, as they intoned, If You Can't Say Anything Nice, Don't Say Anything At All? Hadn't men been giving women a bad reputation for centuries? Shouldn't we form a wall of silence around the badness of women, or at best explain it away by saying it was the fault of Big Daddy, or — permissible too, it seems — of Big Mom? Big Mom, that agent of the patriarchy, that pronatalist, got it in the neck from certain 1970s feminists; though mothers were admitted into the fold again once some of these women turned into them. In a word: were women to be homogenized — one woman is the same as another — and deprived of free will — as in, *The patriarchy made her do it?*

Or, in another word — were men to get all the juicy parts? Literature cannot do without bad behaviour, but was all the bad behaviour to be reserved for men? Was it to be all Iago and Mephistopheles, and were Jezebel and Medea and Medusa and Delilah and Regan and Goneril and spotty-handed Lady Macbeth and H. Rider Haggard's powerful super–femme fatale in *She*, and Toni Morrison's mean Sula, to be banished from view? I hope not. Women characters, arise! Take back the night! In particular, take back The Queen of the Night, from Mozart's *The Magic Flute*. It's a great part, and due for revision.

I have always known that there were spellbinding evil parts for women. For one thing, I was taken at an early age to see *Snow White and the Seven Dwarfs*. Never mind the Protestant work ethic of the dwarfs. Never mind the tedious housework-is-virtuous motif. Never mind the fact that Snow White is a vampire — anyone who lies in a glass coffin without decaying and then comes to life again must be. The truth is that I was paralyzed by the scene in which the evil queen drinks the magic potion and changes her shape. What power, what untold possibilities!

Also, I was exposed to the complete, unexpurgated *Grimm's Fairy Tales* at an impressionable age. Fairy tales had a bad reputation among feminists for a while — partly because they'd been cleaned up, on the erroneous supposition that little children don't like gruesome gore, and partly because they'd been selected to fit the 1950s Prince Charming Is Your Goal ethos. So Cinderella and the Sleeping Beauty were okay, though The Youth Who Set Out to Learn What Fear Was, which featured a good many rotting corpses, plus a woman who was smarter than her husband, were not. But many of these tales were originally told and retold by women, and these unknown women left their mark. There is a wide range of heroines in these tales; passive good girls, yes, but adventurous, resourceful women as well, and proud ones, and slothful ones, and foolish ones, and envious and greedy ones, and also many wise women and a variety of evil witches, both in disguise and not, and bad stepmothers and wicked ugly sisters and false brides as well. The stories, and the figures themselves, have immense vitality, partly because no punches are pulled — in the versions I read, the barrels of nails and the red-hot shoes were left intact — and also because no emotion is unrepresented. Singly, the female characters are limited and two-dimensional. But put all together, they form a rich, five-dimensional picture.

Female characters who behave badly can of course be used as sticks to beat other women — though so can female characters who behave well, witness the cult of the Virgin Mary, better than you'll ever be, and the legends of the female saints and martyrs — just cut on the dotted line, and, minus one body part, there's your saint, and the only really good woman is a dead woman, so if you're so good why aren't you dead?

But female bad characters can also act as keys to doors we need to open, and as mirrors in which we can see more than just a pretty face. They can be explorations of moral freedom — because everyone's choices are limited, and women's choices have been more limited than men's, but that doesn't mean women can't make choices. Such characters can pose the question of responsibility, because if you want power you have to accept responsibility, and actions produce consequences. I'm not suggesting an agenda here, just some possi-bilities; nor am I prescribing, just wondering. If there's a closed-off road, the curious speculate about why it's closed off, and where it might lead if followed; and evil women have been, for a while recently, a somewhat closed-off road, at least for fiction writers.

While pondering these matters, I thought back over the numer-ous bad female literary characters I have known and tried to sort them into categories. If you were doing this on a blackboard, you might set up a kind of grid: bad women who do bad things for bad reasons, good women who do good things for good reasons, good women who do bad things for good reasons, bad women who do bad things for good reasons, and so forth. But a grid would just be a beginning, because there are so many factors involved: for instance, what the character thinks is bad, what the reader thinks is bad, and what the author thinks is bad, may all be different. But let me define a thoroughly evil person as one who intends to do evil, and for purely selfish reasons. The Queen in Snow White would fit that.

So would Regan and Goneril, Lear's evil daughters; very little can be said in their defence, except that they seem to have been against the patriarchy. Lady Macbeth, however, did her wicked murder for a conventionally acceptable reason, one that would win approval for her in corporate business circles — she was furthering her husband's career. She pays the corporate-wife price too — she subdues her own nature, and has a nervous breakdown as a result. Similarly, Jezebel was merely trying to please a sulky husband; he refused to eat his dinner until he got hold of Naboth's vineyard, so Jezebel had its owner bumped off. Wifely devotion, as I say. The amount of sexual baggage that has accumulated around this figure is astounding, since she doesn't do anything remotely sexual in the orig-inal story, except put on makeup.

The story of Medea, whose husband Jason married a new princess, and who then poisoned the bride and murdered her own two children, has been interpreted in various ways. In some versions

Medea is a witch and commits infanticide out of revenge; but the play by Euripides is surprisingly neofeminist. There's quite a lot about how tough it is to be a woman, and Medea's motivation is commendable — she doesn't want her children to fall into hostile hands and be cruelly abused — which is also the situation of the child-killing mother in Toni Morrison's *Beloved*. A good woman, then, who does a bad thing for a good reason. Hardy's *Tess of the D'Urbervilles* kills her nasty lover due to sexual complications; here too we are in the realm of female-as-victim, doing a bad thing for a good reason. (Which, I suppose, places such stories right beside the front page, along with women who kill their abusive husbands. According to a recent *Time* story, the average jail sentence in the U.S. for men who kill their wives is four years, but for women who kill their husbands — no matter what the provocation — it's twenty. For those who think equality is already with us, I leave the statistics to speak for themselves.)

These women characters are all murderers. Then there are the seducers; here again, the motive varies. I have to say too that with the change in sexual mores, the mere seduction of a man no longer rates very high on the sin scale. But try asking a number of women what the worst thing is that a woman friend could possibly do to them. Chances are the answer will involve the theft of a sexual partner.

Some famous seductresses have really been patriotic espionage agents. Delilah, for instance, was an early Mata Hari, working for the Philistines, trading sex for military information. Judith, who all but seduced the enemy general Holofernes and then cut off his head and brought it home in a sack, was treated as a heroine, although she has troubled men's imaginations through the centuries — witness the number of male painters who have depicted her — because she combines sex with violence in a way they aren't accustomed to and don't much like. Then there are figures like Hawthorne's adulterous Hester Prynne, she of *The Scarlet Letter*, who becomes a kind of sex-saint through suffering — we assume she did what she did through Love, and thus she becomes a good woman who did a bad thing for a good reason — and Madame Bovary, who not only indulged her romantic temperament and voluptuous sensual appetites but spent too much of her husband's money doing it, which was her downfall. A good course in double-entry bookkeeping would have saved the day. I suppose she is a foolish woman who did a stupid thing for an insufficient reason, since the men in question were dolts. Neither the modern reader nor the author consider her very evil, though many contemporaries did, as you can see if you read the transcript of the court case in which the forces of moral rectitude tried to get the book censored.

One of my favourite bad women is Becky Sharpe, of Thackeray's *Vanity Fair*. She makes no pretensions to goodness. She is wicked, she enjoys being wicked, and she does it out of vanity and for her own profit, tricking and deluding English society in the process — which, the author implies, deserves to be tricked and deluded, since it is hypocritical and selfish to the core. Becky, like Undine Spragg in Edith Wharton's *The Custom of the Country*, is an adventuress; she lives by her wits and uses men as ambulatory bank accounts. Many literary adventurers are male — consider Thomas Mann's *Felix Krull, Confidence Man* — but it does make a difference if you change the gender. For one thing, the nature of the loot changes. For a male adventurer, the loot is money and women; but for a female one, the loot is money and men.

Becky Sharpe is a bad mother too, and that's a whole other subject — bad mothers and wicked stepmothers and oppressive aunts, like the one in *Jane Eyre*, and nasty female teachers, and depraved governesses, and evil grannies. The possibilities are many.

But I think that's enough reprehensible female behaviour for you today. Life is short, art is long, motives are complex, and human nature is endlessly fascinating. Many doors stand ajar; others beg to be unlocked. What is in the forbidden room? Something different for everyone, but something you need to know and will never find out unless you step across the threshold. If you are a man, the bad female character in a novel may be — in Jungian terms — your anima; but if you're a woman, the bad female character is your shadow; and as we know from the Offenbach opera *Tales of Hoffman*, she who loses her shadow also loses her soul.

Evil women are necessary in story traditions for two much more obvious reasons, of course. First, they exist in life, so why shouldn't they exist in literature? Second — which may be another way of saying the same thing — women have more to them than virtue. They are fully dimensional human beings; they too have subterranean depths; why shouldn't their many-dimensionality be given literary expression? And when it is, female readers do not automatically recoil in horror. In Aldous Huxley's novel *Point Counter Point*, Lucy Tantamount, the man-destroying vamp, is preferred by the other female characters to the earnest, snivelling woman whose man she has reduced to a wet bath sponge. As one of them says, "Lucy's obviously a force. You may not like that kind of force. But you can't help admiring the force in itself. It's like Niagara." In other words, awesome. Or, as one Englishwoman said to me recently, "Women are tired of being *good* all the time."

I will leave you with a final quotation. It's from Dame Rebecca West, speaking in 1912: "Ladies of Great Britain . . . we have not enough evil in us."

Note where she locates the desired evil. In *us*.

THE GRUNGE LOOK

I FIRST WENT to Europe on May 13, 1964. I had been told I was going to do this five months earlier by a male psychic working out of a Toronto tea shop. "You will be going to Europe in May," he said.

"No I won't," I said.

"Yes you will," he said, smugly reshuffling his cards.

I did.

Fleeing a personal life of Gordian complexity, and leaving behind a poetry manuscript rejected by all, and a first novel ditto, I scraped together what was left after a winter of living in a Charles Street rooming house and writing tours-de-force of undiscovered genius while working by day at a market research company, borrowed six hundred dollars from my parents, who were understandably somewhat nervous about my choice of the literary life by then, and climbed onto a plane. In the fall I would be teaching grammar to engineering students at eight-thirty in the morning in a Quonset hut at the University of British Columbia, so I had about three months. In this period of time I intended to become — what? I wasn't sure exactly, but I had some notion that the viewing of various significant pieces of architecture would improve my soul — would fill in a few potholes in it, get rid of a few cultural hangnails, as it were. Here,

I had been studying English literature for six years — I even had an MA, which had got me rejected for employment by the Bell Telephone Company on the grounds of overqualification — and I had never even seen, well, things. Stonehenge, for instance. A visit to Stonehenge would surely improve my understanding of Thomas Hardy. Or someone. Anyway, a lot of my friends from college had already run to England, intending to be actors and the like. So England was my first stop.

The truth is that I didn't have much idea of what I was really doing. Certainly, I had almost no idea at all of where I was really going, and how much it had changed since I'd last checked in via the pages of Charles Dickens. Everything was so much smaller and shabbier than I had imagined. I was like the sort of Englishman who arrives in Canada expecting to find a grizzly bear on every street corner. "Why are there so many *trucks*?" I thought. There were no trucks in Dickens. There weren't even any in T. S. Eliot. "I did not know Death had undone so many," I murmured hopefully, as I made my way across Trafalgar Square. But the people there somehow refused to be as hollow-cheeked and plangent as I'd expected. They appeared to be mostly tourists, like myself, and were busy taking pictures of one another with pigeons on their heads.

My goal, of course, was Canada House, the first stop of every jet-stunned, impecunious young Canadian traveller in those days. But before I go on, let me say a few words about those days. What sort of year was 1964?

It was the year after 1963, in which John Kennedy had been so notably shot. It was the year before the first (to my knowledge) anti-Vietnam peace march; it was roughly four years before the great hippie explosion, and five years before the onset of the early-1970s wave of feminism. Miniskirts had not yet arrived; pantyhose were approaching, but I don't believe they had as yet squeezed out the indigenous population of garter belts and stockings. In hair, something called the bubble cut was favoured: women rolled their hair in big bristle-filled rollers to achieve a smoothly swollen look, as if someone had inserted a tube into one of their ears and blown up their heads like balloons. I indulged in this practice too, though with mixed results, since my hair was ferociously curly. At best it resembled a field of weeds gone over with a lawn roller — still squiggly, though somewhat mashed. At worst it looked as if I'd stuck my finger in a light socket. This silhouette was later to become stylish, but was not so yet. As a result I went in for head scarves, of the Queen-Elizabeth-at-Balmoral type. Paired with the slanty-eyed, horn-rimmed glasses I wore in an attempt to take myself seriously, they were not at all flattering.

Come to think of it, neither was anything in my suitcase. (Hitchhiking backpackers had not yet overrun Europe, so it was, still, a suitcase.) Fashion-wise, 1964 was not really my year. Beatniks had faded, and I hadn't discovered the romantic raggle-taggle gypsy mode; but then, neither had anyone else. Jeans had not yet swept all before them, and for ventures to such places as churches and museums, skirts were still required; grey-flannel jumpers with Peter Pan–collared blouses were my uniform of choice. High heels were the norm for most occasions, and about the only thing you could actually walk in were some rubber-soled suede items known as Hush Puppies.

Lugging my suitcase, then, I Hush-Puppied my way up the imposing steps of Canada House. At that time it offered — among other things, such as a full shelf of geological surveys — a reading room with newspapers in it. I riffled anxiously through the Rooms To Let, since I had no place to stay that night. By pay telephone, I rented the cheapest thing available, which was located in a suburb called Willesden Green. This turned out to be about as far away from everything as you could get, via the London Underground, which I promptly took (here at last, I thought, looking at my intermittently bathed, cadaverous and/or dentally challenged fellow passengers, were a few people Death had in fact undone, or was about to). The rooming-house furnishings smelled of old, sad cigarette smoke, and were of such hideous dinginess that I felt I'd landed in a Graham

Greene novel; and the sheets, when I finally slid between them, were not just cold and damp, they were wet. ("North Americans like that kind of thing," an Englishwoman said to me, much later. "Unless they freeze in the bathroom they think they've been cheated of the English experience.")

The next day I set out on what appears to me in retrospect a dauntingly ambitious quest for cultural trophies. My progress through the accumulated bric-a-brac of centuries was marked by the purchase of dozens of brochures and postcards, which I collected to remind myself that I'd actually been wherever it was I'd been. At breakneck speed I gawped my way through Westminster Abbey, the Houses of Parliament, St. Paul's Cathedral, the Tower of London, the Victoria and Albert Museum, the National Portrait Gallery, the Tate, the house of Samuel Johnson, Buckingham Palace, and the Albert Memorial. At some point I fell off a double-decker bus and sprained my foot, but even this, although it slowed me down, did not stop me in my headlong and reckless pursuit. After a week of this, my eyes were rolling around like loose change, and my head, although several sizes larger, was actually a good deal emptier than it had been before. This was a mystery to me.

Another mystery was why so many men tried to pick me up. It was hardly as if I was, in my little grey-flannel jumpers, dressed to kill. Museums were the usual locale, and I suppose there was something about a woman standing still with her head tilted at a ninety-degree angle that made solicitation more possible. None of these men was particularly rude. "American?" they would ask, and when I said Canadian, they would look either puzzled or disappointed, and would proceed only tentatively to the next question. When they got no for an answer, they simply moved along to the next upstretched neck. Possibly, they hung around tourist lodestones on the theory that female travellers travelled for the same kinds of sexual-adventure reasons they would have travelled, had they been travelling themselves. But in this there was — and possibly still is —

a gender difference. Ulysses was a sailor, Circe was a stay-at-home with commodious outbuildings.

When not injecting myself with culture, I was looking for something to eat. In England in 1964, this was quite difficult, especially if you didn't have much money. I made the mistake of trying a hamburger and a milkshake, but the English didn't yet have the concept: the former was fried in rancid lamb fat, the latter fortified with what tasted like ground-up chalk. The best places were the fish-and-chip shops, or, barring that, the cafés, where you could get eggs, sausages, chips, and peas, in any combination. Finally, I ran into some fellow Canadians, who'd been in England longer than I had, and who put me onto a Greek place in Soho, which actually had salads, a few reliable pubs, and the Lyons' Corner House on Trafalgar Square, which had a roast-beef all-you-can-eat for a set price. A mistake, as the Canadian journalists would starve themselves for a week, then hit the Lyons' Corner House like a swarm of locusts. (The Lyons' Corner House did not survive.)

It must have been through these expatriates that I hooked up with Alison Cunningham, whom I'd known at university and who was now in London, studying modern dance and sharing a second-floor flat in South Kensington with two other young women. Into this flat, Alison — when she heard of my wet-sheeted Willesden Green circumstances — generously offered to smuggle me. "Smuggle" is appropriate; the flat was owned by aristocratic twins called Lord Cork and Lady Hoare, but as they were ninety and in nursing homes, it was actually run by a suspicious dragon of a housekeeper; so for purposes of being in the flat I had to pretend I didn't exist.

In Alison's flat I learned some culturally useful things that have stuck with me through the years: how to tell a good kipper from a bad one, for instance; how to use an English plate-drying rack; and how to make coffee in a pot when you don't have any other device. I continued with my tourist program — stuffing in Cheyne Walk, several lesser-known churches, and the Inns of Court — and Alison practised a dance, which was a reinterpretation of *The Seagull*, set to several of the Goldberg Variations as played by Glenn Gould. I can never hear that piece of music without seeing Alison, in a black leotard and wearing the severe smile of a Greek caryatid of the Archaic period, bending herself into a semipretzel on that South Kensington sitting-room floor. Meanwhile, I was not shirking in the salt mines of Art. Already, my notebook contained several new proto-gems, none of which, oddly, busied itself with the age-old masterworks of Europe. Instead, they were about rocks.

When things got too close for comfort with the dragon house-keeper, I would have to skip town for a few days. This I did by cashing in some miles on the rail pass I had purchased in Canada — one of the few sensible preparations for my trip I had managed to make. (Why no Pepto-Bismol, I ask myself; why no acetaminophen with codeine; why no Gravol? I would never think of leaving the house without them now.) On this rail pass you could go anywhere the railways went, using up miles as you did so. My first journeys were quite ambitious. I went to the Lake District, overshooting it and getting as far north as Carlisle before I had to double back; whereupon I took a bus tour of the Lakes, viewing them through fumes of cigar smoke and nausea, and, although surprised by their smallness, was reassured to hear that people still drowned in them every year. Then I went to Glastonbury, where after seeing the cathedral, I was waylaid by an elderly lady who got five pounds out of me to help save King Arthur's Well, which — she said — was in her backyard and would be ruined by a brewery unless I contributed to the cause. I made it to Cardiff with its genuine-ersatz castle, and to Nottingham and the ancestral home of the Byrons, and to York, and to the Brontë manse, where I was astonished to learn, from the size of their tiny boots and gloves, that the Brontës had been scarcely bigger than children. As a writer of less than Olympian stature, I found this encouraging.

But as my rail pass dwindled, my trips became shorter. Why did I go to Colchester? To the Cheddar Gorge? To Ripon? My motives escape me, but I went to these places; I have the postcards to prove it. Julius Caesar visited Colchester too, so there must have been something to it; but I was driven by frugality rather than by the historicist imperative: I didn't want any of my rail pass miles to go to waste.

Around about July, Alison decided that France would be even more improving for me than England had been, so in the company of a male friend of mine from Harvard, in full retreat from a Southern girlfriend who had brought several ball gowns to a student archaeological graveyard excavation, we took the night boat-train. It was an average Channel crossing, during which we all turned gently green. Alison bravely continued to discourse on intellectual matters, but finally turned her head and, with a dancer's casual grace, threw up over her left shoulder. These are the moments one remembers.

By the time we'd been two days in Paris, where we subsisted on a diet of baguettes, café au lait, oranges, pieces of cheese, and the occasional bean-heavy bistro meal, I was in an advanced state of dysentery. We were shunting around from cheap *pension* to cheap *pension*; the rooms were always up gloomy flights of stairs, with lights that went off when you were halfway up and cockroaches that rustled and crackled underfoot. None of these establishments allowed you to stay in them during the day; so I lay moaning softly on hard French park benches, in gravelly French parks, while Alison, with a sense of duty Florence Nightingale would have envied, read me long improving passages from Doris Lessing's *The Golden Notebook*. Every fifteen minutes a policeman would come by and tell me I had to sit up, since lying on the park benches was forbidden; and every half hour I would make a dash for the nearest establishment with a toilet, which featured not the modern plumbing that has taken over today but a hole in the ground and two footrests, and many previous visitors with imperfect aims.

A diet of bread and water, and some potent French emulsion, administered by Alison, improved my condition, and I dutifully hiked around to Notre Dame, the Eiffel Tower, and the Louvre. In Paris,

BENEFITS OF EUROPEAN TRAVEL

BEFORE
photo credit:
unknown

DURING
A Pre-Raphaelite pose
photo credit: photo machine,
Gare du Nord, Paris

AFTER
Montreal, 1968
photo credit: Jim Polk

the men bent on pickups didn't bother to wait until you had stopped and were craning your neck; they approached at all times, even when you were crossing the street. "Americaine?" they would ask hopefully. They were polite — some of them even used the subjunctive, as in "Voudriez-vous coucher avec moi" — and, when refused, would turn away with a beaglelike melancholy that I chose to find both existential and Gallic.

When we had only a week and a half left, the three of us pooled our resources and rented a car, with which we toured the Châteaux of the Loire, viewing a great many eighteenth-century gilded chairs and staying in youth hostels, and living on more cheese. By this time I was supersaturated with culture; waterlogged, so to speak. If someone had stepped on my head, a stream of dissolved brochures would have poured forth.

Then, for some reason now lost in the mists of history, I decided to go to Luxembourg. On the way there, a middle-aged conductor chased me around the train compartment; when I explained that I was not in fact American, as he had supposed, he shrugged and said "Ah," as if that explained my reluctance. By this time I was getting somewhat fed up with the excess of dog-and-fire-hydrant male attention, and I let my irritation spill over onto the cultural agenda; when I finally got to Luxembourg, I did not go to visit a single church. Instead, I saw *Some Like It Hot*, with subtitles in Flemish, French, and German, where I was the only person in the theatre who laughed in the right places.

This seemed an appropriate point of re-entry to North America. Culture is as culture does, I thought to myself, as I returned to England, steered myself and my Hush Puppies toward the plane, and prepared for decompression.

At that moment my trip in retrospect felt a lot like stumbling around in the dark, bumping into heavy, expensive pieces of furniture, while being mistaken for someone else. But distance adds perspective, and in the months that followed, I tried hard for it. Had my soul been improved? Possibly, but not in the ways I'd anticipated. What I took back with me was not so much the churches and museums and the postcards of them I'd collected but various conversations, in buses, on trains, and with the pickup men at the museums. I remembered especially the general bafflement when it turned out that I was not what I appeared to be; namely, an American. For the Europeans, there was a flag-shaped blank where my nationality should have been. What was visible to me was invisible to them; nor could I help them out by falling back on any internationally famous architectural constructs. About all I had to offer as a referent was a troop of horsey policemen, which hardly seemed enough.

But one person's void is another person's scope, and that was where the new poems I'd brought back squashed at the bottom of my suitcase would come in, or so I thought. Speaking of which, my grey-flannel wardrobe — I could see it now — definitely had to go. As a deterrent to stray men it was inadequate, as a disguise irrelevant, as a poetic manifesto incoherent. I did not look serious in it, merely earnest, and also — by now — somewhat grubby. I had picked up a brown suede vest, on sale at Liberty's, which, with the addition of a lot of black and some innovation with the hair, would transform me into something a lot more formidable; or so I intended.

I did get to Stonehenge, incidentally. I felt at home with it. It was prerational, and pre-British, and geological. Nobody knew how it had arrived where it was, or why, or why it had continued to exist; but there it sat, challenging gravity, defying analysis. In fact, it was sort of Canadian. "Stonehenge," I would say to the next mournful-looking European man who tried to pick me up. That would do the trick.

NOT SO GRIMM:
THE STAYING POWER OF FAIRY TALES

FROM THE BEAST TO THE BLONDE:
ON FAIRY TALES AND THEIR TELLERS
BY MARINA WARNER

THE ACCOMPLISHED British novelist Marina Warner is also the author of several intriguing works of nonfiction, including *Alone of All Her Sex*, an examination of the Virgin Mary cult, and *Monuments and Maidens*, an analysis of female allegorical figures. Her new book inhabits roughly the same territory — the widespread icon, the popular image, the much-told tale — but is even more ambitious in scope.

From the Beast to the Blonde is what its subtitle proclaims: a book about fairy tales and also about those who have told them. As befits its subject, it is a thing of splendour — marvellous, bizarre, exotic — but at the same time familiar as porridge. It's crammed full of goodies — stick your thumb into it anywhere and out comes a plum — and profusely illustrated. It is also simply essential reading for anyone concerned not only with fairy tales, myth, and legends but also with how stories of all kinds get told.

Like many children, I devoured fairy tales. Having cut my milk teeth on the unexpurgated *Grimm's* — despite my parents' fears that the red-hot shoes and poked-out eyeballs might be too much for a six-year-old — I went on to the Andrew Lang collections, the *Arabian Nights*, and anything else I could get my hands on — if eerily illustrated by Arthur Rackham or Edmund Dulac, so much the better. By the time I hit college I was well prepared for the more Jungian of my professors, who, in those myth-oriented days of the late 1950s, referred casually to such fairy-tale denizens as woms (Wise Old Men) and wows (Wise Old Women).

Fairy tales were said to contain universal archetypes, and to teach deep and timeless psychic lessons. Of course, a wom could just as easily be a Wandering Old Molester and a wow a Wicked Old Witch, and if encountered in the forest, or, say, the corner drugstore, a girl was hard pressed to know whether to give them her crust of bread or a very wide berth. Still, there was a definite mystique.

Then fairy tales fell on hard times. Despite such thoughtful studies as Bruno Bettelheim's *The Uses of Enchantment*, they were prettied up and weeded — adventurous heroines as well as grisly doings were downplayed, and the prone or Sleeping Beauty position was favoured. After that, the tales were — understandably — attacked by feminists as brainwashing devices, aimed at turning women into beautiful, dutiful automatons, at extolling the phallic power of sword-sporting princes, and at slandering nonbiological parental units and the chronologically enhanced. Like corsets, they were designed to confine, and as such were reprehensibly outmoded.

But now Marina Warner rides to the rescue. Fiddle-dee-dee, says she, in true Wise Woman fashion, as she rolls up her sleeves and sets to work salvaging things from the closet of discards. Look! Not musty old straw at all, she proclaims. Real gold! You just have to know how to spin it. And quicker than you can say Rumpelstiltskin backward, out the window goes the theory of timeless archetypes, as well as the Volkish idea that these stories were authentic, indigenous, preliterate, out-of-the-soul-of-the-soil emanations. (Her impressive collection of sources and variants puts paid to that.)

Away, too, goes the recent school of disparagement. If you want a feminist heroine, she suggests, how about Mother Goose? Reconsider the beaky nose, the funny bonnet, and the nursery pinafore.

Mother Goose dresses like a featherbrain for the same reason that female "tourists" are favoured as espionage couriers: Both disarm suspicion. But underneath, what surprises! Disguise! Ambiguity! Subversion!

Warner's theory of narrative, once put forth, is eminently sensible: For any tale told, there is a teller, but also a tellee. Also a social context, which changes over time: "Historical realism" is a term she favours. Even when the narrative events themselves remain constant, the moral spin put on them may not, for both the tellers and the tellees have their own fluctuating agendas.

Is it a coincidence that "old wives' tales" about the advisability of being nice to elderly women were once told by elderly women, who needed all the help they could get? Or that Bluebeard stories about young girls being married off to murderous husbands should have peaked during a reaction against made-for-money forced nuptials? Or that the beastliness of the fur-bearing Beast, he of Beauty-and-the, should once have been held against him, but in these green times is seen as a plus? (This book surely contains the definitive in-depth analysis of the Disney film of the tale, if "in-depth" here is not oxymoronic.)

The first section of Warner's book is about the tellers. It deals engagingly with those who collected, rewrote, and concocted such stories, from Marie-Jeanne L'Heritier to Perrault, to the studious Grimm brothers and the melancholy Hans Anderson. But also, even more entertainingly, it considers the imagined teller of tales, she (and it is mostly a "she") from whom story itself was perceived to flow. Who would have suspected that the Mother Goose whose comical portrait adorned so many early collections had such an ancient and august lineage? The cackly-voiced bird-woman, it appears, goes all the way back to the feather-bodied sirens. The sibyl figures in her genealogy too, as does the Queen of Sheba, who was thought by medieval artists to have a bird's foot. So do such disparate figures as the hard-pressed but cool Scheherazade, the pious and instructive

Saint Anne, and a bevy of raucous crones, who, like Juliet's nurse, are vulgar in their speech and erotic in their interests.

But the more women as a group were misprized by society, the greater the level of disguise required by any who dared to break silence. In times of oppression, wisdom of certain kinds can safely be spoken only through the mouths of those playing the fool. Thus the goose face.

The second part of the book deals with the tales themselves — not only in their verbal forms but also as they feature in plays, operas, films, and pictures. Warner focuses on stories with female protagonists — beanstalk Jack and his bravely bladed brethren get short shrift, while maiden-devouring ogres, demon lovers, and incest-inclined fathers are bathed in the lurid spotlight — but then, this book does not pretend to be an encyclopedia. Nor are all the girls in it goody-goodies: Unpleasant females such as ugly sisters, bad fairies, and wicked stepmothers get a thorough going-over, with the caveat that stepmothers in our changed socioeconomic times need no longer be wicked. (I was relieved to hear that, being one.)

Why so many dead mothers? Why so many blonde heroines? Why indeed a chapter called, enticingly, "The Language of Hair"? From which Rapunzel-like German hair-water ad did the Dadaists pinch their name? Only list, Dear Reader — Warner herself is a dab hand at lists — and you shall know all. Or if not all, at least a good deal more than you did when you came in.

At times, you may feel you're at risk of falling into a charmed sleep, having pricked your finger on one spinster too many, but that just means you've been reading too fast. This is a complex tapestry woven of many yarns, and you shouldn't try to unravel all of its threads at once.

Although Warner is entranced by the vitality and metamorphic properties of the fairy tale as form, she does not try to make a case for it as at all times politically appropriate. She recognizes "the contrary directions of the genre," which pull it "toward acquiescence on one hand and rebellion on the other." Because a story — any story, but especially one that exists in such a vernacular domain — is a negotiation between teller and audience, the listeners are accomplices. The aim of the tale may well be to instruct, but if it does not also delight, it will play to empty houses. As Warner says, "Fairystorytellers know that a tale, if it is to enthrall, must move the listeners to pleasure, laughter or tears. . . . The sultan is always there, half asleep, but quite awake enough to rouse himself and remember that death sentence he threatened."

We the audience are the collective sultan. If we want insipid heroines, that's what we'll get, and ditto for bigotries and prejudices and superheated shoes. But not forever. As Warner also says, "What is applauded and who sets the terms of the recognition and acceptance are always in question." We need not content ourselves with limp compliance or sullen revenge: The creative retelling, the utopian dream, the mischievous reversal, the rightly chosen wish, and the renewed sense of wonder may instead be ours.

This is a happy ending — and Warner knows her genre far too well not to give us one — but it is also a challenge. The uses of enchantment, it seems, are in our hands.

23

A RICH DESSERT FROM A
SAUCY CARTER

BURNING YOUR BOATS: THE COLLECTED SHORT STORIES
BY ANGELA CARTER

THE BRITISH WRITER Angela Carter died too early, at the age of fifty-three. Her career spanned four decades, and produced several acclaimed novels and much astute criticism. It also produced four collections of the extravagant, baroque, and disconcertingly down-to-earth short pieces — such as *The Company of Wolves* — that have become her trademark; so much so that publishers are now sending out requests for fabulist fiction "in the manner of Angela Carter." Ironically, she's become more widely appreciated since her death than she ever was before and is now the most frequently studied author in British universities. She's even become that rarest of creatures, an unabashed feminist it's okay for the guys to like. Maybe it's because her feminism is not of a very puritanical sort. She's a rowdy girl rather than a goody-two-shoes: she can say *tits and bum* with the best of them, and does so quite frequently. If she were a character in a work of fiction in the style of Angela Carter, she'd now, in spirit form, be guffawing raucously down the chimney. "In the manner of," indeed! Who would dare?

Burning Your Boats is a collection of her short fictional pieces, including some very early ones and some that were unpublished at the time of her death. It's an amazing plum pudding. If Carter were a colour she'd be purple, if a flower a cross between a wild rose with lots of thorns and a Venus flytrap, if an animal a cunning fox with gryphon claws, if a bird or other airborne device, hybrid lyre-bird-cum-Siren, with a bit of jackdaw thrown in — for all things bright and beautiful, as well as all things gnarled and macabre, appeal to her, and she filches them with abandon, picks them apart, sticks them together again in a new order, and adds them to her deliberately cluttered verbal nest. Not for her Hemingway's clean, well-lighted place, or Orwell's clear prose like a pane of glass. She prefers instead a dirty, badly lit place, with gnawed bones in the corner and dusty mirrors you'd best not consult. Prose like glass, yes — but it's stained glass. Many of her best effects are achieved by overloading. She piles the adjectives up into a towering chocolate-and-cherries mound, then pulls the tablecloth out from under it so the whole edifice comes crashing delightfully down. She loves blowing bubbles, and she also loves bursting them.

If you were writing her literary *naissance* in the manner of Angela Carter, you'd have to provide a troupe of ghostly godpersons gathered round her typewriter. Oscar Wilde would be there, whispering "Nothing succeeds like excess" and bestowing the gift of the inversion of truisms; Sylvia Townsend Warner, with her clutch of ruthless fairies; Edgar Allan Poe, the subject of one of her more spectacular stories, although Carter wears her Rue Morgue with a difference. And Bram Stoker, and Perrault, and Sheridan LeFanu, and George Macdonald, and Mary Shelley, and perhaps even Carson McCullers, and a whole gaggle of disreputable tale-telling old grannies. Although like every child she had ancestors, like every child she was unique; though Carter, it must be said, was more unique than most. (I know: *more unique* is a contradiction; but I said this was *in the manner of*.)

Burning Your Boats is an apt title: It's what you do when you're fighting on perilous ground and choose to cut off your own retreat. At the outset Carter was obstinately unfashionable, both in manner and in matter, but she didn't give a toss. She became herself almost immediately, and never looked back: "A Very, Very Great Lady and Her Son At Home," one of her first stories, is about the deadening grip of dominating mothers on their children, and so is one of her last: "Ashputtle or The Mother's Ghost." "A Victorian Fable (with Glossary)" is an early piece written in Victorian thieves' cant, and illustrates both Carter's penchant for combining scholarship with little bits of junk picked up in curio shops, and the lifelong delight she took in the gaudiness, multiplicity, and untidiness of language itself. Sow's ears into silk purses, and vice versa; the smart-as-a-whip intellectual essay blending into the sensual narrative mode, and vice versa: What concerned her was the magical act of transformation. She knew no bounds, and also no boundaries.

She's best known for her haunted European forests, replete with wolves and werewolves, but England is here too — the polymorphous-perverse Pantomime, and a wonderful country-house kitchen, and Shakespeare's enchanted woods. So is America, the mythological America that is. Carter redoes John Ford's Jacobean shocker *'Tis Pity She's a Whore* as a Western movie directed by the *other* John Ford, and provides two renderings of Lizzie Borden, and a bravura piece in which she transmutes *Der Freischutz* into a Mexican-border melodrama, and an Indian captivity narrative in which the captured white heroine prefers the Indians, as they frequently did in real life.

But the attempt to summarize is hopeless. Suffice to say that you should not miss this book nor should you try to read it all at once, as, like a pound of Turkish Delight, it's too rich for a single mouthful. There's a warm and perceptive introduction by Carter's old friend Salman Rushdie, in which he pays tribute both to the woman — "sharp, foulmouthed, passionate" — and to her work. As he says, "She hadn't finished. . . . The stories in this volume are the measure of our loss. But they are also our treasure, to savour and to hoard."

24

AN EXPERIMENT IN LOVE

BY HILARY MANTEL

HILARY MANTEL's seventh novel, *An Experiment in Love*, is only the second to be published in the United States. This is a shame, because Ms. Mantel is an exceptionally good writer. Her book's title, however, is somewhat misleading. "Experiment" suggests clinical detachment; but if experiments are going on, they're more like what Dr. Frankenstein got up to with the body parts: intense, unholy, and messy. As for "love," the inaccuracy is that it's singular: there are many kinds of love in this book, almost all contaminated. "Enter the Dragoness" might be a more likely title, for this is a story about emotional kung fu, female style — except that by the end although all are wounded or worse, there's no clear winner.

The playing field is England, with its bafflingly complex and minutely calibrated systems of class and status, of region and religion; the players are little girls, larger girls, young women, and, looming huge over all, mothers. The weapons are clothing, schools, intelligence, friendships, insults, accents, trophy boyfriends, material possessions, and food. The battle cry is *"Sauve qui peut!"*

The narrator is Carmel McBain, who — having somehow survived to adulthood — kicks off the action with a Proustian time-warp experience, triggered by a newspaper photograph of her former roommate. Back she goes, sucked through the plug hole of memory into her dire childhood. One of her quirks is that she's dogged by lines from the poems she's learned at school, "The Rime of the Ancient Mariner" among them. Carmel is both the Mariner, doomed to relate, and the Wedding Guest, doomed to listen; and we too are held enthralled while she unwraps her own personal albatross and tells us how she got sadder but wiser.

"I wanted to separate myself from the common fate of girls who are called Carmel," she tells us, "and identify myself with girls with casual names, names which their parents didn't think about too hard." Carmel is the name of the mountain where the prophet Elijah slaughtered the priests of Baal: it's not quite like being called Linda. Indeed, Carmel is sometimes less a person than a geographic site, where embattled forces play themselves out despite her.

It's her mother who saddled her with this weighty name: a formidable north-of-England–working-class mother, of wrathful temperament and Irish Catholic descent, who covers her daughter with her own elaborate embroidery, crams her with homework, and launches her like a missile at the social establishment she both despises and envies. Carmel's mother expects her to climb the heights: "The task in life that she set for me was to build my own mountain, build a step-by-step success: the kind didn't matter as long as it was high and it shone. And as she had told me that it is ruthless people who rise highest in this life, I would slash through the ropes of anyone who tried to climb after me . . . and jump about on the summit alone."

Carmel's forced climb leads from the grim 1950s Catholic primary school of her small, decrepit mill town to the Holy Redeemer, a superior establishment run by sarcastic nuns. There she wears a uniform that includes both a tie and a girdle, and is "stuffed with education," though other nutrients are scarce. The aim is to turn women into "little chappies with breasts." "Women were forced to imitate men, and bound not to succeed at it." Nevertheless, Carmel achieves a meagre scholarship and a bed in Tonbridge Hall, a neo-Brontëan women's residence at London University. Among other things, this novel is a *Bildungsroman*, and one of the issues raised is the form of education appropriate for women.

All along the way, Carmel has a fellow climber, her doppel-gänger and nemesis, the stolid and implacable Karina. Karina's parents are immigrants. They have undergone the war — cattle cars are mentioned — although they are not Jewish. Out of compunction, Carmel's mother insists on a friendship between the girls; thereafter Karina is linked to Carmel, and where Carmel goes Karina follows. Like Carmel's mother, she too envies and despises, but the object of these emotions is Carmel herself. Whatever Carmel has, Karina takes or else destroys, though it is not a one-sided war. Carmel gets her licks in too, and may even have started it all in kindergarten by kicking Karina's baby doll: an early recognition, perhaps, that all was not well in the world of mums and tots. Over the years, Karina is Carmel's enemy, but also — when the girls enter the alien territory of upmarket nuns and middle-class southerners — her oldest friend and grudging ally. "I never thought she was dangerous, except to me," thinks Carmel, wrongly, as it turns out.

They are a Jack-Spratt-and-his-wife couple: Carmel thin and childish, not even allowed to help burn the sparse family dinner; Karina rotund and prematurely competent, a little housewife at the age of twelve. Carmel is cold and hungry and watery, and dreams of drowning; Karina is warm and wool-covered, associated with Catherine wheels and fire. Above all, Karina is the protégée and voice of the mothers, especially Carmel's mother: angry, self-righteous, annihilating.

Although she is acquiescent and browbeaten, Carmel has ways of rebelling. At school she practises "dumb insolence," and her first act on reaching the university is to chop off her hair, which, via the torturing use of curl rags, has been one of the instruments of maternal control. But she also takes over her mother's role. Her mother has deprived her not only of affection and approval but of actual nourishment, and now Carmel begins to deprive herself. Karina, on the other hand, is gorging herself to blimplike proportions. As one character comments, "More and more of Karina. Less and less of Carmel."

We are warned against considering this a story about anorexia; too middle class. Rather, claims the narrator, it is a story about "appetite." Well, perhaps. This portion of the book is set in 1970, at the precise time when anorexia was becoming common but was not yet common knowledge; any later and Carmel could not have been so unselfconscious about her plight. In any case, the dwindling of Carmel has complex causes. There is the nuns' connection of eating with sin and their emphasis on self-denial — but how much self can you do without and still remain alive? There's also Carmel's poverty, and the dreadful food of Tonbridge Hall. But the difficulty for Carmel goes well beyond the pinched pennies and the underdone vegetables: How much of life does she dare to eat? How much to enjoy? The pleasure principle has not been exactly fostered.

The pleasures of the novel, however, are many. The women's-residence portions of *An Experiment in Love* are as harshly delicious as those in *The Group*; the childhood sections are immediate and vivid, funny and bleak, and the intricate love and love-hate relationships among the women, which as the narrator says, have nothing to do with sex, are right on target. This is Carmel's story, but it is that of her generation as well: girls at the end of the 1960s, caught between two sets of values, who had the pill but still ironed their boyfriends' shirts.

Moral confusion reigns, and moral questions also: What makes bad people bad? Even more mysteriously, what makes good people good? Why Karina, and why the heartbreakingly kind Lynette, Karina's affluent roommate, rebuffed by her at every turn? Carmel's weak father, who has retreated into jigsaw puzzles, can't find the missing part of Judas, and neither can Carmel.

"Descriptions are your strong point," Carmel is told, and they are Ms. Mantel's as well. Never have dripping tights hung over a radiator or the smell of a child's wooden ruler been so meticulously rendered. The similes and metaphors glint brightly: the sheets in the dormitory are "tucked strap-tight into the bed's frame, as if to harness a lunatic"; the residence soup is "an uncleaned aquarium, where vegetable matter swam." Much of this verbal dexterity is exercised on food, but as a narrator Carmel is like her mother: she does a little embroidery on everything.

If there's any complaint, it's that we want to know more; like Carmel herself, the book could have been a little fatter. What happened to Karina and Carmel after the horrifying denouement? But perhaps that's the point: it's what you'll never know that haunts you; and with all its brilliance, its sharpness, and its clear-eyed wit, *An Experiment in Love* is a haunting book.

25

IN SEARCH OF ALIAS GRACE:
ON WRITING CANADIAN
HISTORICAL FICTION

WHAT I AM GOING to talk about this evening has to do with the Canadian novel and, more particularly, the Canadian historical novel. I will address the nature of this genre insofar as it has to do with the mysteries of time and memory; I will meditate on why so many of this kind of novel have been written by English-speaking Canadian authors lately; and after that I'll talk a little about my own recent attempt to write such a novel. At the end I'll attempt some sort of meaning-of-it-all nugget or philosophical summation, as such a thing is implicitly called for in the list of ingredients on the cookie box.

Fiction is where individual memory and experience and collective memory and experience come together, in greater or lesser proportions. The closer the fiction is to us, the more we recognize and claim it as individual rather than collective. Margaret Laurence used to say that her English readers thought *The Stone Angel* was about old age, the Americans thought it was about some old woman they knew, and the Canadians thought it was about their grandmothers. Each character in fiction has an individual life, replete with personal detail — the eating of meals, the flossing of teeth, the making of love, the birthing of children, the attending of funerals, and so forth — but each also exists within a context, a fictional world

comprised of geology, weather, economic forces, social classes, cultural references, and wars and plagues and such big public events;
you'll note that, being Canadian, I put the geology first. This fictional world so lovingly delineated by the writer may bear a more
obvious or a less obvious relation to the world we actually live in, but
bearing no relation to it at all is not an option. We have to write out
of who and where and when we are, whether we like it or not, and
disguise it how we may. As Robertson Davies has remarked, ". . . we
all belong to our own time, and there is nothing whatever that we can
do to escape from it. Whatever we write will be contemporary, even
if we attempt a novel set in a past age . . ."[1] We can't help but be modern, just as the Victorian writers — whenever they set their books —
couldn't help but be Victorian. Like all beings alive on Middle Earth,
we're trapped by time and circumstance.

What I've said about fictional characters is, of course, also true
of every real human being. For example: here I am, giving this
Bronfman Lecture in Ottawa. By what twists of coincidence or fate —
how novelistic these terms sound, but also how faithful to real experience they are — do I find myself back here in my city of origin?

For it was in Ottawa that I was born, fifty-seven years, three
days, and several hours ago. The place was the Ottawa General
Hospital; the date, November 18, 1939. About the exact hour, my
mother — to the despair of many astrologers since — is a little vague,
that being a period when women were routinely conked out with
ether. I do know that I was born after the end of the Grey Cup football game. The doctors thanked my mother for waiting; they'd all
been following the game on the radio. In those days most doctors
were men, which may explain their sportive attitude.

"In those days" — there I am, you see, being born in *those* days,
which are not the same as these days; no ether now, and many a
woman doctor. As for Ottawa, I wouldn't have been there at all if it
hadn't been for the Great Depression: my parents were economic
refugees from Nova Scotia — there's your economic force — from

which they were then cut off by the Second World War — there's your big public event.

We lived — here's your personal detail — in a long, dark, railroad-car-shaped second-storey apartment on Patterson Avenue, near the Rideau Canal — there's your geology, more or less — an apartment in which my mother once caused a flood by rinsing the diapers in the toilet, where they got stuck — in *those* days there were no disposable diapers, and not even any diaper services. In *those* days, as I'm sure some of you believe you remember, there was much more snow — there's your weather — and it was much whiter and more beautiful than any snow they ever come up with nowadays. As a child I helped to build snow forts that were much bigger than the Parliament Buildings, and even more labyrinthine — there's your cultural reference. I remember this very clearly, so it must be true, and there's your individual memory.

What's my point? It's out of such individual particulars that fiction is constructed; and so is autobiography, including the kind of autobiography we are each always writing, but haven't yet got around to writing down; and so, too, is history. History may intend to provide us with grand patterns and overall schemes, but without its brick-by-brick, life-by-life, day-by-day foundations it would collapse. Whoever tells you that history is not about individuals, only about large trends and movements, is lying. The shot heard round the world was fired on a certain date, under certain weather conditions, out of a certain rather inefficient type of gun. After the Rebellion of 1837, William Lyon Mackenzie escaped to the United States dressed in women's clothing; I know the year, so I can guess the style of his dress. When I lived in the rural Ontario countryside north of Toronto, a local man said, "There's the barn where we hid the women and children, that time the Fenians invaded." An individual barn; individual women and children. The man who told me about the barn was born some sixty years after the Fenian attack, but he said *we*, not *they*: he was remembering as a personal experience and event at which he had not been present in the flesh, and I believe we have all done that. It's at such points that memory, history, and story all intersect; it would take only one step more to bring all of them into the realm of fiction.

We live in a period in which memory of all kinds, including the sort of larger memory we call history, is being called into question. For history as for the individual, forgetting can be just as convenient as remembering, and remembering what was once forgotten can be distinctly uncomfortable. As a rule, we tend to remember the awful things done to us, and to forget the awful things we did. The Blitz is still remembered; the fire bombing of Dresden, well, not so much, or not by us. To challenge an accepted version of history — what we've decided it's proper to remember — by dredging up things that society has decided are better forgotten, can cause cries of anguish and outrage, as the makers of a recent documentary about the Second World War could testify. Remembrance Day, like Mother's Day, is a highly ritualized occasion; for instance, we are not allowed, on Mother's Day, to commemorate *bad* mothers, and even to acknowledge that such persons exist would be considered — on that date — to be in shoddy taste.

Here is the conundrum, for history and individual memory alike, and therefore for fiction also: How do we *know* we know what we think we know? And if we find that after all we don't know what it is that we once thought we knew, how do we know we are who we think we are, or thought we were yesterday, or thought we were — for instance — a hundred years ago? These are the questions one asks oneself, at my age, whenever one says *Whatever happened to old what's-his-name?*; they are also the questions that arise in connection with Canadian history, or indeed with any other kind of history. They are also the questions that arise in any contemplation of what used to be called "character"; they are thus central to any conception of the novel. For the novel concerns itself, above all, with time. Any plot is a *this* followed by a *that*; there must be change in a novel, and change can only take place over time, and this change can only have significance if either the character in the book, or, at the very least, the reader, can remember what came before. As Henry James's biographer Leon Edel has said, if there's a clock in it, you know it's a novel.

Thus there can be no history, and no novel either, without memory of some sort; but when it comes right down to it, how reliable is memory itself — our individual memory, or our collective memory as a society? Once, memory was a given. You could lose it and you could recover it, but the thing lost and then recovered was as solid and all-of-a-piece, was as much a *thing*, as a gold coin. "Now it all comes back to me," or some version of it, was a staple of the recovering-from-amnesia scenes in Victorian melodramas — indeed, even so late as the recovering-from-amnesia scene in Graham Greene's *The Ministry of Fear*; and there was an *it*, there was an *all*. If the seventeenth century revolved around faith — that is, what you believed — and the eighteenth around knowledge — that is, what you could prove — the nineteenth could be said to have revolved around memory. You can't have Tennyson's "Tears, idle tears, . . . O Death in Life, the days that are no more," unless you can remember those days. Nostalgia for what once was, guilt for what you once did, revenge for what someone else once did to you, regret for what you once might have done, but didn't do — how central they all are to the previous century, and how dependent each one of them is on the idea of memory itself. Without memory, and the belief that it can be recovered whole, like treasure fished out of a swamp, Proust's famous madeleine is reduced to a casual snack. The nineteenth-century novel would be unimaginable without a belief in the integrity of memory; for what is the self without a more or less continuous memory of itself, and what is the novel without the self? Or so they would have argued, back then.

As for the twentieth century, at least in Europe, it has been on the whole more interested in forgetting — forgetting as an organic process, and sometimes as a willed act. Dali's famous painting

The Persistence of Memory features a melting clock and a parade of destructive ants; Beckett's famous play *Krapp's Last Tape* is relentless in its depiction of how we erase and rewrite ourselves over time; Milan Kundera's novel *The Book of Laughter and Forgetting* has a touchstone twentieth-century title; the horrifying film *Night and Fog* is only one of many twentieth-century statements about how we industriously and systematically obliterate history to suit our own vile purposes; and in Orwell's *Nineteen Eighty-four*, the place where documents are sent to be destroyed is called, ironically, the Memory Hole. The twentieth century's most prominent theories of the psyche — those that evolved from Freud — taught us that we were not so much the sum of what we could remember, as the sum of what we had forgotten[2]; we were controlled by the Unconscious, where unsavoury repressed memories were stored in our heads like rotten apples in a barrel, festering away but essentially unknowable, except for the suspicious smell. Furthermore, twentieth-century European art as a whole gradually lost faith in the reliability of time itself. No longer an evenly flowing river, it became a collage of freeze-frames, jumbled fragments, and jump-cuts.[3]

The hero of Spanish writer Javier Marias's 1989 novel *All Souls* represents a host of twentieth-century European spiritual relatives when he says,

> . . . I must speak of myself and of my time in the city of Oxford, even though the person speaking is not the same person who was there. He seems to be, but he is not. If I call myself "I," or use a name which has accompanied me since birth and by which some will remember me . . . it is simply because I prefer to speak in the first person and not because I believe that the faculty of memory alone is any guarantee that a person remains the same in different times and different places. The person recounting here and now what he saw and what happened to him then is not the same person who saw those things and to whom those things

happened; neither is he a prolongation of that person, his shadow, his heir or his usurper.[4]

Fine and dandy, we say, with our streetwise postmodern consciousness. However, problems do arise. If the I of now has nothing to do with the I of then, where did the I of now come from? Nothing is made from nothing, or so we used to believe. And, to get back to Canadian Studies — why is it that it's now — within the last fifteen or twenty years, and so near the end of the fragmenting and memory-denying twentieth century — that the Canadian historical novel has become so popular, with writers and readers alike?

But what exactly do we mean by "historical novel"? All novels are in a sense "historical" novels; they can't help it, insofar as they have to, they *must*, make reference to a time that is not the time in which the reader is reading the book. (A reference to science fiction novels will not save us here, as the writer has of course written the book in a time that is already past to the reader.) But there is the past tense — yesterday and yesterday and yesterday, full of tooth flossing and putting the antifreeze into the car, a yesterday not so long ago — and then there is The Past.

Charles Dickens's Scrooge timorously asks the Ghost of Christmas Past whether the past they are about to visit is "long past," and is told, "No — *your* past." For a considerable period it was only "your past" — the personal past of the writer, and, by extension, that of the reader — that was at issue in the Canadian novel. I don't recall any serious writer in the 1960s writing what we think of as historical romances proper, that is, the full-dress–petticoat-and-farthingale kind, which were associated with subjects like Mary Queen of Scots. Perhaps it was thought that Canada lacked the appropriate clothing for such works; perhaps the genre itself was regarded as a form of trash writing, like bodice rippers — which, like any other genre, it either is or it isn't, depending on how it's done.

Once, we as a society were not so squeamish. Major Richardson's hugely popular nineteenth-century novel *Wacousta* was, among other things, a historical novel along the lines of Sir Walter Scott, granddaddy of the form, and Fenimore Cooper, his even more prolix descendant. These were nineteenth-century novelists, and the nineteenth century loved the historic novel. *Vanity Fair, Middlemarch, A Tale of Two Cities, Ivanhoe, Treasure Island* — all are historic novels of one kind or another, and these are only a few. Perhaps the question to be asked is not why we're writing historic novels now, but why we didn't do it before.

In any case, by the 1960s it was as if we'd forgotten that on this continent, and especially north of the 49th parallel, there was ever a bodice to be ripped or a weak-minded lady to be rendered hysterical by the experience. We were instead taken up by the momentous discovery that we actually existed, in what was then the here and now, and we were busily exploring the implications of that.

Our generation of English-speaking Canadians — those of us who were children in the 1940s and adolescents in the 1950s — grew up with the illusion that there was not then and never had been a Canadian literature. I say "illusion," because there had in fact been one; it's just that we weren't told about it. The collapse of old-style English colonial imperialism had abolished the old-style school reader — the kind that used to contain excerpts from English literature, mingled with bits from our native singers and songstresses, usually so termed. Thus you could go through twelve years of schooling, back then, and come out with the impression that there had only ever been one Canadian writer, and that was Stephen Leacock.

The 1950s came right after the 1940s and the 1930s; and the double whammy of the Depression followed by the War had wiped out what in the early part of the century had been a burgeoning indigenous publishing industry, complete with best-sellers. (Remember Mazo de la Roche? We didn't. We were told nothing about her.) Add to that the weight of the paperback book industry — completely controlled, back then, from the United States — and the advent of television, most of which came from south of the border, and you get the picture. There was radio, of course. There was the CBC. There were Wayne and Schuster and Our Pet, Juliette. But it wasn't much of a counterbalance.

When we hit university in the late 1950s and encountered intellectual magazines, we found ourselves being fed large doses of anxiety and contempt, brewed by our very own pundits and even by some of our very own poets and fiction writers, concerning our own inauthenticity, our feebleness from the cultural point of view, our lack of a real literature, and the absence of anything you could dignify by the name of history — by which was meant interesting and copious bloodshed on our own turf. In Quebec, people were more certain of their own existence, and especially of their own persistence, although they had lots of Parisian-oriented voices to tell them how substandard they were. In Angloland, Earle Birney's famous poem that concludes "It's only by our lack of ghosts we're haunted" sums up the prevailing attitude of the time.

Well, we young writers charged ahead anyway. We thought we were pretty daring to be setting our poems and stories in Toronto and Vancouver and Montreal, and even Ottawa, rather than in London or Paris or New York. We were, however, relentlessly contemporary: history, for us, either didn't exist, or it had happened elsewhere, or if ours it was boring.

This is often the attitude among the young, but it was especially true of us, because of the way we'd encountered our own history. Quebec has always had its own version of history, with heroes and villains, and struggle, and heartbreak, and God; God was a main feature until recently. But those of us in English Canada who went to high school when I did weren't dosed with any such strong medicine. Instead we were handed a particularly anemic view of our past, insofar as we were given one at all. For others on more troubled shores the epic battles, the heroes, the stirring speeches, the do-or-die last stands, the freezing to death during the retreat from Moscow. For us the statistics on wheat and the soothing assurances that all was well in the land of the cow and potato, not to mention — although they *were* mentioned — the vein of metallic ore and the stack of lumber. We looked at these things, and saw that they were good, if tedious, but we didn't really examine how they'd been obtained or who was profiting by them, or who did the actual work, or how much they got paid for it. Nor was much said about who inhabited this space before white Europeans arrived, bearing gifts of firearms and smallpox, because weren't we nice people? You bet we were, and nice people do not dwell on morbid subjects. I myself would have been much more interested in Canadian history if I'd known our dull prime minister, Mackenzie King, had believed that the spirit of his mother was inhabiting his dog, which he always consulted on public policy — it explains so much — but nobody knew about such things back then.

The main idea behind the way we were taught Canadian history seemed to be reassurance: as a country, we'd had our little differences, and a few embarrassing moments — the Rebellion of '37, the hanging of Louis Riel, and so forth — but these had just been unseemly burps in one long, gentle after-dinner nap. We were always being told that Canada had come of age. This was even a textbook title: *Canada Comes of Age.* I'm not sure what it was supposed to mean — that we could vote and drink and shave and fornicate, perhaps; or that we had come into our inheritance, and could now manage our own affairs.

Our inheritance. Ah yes — the mysterious sealed box handed over by the family solicitor when young master comes into his majority. But what was inside it? Many things we weren't told about in school, and this is where the interest in historical writing comes in. For it's the very things that *aren't* mentioned that inspire the most curiosity in us. *Why* aren't they mentioned? The lure of the Canadian past, for the writers of my generation, has been partly the lure of the unmentionable — the mysterious, the buried, the forgotten, the discarded, the taboo.

This digging up of buried things began perhaps in poetry; for instance, E. J. Pratt's narrative poems on subjects like the sinking of the *Titanic* and the life of the French Jesuit missionary Brébeuf. Pratt was followed by certain younger writers; I think of Gwendolyn MacEwen's mid-1960s verse play *Terror and Erebus*, about the failure of the Franklin expedition. I blush to mention Margaret Atwood's *The Journals of Susanna Moodie* of 1970, but since I'll need to mention it later on anyway, I'll get the blushing over with now. Other poets — Doug Jones and Al Purdy in particular, but there were more — used historic events as subject for individual poems. James Reaney was a pioneer in the use of local history — he was writing the Donnelly trilogy in the late 1960s, although the plays were not produced until later. There were other plays in the 1970s too — Rick Salutin's *The Farmers' Rebellion*, about the Upper Canadian Rebellion, springs to mind.

Then came the novels. These weren't historical romances of the bodice-ripping kind; instead they were what we should probably term "novels set in the historic past," to distinguish them from the kind of thing you find in drugstores that have cloaks on them and raised silver scrollwork titles. When is the past old enough to be considered historic? Well, roughly, I suppose you could say it's anything before the time at which the novel-writer came to consciousness; that seems fair enough.

In the novel, then, we had Anne Hébert's excellent *Kamouraska*, as early as 1970. It was written in French, but it was translated, and many English-speaking writers read it. As far back as Margaret Laurence's *The Diviners* in 1974 and Marian Engel's *Bear* in 1976, figures from the Canadian past were used as a point of reference for the Canadian present — Catharine Parr Traill by Laurence, an obscure and probably invented nineteenth-century English emigrant by Engel. Rudy Wiebe's *The Temptations of Big Bear* in 1973 and *The Scorched Wood People* in 1977 are usually thought of as being enclosed by the parentheses *Native People*, but they are of course set entirely in the past. Then there's Timothy Findley's *The Wars* in 1977.

In the 1980s and 1990s, the trend intensified. Graeme Gibson's *Perpetual Motion* was published in 1982. After that their names are legion. Robertson Davies's *Murther and Walking Spirits* is a historical novel. So — using my definition of historic — are Michael Ondaatje's *In the Skin of a Lion* and *The English Patient*, and Brian Moore's *Blackrobe*. So are Alice Munro's two stories "Meneseteung" and "A Wilderness Station." So are George Bowering's *Burning Waters* and Daphne Marlatt's *Ana Historic*, and Jane Urquhart's *The Whirlpool* and *Away*; so is Carol Shields's *The Stone Diaries*; so is Timothy Findley's *The Piano Man's Daughter*. In this year alone, we have Findley's *You Went Away*, Anne-Marie MacDonald's *Fall on Your Knees*, Katherine Govier's *Angel Walk*, Anne Michaels's *Fugitive Pieces*, Gail Anderson-Dargatz's *The Cure for Death by Lightning*, and Guy Vanderhaeghe's *The Englishman's Boy*.

All of these are set in the past — Dickens's *long* past — but not all use the past for the same purposes. Of course not; the authors of them are individuals, and each novel has its own preoccupations. Some attempt to give more or less faithful accounts of actual events, in answer perhaps to such questions as "Where did we come from and how did we get here?" Some attempt restitution of a sort, or at least an acknowledgement of past wrongs — I'd put the Rudy Wiebe novels and Guy Vanderhaeghe's book in this category, dealing as they do with the deplorable North American record on the treatment of Native peoples. Others, such as Graeme Gibson's, look at what we have killed and destroyed in our obsessive search for the pot of gold. Others delve into class structure and political struggles — Ondaatje's *In the Skin of a Lion*, for instance. Yet others unearth a past as it was lived by women, under conditions a good deal more stringent than our own; yet others use the past as background to family sagas — tales of betrayal and tragedy and even madness. "The past is another country," begins the English novel *The Go-Between*[5]; "they do things differently there." Yes, they do, and these books point that out; but they also do quite a few things the same, and these books point that out as well.

Why then has there been such a spate of historical novels in the past twenty years, and especially in the past decade? Earlier, I gave some possible reasons as to why this trend didn't occur earlier; but why is it happening now?

Some might say that we're more confident about ourselves — that we're now allowed to find ourselves more interesting than we once did; and I think they would be right. In this, we're part of a worldwide movement that has found writers and readers, especially in ex-colonies, turning back toward their own roots, while not rejecting developments in the imperial centres. London and Paris are still wonderful places, but they are no longer seen as the only homes of the good, the true, and the beautiful, as well as of those more typical twentieth-century tastes, the bad, the false, and the ugly. You want squalor, lies, and corruption? Hell, we've got 'em homegrown, and not only that, we always have had, and there's where the past comes in.

Some might say that, on the other hand, the past is safer; that at a time when our country feels very much under threat — the threat of splitting apart, and the threat of having its established institutions and its social fabric and its sense of itself literally torn apart — it feels comforting to escape backwards, to a time when these things were not the problems. With the past, at least we know what happened: while visiting there, we suffer from no uncertainties about the future, or at least the part of it that comes in between them and us; we've read about it. The *Titanic* may be sinking, but we're not on it. Watching it subside, we're diverted for a short time from the leaking lifeboat we're actually in right now.

Of course the past was not really safer. As a local museum custodian has commented, "Nostalgia is the past without the pain,"[6] and for those living in it, the past was their present, and just as painful as

our present is to us — and perhaps more so, considering the incur-
able diseases and the absence of anesthesia, central heating, and
indoor plumbing back then, to mention a few of the drawbacks.
Those who long for a return to the supposed values of the nineteenth
century should turn away from the frilly-pillow magazines devoted to
that era and take a good hard look at what was really going on. So
although coziness may be an attraction, it's also an illusion; and not
many of the Canadian historical novels I've mentioned depict the
past as a very soothing place.

There's also the lure of time travel, which appeals to the little
cultural anthropologist in each one of us. It's such fun to snoop, as it
were; to peek in the windows. What did they eat, back then? What
did they wear, how did they wash their clothes, or treat their sick, or
bury their dead? What did they think about? What lies did they tell,
and why? Who were they really? The questions, once they begin, are
endless. It's like questioning your dead great-grandparents — does
any of what they did or thought live on in us?

I think there's another reason for the appeal, and it has to do
with the age we are now. Nothing is more boring to a fifteen-year-
old than Aunt Agatha's ramblings about the family tree; but often,
nothing is more intriguing to a fifty-year-old. It's not the individual
authors who are now fifty — some of them are a good deal younger
than that. I think it's the culture.

I once took a graduate course entitled "The Literature of the
American Revolution," which began with the professor saying that
there actually *was* no literature of the American Revolution, because
everyone was too busy being too revolting during that period to write
any, so we were going to study the literature just before it, and the literature just after it. What came after it was a lot of hand-wringing
and soul-searching on the part of the American artistic community,
such as it was. Now that we've had the Revolution, they fretted,
where is the great American genius that ought to burst forth? What
should the wondrous novel or poem or painting be like, to be truly

American? Why can't we have an American fashion industry? And so on. When *Moby Dick* and Walt Whitman finally did appear, most right-thinking people wiped their feet on them; but such is life.

However, it was out of this questioning and assessing climate — where did we come from, how did we get from there to here, where are we going, who are we now — that Nathaniel Hawthorne wrote *The Scarlet Letter*, a historic novel set in seventeenth-century New England. The eighteenth century had mostly been embarrassed by the Puritans, and especially by their crazed zeal during the Salem witchcraft trials, and had tried to forget about them; but Hawthorne dug them up again. *The Scarlet Letter* is not of course seventeenth century in any way the Puritans would have recognized; in good nineteenth-century style, it's far too admiring and respectful of that adulterous baggage, Hester Prynne. Instead it's a novel that uses a seventeenth-century English Colonial setting for the purposes of a newly forged nineteenth-century American Republic. And I think that's part of the interest for writers and readers of Canadian historical fiction now: by looking backwards, we place ourselves.

Having more or less delivered two of the three main things I promised you, I'll now turn to the third, that is, my own attempt to write a piece of fiction set in the past. I didn't plan to do it, but I somehow ended up doing it anyway; which is how my novels generally occur. Nor was I conscious of any of the motives I've just outlined. I think novelists begin with hints and images and scenes and voices, rather than with theories and grand schemes. It's individual characters interacting with and acted upon by the world that surrounds them that the novel has to do; with the details, not the large pattern; although a large pattern may then of course emerge.

The book in question is *Alias Grace*, and here is how it came about. In the 1960s, for reasons that can't be rationally explained, I found myself writing a sequence of poems called *The Journals of Susanna Moodie*, which was about an English emigrant who came to what is now Ontario in the 1830s and had a truly awful time in a swamp north of Peterborough, and wrote about her experiences in a book called *Roughing It in the Bush*, which warned English gentlefolk not to do the same. Canada, in her opinion, was a land suited only to horny-handed peasants, otherwise known as honest sons of toil. After she escaped from the woods she wrote *Life in the Clearings*, which contains her version of the Grace Marks story.

Susanna Moodie describes her meeting with Grace in the Kingston Penitentiary in 1851; she then retells the double murder in which Grace was involved. The motive, according to Moodie, was Grace's passion for her employer, the gentleman Thomas Kinnear, and her demented jealousy of Nancy Montgomery, Kinnear's housekeeper and mistress. Moodie portrays Grace as the driving engine of the affair — a scowling, sullen teenage temptress — with the co-murderer, the manservant James McDermott, shown as a mere dupe, driven on by his own lust for Grace as well as by her taunts and blandishments.

Thomas Kinnear and Nancy Montgomery ended up dead in the cellar, and Grace and McDermott made it across Lake Ontario to the States with a wagonful of stolen goods. They were caught and brought back, and tried for the murder of Thomas Kinnear; the murder of Nancy was never tried, as both were convicted and condemned to death. McDermott was hanged. Grace was sentenced as an accessory, but as a result of petitions by her well-wishers, and in consideration of her feebler sex and extreme youth — she was barely sixteen — her sentence was commuted to life.

Moodie saw Grace again, this time in the violent ward of the newly built Lunatic Asylum in Toronto; and there her account ends, with a pious hope that perhaps the poor girl was deranged all along, which would explain her shocking behaviour and also afford her forgiveness in the Afterlife. That was the first version of the story I came across, and being young, and still believing that "nonfiction" meant "true," I did not question it.

Time passed. Then, in the 1970s, I was asked by CBC producer George Jonas to write a script for television. My script was about Grace Marks, using Moodie's version, which was already highly dramatic in form. In it, Grace is brooding and obsessive, and McDermott is putty in her hands. I did leave out Moodie's detail about Grace and McDermott cutting Nancy up into four pieces before hiding her under a washtub. I thought it would be hard to film, and anyway why would they have bothered?

I then received an invitation to turn my television script into a theatre piece. I did give this a try. I hoped to use a multilevelled stage, so the main floor, the upstairs, and the cellar could all be seen at once. I wanted to open it in the Penitentiary and close it in the Lunatic Asylum, and I had some idea of having the spirit of Susanna Moodie flown in on wires, in a black silk dress, like a cross between Peter Pan and a bat; but it was all too much for me, and I gave it up, and then forgot about it.

More time passed. Soon enough it was the early 1990s, and I was on a book tour, and sitting in a hotel room in Zurich. A scene came to me vividly, in the way that scenes often do. I wrote it down on a piece of hotel writing paper, lacking any other kind; it was much the same as the opening scene of the book as it now exists. I recognized the locale: it was the cellar of the Kinnear house, and the female figure in it was Grace Marks. Not immediately, but after a while, I continued with the novel. This time however I did what neither Moodie nor I had done before: I went back to the past.

The past is made of paper; sometimes, now, it's made of microfilm and CD-ROMs, but ultimately they too are made of paper. Sometimes there's a building or a picture or a grave, but mostly it's paper. Paper must be taken care of; archivists and librarians are the guardian angels of paper; without them there would be a lot less of the past than there is, and I and many other writers owe them a huge debt of thanks.

What's on the paper? The same things that are on paper now. Records, documents, newspaper stories, eyewitness reports, gossip and rumour and opinion and contradiction. There is — as I increasingly came to discover — no more reason to trust something written down on paper then than there is now. After all, the writers-down were, and are, human beings, and are subject to error, intentional or not, and to the very human desire to magnify a scandal, and to their own biases. I was often deeply frustrated as well not by what those past recorders had written down but by what they'd left out. History is more than willing to tell you who won the Battle of Trafalgar and which world leader signed this or that treaty, but it's more reluctant about the now-obscure details of daily life. Nobody wrote these things down, because everybody knew them, and considered them too mundane and unimportant to record. Thus I found myself wrestling not only with who said what about Grace, but also with how to clean a chamber pot, what footgear would have been worn in winter, the origins of quilt pattern names, and how to store parsnips. If you're after the truth, the whole and detailed truth, and nothing but the truth, you're going to have a thin time of it if you trust to paper; but with the past, it's almost all you've got.

Susanna Moodie said at the outset of her account that she was writing the story from memory, and as it turns out, her memory was no better than most. She got the location wrong, and the names of some of the participants, just for starters. Not only that, the story was much more problematic, although less neatly dramatic, than the one Moodie had told. For one thing, the witnesses — even eyewitnesses, even at the trial itself — could often not agree; but then, how is this different from most trials? For instance, one says the Kinnear house was left in great disarray by the criminals, another says it was tidy and it was not realized at first that anything had been taken. Confronted with such discrepancies, I tried to deduce which account was the most plausible.

Then there was the matter of the central figure, about whom opinion was very divided indeed. All commentators agreed that Grace was uncommonly good-looking, but they could not agree on her height or the colour of her hair. Some said Grace was jealous of

Nancy, others that Nancy was, on the contrary, jealous of Grace. Some viewed Grace as a cunning female demon, others considered her a simple-minded and terrorized victim, who had only run away with McDermott out of fear for her own life.

I discovered as I read that the newspapers of the time had their own political agendas. Canada West was still reeling from the effects of the 1837 Rebellion, and this influenced both Grace's life before the murders and her treatment at the hands of the press. A large per-centage of the population — some say up to a third — left the country after the Rebellion; the poorer and more radical third, we may assume, which may account for the Tory flavour of those who remained. The exodus meant a shortage of servants, which in turn meant that Grace could change jobs more frequently than her coun-terparts in England. In 1843 — the year of the murder — editorials were still being written about the badness or worthiness of William Lyon Mackenzie; and as a rule, the Tory newspapers that vilified him also vilified Grace — she had after all been involved in the murder of her Tory employer, an act of grave insubordination; but the Reform newspapers that praised Mackenzie were also inclined to clemency toward Grace. This split in opinion continued through later writers on the case, right up to the end of the nineteenth century.

I felt that, to be fair, I had to represent all points of view. I devised the following set of guidelines for myself: when there was a solid fact, I could not alter it; long as I might to have Grace witness McDermott's execution, it could not be done, because, worse luck, she was already in the Penitentiary on that day. Also, every major ele-ment in the book had to be suggested by something in the writing about Grace and her times, however dubious such writing might be; but in the gaps left unfilled, I was free to invent. Since there were a lot of gaps, there is a lot of invention. *Alias Grace* is very much a novel rather than a documentary.

As I wrote, I found myself considering the number and variety of the stories that had been told: Grace's own versions — there were several — as reported in the newspapers and in her "Confession"; McDermott's versions, also multiple; Moodie's version; and those of the later commentators. For each story, there was a teller, but — as is true of all stories — there was also an audience; both were influenced by received climates of opinion, about politics, but also about criminality and its proper treatment, about the nature of women — their weakness and seductive qualities, for instance — and about insanity; in fact about everything that had a bearing on the case.

In my fiction, Grace too — whatever else she is — is a storyteller, with strong motives to narrate, but also strong motives to withhold; the only power left to her as a convicted and imprisoned criminal comes from a blend of these two motives. What is told by her to her audience of one, Dr. Simon Jordan — who is not only a more educated person than she is, but a man, which gave him an automatic edge in the nineteenth century, and a man with the potential to be of help to her — is selective, of course. It's dependent on what she remembers; or is it what she says she remembers, which can be quite a different thing? And how can her audience tell the difference? Here we are, right back at the end of the twentieth century, with our own uneasiness about the trustworthiness of memory, the reliability of story, and the continuity of time. In a Victorian novel, Grace would say, "Now it all comes back to me;" but as *Alias Grace* is not a Victorian novel, she does not say that; and if she did, would we — any longer — believe her?

These are the sorts of questions that my own fictional excursion into the nevertheless real Canadian past left me asking. Nor did it escape me that a different writer, with access to exactly the same historical records, could have — and without doubt would have — written a very different sort of novel. I'm not one of those who believes there is no truth to be known; but I have to conclude that, although there undoubtedly was a truth — somebody did kill Nancy Montgomery — truth is sometimes unknowable, at least by us.

What does the past tell us? In and of itself, it tells us nothing. We have to be listening first, before it will say a word; and even so, listening means telling, and then retelling. It's we ourselves who must do such telling, about the past, if anything is to be said about it; and our audience is one another. After we in our turn have become the past, others will tell stories about us, and about our times; or not, as the case may be. Unlikely as it seems, it's possible we may not interest them.

But meanwhile, while we still have the chance, what should we ourselves tell? Or rather, what *do* we tell? Individual memory, history, and the novel are all selective: no one remembers everything, each historian picks out the facts he or she chooses to find significant, and every novel, whether historical or not, must limit its own scope. No one can tell all the stories there are. As for novelists, it's best if they confine themselves to the Ancient Mariner stories; that is, the stories that seize hold of them and torment them until they've grabbed a batch of unsuspecting Wedding Guests with their skinny hands, and held them with their glittering eyes or else their glittering prose, and told them a tale they cannot choose but hear.

Such stories are not about this or that slice of the past, or this or that political or social event, or this or that city or country or nationality, although of course these may enter into it, and often do. They are about human nature, which usually means they are about pride, envy, avarice, lust, sloth, gluttony, and anger. They are about truth and lies, and disguises and revelations; they are about crime and punishment; they are about love and forgiveness and long-suffering and charity, they are about sin and retribution and sometimes even redemption.

In the recent film *Il Postino*, the great poet Pablo Neruda upbraids his friend, a lowly postman, for having filched one of Neruda's poems to use in his courtship of a local girl. "But," replies the postman, "poems do not belong to those who write them. Poems belong to those who need them." And so it is with stories about the past. The past no longer belongs only to those who lived in it; the past belongs to those who claim it, and are willing to explore it, and to infuse it with meaning for those alive today. The past belongs to us, because we are the ones who need it.

1. Robertson Davies, *The Merry Heart*, McClelland and Stewart, 1996, p. 358.
2. See, for instance, Ian Hacking, *Rewriting the Soul*, Princeton University Press, Princeton, 1995.
3. See, for instance, Paul Fussell's *The Great War and Modern Memory*.
4. Javier Marias, *All Souls*, The Harvill Press, London, 1995.
5. L. P. Hartley, *The Go-Between*, Hamish Hamilton, 1953.
6. CBC show about local museums, summer 1996.

26

MASTERPIECE THEATRE

TRICKSTER MAKES THIS WORLD: MISCHIEF, MYTH AND ART
THE GIFT: IMAGINATION AND THE EROTIC LIFE OF PROPERTY
BY LEWIS HYDE

TRICKSTER MAKES THIS WORLD: MISCHIEF, MYTH AND ART is Lewis Hyde's second masterpiece of — well, of what? Of wondering, of pertinent storytelling, pondering. Of making connections that seem both absolutely true and absolutely obvious once Hyde has made them but which we've somehow never noticed before. He's one of those quirky, eccentric Wise Children the United States sometimes throws up — a sort of Thoreau-cum-anthropologist-cum-seer, an asker of naive questions that turn out to be the reverse of naive, fascinated by why we behave the way we do, and why our right hand is often so blind to what our left hand is up to, and why it matters, especially to that elusive entity we've named the soul. Robert Bly calls Hyde a mythologist, which sort of fits, but perhaps he could also be called an illuminationist. In short, he casts light.

It's hard to discuss *Trickster Makes This World* apart from Hyde's first such syncretic masterpiece, *The Gift: Imagination and the Erotic Life of Property*. The classification on *The Gift*'s back cover reads "Literary Criticism/Sociology," but I expect many distraught bookstore workers have attempted to jam it also into "Anthropology," "Economics," "Theology," or "Philosophy." *The Gift* was first published in 1979 and has been in print ever since. It passes from hand to hand, primarily the hands of those in any way connected with the arts but also the hands of all who are interested in the sometimes arbitrary values placed on the material goods of this world. The primary question it poses is simple: Why is a poet, in our society, unlikely ever to be rich? Or, in another form: What is it about a series of romance novels designed entirely through market research that leads us to believe none of them will ever be a work of art? Or else: What is Keats's "Ode to a Nightingale" worth in dollar terms? In the course of explaining why the answer is both "nothing" and "it's priceless," Hyde stitches together not only folk tale and impressive erudition but biographical anecdote, personal observation, and anything else he finds useful, and on this flying patchwork he covers an immense amount of essential human ground.

By the pressures of the market economy we live in, he says, we've been fooled into believing that there is only one way in which things are exchanged: through money transactions, or buying and selling. Yet on some level we know there's another economy at work in human societies: the gift economy, which has quite different rules and consequences. It's the relation between the two economies that *The Gift* explores. In the course of reading it, we discover how "Indian givers" got their undeserved name, why usury developed the way it did, why you don't normally charge for donating a kidney to your brother, why women were traditionally "given" in marriage and sons were "given" by mothers in war, and why the Welsh passed free meals over the coffins of their dead.

Money transactions create no bonds of love or gratitude and imply no obligations. Gifts, on the other hand, are reciprocal and also emotionally loaded: market exchanges move through the bank account, gifts through the heart. Where the gift circulates, spiritual life flourishes. All societies exist in both economies, says Hyde, but each tends to value one economy over the other. Our own society has overemphasized the market and denied the gift, and the result is stagnant wealth on the one hand and spiritual death and material poverty on the other.

The artist belongs primarily to the gift economy; without that element of creation that arrives uncommanded and cannot be bought, the work is unlikely to be alive. *The Gift* is the best book I know of for the aspiring young, for talented but unacknowledged creators, or even for those who have achieved material success and are worried that this means they've sold out. It gets to the core of their dilemma: how to maintain yourself alive in the world of money when the essential part of what you do cannot be bought or sold. All literary and theatrical and film agents should read this book; they may be surprised to learn what a mythological role they play as guardians of the threshold that separates gift from dollar transaction but which must somehow be crossed if the artist is to eat. *The Gift* should also be read by every patron, every legislator, and every diehard opponent of arts funding. It lights up the dark corners.

Trickster Makes This World picks up a motif from *The Gift* in which the god Hermes, or Mercury, makes an appearance as that part of the human imagination that governs quick changes, as well as quick money exchanges. If you pray to Hermes, Hyde notes, you'll get action, but it will be action with no moral strings attached and no guarantees: Hermes goes in for one-night stands. (He's also the patron of thieves, liars, crossroads, footloose wandering, and the guide for souls on their way to the underworld. In his role as messenger to the gods, he used to appear on the cover of our telephone book, with his midsection modestly wreathed in trunk line cables.)

As Hyde points out, Hermes has many brothers in cultures worldwide. Coyote and Raven in North America; Eshu and Legba in Africa; the Monkey King in China; Krishna in India; not to mention Brer Rabbit of the American South: these are a few of the trickster figures whose devious ways Hyde explores. (Why are they all male? That would be telling. Read on!) In every culture that has a trickster god, it's the other gods who have made the various forms of perfection, but it's the trickster who's responsible for the changes — the mistakes, if you like — that have brought about the sometimes deplorable mess and the sometimes joyful muddle of this world as it is.

And what an ambiguous creature trickster is! He's cunning personified, a sleight-of-hand artist and a cheat, yet through his overweening curiosity and his tendency to meddle in things about which he lacks true knowledge, he often makes a fool of himself. He steals fire and burns his fingers. He lives by his wits, yet he falls into traps. He's subversive in that he disrupts conventions and transgressive because he crosses forbidden boundaries, yet he displays no overtly high and solemn purpose in these activities. He's a god, but a god of dirt and mixture and of shameless, unsanctioned sex. He's a teller of lies, but of lies without malice. He lies in order to cover up his thefts — thefts made from the motive of simple appetite or simply for the fun of stealing — or merely to fool people or to concoct stories or to stir things up. "Trickster," says Hyde, "feels no anxiety when he deceives. . . . He . . . can tell his lies with creative abandon, charm, playfulness, and by that affirm the pleasures of fabulation." As Hyde says, "Almost everything that can be said about psychopaths can also be said about tricksters," although the reverse is not the case. "Trickster is among other things the gatekeeper who opens the door into the next world; those who mistake him for a psychopath never even know such a door exists."

What is "the next world?" It might be the underworld or the world of the imagination, or — in real-life terms — the unobtainable, the denied, the forbidden: other cultures, other nations, other forms of sexuality, other classes and races. Hyde illustrates his theme not only with tales of the ancient gods and heroes but also with the work of present-day creators such as Maxine Hong Kingston and Allen Ginsberg — crossers of boundaries themselves and explorers of the crossing — and with the real people in whom the spirit of trickster has been incarnate. Foremost among these is Frederick Douglass, who in the nineteenth century crossed the perilous line dividing black from white, slave from free man, and in doing so turned the assumptions that governed such divisions upside down. Such figures remind us that it's Odysseus the trickster who tells a lie good enough to get his men alive out of the monster Cyclops's cave and Prometheus the trickster who steals fire from the gods and makes a gift of it to man. Through his daring and wiliness, trickster too can be a hero.

The pleasures of fabulation, the charming and playful lie — this line of thought leads Hyde to the last link in his subtitle, the connection of the trickster to art. Hyde reminds us that the wall between the artist and that American favourite son, the con artist, can be a thin one indeed; that craft and crafty rub shoulders; and that the words *artifice, artifact, articulation*, and *art* all come from the same ancient root, a word meaning "to join," "to fit," and "to make." If it's a seamless whole you want, pray to Apollo, who sets the limits within which such a work can exist. Tricksters, however, stand where the door swings open on its hinges and the horizon expands; they operate where things are joined together and, thus, can also come apart.

At the end of James Joyce's *A Portrait of the Artist as a Young Man*, cunning is one of the virtues invoked, and it's Daedalus, maker of mazes, to whom Stephen Dedalus addresses his invocation: "Old father, old artificer, stand me now and ever in good stead"; we can guess by this that Joyce has crafty disruption on his mind. Tricksters aren't the only kind of artists who exist, but there's a healthy population of trickster artists. Picasso and Marcel Duchamp — he of the urinal as found art — are just a couple of those on Hyde's list. Such artists can be mere lightweight playful brats, but they can also be those who come along when a tradition has become too set in its ways, too orderly, too Apollonian, and shake it out of its rut. And artists of whatever sort need trickster's help from time to time: When you're blocked or stuck, take an aimless walk and let your mind off its leash and call on trickster. He's the opener of dreams, of roads, and of possibilities. Like T. S. Eliot and Walt Whitman, both apple-cart upsetters in their day, he can tell you there are diamonds in the mud.

I've suggested just a few of the reasons why *Trickster Makes This World* will be as widely read by those in the arts as *The Gift* has been, but there are lots of other reasons, and lots of reasons too why this book should be read by anyone interested in the grand and squalid matter of all things human. Hyde's book is a glorious grab bag stuffed with necessary loot, a joyful plum pudding rich in treasures. Once more, we are indebted to him.

27

THE AWKWARD SUBLIME

I BEGAN TO READ Al Purdy's poetry about the same time it changed from being odd and ungainly to being remarkable — in the early 1960s. I was just into my twenties, writing a lot of poetry but not liking much of it; like most young poets then, I wanted to be published by Contact Press — a highly respected, poet-run co-operative — and I read everything they issued; and thus I read Al Purdy's *Poems for All the Annettes* in 1962, when it first came out.

I was somewhat frightened by it, and did not fully understand what he was doing. This was a new sort of voice for me, an over-powering one, and a little too much like being backed into the corner of a seedy bar by a large, insistent, untidy drunk, who is waxing by turns both sentimental and obscene. For a young male poet of those days, this kind of energy and this approach — casual, slangy, subversive of recent poetic convention — could be liberating and inspirational, and some found in him an ersatz father figure. But for a young female poet — well, this was not the sort of father figure it would be altogether steadying to have.

Then, in 1965, *The Cariboo Horses* — Purdy's breakthrough book — came out, and I found that the drunk in the bar was also a major storyteller and mythmaker, though still wearing his offhand and rather shabby disguise. This was poetry for the spoken voice par excellence — not an obviously rhetorical voice but an anecdotal one, the voice of the Canadian vernacular. Yet not only that either, for no sooner had Purdy set up his own limits than he'd either transcend or subvert them. He was always questioning, always probing, and among those things that he questioned and probed were himself and his own poetic methods. In a Purdy poem, high diction can meet the scrawl on the washroom wall, and, as in a collision between matter and antimatter, both explode.

It would be folly to attempt to sum up Purdy's poetic universe: like Walt Whitman's it's too vast for a précis. What interested him could be anything, but above all the wonder that anything at all can be interesting. He was always turning banality inside out. For me, he was, above all, an explorer — pushing into nameless areas of landscape, articulating the inarticulate, poking around in dusty corners of memory and discovering treasure there, digging up the bones and shards of a forgotten ancestral past. When he wasn't capering about and joking and scratching his head over the idiocy and pain and delight of being alive, he was composing lyric elegies for what was no longer alive, but had been — and, through his words, still is. For underneath that flapping overcoat and that tie with a mermaid on it and that pretence of shambling awkwardness — yes, it was a pretence, but only partly, for among other things Purdy was doing a true impersonation of himself — there was a skilful master conjurer. Listen to the voice, and watch the hands at work: just hands, a bit grubby too, not doing anything remarkable, and you can't see how it's done, but suddenly, where a second ago there was only a broken vase, there's a fistful of brilliant flowers.

PART III

2001–2004

2001–2004

In the first part of 2001 I was still on book tour for *The Blind Assassin*. I'd got as far as New Zealand and Australia and was taking a break in Queensland to do some birdwatching with friends when I unaccountably found myself beginning another novel — a process described in the short piece, "Writing *Oryx and Crake*."

I continued with this novel back in Canada. I wrote part of it on an island in Lake Erie, where my novel-writing was sadly interrupted by the untimely death of Mordecai Richler. Several other friends and fellow writers also died during this period, and I wrote about some of them. "The Wrong Box" was written for a collection dedicated to the work of Matt Cohen, who died of cancer in 1999. The tribute given at Timothy Findley's memorial and my celebration of Carol Shields are also reprinted here.

I wrote some of *Oryx and Crake* on a boat in the Arctic. On September 11, 2001, I was in the Toronto airport waiting for a plane to New York for the paperback launch of *The Blind Assassin* when the catastrophe took place. One of the pieces in this section is connected with that event. At that period I was working on an introduction to H. Rider Haggard's peculiar novel *She*; the editor on this quixotic project was a young man called Benjamin Dreyer, and it was from him that I was able to learn — via e-mail, during that time of blocked phone lines — that my friends and colleagues in New York were safe.

In times of crisis, the temptation is to throw everything into defence mode, to believe that the best defence is offence — which can lead, in the human body, to death from your own immune response — and to jettison the very values you thought you were defending in the first place. Too often, the operation can be a success, but the patient dies. Urgers of moderation and multilateralism are seen as wimps, and chest-thumping becomes the order of the day. My "Letter to America" was written because back in the summer of 2002 I made a promise to Victor Navasky, the editor of *The Nation*, to write such a thing, before the invasion of Iraq was even mentioned. It appeared just before that invasion began, was widely reprinted, and generated a great deal of response from around the world. The essay on Napoleon's mistakes came from my reading of history and my sense of caution.

This section might well be called "A Fistful of Editors," in tribute to the many editors I have worked with over the years. In occasional writing, it is usually the editors who come up with the occasions. Then they cajole you into writing about them, hold your hand while you're doing it, and attempt to save you from your more embarrassing mistakes. There have been magazine editors, newspaper editors, editors of anthologies, editors in charge of introductions and afterwords. They've all been wonderful. Some new editors came into my life at this period — Erica Wagner of *The Times*, Robert Silvers of the *New York Review of Books*. Mr. Silvers is the only editor I know who seems to be at his most elegant and charming — at least on the subject of semicolons — over the phone and in the middle of the night. That is probably why he always gets his way.

Whenever I think I'm coming to resemble Melmoth the Ponderer, or The Restless Unread, prowling by night and pouncing on unwary readers, or one of the Scribes of Dracula, chained in a cellar, eating flies, and doomed to scribble endlessly — whenever I resolve to write less and do something healthful instead, like ice dancing — some honey-tongued editor is sure to call me up and make me an offer I can't refuse.

The last piece in this collection was written for yet another editor, Robin Robertson, a poet and fellow trustee of the Griffin Poetry Prizes. The piece, called "Mortification," was written for a collection of anecdotes by writers about the gruesome things that have happened to them in public. Most of these gruesome things have been connected with the publication of one or another of their books, but despite the gruesome things — which can go well beyond a joke in countries that discourage free public speech — the writers are not deterred.

What is it, this compulsion? Why this boundless outflowing of words? What drives them to it? Is writing some sort of disease, or — being speech in visual form — is it simply a manifestation of being human?

28

MORDECAI RICHLER: 1931–2001

DIOGENES OF MONTREAL

MORDECAI RICHLER is gone, and a major light has been snuffed out. But what sort of light? No athlete's torch, no angel's halo. Picture instead the lantern of grumpy, scathing, barrel-dwelling Diogenes, who walked around in daylight searching for an honest man.

Mordecai was the searcher and the honest man both, and equally distrustful of fine feathers. Tarted up for grand events, he somehow gave the impression that he'd be happier in the barrel. Rumpled, tie askew, glass of Scotch at his elbow, thin cigar in mouth, his sad bloodhound's gaze fixed on the bogusness of the passing scene, while in one hand he held the pen that was both lance (as in chivalry, as in boil) and balloon-puncturing pin — this is the image of him beloved by his public and perfected by his friend Aislin, the celebrated cartoonist. Mordecai seemed so permanent, so substantial, so on top of things, so much to be depended on when each new hot-air blimp loomed into view, that it's difficult to believe in his mortality.

But — as with all fine writers — mortality was his subject. Human nature, in all its nakedness, paltriness, silliness, avariciousness, crassness, meanness, and downright evil — he knew it inside out, having had a ringside view as he came of age in a poor Jewish area of Montreal during the Depression and then witnessed not only the atrocities but also the hypocrisies of the Second World War, followed — for him — by the hard scrabbling of the literary life in London, as seen from the bottom.

He'd paid — as we say — his dues. His bullshit radar was acute, his hopes for the innate goodness of the human species not very high, and in this he was a satirist, a true child of Jonathan Swift. When he went after separatism in Quebec, he rubbed fur the wrong way; but all of his fur-rubbing was deliberate — he would have been horrified to have wounded the innocent, unintentionally. Quebec was hardly alone: anyone was fair game, so long as the target had committed the ultimate sin in his eyes, which was — or so I'd guess — pomposity.

His propensity for skewering the inflated, coupled with a wonderful sense of mischief, produced some of the most hilarious moments in Canadian literature. The pretentious "art" film of a bar mitzvah in *The Apprenticeship of Duddy Kravitz*, the travesty of the Franklin expedition in *Solomon Gursky Was Here*, in which the heroic sailors dress up in ladies' frillies — this is Mordecai at his most inventively outrageous. But every satirist cherishes an alternative to the vices and follies he depicts, and so did Mordecai. His alternative was not so far from that of Charles Dickens — the warm-hearted, sane, and decent human being — and this side of him comes to the fore in his novels, most particularly in his tragicomic meditation on fallibility, *Barney's Version*. Behind the formidable public persona was a shy and generous man, who gave his time to efforts he believed in — most recently, the "best-book-only" Giller Prize, for which he served as an architect and first-year juror.

He was a consummate professional with high standards and no time for fools, but he was also a dear man who was loved by everyone who knew him well, respected by his fellow writers, and trusted by his many devoted readers to tell it straight. For my generation, he was a trailblazer who went on to create and occupy a unique place in our national life and literature, and we will miss him very much.

29

INTRODUCTION

SHE

BY H. RIDER HAGGARD

WHEN I FIRST READ H. Rider Haggard's highly famous novel *She*, I didn't know it was highly famous. I was a teenager, it was the 1950s, and *She* was just one of the many books in the cellar. My father unwittingly shared with Jorge Luis Borges a liking for nineteenth-century yarns with touches of the uncanny coupled with rip-roaring plots; and so, in the cellar, where I was supposed to be doing my homework, I read my way through Rudyard Kipling and Conan Doyle, and *Dracula* and *Frankenstein*, and Robert Louis Stevenson and H. G. Wells, and also Henry Rider Haggard. I read *King Solomon's Mines* first, with its adventures and tunnels and lost treasure, and then *Allan Quatermain*, with its adventures and tunnels and lost civilization. And then I read *She*.

I had no sociocultural context for these books then — the British Empire was the pink part of the map, "imperialism and colonialism" had not yet acquired their special negative charge, and the accusation "sexist" was far in the future. Nor did I make any distinctions between great literature and any other kind. I just liked reading. Any book that began with some mysterious inscriptions on a very old broken pot was fine with me, and that is how *She* begins. There was even a picture at the front of my edition — not a drawing of the pot but a *photograph* of it, to make the yarn really convincing. (The pot was made to order by Haggard's sister-in-law; he intended it to function like the pirate map at the beginning of *Treasure Island* — a book the popularity of which he hoped to rival — and it did.)

Most outrageous tales state at the very beginning that what follows is so incredible the reader will have trouble believing it, which is both a come-on and a challenge. The messages on the pot stretch credulity, but having deciphered them, the two heroes of *She* — the gorgeous but none too bright Leo Vincey and the ugly but intelligent Horace Holly — are off to Africa to hunt up the beautiful, undying sorceress who is supposed to have killed Leo's distant ancestor. Curiosity is their driving force, vengeance is their goal. Many a hardship later, and after having narrowly escaped death at the hands of the savage and matrilineal tribe of the Amahagger, they find not only the ruins of a vast and once-powerful civilization and the numerous mummified bodies of the same but also, dwelling among the tombs, the self-same undying sorceress, ten times lovelier, wiser, and more ruthless than they had dared to imagine.

As Queen of the Amahagger, "She-who-must-be-obeyed" wafts around wrapped up like a corpse in order to inspire fear; but once tantalizingly peeled, under those gauzy wrappings is a stunner, and — what's more — a virgin. "She," it turns out, is two thousand years old. Her real name is Ayesha. She claims she was once a priestess of the Egyptian nature-goddess Isis. She's been saving herself for two millennia, waiting for the man she loves: one Kallikrates, a very good-looking priest of Isis and the ancestor of Leo Vincey. This man broke his vows and ran off with Leo's ancestress, whereupon Ayesha slew him in a fit of jealous rage. For two thousand years she's been waiting for him to be reincarnated; she's even got his preserved corpse enshrined in a side room, where she laments over it every night. A point-by-point comparison reveals — what a surprise! — that Kallikrates and Leo Vincey are identical.

Having brought Leo to his knees with her knockout charms, and having polished off Ustane, a more normal sort of woman with whom Leo has formed a sexual pair-bond, and who just happens to be a reincarnation of Ayesha's ancient Kallikrates-stealing enemy, She now demands that Leo accompany her into the depths of a nearby mountain. There, She says, is where the secret of extremely long and more abundant life is to be found. Not only that, She and Leo can't be One until he is as powerful as She — the union might otherwise kill him (as it does, in the sequel, *Ayesha: The Vengeance of She*). So off to the mountain they go, via the ruins of the ancient, once-imperial city of Kôr. To get the renewed life, all one has to do — after the usual Haggard adventures and tunnels — is to traverse some caverns measureless to man, step into a very noisy rolling pillar of fire, and then make one's getaway across a bottomless chasm.

This is how She acquired her powers two thousand years before, and to show a hesitating Leo how easy it is, She does it again. Alas, this time the thing works backward, and in a few instants Ayesha shrivels up into a very elderly bald monkey and then crumbles into dust. Leo and Holly, both hopelessly in love with She and both devastated, totter back to civilization, trusting in Her promise that She will return.

As a good read in the cellar, this was all very satisfactory, despite the overblown way in which She tended to express herself. *She* was an odd book in that it placed a preternaturally powerful woman at the centre of things: the only other such woman I'd run into so far had been the Wonder Woman of the comics, with her sparkly lasso and star-spangled panties. Both Ayesha and Wonder Woman went all weak-kneed when it came to the man they loved — Wonder Woman lost her magic powers when kissed by her boyfriend, Steve Trevor; Ayesha couldn't focus on conquering the world unless Leo Vincey would join her in that dubious enterprise — and I was callow enough, at fifteen, to find this part of it not only soppily romantic but pretty hilarious. Then I graduated from high school and discovered good taste, and forgot for a while about *She*.

For a while, but not forever. In the early 1960s I found myself in graduate school, in Cambridge, Massachusetts. There I was exposed to Widener Library, a much larger and more organized version of the cellar; that is, it contained many sorts of books, not all of which bore the Great Literature Seal of Approval. Once I was let loose in the stacks, my penchant for not doing my homework soon reasserted itself, and it wasn't long before I was snuffling around in Rider Haggard and his ilk once more.

This time, however, I had some excuse. My field of specialization was the nineteenth century, and I was busying myself with Victorian quasi-goddesses; and no one could accuse Haggard of not being Victorian. Like his age, which practically invented archaeology, he was an amateur of vanished civilizations; also like his age, he was fascinated by the exploration of unmapped territories and encounters with "undiscovered" native peoples. As an individual, he was such a cookie-cutter county gentleman — albeit with some African travelling in his past — that it was hard to fathom where his overheated imagination had come from, though it may have been this by-the-book-English-establishment quality that allowed him to bypass intellectual analysis completely. He could sink a core-sampling drill straight down into the great English Victorian unconscious, where fears and desires — especially male fears and desires — swarmed in the darkness like blind fish. Or so claimed Henry Miller, among others.

Where did it all come from? In particular, where did the figure of She come from — old-young, powerful-powerless, beautiful-hideous, dweller among tombs, obsessed with an undying love, deeply in touch with the forces of Nature and thus of Life and Death? Haggard and his siblings were said to have been terrorized by an ugly rag doll that lived in a dark cupboard and was named "She-who-must-be-obeyed," but there is more to it than that. *She* was published in 1887, and thus came at the height of the fashion for sinister but seductive women. It looked back also on a long tradition of the same.

Ayesha's literary ancestresses include the young-but-old supernatural women in George MacDonald's "Curdie" fantasies, but also various Victorian femmes fatales: Tennyson's Vivien in *Idylls of the King*, bent on stealing Merlin's magic; the Pre-Raphaelite temptresses created in both poem and picture by Rossetti and William Morris; Swinburne's dominatrixes; Wagner's nasty pieces of female work, including the very old but still toothsome Kundry of *Parsifal*; and, most especially, the Mona Lisa of Walter Pater's famous prose poem, older than the rocks upon which she sits, yet young and lovely, and mysterious, and filled to the brim with experiences of a distinctly suspect nature.

As Sandra Gilbert and Susan Gubar pointed out in their 1989 book, *No Man's Land*, the ascendency in the arts of these potent but dangerous female figures is by no means unconnected with the rise of "Woman" in the nineteenth century, and with the hotly debated issues of her "true nature" and her "rights," and also with the anxieties and fantasies these controversies generated. If women ever came to wield political power — to which they were surely, by their natures, unsuited — what would they do with it? And if they were beautiful and desirable women, capable of attacking on the sexual as well as the political front, wouldn't they drink men's blood, sap their vitality, and reduce them to grovelling serfs? As the century opened, Wordsworth's Mother Nature was benign, and "never would betray / The heart that loved her"; but by the end of the century, Nature and the women so firmly linked to her were much more likely to be red in tooth and claw — Darwinian goddesses rather than Wordsworthian ones. When, in *She*, Ayesha appropriates the fiery phallic pillar at the heart of Nature for the second time, it's just as well that it works backward. Otherwise men could kiss their own phallic pillars goodbye.

"You are a whale at parables and allegories and one thing reflecting another," wrote Rudyard Kipling in a letter to Rider Haggard, and there appear to be various hints and verbal signposts scattered over the landscape of *She*. For instance, the Amahagger, the tribe ruled by She, bears a name that not only encapsulates *hag* but also conflates the Latin root for *love* with the name of Abraham's banished wilderness-dwelling concubine, Hagar, and thus brings to mind a story of two women competing for one man. The ancient city of Kôr is named perhaps for *core*, cognate with the French *coeur*, but suggesting also *corps*, for body, and thus *corpse*, for dead body; for She is in part a Nightmare Life-in-Death. Her horrid end is reminiscent of Darwinian evolution played backward — woman into monkey — but also of vampires after the stake-into-the-heart manoeuvre. (Bram Stoker's *Dracula* appeared after *She*, but Sheridan LeFanu's *Carmilla* predates it, as does many another vampire story.) These associations and more point toward some central significance that Haggard himself could never fully explicate, though he chalked up a sequel and a couple of prequels trying. "*She*," he said, was "some gigantic allegory of which I could not catch the meaning."

Haggard claimed to have written *She* "at white heat," in six weeks — "It came," he said, "faster than my poor aching hand could set it down," which would suggest hypnotic trance or possession. In the heyday of Freudian and Jungian analysis, *She* was much explored and admired, by Freudians for its womb-and-phallus images, by Jungians for its anima figures and thresholds. Northrop Frye, proponent of the theory of archetypes in literature, says this of *She* in his 1975 book, *The Secular Scripture: A Study of the Structure of Romance*:

> In the theme of the apparently dead and buried heroine who comes to life again, one of the themes of Shakespeare's *Cymbeline*, we seem to be getting a more undisplaced glimpse of the earth-mother at the bottom of the world. In later romance there is another glimpse of such a figure in Rider Haggard's *She*, a beautiful and sinister female ruler, buried in the depths of a dark continent, who is much involved with archetypes of death and rebirth. . . . Embalmed mummies suggest Egypt, which is

preeminently the land of death and burial, and, largely because of its Biblical role, of descent to a lower world.

Whatever *She* may have been thought to signify, its impact upon publication was tremendous. *Everyone* read it, especially men; a whole generation was influenced by it, and the generation after that. A dozen or so films have been based on it, and a huge amount of the pulp-magazine fiction churned out in the early twentieth century bears its impress. Every time a young but possibly old and/or dead woman turns up, especially if she's ruling a lost tribe in a wilderness and is a hypnotic seductress, you're looking at a descendant of She.

Literary writers too felt Her foot on their necks. Conrad's *Heart of Darkness* owes a lot to Her, as Gilbert and Gubar have indicated. James Hilton's Shangri-La, with its ancient, beautiful, and eventually crumbling heroine, is an obvious relative. C. S. Lewis felt Her power, fond as he was of creating sweet-talking, good-looking evil queens; and in Tolkien's *The Lord of the Rings*, She splits into two: Galadriel, powerful but good, who's got exactly the same water mirror as the one possessed by She; and a very ancient cave-dwelling man-devouring spider-creature named, tellingly, Shelob.

Would it be out of the question to connect the destructive Female Will, so feared by D. H. Lawrence and others, with the malign aspect of She? For Ayesha is a supremely transgressive female who challenges male power; though her shoe size is tiny and her fingernails are pink, she's a rebel at heart. If only she hadn't been hobbled by love, she would have used her formidable energies to overthrow the established civilized order. That the established civilized order was white and male and European goes without saying; thus She's power was not only female — of the heart, of the body — but barbaric, and "dark."

By the time we find John Mortimer's Rumpole of the Bailey referring to his dumpy, kitchen-cleanser-conscious wife as "she who must be obeyed," the once-potent figure has been secularized and demythologized, and has dwindled into the combination of joke and rag doll that it may have been in its origins. Nevertheless, we must not forget one of Ayesha's pre-eminent powers — the ability to reincarnate herself. Like the vampire dust at the end of Christopher Lee movies, blowing away only to reassemble itself at the outset of the next film, She could come back. And back. And back.

No doubt this is because She is in some ways a permanent feature of the human imagination. She's one of the giants of the nursery, a threatening but compelling figure, bigger and better than life. Also worse, of course. And therein lies her attraction.

Sources

Atwood, Margaret. "Superwoman Drawn and Quartered: The Early Forms of *She*." *Alphabet* magazine vol. 10, July 1965.

Frye, Northrop. *The Secular Scripture: A Study of the Structure of Romance*. Cambridge, Mass.: Harvard University Press, 1976.

Gilbert, Sandra M., and Susan Gubar. *No Man's Land: The Place of the Woman Writer in the Twentieth Century, vol. 2: Sexchanges*. New Haven: Yale University Press, 1989.

Karlin, Daniel. Introduction, in Haggard, H. Rider, *She*. Oxford: Oxford University Press, 1991.

30

WHEN AFGHANISTAN WAS AT PEACE

IN FEBRUARY 1978, almost twenty-three years ago, I visited Afghanistan with my spouse, Graeme Gibson, and our eighteen-month-old daughter. We went there almost by chance: we were on our way to the Adelaide literary festival in Australia. Pausing at intervals, we felt, would surely be easier on a child's time clock. (Wrong, as it turned out.) We thought Afghanistan would make a fascinating two-week stopover. Its military history impressed us — neither Alexander the Great nor the British in the nineteenth century had stayed in the country long because of the ferocity of its warriors.

"Don't go to Afghanistan," my father said when told of our plans. "There's going to be a war there." He was fond of reading history books. "As Alexander the Great said, Afghanistan is easy to march into but hard to march out of." But we hadn't heard any other rumours of war, so off we went.

We were among the last to see Afghanistan in its days of relative peace — relative, because even then there were tribal disputes and superpowers in play. The three biggest buildings in Kabul were the Chinese embassy, the Soviet embassy, and the American embassy, and the head of the country was reportedly playing the three against one another.

The houses of Kabul were carved wood, and the streets were like a living *Book of Hours*: people in flowing robes, camels, donkeys, carts with huge wooden wheels being pushed and pulled by men at either end. There were few motorized vehicles. Among them were buses covered with ornate Arabic script, with eyes painted on the front so the buses could see where they were going.

We managed to hire a car in order to see the terrain of the famous and disastrous British retreat from Kabul to Jalalabad. The scenery was breathtaking: jagged mountains and the *Arabian Nights* dwellings in the valleys — part houses, part fortresses — reflected in the enchanted blue-green of the rivers. Our driver took the switchback road at breakneck speed since we had to be back before sundown because of bandits.

The men we encountered were friendly and fond of children: our curly-headed, fair-haired child got a lot of attention. The winter coat I wore had a large hood so that I was sufficiently covered and did not attract undue notice. Many wanted to talk; some knew English, while others spoke through our driver. But they all addressed Graeme exclusively. To have spoken to me would have been impolite. And yet when our interpreter negotiated our entry into an all-male tea house, I received nothing worse than uneasy glances. The law of hospitality toward visitors ranked higher than the no-women-in-the-tea-house custom. In the hotel, those who served meals and cleaned rooms were men, tall men with scars either from duelling or from the national sport, played on horseback, in which gaining possession of a headless calf is the aim.

Girls and women we glimpsed on the street wore the chador, the long, pleated garment with a crocheted grill for the eyes that is more comprehensive than any other Muslim cover-up. At that time, you often saw chic boots and shoes peeking out from the hem. The chador wasn't obligatory back then; Hindu women didn't wear it. It was a cultural custom, and since I had grown up hearing that you weren't decently dressed without a girdle and white gloves, I thought

I could understand such a thing. I also knew that clothing is a symbol, that all symbols are ambiguous, and that this one might signify a fear of women or a desire to protect them from the gaze of strangers. But it could also mean more negative things, just as the colour red can mean love, blood, life, royalty, good luck — or sin.

I bought a chador in the market. A jovial crowd of men gathered around, amused by the spectacle of a Western woman picking out such a non-Western item. They offered advice about colour and quality. Purple was better than light green or the blue, they said. (I bought the purple.) Every writer wants the Cloak of Invisibility — the power to see without being seen — or so I was thinking as I donned the chador. But once I had put it on, I had an odd sense of having been turned into negative space, a blank in the visual field, a sort of antimatter — both there and not there. Such a space has power of a sort, but it is a passive power, the power of taboo.

Several weeks after we left Afghanistan, the war broke out. My father was right, after all. Over the next years, we often remembered the people we met and their courtesy and curiosity. How many of them are now dead, through no fault of their own?

Six years after our trip, I wrote *The Handmaid's Tale*, a speculative fiction about an American theocracy. The women in that book wear outfits derived in part from nuns' costumes, partly from girls' school hemlines, and partly — I must admit — from the faceless woman on the Old Dutch Cleanser box, but also partly from the chador I acquired in Afghanistan and its conflicting associations. As one character says, there is freedom to and freedom from. But how much of the first should you have to give up in order to assure the second? All cultures have had to grapple with that, and our own — as we are now seeing — is no exception. Would I have written the book if I never visited Afghanistan? Possibly. Would it have been the same? Unlikely.

31

MYSTERY MAN

SOME CLUES TO DASHIELL HAMMETT

The Selected Letters of Dashiell Hammett, 1921–1960
Edited by Richard Layman with Julie M. Rivett

Dashiell Hammett: A Daughter Remembers
By Jo Hammett, edited by Richard Layman with Julie M. Rivett

Dashiell Hammett: Crime Stories and Other Writings
Selected and edited by Steven Marcus

WHEN I WAS a preadolescent spending summers in northern Canada, I read a lot of old detective fiction because it was there. When I'd got through the pile I read some of it over again, there being no library where I could go and get more. I didn't reread Erle Stanley Gardner or Ellery Queen: I found them dry. But I did reread Dashiell Hammett.

What was it about these books that intrigued me as an avid but ignorant child reader? Their world was fast-paced, sharp-edged, and filled with zippy dialogue and words I'd never heard pronounced — slang words like *gunsel*, fancy words like *punctilious*. This was not the Agatha Christie sort of story — there were fewer clues, and these were more likely to be lies people told rather than cuff buttons they'd left strewn around. There were more corpses, with less importance bestowed on each: a new character would appear, only to be gunned down by a fire-spitting revolver. In a "clues" novel, everything depended on who was where; in a Hammett one, it was more likely to be who was who, given to disguises and false names as these folk were. The action was dispersed, not sealed up as in a nobody-leaves-this-house puzzle: dark mean streets were prowled, cars were driven at speed, people blew in from elsewhere and hid out and skipped town. Oddly enough, clothing was described in more detail than in many country-house murders — a feature I appreciated. There was a lot of drinking, of substances I had never heard of, and a great deal of smoking. As an eleven-year-old I found this world very, very sophisticated.

It's odd to think that in July of 1951, while I was trying to figure out why a man would turn a strange shade of yellow, with bloodshot eyes, while telling a woman that maybe he loved her and maybe she loved him but he wasn't going to play the sap for her, the author of the books that so fascinated me was about to be jailed. The McCarthy Red Scare was at its height, and Hammett had been called into U.S. district court as a representative of the Civil Rights Congress Bail Fund to be questioned about four fugitives. Notoriously, he refused to testify. He wouldn't even give his name. The man whose books had been legends in their time had now become a legend of a different kind: exemplary not only of a certain kind of American fiction but also of a certain kind of American life.

Forty years after his death, Dashiell Hammett continues to intrigue. While he was still alive, Raymond Chandler wrote his famous 1944 tribute to him, *The Simple Art of Murder*. After his death, his companion of many years and literary executrix, Lillian Hellman, served him up as a dreamlike portrait in her 1973 memoir, *Pentimento*. Attempting to control the legend, Hellman then authorized a biography[1]; there have been several unauthorized biographies as well.

In 2001, there were three new additions to works by and about Hammett: *The Selected Letters of Dashiell Hammett, 1921–1960*, edited by Richard Layman with Hammett's granddaughter Julie M. Rivett; *Dashiell Hammett: A Daughter Remembers*, a personal memoir by Hammett's second daughter, Josephine, who also supplied a foreword for the *Selected Letters*; and *Dashiell Hammett: Crime Stories and Other Writings*, selected and edited by Steven Marcus.

The man who created and solved so many mysteries left quite a few of his own behind him, it seems: many have been the attempts to explicate him. Where did his talent come from? Why the extreme drinking, the reckless spending? Why the communism, in such a patriotic American? Why the sudden creative silence, and then that other silence, the one that landed him in jail? Did Lillian Hellman exhaust him, or was she on the contrary his right-hand gal and kindly keeper? These are the sorts of questions that have raised themselves over time.

Those who have read even a little about Hammett know the main outlines of the plot. It's laid before us in condensed form at the end of *Dashiell Hammett: Crime Stories and Other Writings*, and again in the excellent summaries dividing the periods of his life in the *Selected Letters*, and yet again, in a different mode, in Jo Hammett's memoir.

This last is exactly what the jacket says it is: a reminiscence presented in "straightforward prose, with unaffected charm." It contains a lot of photos, and some new, suggestive information about Hammett's family background. It also tells the story of how the photos came to light — one of those proverbial stashes of old cardboard boxes in the garage that turn out to be a treasure trove. Jo Hammett writes concisely, with much personal anecdote and wry observation. She sees her father from a necessarily intimate angle, and though she adored him, she also naturally resented his treatment of the family — of her mother Jose, her older sister Mary, and herself. Hammett wasn't evil or violent, and he tried to send sufficient money; he gave the daughters lavish treats; he wrote them loving, funny letters; but he was seldom there.

Jo Hammett saves the largest part of her resentment for Lillian Hellman, who seems to have deserved it. Ms. Hammett tries her best to acknowledge Hellman's virtues — she was smart, she had good taste, she took care of Hammett during his last, broke decade — but it costs her a lot of teeth grinding to do so. Hellman, it seems, was close to being a mythomaniac, and a ruthless power player; gaining control of Hammett's copyrights was one of her milder gambits. No Other Woman would have come out well from the daughter's point of view, but this portrait of Hellman does raise a question: What did Hammett see in her? As his daughter says, he appreciated people who went too far, as he often did himself; and his admiration for attractive women who lied outrageously — so evident in *The Maltese Falcon* and elsewhere — predates Hellman. It's another of Hammett's enigmas, for otherwise he set great store by speaking honestly.

Samuel Dashiell Hammett was born in rural Maryland in 1894. As a boy he wanted to read all the books in the Baltimore public library, but he had to quit high school at the age of fourteen to help out with the shaky family finances. (His father, whom he didn't like, was a spendthrift, drinker, sharp dresser, and womanizer; but unlike Hammett, who resembled him in all these respects, he was mean and stingy.) At twenty-one, Hammett got a job as a Pinkerton's detective agency operative, which he left in 1918 to join the army. He suffered the first of many severe respiratory illnesses then. During one recuperation he married a nurse he met at the infirmary; then he signed on at Pinkerton's once more, but his health broke down. It was then that he began writing crime stories for the pulps.[2]

Once Hammett had teamed up with the magazine *Black Mask*, an astonishing burst of creativity followed. He turned out stories at an amazing rate, followed by five highly successful novels, including *Red Harvest*, *The Dain Curse*, *The Glass Key*, and *The Maltese Falcon*, this last perhaps the best-known American crime novel of all time. By that time he was famous and rich, but he was also drinking and spending money, both at a prodigal rate. Then followed the liaison with Lillian Hellman and his silence as a writer. Later in the 1930s he became involved in the activities of the Communist Party of America, as did many who were appalled by the rise of fascism. That he had been a witness to violent union busting during his Pinkerton days may also have played a part.[3] After serving in the army during the Second World War — he edited an army paper in the Aleutians — he was caught in the Red Scare dragnet and jailed for contempt of court. His books and the radio shows based on them were blacklisted and the IRS went after him for back taxes. He came out of prison minus his health and his money, neither of which he ever regained. He died in 1961, at the age of sixty-six.

The *Selected Letters* was made possible by the same lucky garage find that enabled Jo Hammett to piece together her memoir. All of the letters are by Hammett: the answers to them have disappeared. Most of the letters are to women — his wife, his daughters, Lillian Hellman, other mistresses, and women friends — either because women saved the letters, or because Hammett felt more comfortable writing to women than to men. Reading them is like reading the letters of anyone you don't know — first names you can't place, books you've never heard of, private jokes you don't get — but then some bon mot or caustic remark will liven things up again. ("Bruce Lockwood, who has been borrowing money from me, sent me a dozen of his wife's horrible watercolors, from which I'm supposed to select a couple to be gifted with.") Many letters are ornamented with drawings or stuck with newspaper clippings; some are whimsical pieces of wordplay. They're the letters of a man who loved to write, to flirt, and to amuse others. It's plain to see why women liked him.

The letters have been meticulously edited, and among them are some documents that will be very helpful to anyone studying — for instance — American intellectual and political life of the 1930s and

1940s. The letters to Hammett's first daughter, Mary, in which he tries to answer her questions about the chief issues of the day — Why support the Republican side in the Spanish Civil War?, What's the scoop on Hitler — are particularly sober and thoughtful. The letters to Lillian Hellman show that the two of them had — whatever their respective failings — a deep-rooted, enduring, and often frisky relationship, though it's somewhat unnerving to come across the tough and ambitious Hellman being addressed as "my little cabbage."

The letters begin in 1921, with a series to Josephine Dolan, soon to become Hammett's wife. Anyone who was around in the first half of the twentieth century will recognize the young-man-to-girlfriend style. He teases her and sweet-talks, and brags about how much hell he's been raising. Presumably she scolded him about his health and teased him in return. It's a sweet beginning.

Another sweet beginning is his letters to the editor of *Black Mask*. Already, in 1923, he's making fun of himself: Creda Dexter in "The Tenth Clew" is described as looking like a kitten, but Hammett confesses to the *Black Mask* editor that her original looked "exactly like a young white-faced bull pup." Then, he claims, his nerve failed him:

> "Nobody will believe you if you write a thing like that," I told myself. "They'll think you're trying to spoof them." So, for the sake of plausibility, I lied about her. . . .

But such gentle ridicule of the genre alternates with earnestness: in a 1928 letter to his book publisher, he says he wants to try adapting the "stream-of-consciousness method" to the detective story. "I'm one of the few — if there are any more — people moderately literate who take the detective story seriously," he says.

> I don't mean that I necessarily take my own or anybody else's seriously — but the detective story as a form. Some day

somebody's going to make "literature" out of it . . . and I'm selfish enough to have my hopes. . . .

Dashiell Hammett: Crime Stories and Other Writings contains
the foundation for those hopes. The "other writings" are two small
and admired nonfiction pieces, "From the Memoirs of a Private
Detective" and "Suggestions to Detective Story Writers." The first is
a string of anecdotes about human stupidity and bits of cynical, tongue-
in-cheek wisdom reminiscent of Ambrose Bierce: "Pocket-picking is
the easiest to master of all the criminal trades. Anyone who is not crippled can become an adept in a day." The second — the "Suggestions"
— displays the practical seriousness with which Hammett viewed his
craft, while at the same time it's hilariously scathing at the expense of
other, sloppier detective story writers. "A pistol, to be a revolver, must
have something on it that revolves," he remarks. "'Youse' is the plural
of 'you.'" "A trained detective shadowing a subject does not ordinarily leap from doorway to doorway. . . ."

This approach brings to mind that other American Samuel, Sam
Clemens (Mark Twain), who so famously took the stuffing out of
Fenimore Cooper's standards of accuracy. Indeed, the two Samuels[4]
have a lot in common: the combination of steely-eyed observation of
the dirty underbelly of America and the idealistic wish that it would
live up to its founding principles, the deadpan humour, and above all
the dedication to language. This last, in both, took the form of an
attempt to capture the tone and cadence of the American vernacular
in literature, of which *Huckleberry Finn* is surely the first fully triumphant example.

Seen in this light, Hammett, with his word-collecting and ear for
slang dialects,[5] is part of the project of American linguistic self-
definition that began with Noah Webster's 1783 *Spelling Book* and his
later dictionary. The effort was continued through Fenimore
Cooper's Natty Bumppo of the *Leatherstocking Tales*, and gathered

speed with various dialect and regional writers of the nineteenth century, as well as with Whitman and his barbaric yawp. Owen Wister and his creation of the western — its ur-plot, its tall tales and talk — belongs here too, and Bret Harte, and many after them. The hard-boiled detective story lent itself to this sort of exploration, criminal slang being not only colourful but often indigenous.

If this is Hammett's literary ancestry, or part of it, his subsequent family tree is equally noteworthy. He was an admirer of Sherwood Anderson, who wrote concisely about hitherto overlooked corners of small-town life. He respected Faulkner as one might respect a very bright but weird second cousin.[6] He found Hemingway irritating, like a brother who is also a rival, and took little pokes at him — in "The Main Death" he has a particularly vacuous rich girl reading *The Sun Also Rises*. He must have found it gratifying to be called "better than Hemingway" in the 1930 publisher's ad for *The Maltese Falcon*.

Like Wister's *Virginian*, the granddaddy of all westerns, Hammett's work had incalculable influence. He was one of those writers whom everyone of a certain age read as a matter of course. He himself said, "I've been as bad an influence on American literature as anyone I can think of." Raymond Chandler is the younger brother: he inherited the battered office furniture and the type of the romantic-loner detective, though Philip Marlowe is more of an intellectual than Sam Spade, and more fascinated with upholstery. Nathanael West was arguably a melancholy cousin. Elmore Leonard — who, like Hammett, began in magazines — has Hammett's pace, descriptive eye, and dead-on ear for dialogue. Carl Hiassen has the outrageousness, the taste for the hilariously bizarre, and the manic inventiveness.[7]

The Hammett prize for experimenting with language in a criminal setting must surely go to Jonathan Lethem's beguiling *Motherless Brooklyn*, in which the sleuth has Tourette's syndrome. And there are many, many more. Even the pratfalling body pile-ups were inherited by an unlikely third cousin: read Hammett's "Dead Yellow Women" or "The Big Knockover," then the riot-in-the-bar sequence in the first chapter of Thomas Pynchon's *V*, just for fun. The most recent addition is the fine Spanish thriller writer Pérez-Reverte, who pays direct homage to *The Maltese Falcon*.

Dashiell Hammett: Crime Stories and Other Writings takes us back to the beginning of the line. Twenty-four of the early magazine stories have been selected. In addition, there's the manuscript of *The Thin Man*, much shorter and almost completely different from the published book. (No Nick and Nora Charles tossing back the booze in their chic apartment, no Asta the dog.) The stories give us a good look at the young Hammett staking out his territory. They're best read one at a time, with pauses between, since too much at once dulls the edge. They are very much of their period and genre — *hard-boiled* was the term used of this kind of side-of-the-mouth crime fiction. (Hard-boiled eggs were what blue-collar workers had in their lunch boxes.) But despite their adherence to formulas it's easy to see from the stories why Hammett rose so rapidly.

Low life and high life are his interests: each set is motivated largely by money, power, and sex, and each behaves badly, though the high-lifes are less likely to have poor complexions, perhaps because they don't eat at grease joints — about the only places in Hammett stories where people consume food. The cozy middle-class Norman Rockwell front-porch folks do not concern him; when their representatives appear, they are likely to be thugs in disguise, like the "affectionate old couple" with their twinkling eyes in "The House in Turk Street" who are fronting for a mob, or the entire population of the town of Izzard, in "Nightmare Town," including the jolly banker and the kindly doctor, who are all part of a huge criminal conspiracy.[8]

Realism is a word often used to describe Hammett's writing, but the stories are realistic only in their settings and details — the pimples on nasty youths, the dingy office furniture of the cheap private eyes — and in their forthright use of the vernacular. The dialogue was influenced by its period, when the wisecrack and the vaudeville one-liner were valued and a smart mouth like Dorothy Parker's was an asset. The plots are Jacobean in their doubled and redoubled vengeance, and also in their carnage: they resemble multiple car crashes. This was the age of the Keystone Cops, when mayhem was first being portrayed on the screen,[9] and surely some of the brawls and corpse-fests in Hammett were intended to be funny in this quasi-slapstick way. The exuberance of language, the relish with which seediness is described, the playing with aphorisms, the joy of bizarre invention — it's a pleasure to imagine the young Hammett cutting loose with whatever rascally hijinks he could cook up and put over. The aim was not realism, but to make things seem real — "real as a dime," as one narrator says of a far-fetched yarn he's been reading.

For the pulp adventure-crime stories of this era are not real realism. Instead they're romances in the Northrop Frye sense, with knights-errant disguised as detectives, and treasures with criminal-mastermind ogres guarding them. There are trolls in the guise of goons with huge chins, pasty faces, dead eyes, or other physical distortions, and threatened maidens who sometimes really are maidens — innocent heiresses transgressing social boundaries — but most likely instead femmes fatales with silver eyes or other enchantments. These latter turn into clawing cats or foulmouthed banshees when the hero calls their bluff. Quite often the spell-breaking words are "You are a liar," or words to that effect; for like Sam Spade after him, the hero always resists female blandishments in pursuit of his higher mission. This mission is not exactly justice; it's more like professionalism. The hero has a job to do and is good at his job. He's a working man, and this kind of thoroughness gets Hammett's respect. Also this kind of toughness, for toughness was a cardinal virtue for him.[10]

The hero who most frequently appears in these stories, and the one that made Hammett so popular with his readers, is a man without a name. He's known as the Continental Op — an operative working for the Continental Detective Agency. The Op reports to

The Old Man — surely the original of James Bond's M, George Smiley's Control, and Charlie of *Charlie's Angels*. This hero makes a point of avoiding heroics, as his aim is not to get himself killed but to catch the criminals. He's short and fat and down-to-earth, playing a grouchy Sancho Panza to the thin, idealistic tilter at windmills who was lurking inside Hammett and would make such a decisive appearance in the courtroom in his later life.

Fatness and thinness are distinguishing markers in the stories and novels, but they're also recurring motifs in the letters. Time and again Hammett tells his correspondents that he's eating again, that he's gaining weight, or — when illness or drink have got the better of him — that he hasn't been able to eat at all. In the light of this constant struggle with his thinness — at bottom a struggle to remain alive — the title of Hammett's last novel, *The Thin Man*, may have been a wry joke, the subject of which was Hammett himself. The thin man in the book is a mad genius who's dead before the book begins. He appears to be alive only because other people say he is; in reality, he's so thin he isn't there at all. "Count me out," Hammett may have been saying. "I've run out of energy, I'm gone." And he was gone, from the writing scene at least.

Which brings us to the two silences: the literary silence, and the dramatic public one in federal court. Of the literary one — the absence of any new books after the mid-1930s — Jo Hammett makes short work. "He didn't stop writing. Not until the very last. What he stopped was finishing." And indeed the letters are sprinkled with references to books he was beginning or continuing, and to possibilities for having the free time and the space in which to write.[11] This part of the story makes painful reading for anyone who's trying to write books, since the moves — the setting out with optimism, the evasion, the fading away of purpose — are so familiar.

None of the attempts came to anything. Drink has been suggested as the reason, and illness, and other activities that interfered, though it was Hammett's choice to let them. Then there were ambition and high standards: Hammett wanted to go "mainstream" — to get outside what he felt was the limiting circle of crime writing — and that was a big leap. Perhaps, however, his fundamental problem was with language. "I stopped writing because I was repeating myself," he said in 1956. "It is the beginning of the end when you discover you have style." And he did have style, or rather a style — a mannered implement he'd worked up and polished, but an implement very much of its time. Possibly he could no longer settle on a language equal to the occasion; or rather, the occasion itself had passed by. By the 1940s and 1950s the scene had changed radically, and he must have felt out of his element. He couldn't go to town on the language any more, because that kind of town no longer existed.

Then there's the other silence, the one in court. The virtues of silence as a stratagem had occurred to Hammett early. "It doesn't matter how shrewd a man is, or how good a liar," the Op says in the 1924 story "ZigZags of Treachery": "If he'll talk to you and you play your cards right, you can hook him — can make him help you convict him. But if he won't talk you can't do a thing with him."

Also, if Hammett kept silent, he wouldn't implicate anyone else: only he would suffer. Strangely enough, there's a literary precedent even for that. The young boy who'd wanted to read all the books in the Baltimore public library can hardly have escaped Longfellow, then the most revered of American poets. Longfellow's poem "The Children's Hour"[12] was chosen by Hammett as the title of the play attributed to Lillian Hellman, though Hammett had provided the story for it and did much of the work. So Hammett more than likely knew Longfellow's verse drama, *Giles Corey of the Salem Farms*.

Giles Corey was the man who refused to plead either guilty or not guilty during the Salem witchcraft episode. If he pled, he'd have been tried, and if tried, he'd have been found guilty — all those accused were. His property would then have been confiscated by the State, and his family deprived. He took his stand on principle, but also out of consideration for others, as Hammett himself did. The penalty for failure to plead was "pressing" — stones were piled on top of you until you either pled or died. Giles Corey did the latter.[13] If Hammett considered the Salem trials as a paradigm for the McCarthy "witchhunt," he was not alone. Many used that metaphor, including Arthur Miller in his play *The Crucible*.

In Longfellow's play, the last words spoken about Corey before his death are, "I wonder now / If the old man will die, and will not speak? He's obstinate enough and tough enough / For anything on earth." Silence equals toughness. Could it be that this verbal equation was first planted in young Hammett's head by the author of *Evangeline*?

Well, it's one more clue.

1. Diane Johnson, *Dashiell Hammett: A Life* (Random House, 1983).

2. The term *pulp* didn't refer to the sleaziness of the writing, but to the quality of the paper: the pulps were printed on uncoated paper, as opposed to the more upmarket "slicks." But many good writers got their start in the pulps, and they were a source of income if you could write quickly.

3. As he was already a star by then, he evidently didn't have to suffer the mind bending and humiliation dished out to lesser CPUSA members, such as Richard Wright.

4. The third Samuel in the trio is Sam Spade. Hammett was very conscious of names, and would have given his own to this character quite deliberately.

5. As Jo Hammett remarks, "Papa loved all kinds of word play: thieves' cant, convict argot, Yiddish expressions, restaurant and cowboy talk, Cockney rhyming slang, gangster-lowlife speak."

6. In 1931 he was reading *Sanctuary*, which — with its twisted Popeye and its socialite who plays with the toughs — is probably Faulkner's most Hammett-like book. Hammett didn't think highly of it, but revised his opinion of Faulkner upward in later years.

7. Hiassen's amazing "Velcro-Face" of *Skin Tight* and his road-kill–eating ex-senator exist on a continuum that leads from Hammett's squinty or big-chinned grotesques through Faulkner's twisted Popeye through *Dick Tracy* of the comics, with its gargoyle thugs such as "Anyface," who looked like Swiss cheese.

8. This strain — awfulness behind the apple-pie facade — runs through Hawthorne's "Young Goodman Brown," in which the wholesome townsfolk are in league with the Devil, through Hammett, through Ray Bradbury's *Martian Chronicles*, where the town conceals murderous Martians, through the film *The Stepford Wives*, in which robot wife doubles have replaced real wives, to the television show *Twin Peaks* and certain episodes of *The X Files*. In real life it has played itself out in versions of Satanic cults, as well as its ur-form, the infamous Salem witchcraft trials.

9. Hammett was a moviegoer. It's endearing to find him giving his opinion of the relative merits of *Pinocchio* versus *Snow White*. Needless to say, he liked *Pinocchio* better.

10. Jo Hammett describes all the kinds of toughness Hammett admired: tough men, tough women, tough sports. It was a quality of character as well as a physical quality. "Toughness," she says, "would take him through the last bad years."

11. There were three main attempts: *My Brother Felix*, which was "going to be pretty good for both magazines and movies"; *The Valley Sheep Are Fatter*, a title that comes from one of Thomas Love Peacock's novels; and *Tulip*, this last about a writer who can no longer write.

12. Thought of as a piece of syrupy kitsch by those who haven't read it closely. But Hammett was a good reader, and must have seen it for the creepy poem it is.

13. The only words Corey is said to have uttered were "Put on more stones," but Longfellow has the pressing take place offstage and so does not use them.

32

OF MYTHS AND MEN

ATANARJUAT: THE FAST RUNNER

Atanarjuat: The Fast Runner (directed by Zacharias Kunuk) is the first feature film ever to be made in Inuktitut. It's also the first to be made almost entirely by Inuit — *made* in many ways, for the clothing, the artifacts such as spears and kayaks, and the dwellings were all painstakingly researched and then handmade by artisans to recreate the world of almost a thousand years ago, long before the coming of Europeans. For the people of the community out of which this film emerged, it will be what they have lacked for so many years: a validation of their roots.

The danger might have been that such a film would have only a curio value, but nothing could be farther from the truth. *Atanarjuat* won the Camera d'Or at Cannes for best first feature and then went on to collect six Genie Awards, and no wonder. It's already being called a masterpiece. This film is a knockout.

I've seen it, or parts of it, on three occasions. I'll talk about them in reverse order.

The film was viewable in England before its release in Canada, so I saw it in its entirety in London, at the Institute of Contemporary Art. We went to the matinee, but even so we were lucky to get in: the place was packed. During the screening, my English pal and I — supposed mistresses of sang-froid, both of us — did a lot of arm clutching, and, at the end, some unseemly snivelling. As we staggered out of the theatre, red-eyed and wobbly-kneed, she said, "My god! What a film!" Speechlessness is the best tribute.

I'd known *Atanarjuat* was going to be on in London because, while I'd been in Paris doing my bad imitation of a person who can speak French, we'd happened to turn on the BBC, and the film was being reviewed, complete with excerpts. I don't think I've ever heard an English film critic indulging in this kind of breathless rhapsody. "If Homer had been given a video camera, this is what he would have done," said he, and there's something to that.

Which bit of Homer? The story of the House of Atreus would be my guess, for this is a generational saga with many Homeric elements — love, jealousy, rivalry between young contenders, extraordinary feats of strength, resentments passed from fathers to sons, and crimes that beget consequences years later. The world of Greek myth is one in which gods interact with human beings, dreams have significance, grudges are held, vengeance is exacted, the ways of Fate are dark, food can cast a spell, and animals aren't always what they seem; and if you substitute the word *spirits* for the word *gods*, these things are true as well of *Atanarjuat*.

It helps going into the film to know a couple of things. First, this is not a "made-up" story, any more than Homer would have said *The Iliad* was made up. It's based on oral tradition — on a series of events said to have really happened, in real places. (You can follow the travels of the characters on the film's web site.) So it would be beside the point to fault someone called "the author" for something you don't like about "the plot."

Second, a newborn child was thought to be a reincarnation of someone who'd died. Thus, when the grandmother addresses a young woman as "little mother" — which throws you the first time you hear it — it's not just that the girl is named after the old woman's mother: she is that mother.

Third, spirits are all around. They can confer extra strength, and they can enter into people, and make them behave badly (like the demons cast out by Christ). But they can be mastered to some extent by shamans, who can also call on the dead for help. So, as in Homer, this story isn't just about conflict between human rivals. It's a battle between one lot of spirits and another, kicked off when an evil spirit arrives and sows discord among the members of a hunting group, and enters into one of them.

Fourth, it was forbidden for a woman to speak to or even look at her brother-in-law. That's why the bad sex scene between the wayward second wife of the hero and the hero's brother isn't just any old roll in the fur. It's really bad.

Fifth, there are various kinds of strength. There's the strength conferred by the position of leadership — keep your eye on the teeth-and-tusk necklace, the equivalent of the crown in *Richard III* — and this position is always held by a man, because the group is a hunting group and it's the men who hunt. There's the strength conferred by shamanistic power, which can be used for good or ill; but it helps to know that both the woman (later the grandmother) who gives a talismanic rabbit's foot to her brother, and the brother himself, possess this power.

And finally, there's moral authority. This can be earned or lost. (Watch out for the moment when, in any western genre film, the hero — his enemies finally at his mercy — would blow them to bits. This doesn't happen. Instead, Atanarjuat says, "The killing stops here," thus gaining moral authority. We could use a little of that right now.) But the ultimate moral authority resides with the elders, who wield it sparingly, though to crushing effect. Keep your eye on the grandmother.

These were things I would have liked to have known the first time I saw this film. It was the summer before it was to preview at the Toronto International Film Festival (on September 12, 2001: the preview was cancelled). I was on an icebreaker in the Arctic, with a tour group called Adventure Canada. They'd asked me to come along and

give a couple of talks, a small price to pay for the experience of seeing places I'd only ever dreamed about. Everything about this
voyage was magic; the Arctic light effects alone — the mirages, the
Fata Morgana, the "glories" — were worth the trip. At one point we
all got out and stood on an ice pan, looking forebodingly like a David
Blackwood lithograph.

If we'd taken off all our clothes and leapt from floe to floe, we
might have resembled instead — from a distance — the spectacular
scene in which the hero of *Atanarjuat* runs stark naked across miles
and miles of broken pan ice. I didn't get as far as this during my first
viewing. It wasn't that the film was being shown in episodes on a TV
set and it was hard to read the subtitles. But Pakak Innuksuk — the
man who plays the Strong One, the hero's older brother — was on
the ship with us. He was a man of few but cogent words, a hunter
from much farther north, and in the film he was much as he seemed
in life; more brusque, but recognizable. So I watched up to the place
where Pakak was sleeping in a skin tent along with his brother, and
the three murderous rivals were sneaking up on them. I knew Pakak
was about to be horribly speared, and I didn't think I could go
through with it. (It was okay to watch Pakak being speared in
London. I hadn't just had pancakes with him.)

There's a permeable boundary between reality and art. We
know there's a connection, we know there's a difference, but there's
no stone wall. When I think of *Atanarjuat*, of course I will always
think of Pakak. While we were scrambling around on the Arctic landscape one day, I recalled with some embarrassment having been told
that a native band, lacking a word for "northern tourism," had come
up with an expression that means "white men playing in the woods."
So there we were, mostly white people playing on the rocks, and
there was Pakak, standing on a cliff where he had a good view.

He had a large bear gun. He was watching out for animals. As
he, and all the men of whom (says the lore) he is an incarnation, have
been doing for thousands of years.

33

COPS AND ROBBERS

TISHOMINGO BLUES

BY ELMORE LEONARD

TISHOMINGO BLUES is Elmore Leonard's thirty-seventh novel. At that number you'd think he'd be flagging, but no, the maestro is in top form. If, like Graham Greene, he were in the habit of dividing his books into "novels" and "entertainments" — with, for instance, *Pagan Babies* and *Cuba Libre* in the former list, and *Glitz*, *Get Shorty*, and *Be Cool* in the latter — this one might fall on the "entertainment" side; but, as with Greene, those that might be consigned to the "entertainment" section are not necessarily of poorer quality.

Those offended by what my grandmother called "language," and by what used to be termed, in adventure stories, "fearful oaths," and by the derogatory epithets and salacious jokes that used to pass from mouth to ear in the smoking cars of trains and now whiz to and fro over the Internet, should avoid *Tishomingo Blues*. But Leonard is often and justly praised for his mastery of the demotic, and the demotic would not be itself without this kind of thing. Anyway it's pretty much always apt: each character speaks in character. Here's one of the more villainous heavies:

> No mention of the smoke or the two greasers — Newton think-
> ing of the one he'd asked that time where the nigger was and the

one said he'd gone to fuck your wife. It had set him off, sure, even knowing it wasn't true. One, Myrna wasn't ever home, she played bingo every night of her life. And two, not even a smoke'd want to fuck her, Myrna going four hundred pounds on the hoof. Try and find the wet spot on her.

This is an object lesson in economy worthy of a short essay in *Maladicta*, the defunct scholarly journal devoted to foul language (still available on the Internet): three racial slurs, two F-words, misogyny combined with lookism, and a sneer at bingo players, all wrapped up in five terse lines. The man who speaks this will surely die. ("Good" characters in Leonard swear differently from the way "bad" characters do.)

As to what Leonard is up to beyond the texture of his prose, it's what he's been up to for some time. A good deal of any Leonard novel — or those of, say, the last twenty years — consists of deadpan social observation. John le Carré has maintained that, for the late twentieth century at least, the spy novel is the central fictional form, because it alone tackles the implementation of the hidden agendas that — we suspect, and as the evening news tends to confirm — surround us on all sides.[1] Similarly, Elmore Leonard might argue — if he were given to argument, which he is not — that a novel without some sort of crime or scam in it can hardly claim to be an accurate representation of today's reality. He might add that this is especially true when that reality is situated in America, home of Enron and of the world's largest privately held arsenal, where casual murders are so common that most aren't reported, and where the CIA encourages the growing and trading of narcotics to finance its foreign adventures.

Not only that — Leonard might continue, and it's a point he's copiously illustrated — the line between the law and the lawbreakers is, in his native land at any rate, not a firm one. (One of the nasties in this book is an ex-sheriff's deputy, an employment category about which few have a good word to say.) In fact, the uncertainties about this division — law enforcers versus lawbreakers, with coins tossed over who the villains are to be — goes far back, and is firmly embedded in American folklore. The Revolutionaries of 1776 were in essence rebels against the established government of their time, and ever since then there has been some question about who is entitled to impose what sort of legal code upon whom, and by what means. The Klan vigilantes and the lynch mob have been — as Leonard reminds us in this book — two of the less pleasant historical responses.

There are righteous causes in aid of which breaking the law is surely the moral thing to do, but who is to decide what those causes are? It's a series of short steps from the rude bridge that spanned the flood, where the embattled and incidentally lawbreaking Concord farmers stood, to John Brown's celebrated abolitionist and also homicidal Body, to Thoreau's classic "Civil Disobedience," to Darlin' Corrie of the well-known folk song, who has to wake up and get her shotgun because the Revenooers are a-comin' to tear her still-house down.

Like all writers who concern themselves with crimes and punishments, Leonard is interested in moral issues, but these issues are for him by no means clear-cut. Having been born in 1925, he entered the scene as a conscious observer during the half century when this tendency — the questioning of law, the admiration of its breakers — was at its peak. It was the 1930s, and the Depression was causing much real desperation. No wonder that many followed the exploits of the James brothers and Bonnie and Clyde with a great deal of interest — young Leonard, by his own account, among them. For if oppression is economic, and the bank has grabbed your farm and turfed out your family, isn't it at least slightly heroic to stick your hand in the till? The father who hangs in connection with such a crime in Davis Grubb's 1930s-era novel *The Night of the Hunter* is not a bad guy: he's a good guy, and it's the system that hangs him that bears the moral taint.

But the James brothers and Bonnie and Clyde were not Robin Hoods, even in mythologized retellings. The American version of the robber as folk hero is very potent, but it doesn't include giving to the poor: that would be sappy, and perhaps Communist as well. The best thing to do with the poor is to remove yourself from their number by any means at your disposal, and this is largely what Leonard's crooks set out to accomplish. Thus, quite often in Leonard's books you don't get a choice between good noncriminals and bad criminals: instead, you get a choice between good guys and bad guys, period. There are many factors that determine whether a guy is good or bad — more specifically, whether he is an asshole, a pompous blowhard, a coward, a condescending jerk, a moron, or a man a man can respect — but which side of the legal line he happens to be on is not among them.

As every child who has ever played cops and robbers knows, it was more fun being a robber, because you could fool people and get away with forbidden behaviour, and there was more risk. In *Tishomingo Blues*, fun, risk, forbidden behaviour, and fooling people go together. There are two main characters. The first is not a criminal. Instead he's an edge dweller and risk taker of another sort. He's a professional high diver called Dennis Lenahan, who makes a living at amusement parks going off an eighty-foot tower into a tank that looks, from above, to be the size of a fifty-cent piece. He does this, as far as we can tell, for three reasons: it gives him a rush, it helps him to pick up girls, and he has no other marketable skills. When we enter his picture he's beginning to worry about how much longer he'll be able to keep up the performances without breaking his neck. (Or rupturing his anus and ruining his genitalia, two other hazards of high diving about which we are duly informed on the first page.) Dennis is not someone who's ever given a thought to stock options or gated retirement communities — his first marriage failed because he was "too young," and, although nearing forty, he's still too young — so these are new and depressing thoughts for the likeable lad.

Dennis soothes his anxieties by wafting into bed with nice women who never turn him down — well, he's very fit — and this is the one matter that may give the female reader thoughtful pause. Leonard is precise about physicality in other respects. His characters piss, take dumps, fart, have bad breath, and much else. Unlike some fictional characters, they eat and drink, and they do this accurately, brand names and all. (Early Times, Pepsis, and Lean Cuisines are featured.) But Dennis floats into the sack with nary a question and nary a precaution: no thoughts of STDS trouble his enthusiastic head. Maybe this is accurate too — probably it is, or there wouldn't be so many cases of herpes, not to mention AIDS. But you want to whisper — especially when Dennis is tumbling around with the disaffected wife of a morally disgusting man who's done hard time in an unsanitary prison — "Dennis, honey, don't you know who's been in there before you?" Dennis, we fear, will wake up one morning with a dose of something he can't get rid of. But such dismal futures lie outside the margins of the book, and to dwell too long on them would be like anticipating Cinderella's wedding night, when she will pop out of her trance and realize that Prince Charming is a shoe fetishist.

The second main character has a lot more bulbs in his chandelier. The name he's going by is Robert Taylor — we assume it's assumed[2] — and he's definitely a criminal element. He's handsome, slick, personable, cool, well dressed, Jaguar-driving, and from Detroit. (He also carries an attaché case with a gun in it, but this is a part of the country — Tunica, Mississippi — where people have guns the way most people have noses, so it elicits scant surprise.) In addition to all of the above, Robert is black. Add in the setting and an upcoming historical reenactment of a Civil War battle, and you've got the nitroglycerine for the dynamite.

When I started reading about Tunica, Mississippi, as described by Elmore Leonard, it seemed so extravagantly over the top — even just architecturally — that I thought I'd stumbled upon a made-up place, like the Emerald City of Oz, which it somewhat resembles. (Oz too is a city of illusions controlled by a scam artist who deceives people and holds out false promises.) But I should have known better, because Leonard doesn't make up this sort of stuff. He doesn't need to: it's right there for the taking, in all its full-blown weirdness. Tunica is real — it's "The Casino Capital of the South." But it's *also* made up, because the business of gambling is nothing if not the successful selling of illusion.

The connection between illusion and reality, lie and truth — and also the gap between them — is one of the leitmotifs that runs through *Tishomingo Blues*. Everything in Tunica is faux, including the whore-in-a-trailer pretending to be Barbie, and the "Southern Living Village," a complex in the throes of development where all the dwellings are imitations of something else and the entire operation is a front for the drug trade. The focus of the story is the Tishomingo Lodge & Casino. Its name is ripped off from a real Native American chief; its form is a kitschy teepee; its cocktail waitresses wear fringed fake-buckskin miniskirts; its foyer mural is horrendously inaccurate. But though the decor in Tunica may be fake, the danger is real.

Dennis the diver lands in Tunica because he's talked the manager of the casino into engaging his high-dive act as a customer attraction. Almost immediately he's in trouble. While up on his tower and about to do a test dive, he sees two men down below shoot a third man. They see him seeing them. They're about to pot him, but they get distracted. Robert Taylor, the black criminal, has witnessed the shooting too. He has also witnessed Dennis witnessing it. They strike up a curious symbiotic palship.

What does each want of the other? What Dennis ought to want is a goodbye handshake and a bus ticket to Nome, Alaska, but he's a bit of an innocent and doesn't know how afraid he ought to be. Also he doesn't want to abandon his tower and his tank. So he sticks around, and Robert Taylor presents himself as a fellow who can help Dennis do that. Without Robert present, we fear, young Dennis's brain will shortly be "red Cream of Wheat," as other brains have been before. So Robert is our man.

But what does Robert Taylor want of Dennis? That's more complicated. First version, he wants Dennis and his diving act to function as the laundry for his drug money, because he plans to take over the market from the local-yokel Dixie Mafia. Second version, he wants to buy Dennis's soul. He puts that right on the table. "You at the crossroads, Dennis. I'm about to make an offer to buy your soul." "Like Faust, man. Sell your soul, you get anything you want." If Dennis sells, what he'll get is mojo, and this mojo will enable him to realize his innermost dreams; but he'll have to really believe it — otherwise it won't work — and they have the one chance to grab it.[3]

For Robert isn't just any old gangster. He's invested with more significance than that. He's the Master of the Crossroads, the deceiving prankster born and bred in the briar patch, the man who makes things happen. He's the fast-talking salesman selling himself and riding on a shoeshine and a smile[4]; he's the gambler with his sleeves stuffed with aces. He's the deity you pray to when you want change and action, though there's no guarantee of what kind of action you will get. He's Mercury, god of thieves and commerce and communication and conductor of souls to the underworld, and he's Anansi, African web spinner, catcher of flies in traps. He teases Dennis by implying he's the Devil, but if so he's hardly the Biblical Satan. Instead he's the devil of folklore, whose bargains could work out in your favour, especially if you do what Dennis is urged to do — no matter what you see, keep your mouth shut.[5] Robert is — in other words — a particularly engaging example of a trickster figure.[6] "You gonna miss me, you know it?" he says toward the end of the book, as much to the reader as to the lady he's taking leave of. "You gonna miss the fun."

And he's on solid home ground in Tunica. His roots — he claims — are right here, on the banks of the Mississippi River, the ur-river, the Old Man River. The Mississippi divides and binds all elements — North and South, white, black, and Indian, rich and poor, travellers and gamblers. It's the river of *Showboat*, and, yes, Leonard dutifully supplies a beautiful quadroon who's concealing her ancestry. It's the river of Huck and Jim, the first white-black pair out to beat the odds and the scoundrels. It's the river of the King and the Duke, seedy but amusing scammers-for-profit; and it's the river of Melville's Confidence Man, an elusive and ambiguous figure whose masquerades result — sometimes — in good.

Robert Taylor is the inheritor, then, of a long and many-stranded tradition. To watch him in action as he mines this rich lode is a pleasure, though it's somewhat like what Monty Python did with Botticelli's *Venus* — part humorous travesty, part straight aggression. Robert, for instance, is a history buff. "History can work for you," he says, "you know how to use it," and he does know how. He's gone to college — he paid his tuition by dealing, but he wouldn't sell to students because he figured their minds were already too addled:

> I took eighteen hours of history — ask me a question about it, anything, like the names of famous assassins in history. Who shot Lincoln, Grover Cleveland. I took history 'cause I loved it, man, not to get a job from it. I knew about the Civil War even before I saw it on TV, the one Ken Burns did. I stole the entire set of videos from Blockbuster.

Robert's first history trick is to get hold of a 1915 souvenir postcard of a lynching, and to tell two different Tunica white bad guys that it's his great-grandpa dangling from the bridge and their great-grandpa doing the hanging:

> I thought maybe you already knew your great-granddaddy lynched that man in the picture, my own great-granddaddy, rest his soul. And cut his dick off. Can you imagine a man doing that

to another man . . . ? . . . I thought to myself, Lookit how our heritage is tied together, going back to our ancestors. Yeah, I'm gonna show him the historical fact of it.

Robert says this to a diehard racist and violent creep. This is *Roots* with a vengeance. "You only used it to set [him] up," says Dennis of the postcard. "That don't mean it ain't real," Robert replies.

Robert's aim is to scam his way as an "African Confederate" into the reenactment of the Battle of Brice's Cross Roads (which will not take place at the real Brice's Cross Roads, needless to say). That way, he can arrange for his opponents to be dispatched with real bullets — putting the history back into History, you might say. The Dixie Mafia's tribute to authenticity, on the other hand, is to attempt to reenact the postcard lynching, with Robert playing the role of dickless corpse. As usual, Leonard has done his research; he has the rules and attitudes of the reenactment movement down pat, and he plays them for all they're worth. If you didn't know about Naughty Child Pie and the Robert E. Lee and Stonewall Jackson salt-and-pepper shakers, and what farbs and hard-cores are, you'll find out here.

Leonard doesn't write whodunits — we always know who done it because we see them doing it. You might say he writes howdunits. His plots are like chess games — the pieces are all out in the open, we can watch the set-up, but it's the rapid moves of the endgame that surprise. They're also like Feydeau farces, which is in no way to disparage them. Such performances are very hard to pull off successfully, and timing is everything: Feydeau used to compose with a stopwatch. The reader knows who is in which cupboard and under what bed and behind which bush, but the characters don't know. Then they start figuring it out, and things move very quickly after that. The sleight-of-hand machinery in this book is engineered by Robert, of course: as chief trickster, he is after all the Master of Illusion.

But in this world of the amusement park and the dress-ups and the reenactment, of the facade, the disguise, and the sham, where does reality lie, and what's actually worth having, and who has it? I'd say there's one main thing, and that is the respect — not of everyone, because men who want that are vain and foolish — but of a man whose respect counts for something. (These are boys' rules. Women aren't players in the respect game, in the world of *Tishomingo Blues*: they earn favourable attention in other ways.) The ways of obtaining and evaluating this and other kinds of man-to-man respect could form the basis for a dissertation in sociobiology — the male primate stare, for instance, or who looks at whom, and how, and what it means.

Apart from being able to do the stare, you get respect — as far as I can figure out — by being serious about things that count, by not talking too much, by knowing what you're talking about — there's a lot of lore exchanging in this book, about the blues and their singers, about the Civil War, about how to set up a diving tank, and, rather less enchantingly, about baseball games of yore.[7] If you already have respect, and especially if you're a criminal kingpin, you have to keep the respect by not getting lazy and arrogant, or it'll be the Cream of Wheat brain for you.

But most of all you get the respect by making a hard thing look easy. This is how Dennis gets Robert's respect. "I love to watch people who make what they do look easy. No flaws, nothing sticking out," he says about Dennis's act. A third party comments, "The guy high in the air, twisting and turning, is in control of himself, showing how cool he is. And Robert's cool. He keeps Dennis around because he respects him as a man." Women don't evaluate this kind of behaviour in quite the same way. When Dennis doses his clothing in high-test gasoline and torches himself for a fireball jump, Robert says, "Man." But his female companion says, "Big fucking deal." When women do admire Dennis, they're looking at his body — what might be in it for them. But Robert's admiring the guts and the technique.

Billy Darwin, Dennis's employer, has his own version of "big fucking deal." He makes the mistake of thinking that the thing is easy because it looks easy. He belittles what Dennis does, "sounding like a nice guy while putting you in your place, looking down at what you did for a living," and then he tries diving off the tower himself to demonstrate his cool and to show what a snap it is. He comes to grief.

And this, possibly, is our one small peek behind the scenes, to the shadows where the author lurks. Could it be that Mr. Leonard has heard a few too many times that the thing he's done professionally now for four decades, or thirty-seven times, is really easy because he makes it look easy? Just because it's an amusement park and people are entertained by what you do, does that mean it's not a serious skill? Could it be that he'd like to see a few of those kinds of commentators try jumping off the tower themselves? If you've been to the crossroads, and made the deal, and got the mojo — which turns out to be dependent on a great deal of hard work and practice, just like sleight of hand — wouldn't you maybe get a trifle riled by that kind of misjudgement from time to time?

Not so as to lose your cool, mind you. Not so much as that.

1. Le Carré gave these views in his acceptance speech when granted an honorary degree by the University of Edinburgh.

2. "Robert Taylor" was the assumed name of the actor who, besides being a famous romantic lead, starred in a huge number of crime and Western films. He played, for instance, Billy the Kid in the eponymous film in 1941. As someone says in *Tishomingo Blues*, "working for Robert . . . was like being in the fucking movies."

3. It's odd to find the sentiments of the Blue Fairy in *Pinocchio* on the lips of Robert Taylor. But then, wishing upon a star, makes no difference who you are, is partly what distinguishes Taylor from the bad guys: he's dreaming his own version of the American Dream.

4. Robert Taylor is the mirror image of Willy Loman of *Death of a*

Salesman. The latter is the dishonest "honest" man, the former the honest dishonest one.

5. See for instance the Grimms' tale "The Devil's Sooty Brother." In such stories the hero, if lucky and prompt, can obtain the Devil's bounty and keep his own soul too, and this is what Dennis does.

6. For much more, see Lewis Hyde's thorough study, *Trickster Makes This World* (Farrar, Straus and Giroux, 1998). Hyde makes the point however that in a nation paved from end to end with snake-oil salesmen, the Trickster doesn't function quite as usual.

7. The character who drones on about baseball is intended to be boring. The trick is to see how he interjects his obsession into any topic whatsoever. If you get tired of it you can do what Dennis does — tune out.

34

TIFF AND THE ANIMALS

**(ON THE OCCASION OF THE TIMOTHY FINDLEY
MEMORIAL EVENING, CONVOCATION HALL,
UNIVERSITY OF TORONTO, SEPTEMBER 29, 2002)**

WHAT DO YOU SAY when everything has been said? How about: *It won't be the same. We'll miss him. He was creative, extravagantly generous, humane, unique.* What more?

What more? I said to Tiff — figuratively, as I am not yet a truly crazy person out of one of his books. Tiff gave one of those big smoke-filled laughs of his and said, What about the animals?

Well, yes. There were always animals, in the life and in the work. Cats, a lot of those. At Stone Orchard, his farm, a cathouse full. Dogs, sometimes. Birds, occasionally. A bear once. The entire menagerie, in *Not Wanted on the Voyage*. And a whole slew of rabbits.

What's this *thing* you had about Peter Rabbit? I said to Tiff. You did manage to get him in a lot. It wasn't just whimsy, was it? You knew he wasn't a cuddly stuffed toy or a kiddie's milk mug, although you collected those. It's a dark story when you come to think of it. But what was it with you and him, precisely? You even chose him as your Banned Book, once.

Peter Rabbit, Tiff pronounced, in that voice that was always *his* voice — although he was known to do some wicked imitations of, for instance, me — Peter Rabbit, he pronounced, was Oscar Wilde backwards.

He must have meant the Oscar who said, I live in fear of not being misunderstood. That, in an age in which being gay was not only a dangerous thing to be but a crime, as it was too when Tiff was young.

And a lot of his work revolves around that — being misunderstood, and also not being misunderstood, which could be even worse. And the fear of both. What to disguise, what to reveal, when to lie and when to blurt, what are the consequences of each? But though this fear is omnipresent in Tiff's writing, it's most often shown in a social context — the context of other people. Being different and going your own way can shatter the family, which sometimes rejects you, but sometimes takes you back.

In the very early novel *The Last of the Crazy People*, the young boy bumps off every single one of his relatives, which is one solution. In *The Wars*, the boy shatters the family not only by going off to war but also through a forbidden act; then he escapes into permanent wounded mindlessness. In *Pilgrim*, the boy-man is a mute in a lunatic asylum. (Being mute — being voiceless — having your voice taken away — being unable to speak, or to speak out — these motifs recur.) However, in the last novel, *Spadework*, the family is shattered by the defection of its husband/father, who falls in love with a man; but then it accepts the shatterer back, and integrates him again into the social group.

This is the Peter Rabbit solution; and in the days of Tiff's adolescence, when gay people were so frequently shunned by their relations and gay-bashing was official state policy, how difficult it was to achieve, and therefore how desired. It's the wounds of youth that leave the deepest scars.

Consider how the Peter Rabbit story goes. Peter's father is dead. Peter is the sole son in a family consisting of a widow and three conventionally well-behaved daughters. Mother Rabbit issues a taboo — no Mr. McGregor's garden for Peter, no forbidden fruits and especially vegetables, no great big dangerous man with huge boots and a rake with a very, very long handle.

But Peter promptly violates this taboo. In doing so, he runs the risk of devastating the precarious Rabbit family even further. Off he goes to do the forbidden thing, involving, in his case, lettuces. He comes to grief, and like Oscar Wilde is found out and pursued and incarcerated — not in Reading Jail, but in a watering pot. However, he makes a dash for it, and although by now he's feeling quite ill, he manages to get back to the safety and warmth of his family, where he is cared for and given camomile tea and tucked into bed. And I have to say that nobody has written about the comforting pleasures of clean, fresh, crisp pyjamas better than Tiff.

In so many of Tiff's books, the character feels like (and sometimes actually is) a small, helpless animal on the run, excluded by definition, ill or blind, lacerated in body or heart, seeking a place of shelter, where he will no longer be alone but part of a loving group; no longer an *I*, but an *us*.

So, there's my interpretation, I said to Tiff. You always wanted more academic literary criticism of your work. D'you buy it?

Not bad about Peter, he said. Though a little overdone about the rake. But you've missed something about animals in general.

What's that? I said. Apart from the simple fact that you were fond of them.

They can't *talk*, he said. They are allowed no *voices*. We don't *listen*. They live in fear of being misunderstood. They are so often . . . *excluded*. They are at our mercy. And we have had the unmitigated *gall* to proclaim that they have no souls!

So, are there any rabbits in Heaven? I said. Now that you're in a position to know. Not to mention cats.

I *demanded* them, said Tiff. It wouldn't have been Heaven without them.

35

THE INDELIBLE WOMAN

TO THE LIGHTHOUSE
BY VIRGINIA WOOLF

I FIRST READ Virginia Woolf's *To the Lighthouse* when I was nineteen. I had to. It was on a course — "The Twentieth-Century Novel," or some such. I got on all right with the nineteenth-century novel — the works of Dickens were, I felt, just as such things should be, at least in England: lots of mad people and fog. Nor did I do too badly with certain twentieth-century novels. Hemingway I could more or less fathom — I'd played war as a child, I'd gone fishing a lot, I knew the approximate rules of both, I was aware that boys were laconic. Camus was depressing enough for the late-adolescent me, with existential angst and gritty, unpleasant sex into the bargain. Faulkner was my idea of what could be possible for — well, for myself as a writer (which was what I wanted to be), hysteria in steaming, bug-infested swamps being my notion of artistic verisimilitude. (I knew those bugs. I knew those swamps, or swamps very like them. I knew that hysteria.) That Faulkner could also be outrageously funny went — at the age I was then — right past me.

But Virginia Woolf was off on a siding as far as my nineteen-year-old self was concerned. Why go to the lighthouse at all, and why make such a fuss about going or not going? What was the book about? Why was everyone so stuck on Mrs. Ramsay, who went around in floppy old hats and fooled around in her garden, and indulged her husband with spoonfuls of tactful acquiescence, just like my surely boring mother? Why would anyone put up with Mr. Ramsay, that Tennyson-quoting tyrant, eccentric disappointed genius though he might be? Someone had blundered, he shouts, but this did not cut any ice with me. And what about Lily Briscoe, who wanted to be an artist and made much of this desire, but who didn't seem to be able to paint very well, or not to her own satisfaction? In Woolfland, things were so tenuous. They were so elusive. They were so inconclusive. They were so deeply unfathomable. They were like the line written by a wispy poet in a Katherine Mansfield short story: "Why must it always be tomato soup?"

At nineteen, I'd never known anyone who had died, with the exception of my grandfather, who'd been old and far away. I'd never been to a funeral. I understood nothing of that kind of loss — of the crumbling of the physical texture of lives lived, the way the meaning of a place could change because those who used to be in it were no longer there. I knew nothing about the hopelessness and the necessity of trying to capture such lives — to rescue them, to keep them from vanishing altogether.

Although I'd been guilty of many artistic failures, such was my callowness that I did not yet recognize them as such. Lily Briscoe suffers the aggression of an insecure man who keeps telling her that women can't paint and women can't write, but I didn't see why she should be so upset about it: the guy was obviously a drip, so who cared what he thought? Anyway, no one had ever said that sort of thing to me, not yet. (Little did I know they would soon begin.) I didn't realize what weight such pronouncements could have, even when uttered by fools, because of the many centuries of heavily respectable authority that lay behind them.

This past summer, forty-three years later, I read *To the Lighthouse* again. No particular reason: I was in that very Canadian space, "the cottage," and so was the book, and I'd read all the murder mysteries. So I thought I'd try again.

How was it that, this time, everything in the book fell so completely into place? How could I have missed it — above all, the patterns, the artistry — the first time through? How could I have missed the resonance of Mr. Ramsay's Tennyson quotation, coming as it does like a prophecy of the First World War? How could I not have grasped that the person painting and the one writing were in effect the same? ("Women can't write, women can't paint . . .") And the way time passes over everything like a cloud, and solid objects flicker and dissolve? And the way Lily's picture of Mrs. Ramsay — incomplete, insufficient, doomed to be stuck in an attic — becomes, as she adds the one line that ties it all together at the end, the book we've just read?

Some books have to wait until you're ready for them. So much, in reading, is a matter of luck. And what luck I'd just had! (Or so I muttered to myself, putting on my floppy old hat, going out to fool around in my unfathomable garden . . .)

36

THE QUEEN OF QUINKDOM

THE BIRTHDAY OF THE WORLD AND OTHER STORIES
BY URSULA K. LE GUIN

THE BIRTHDAY OF THE WORLD is Ursula K. Le Guin's tenth collection of stories. In it she demonstrates once again why she is the reigning queen of . . . but immediately we come to a difficulty, for what is the fitting name of her kingdom? Or, in view of her abiding concern with the ambiguities of gender, her queendom, or perhaps — considering how she likes to mix and match — her quinkdom? Or may she more properly be said to have not one such realm, but two?

"Science fiction" is the box in which her work is usually placed, but it's an awkward box: it bulges with discards from elsewhere. Into it have been crammed all those stories that don't fit comfortably into the family room of the socially realistic novel or the more formal parlour of historical fiction, or other compartmentalized genres: westerns, gothics, horrors, gothic romances, and the novels of war, crime, and spies. Its subdivisions include science fiction proper (gizmo-riddled and theory-based space travel, time travel, or cybertravel to other worlds, with aliens frequent); science-fiction fantasy (dragons are common; the gizmos are less plausible, and may include wands); and speculative fiction (human society and its possible future forms, which are either much better than what we have now, or much worse). However, the membranes separating these subdivisions are permeable, and osmotic flow from one to another is the norm.

The lineage of "science fiction," broadly considered, is very long, and some of its literary ancestors are of the utmost respectability. Alberto Manguel has catalogued many in *The Dictionary of Imaginary Places*: Plato's account of Atlantis is among them, and Sir Thomas More's *Utopia* and Jonathan Swift's *Gulliver's Travels*. Accounts of voyages to unknown realms with bizarre inhabitants are as old as Herodotus in his wilder moments, as old as *The Thousand and One Nights*, as old as Thomas the Rhymer. Folk tales, the Norse sagas, and the adventure-romances of chivalry are not-so-distant cousins of such tales, and have been drawn on by hundreds of imitators of *The Lord of the Rings* and/or *Conan the Conqueror* — works which previously fetched their water from the same wells, as did their precursors, George MacDonald and the H. Rider Haggard of *She*.

Jules Verne is probably the best known of the early gizmo-fictionalists, but Mary Shelley's *Frankenstein* could be thought of as the first "science fiction" — that is, the first fiction that had real science in it — inspired as it was by experiments with electricity, in particular the galvanizing of corpses. Some of her preoccupations have stayed with the genre (or genres) ever since: most specifically, what is the price that must be paid by Promethean Man for stealing fire from Heaven? Indeed, some commentators have proposed "science fiction" as the last fictional repository for theological speculation. Heaven, Hell, and aerial transport by means of wings having been more or less abandoned after Milton, outer space was the only remaining neighbourhood where beings resembling gods, angels, and demons might still be found. J. R. R. Tolkien's friend and fellow fantasist C. S. Lewis even went so far as to compose a "science fiction" trilogy — very light on science, but heavy on theology, the "space ship" being a coffin filled with roses and the temptation of Eve being reenacted on the planet of Venus, complete with luscious fruit.

Rearranged human societies have been a constant in the tradition as well, and they have been used both to criticize our present state of affairs and to suggest more pleasant alternatives. Swift depicted an ideal civilization, although — how English! — it was populated by horses. The nineteenth century, cheered on by its successes with sewage systems and prison reform, produced a number of earnestly hopeful speculative fictions. William Morris's *News from Nowhere* and Edward Bellamy's *Looking Backward* are foremost among them, but this approach became such a vogue that it was satirized not only by Gilbert and Sullivan's operetta *Utopia Limited* but also by Samuel Butler's *Erewhon*, where illness is a crime and crime is an illness.

However, as the optimism of the nineteenth century gave way to the Procrustean social dislocations of the twentieth — most notably in the former Soviet Union and the former Third Reich — literary utopias, whether serious or sardonic, were displaced by darker versions of themselves. H. G. Wells's *The Time Machine*, *The War of the Worlds*, and *The Island of Dr. Moreau* prefigure what was shortly to follow. *Brave New World* and *Nineteen Eighty-four* are of course the best known of these many prescient badlands, with Karel Čapek's *R.U.R.* and the nightmarish fables of John Wyndham running close behind.

It's too bad that one term — *science fiction* — has served for so many variants, and too bad also that this term has acquired a dubious if not downright sluttish reputation. True, the proliferation of sci-fi in the 1920s and 1930s gave rise to a great many bug-eyed-monster-bestrewn space operas that were published in pulp magazines and followed by films and television shows that drew heavily on this odoriferous cache. (Who could ever forget *The Creeping Eye*, *The Head that Wouldn't Die*, or *The Attack of the Sixty-Foot Woman*? A better question: Why can't we forget them?)

In brilliant hands, however, the form can be brilliant, as witness the virtuoso use of sci-trash material in Kurt Vonnegut's *Slaughterhouse Five*, or Russell Hoban's linguistically inventive *Riddley Walker*, or Ray Bradbury's *Fahrenheit 451* and *The Martian Chronicles*. (Jorge Luis Borges was a fan of this last book, which is no surprise.) Sci-fi is sometimes just an excuse for dressed-up swashbuckling and kinky sex, but it can also provide a kit for examining the paradoxes and torments of what was once fondly referred to as the human condition: What is our true nature, where did we come from, where are we going, what are we doing to ourselves, of what extremes might we be capable? Within the frequently messy sandbox of sci-fi fantasy, some of the most accomplished and suggestive intellectual play of the last century has taken place.

Which brings us to Ursula K. Le Guin. No question about her literary quality: her graceful prose, carefully thought-through premises, psychological insight, and intelligent perception have earned her the National Book Award, the Kafka Award, five Hugos, five Nebulas, a Newberry, a Jupiter, a Gandalf, and an armful of other awards, great and small. Her first two books, *Planet of Exile* and *Rocannon's World*, were published in 1966, and since then she has published sixteen novels, as well as ten collections of stories.

Collectively, these books have created two major parallel universes: the universe of the Ekumen, which is sci-fi proper — space ships, travel among worlds, and so forth — and the world of Earthsea. The latter must be called "fantasy," I suppose, since it contains dragons and witches and even a school for wizards, though this institution is a long way from the Hogwarts of *Harry Potter*. The Ekumen series may be said — very broadly — to concern itself with the nature of human nature: How far can we stretch and still remain human? What is essential to our being, what is contingent? The Earthsea series is occupied — again, very broadly speaking — with the nature of reality and the necessity of mortality, and also with language in relation to its matrix. (That's heavy weather to make of a series that has been promoted as suitable for age twelve, but perhaps the fault lies in the marketing directors. Like *Alice in Wonderland,* these tales speak to readers on many levels.)

Le Guin's preoccupations are not divided into two strictly separate packages, of course: both of her worlds are scrupulously attentive to the uses and misuses of language; both have their characters fret over social gaffes and get snarled up in foreign customs; both worry about death. But in the Ekumen universe, although there is much strangeness, there is no magic, apart from the magic inherent in creation itself.

The astonishing thing about Le Guin as a writer is that she managed to create these two realms, not only in parallel, but at the same time. The first Earthsea book, *A Wizard of Earthsea,* appeared in 1968, and *The Left Hand of Darkness,* the famous classic from the Ekumen series, in 1969. Either one would have been sufficient to establish Le Guin's reputation as a mistress of its genre; both together make one suspect that the writer has the benefit of arcane drugs or creative double jointedness or ambidexterity. Not for nothing did Le Guin invoke handedness in her fourth title: as soon as we start talking about the *left* hand, all sorts of Biblical connotations gather. (Although the left hand is the sinister one, God too has a left hand, so left hands can't be all bad. Should your right hand know what your left hand is doing, and if not, why not? And so forth.) As Walter Benjamin once said, the decisive blows are struck left-handed.

Ursula K. Le Guin has continued to explore and describe and dramatize both of her major fictional realms over the thirty-six years that have passed since her first novel was published. But since the stories in *The Birthday of the World* are Ekumen stories — with two exceptions — it's as well to concentrate on the science-fiction world rather than on the fantasy one. The general premises of the Ekumen series are as follows. There are many habitable planets in the universe. Long, long ago they were "seeded" by a people called the Hainish, space travellers from an earthlike planet, after which time passed, disruptions occurred, and each society was left alone to develop along different lines.

Now, a benevolent federation called the Ekumen having been established, explorers are being sent out to see what has become of these far-flung but still hominid or perhaps even human societies. Conquest is not the aim, nor is missionary work: noninvasive, non-directive understanding and recording are the functions required of such explorers or ambassadors, who are known as Mobiles. Various gizmos are provided to allow them to function amid the alien corn, and they are provided with a handy widget called the "ansible," a piece of technology we should all have because it allows for instantaneous transmission of information, thus cancelling out the delaying effects of the fourth dimension. Also, it never seems to crash like your Internet e-mail program. I'm all for it.

Here it is necessary to mention that Le Guin's mother was a writer, her husband is a historian, and her father was an anthropologist; thus she has been surrounded all her life by people whose interests have dovetailed with her own. The writing connection, through her mother, is obvious. Her husband's historical knowledge must have come in very handy: there's more than an echo in her work of the kinds of usually unpleasant events that change what we call "history." But her father's discipline, anthropology, deserves special mention.

If the "fantasy" end of science fiction owes a large debt to folk tale and myth and saga, the "science-fiction" end owes an equally large debt to the development of archaeology and anthropology as serious disciplines, as distinct from the tomb looting and exploration-for-exploitation that preceded them and continued alongside them. Layard's discovery of Nineveh in the 1840s had the effect of a can opener on Victorian thinking about the past; Troy and Pompeii and ancient Egypt were similarly mesmerizing. Through new discoveries and fresh excavations, European concepts of past civilizations were rearranged, imaginative doors were opened, wardrobe choices were expanded. If things were once otherwise, perhaps they could be otherwise again, especially where clothing and sex were concerned — two matters that particularly fascinated Victorian and early-twentieth-century imaginative writers, who longed for less of the former and more of the latter.

Anthropology arrived a little later. Cultures were discovered in remote places that were very different from the modern West, and rather than being wiped out or subjugated, they were taken seriously and studied. How are these people like us? How are they different? Is it possible to understand them? What are their foundation myths, their beliefs about an afterlife? How do they arrange their marriages, how do their kinship systems work? What are their foods? How about their (a) clothing and (b) sex? Which were usually discovered — through the work of various perhaps overeager inquirers such as Margaret Mead — to be (a) scantier and (b) more satisfactory than ours.

Anthropologists do — or are supposed to do — more or less what the Mobiles in Le Guin's Ekumen construction are supposed to do: they go to distant shores, they look, they explore foreign societies and try to figure them out. Then they record, and then they transmit. Le Guin knows the tricks of the trade, and also the pitfalls: her Mobiles are mistrusted and misled while they are in the field, just as real anthropologists have been. They're used as political pawns, they're scorned as outsiders, they're feared because they have unknown powers. But they are also dedicated professionals and trained observers, and human beings with personal lives of their own. This is what makes them and the stories they tell believable, and Le Guin's handling of them engaging as writing in its own right.

It's informative to compare two of Le Guin's introductions: the one she wrote for *The Left Hand of Darkness* in 1976, seven years after the book was first published, and the foreword she's now written for *The Birthday of the World*. *The Left Hand of Darkness* takes place on the planet of Gethen, or Winter, where the inhabitants are neither men nor women nor hermaphrodites. Instead they have phases: a non-sexual phase is followed by a sexual phase, and during the latter each person changes into whichever gender is suitable for the occasion. Thus anyone at all may be, over a lifetime, both mother and father, both penetrator and penetree. As the story opens, the "king" is both mad and pregnant, and the non-Gethenian observer from the Ekumen is nothing if not confused.

This novel appeared at the beginning of the hottest period of 1970s feminism, when emotions were running very high on subjects having to do with genders and their roles. Le Guin was accused of wanting everyone to be an androgyne and of predicting that in the future they would be; conversely, of being antifeminist because she'd used the pronoun "he" to denote persons not in "kemmer" — the sexual phase.

Her introduction to *The Left Hand of Darkness* is therefore somewhat brisk. Science fiction should not be merely extrapolative, she says; it should not take a present trend and project it into the future, thus arriving via logic at a prophetic truth. Science fiction cannot predict, nor can any fiction, the variables being too many. Her own book is a "thought-experiment," like *Frankenstein*. It begins with "Let's say," follows that with a premise, and then watches to see what happens next. "In a story so conceived," she says, "the moral complexity proper to the modern novel need not be sacrificed . . . thought and intuition can move freely within bounds set only by the terms of the experiment, which may be very large indeed."

The purpose of a thought-experiment, she writes, is to "describe reality, the present world." "A novelist's business is lying" — lying interpreted in the novelist's usual way, that is, as a devious method of truth telling. Consequently the androgyny described in her book is neither prediction nor prescription, just description: androgyny, metaphorically speaking, is a feature of all human beings. With those who don't understand that metaphor is metaphor and fiction is fiction, she is more than a little irritated. One suspects she's received a lot of extremely odd fan mail.

The foreword to *The Birthday of the World* is mellower. Twenty-six years later, the author has fought her battles and is an established feature of the sci-fi landscape. She can afford to be less didactic, more charmingly candid, a little scattier. The universe of the Ekumen now feels comfortable to her, like "an old shirt." No sense in expecting it to be consistent, though: "Its Time Line is like something a kitten pulled out of the knitting basket, and its history consists largely of gaps." In this foreword, Le Guin describes process rather than theory: the genesis of each story, the problems she had to think her way through. Typically, she doesn't concoct her worlds: she finds herself in them, and then begins to explore them, just like, well, an anthropologist. "First to create difference," she says, ". . . then to let the fiery arc of human emotion leap and close the gap: this acrobatics of the imagination fascinates and satisfies me as almost no other."

There are seven shorter stories in *The Birthday of the World*, and one that might qualify as a novella. Six of the first seven are Ekumen stories — they're part of the "old shirt." The seventh probably belongs there, though its author isn't sure. The eighth is set in a different universe altogether — the generic, shared, science-fiction "future." All but the eighth are largely concerned with — as Le Guin says — "peculiar arrangements of gender and sexuality."

All imagined worlds must make some provision for sex, with or without black leather and tentacles, and the peculiarity of the arrangements is an old motif in science fiction: one thinks not only of Charlotte Perkins Gilman's *Herland*, where the genders live separately, but also of W. H. Hudson's *A Crystal Age*, featuring an antlike neuter state, or John Wyndham's "Consider Her Ways," also based on a hymenoptera model, or Marge Piercey's *Woman on the Edge of Time*, which tries for absolute gender equality. (Men breast-feed: watch for this trend.) But Le Guin takes things much further. In the first story, "Coming of Age in Karhide," we see Gethen/Winter not through the eyes of a Mobile but through those of a Gethenian just coming into adolescence: Which gender will s/he turn into first? This story is not only erotic, but happy. Why not, in a world where sex is always either spectacular or of no concern whatsoever?

Things aren't so jolly in "The Matter of Seggri," where there's a gender imbalance: far more women than men. The women run everything, and marry each other as life partners. The rare boy children are spoiled by the women, but as men they must live a segregated life in castles, where they dress up, show off, stage public fights, and are rented out as studs. They don't have much fun. It's like being trapped in the World Wrestling Federation, forever.

"Unchosen Love" and "Mountain Ways" take place on a world called O, created by Le Guin in *A Fisherman of the Inland Sea*. On O, you must be married to three other people, but can have sex with only two of them. The quartets must consist of a Morning man and a Morning woman — who can't have sex — and an Evening man and an Evening woman, who also can't have sex. But the Morning man is expected to have sex with the Evening woman and also the Evening man, and the Evening woman is expected to have sex with the Morning man and also the Morning woman. Putting these quartets together is one of the problems the characters face, and keeping them straight — who's for you, who's taboo — is a problem for both reader and writer. Le Guin had to draw charts. As she says, "I like thinking about complex social relationships which produce and frustrate highly charged emotional relationships."

"Solitude" is a meditative story about a world in which conviviality is deeply distrusted. Women live alone in their own houses in an "auntring" or village, where they make baskets and do gardening, and practise the nonverbal art of "being aware." Only the children go from house to house, learning lore. When girls come of age they form part of an auntring, but boys must go off to join adolescent packs and scratch a living in the wilderness. They fight it out, and those who survive become breeding males, living shyly in hermit huts, guarding the auntrings from a distance, and being visited by the women, who "scout" for purposes of mating. This set-up, despite its spiritual satisfactions, would not suit everyone.

"Old Music and the Slave Women" comes very close to home, inspired as it was by a visit to a former plantation in the American South. On the planet of Werel, slavers and antislavers are at war, and sex among the slavers is a matter of raping the field hands. The chief character, an intelligence officer with the Ekumen embassy, gets into arguments over human rights and then bad trouble. Of all the stories, this one comes closest to substantiating Le Guin's claim that science fiction describes our own world. Werel could be any society torn by civil war: wherever it's happening, it's always brutal, and Le Guin, although at times a movingly lyrical writer, has never shied away from necessary gore.

The title story is constructed on an Inca base, with a splash of ancient Egypt. A man and a woman together form God. Both positions are hereditary and created by brother–sister marriage; the duties of God include divination by dancing, which causes the world to be born anew each year. Governance is carried out by God's messengers, or "angels." What happens when a foreign but powerful presence enters this highly structured world and the belief system that sustains it crumbles? You can imagine, or you can read *The Conquest of Peru*. Nevertheless, this delicate story is strangely courageous, strangely hopeful: the world ends, but then, too, it is always beginning.

The last story, "Paradises Lost," continues the note of renewal. Many generations have been born and have died on board a long-distance space ship. During the voyage a new religion has sprung up, whose adherents believe they are actually, now, in Heaven. (If so, Heaven is just as boring as some have always feared.) Then the ship reaches the destination proposed for it centuries earlier, and its inhabitants must decide whether to remain in "Heaven" or to descend to a "dirtball" whose flora, fauna, and microbes are completely alien to them. The most enjoyable part of this story, for me, was the release from claustrophobia: try as I might, I couldn't imagine why anyone would prefer the ship.

Le Guin is on the side of the dirtball too, and, by extension, of our very own dirtball. Whatever else she may do — wherever her curious intelligence may take her, whatever twists and knots of motive and plot and genitalia she may invent — she never loses touch with her reverence for the immense *what is*. All her stories are, as she has said, metaphors for the one human story; all her fantastic planets are this one, however disguised. "Paradises Lost" shows us our own natural world as a freshly discovered Paradise Regained, a realm of wonder; and in this, Le Guin is a quintessentially American writer, of the sort for whom the quest for the Peaceable Kingdom is ongoing. Perhaps, as Jesus hinted, the kingdom of God is within; or perhaps, as William Blake glossed, it is within a wild flower, seen aright.

The story — and the book — ends with a minimalist dance, as an old woman and a crippled old man celebrate, indeed worship, the ordinary dirt that sustains them after they have left the ship. "Swaying, she lifted her bare feet from the dirt and set them down again while he stood still, holding her hands. They danced together that way."

37
INTRODUCTION

GROUND WORKS
EDITED BY CHRISTIAN BÖK

GROUND WORKS is an anthology of experimental fiction by writers who emerged on the wilder shores of literature in this country almost forty years ago.

I admit to being the instigator of this book. I agitated for it because a body of work that deserved to be recalled and set within its original frame was slipping from view, leaving the young with the impression that there was nothing unorthodox in this country before folks started getting their tongues pierced. But I did not want to trust my own now somewhat arthritic judgement, so Christian Bök, a young experimental writer of the twenty-first century, was asked to do the selecting and arranging, and is thus the book's primary editor. The result is a sort of Ogopogo Creature: you've heard the rumours about an invisible, impossible weirdness, now here's the blurry snapshot. See? There was something down there all along!

The term *experimental fiction* covers a lot of territory. It also makes me a little nervous, as I grew up with scientists and know their single-minded ways, and the term itself is a tribute to the early twentieth century's reverence for that particular branch of human knowledge. The reverence may have faded somewhat, but the term remains, leaving behind a faint whiff of formaldehyde and Dr. Frankenstein: the dissection of language and narrative, and their reassembly into talking monsters, can strike us as cold-blooded. Dr. Frankenstein himself was not cold-blooded, however; he was a disrupter of social norms, a breaker of laws, a subversive idealist, a feverish believer in the new and the potential; and so it is with many "experimental" writers.

In what ways can fiction be "experimental"? On the one hand, all fiction is experimental, in that it ventures into the unknown and attempts to prove a hypothesis. Thus:

HYPOTHESIS: a) That this piece of fiction can actually be written by the author attempting it, and b) that it can thereafter hold a reader's attention.

DEMONSTRATION: The piece of fiction.

CONCLUSION: Someone actually reads the book all the way through, without throwing it against the wall.

But that's too broad. What we usually mean by "experimental fiction" is fiction that sets up certain rules for itself — rules that are not the same as those followed by the mainstream fiction of its day — and then proceeds to obey its own new commandments, while subverting the conventions according to which readers have understood what constitutes a proper work of literature. There's a faint air of peeking beneath the skirts, of snooping behind the rhetorical scenes. Pieces like these can border on the parody or the extended joke — Woody Allen's story about the machine that allows real people to get into well-known books as characters, Pozzo's send-up rendition of a sunset description in *Waiting for Godot*, Michael Ondaatje's use of pulp romance conventions to syncopate his Billy the Kid saga — which does not exclude the possibility of their being at the same time deeply unsettling. Accepted narrative lines are turned upside down, language is stretched and pulled inside out, characters don't remain "within character." Thus the writers in this anthology — at least in the work represented here — were more interested in colouring outside the lines than within them, and some even had it in mind to toss the entire colouring book into the fire and start with a whole new sheet of paper.

What was it that made the Canada of the 1960s such fertile ground for this kind of writing? Partly it was a stranger place in many ways than is often supposed — who remembers the LSD that flowed so freely in London, Ontario, in the 1950s — well before the age of Timothy Leary — not to mention the orgies in the cathedral? It was strange in a literary way as well. What other country would have produced a set of Spenserian eclogues spoken in a farmyard by a flock of geese? (*A Suit of Nettles*, James Reaney, 1958.) Partly, also, it was an open field — some might say a vacant lot. Many of the conditions taken for granted today — that there is a Canadian "canon," that a Canadian writer can be widely known, respected, and solvent, that you can get a grant or a film contract or teach creative writing or win big prizes, that there are such things as book-promotion tours and literary festivals, that it is possible to live in Canada and function as a professional writer with a national, indeed an international "career" — these conditions scarcely existed in the writing world of the 1950s and 1960s, when the writers collected here had their toes on the starting line. Nature abhors a vacuum, and so does literature. There is nothing more conducive to scribbling than a blank page.

There had been well-known Canadian fiction writers earlier — L. M. Montgomery of *Anne of Green Gables* fame, for instance, or Mazo de la Roche of the Jalna books, or, on higher literary ground, Morley Callaghan — but as a rule these had entered the scene through non-Canadian publishers, and were then distributed in Canada through agents or branch plants. There was, too, a Canadian-owned publishing industry, which even had a cheap-hardback mass-distribution side to it, but the Depression, the Second World War, and the advent of the U.S.-controlled paperback industry had kicked large holes in that. After the war, the old order changed: the British Empire as a political force was all but defunct, and any writer associated with it was passé; the new wave of money coming into Canada was American, as was the new wave of widely read writers. This was — with a few exceptions — largely a one-way street.

Morley Callaghan had taken it for granted that a young writer would cut his teeth in the U.S. magazine market, and would go on to be published in New York — the route he himself had taken — but this was an increasingly unlikely scenario.[1] Young Canadian "experimental" writers felt cut off — too "Canadian," whatever that meant, to be published internationally, and too radical in their approach to their writing to be published readily in the five or so established but beleaguered Canadian English-language houses functioning at that time. These houses estimated — rightly enough — that in such newly post-colonial times, when the "real" cultural places were thought to be elsewhere, the audience for Canadian writing wasn't large enough to justify their investing in a novel unless a foreign publishing partner could be obtained. But, Canada being viewed in "The States" as the place where the snow came from, and "Canadian writer" being considered an oxymoron by London cultural commentators, foreign partners willing to take the chance were few.

If you were a frustrated young writer who despaired of making a place for yourself in Canada, you could always move, of course; you could live elsewhere and begin publishing there, and that's what some novelists did. Or if you were a poet, you could crank out your own work and that of your friends on small presses and stick it into mimeo magazines, such as *Tish* and *The Sheet*, or even into more beautifully designed productions such as *Emblem Books* and *Alphabet*; there was already a tradition of this sort of publishing in Canada. You could "publish" over the airwaves, on Robert Weaver's show, *Anthology* — about the only venue that would pay you actual money. You could — from 1960 or so on — read your poetry out loud, in a few dark, smoky coffee houses that held reading series; and there you might meet international — usually American — poets who were blowing through town.

Or you could, alone or together with other writers, scrape together a few dollars and start a new small publishing house. And this is what indeed happened, in more or less that order. Contact Press, Coach House Press, House of Anansi Press, Talonbooks, Blew-Ointment Press, Sono Nis, and Quarry Press were among the many such enterprises that began in this way at that time. Many but not all of the writers sampled here were also poets, and many of the presses that first published them began with poetry, in the early to mid-1960s. The overlaps — poets publishing poets in presses devoted to poetry — were considerable. Michael Ondaatje was for years a member of the Coach House collective; I myself worked as an editor with House of Anansi Press. Andreas Schroeder worked with Sono Nis; George Bowering was associated with *Tish*; and these are just a few examples.

This scene was not idyllic. In my own experience, small-press publishing was a hotbed of jealousy and intrigue and puddles of blood on the floor, second only to Rome under Caligula. Coach House Press got around this in the early days by consuming large amounts of mellowing substances — "Printed in Canada by mindless acid freaks," read their logo, right alongside "Copyright is obsolete" — but at House of Anansi it was not so much drugs as drinking, and no one got out of it without a knife between the shoulder blades. No one but a lunatic, or someone brainwashed by the Girl Guides into thinking she had to do Good Deeds For Others, would have stayed in this situation for long. Which was I? A little of both. But that's another story.

The writers in *Ground Works*, as a group, were born in the 1930s or the 1940s. They were not baby boomers: they preceded that wave. As children they were close to Depression times, and also to war times, when Canada had in fact cut a bit of a dash. They came of intellectual age at the zenith of the postwar French intellectuals; they read the great modernists as a matter of course. Existentialism was the philosophical catchword then; Brecht and Sartre and the Theatre of the Absurd were frequently performed on campuses; "experiment" was in the air. This period followed the McCarthy years, transited the age of the beatniks, and led into days of the civil rights movement and then into the era of the Vietnam War. It was a time of ferment and change, and out of that cauldron came — at about this time — the idea of cultural nationalism. This was a modest enough thing in Canada, consisting as it did mainly in a proclamation of one's own existence, but it caused a good deal of uproar nonetheless. (Canada was then, and still is, one of those odd places where large doses of patriotism are considered unpatriotic, and where the powers that be are of the firm belief that a rocked boat always sinks.)

This was also, in writing, perhaps the most thoroughly male-dominated period of the past hundred years. Internationally, the great female modernists belonged to the first third of the twentieth century. (Of the Canadians, Elizabeth Smart was then unknown, Mavis Gallant, if noticed at all, was believed to be an American, and Sheila Watson had composed *The Double Hook* some time before its ultimate publication in 1961, when it appeared just in time to perk a lot of us up.) The hot new writers making their debuts in the late 1940s and the 1950s and the early 1960s were almost all men. Many reasons could be given for this state of affairs, but suffice it to say that such was the reality, and it — as well as the observable fact that men have historically been more interested in literature as a game than women have been — accounts for the scarcity of female writers in this collection. More women writers of all kinds would appear in Canada shortly. Margaret Laurence would come to prominence, Alice Munro and Marian Engel would publish at the tail end of the 1960s, and many more would follow, some of whom wrote "experimental" fiction and are included in this book. But writing in the 1960s was pretty much a guy thing, in Canada as elsewhere, in experimental literature as well as in the "mainstream."

It was also an urban thing. The small town, the wilderness, the Native motifs, and the pioneering past of earlier Canadian writing had been tossed out along with the Empire. They'd be back, but they hadn't come back yet.

I've made the literary climate back then sound like inclement weather, and it was. There wasn't much infrastructure or public recognition — writers, when thought about at all, were pictured as bearded maniacs inhabiting some insalubrious bohemia or drafty ivory tower; or, if female, especially if female poets, as half-baked women, the baked half being the head in the oven, for after the recent, spectacular exit of Sylvia Plath, suicide for such was almost de rigueur. Unless you cracked New York — a snowball's chance in hell — there were scant prospects of being rich and famous. But on the other hand it was an era of tremendous freedom. You didn't have to worry about market forces, because there was hardly any market as such: the numbers for even a Canadian "best-seller" were tiny by today's standards. You could travel strange roads, because there were no highways. You didn't feel weighted down by your country's cultural baggage, because — officially at any rate — there wasn't much of it. You could get lost in the language, because the signposts were few. You could take your influences from wherever you liked, because who was looking?

It was a verbal free-for-all: a rambunctious eclecticism prevailed. There was — strangely enough — a spirit of enormous optimism: not much was actual, therefore everything was potential. All was poised on the verge, about to happen. We felt, for a while, as if we really could stop being who we were often told we were — small, boring, hopelessly provincial — and, like the albatross, go straight from fledgling status to full soaring flight.

Ground Works allows us to look back on those simmering years. (After that, of course, everything changed. As is its habit.)

1. See *Canadian Novelists and the Novel*. Ed. Douglas Daymond and Leslie Monkman. Borealis: Ottawa, 1981. Or contact Canadian Centre for Studies in Publishing.

38
THE WRONG BOX: MATT COHEN, FABULISM, AND CRITICAL TAXONOMY

All the decisive blows are struck left-handed.
— WALTER BENJAMIN, AS QUOTED BY
MATT COHEN AS THE EPIGRAPH TO *Last Seen*

IT'S IMPOSSIBLE to read much of Matt Cohen's work without coming to a self-evident conclusion: Cohen is not at every writing moment a literary realist. At the core of his imagination — though not always on its surface — lies the realm of fable.

Sherwood Anderson and Chekhov accept one set of assumptions about what can be placed inside the parentheses of prose fiction; Poe and Gogol and Kafka and Angela Carter and the Stevenson of *Dr. Jekyll and Mr. Hyde* accept another set. Within the latter — the realm of the fable — a body may house two souls, the dead may return to life, an ambulatory nose may flee from its owner, man and animal may exchange shapes. There has always been a certain amount of crossover between the two modes, but it may be fair to say that elements that appear only as figurative language when bound by the strictures of literary realism appear as physical experience when these strictures are discarded.

Cohen is of course a "realist" quite a lot of the time. He can "do" realism — he knows the moves — but it is not the only thing he can do. Throughout his career he alternated between "realism" and other, more peculiar kinds of writing, and in his most deeply felt and personal novel, which I take to be *Last Seen*, he successfully blended the two.

At times of great emotional crisis, in life as in art, realistic observation of physical detail becomes hyperrealism and can read like a fevered or dream state; and at times of great political and social crisis (wars, revolutions, catastrophes) the same thing happens with events — the stream of ordinary time is disrupted, the sequence of mundane events is broken, and horrific scenes and grotesqueries appear, also as in dreams or fevers. Literary works that attempt to set down or evoke such states will contain instances of the fantastic, as do folklore and myth. In folklore or myth, the hero typically sets off on an adventure and enters an Otherworld where the rules of nature no longer apply; and at times of crises in "real life," elements from that Otherworld seem to break through a barrier and enter the realm of common human experience, distorting it in the direction of the bizarre.

These are my axioms. Another of my axioms is that Matt Cohen was a born fabulist. He was — among other personages — "Teddy Jam," a prolific and effortless writer of children's books. Tale spinning, improvisation, and the invention of wild fantasies came to him easily; it was the "realism" that was hard work.

If Matt Cohen had himself been a character in a fable, he would have been Rumpelstiltskin — the artist as odd little outsider and grumbling isolate. A singularity whose real name is a secret known only to himself, engaged in an improbable activity that transmutes base matter into precious essence — this role was part of Cohen's own self-definition, as any reader of his memoir, *Typing: A Life in 26 Keys*, will quickly learn. In his own eyes he could sometimes spin straw into gold, although on other occasions he suspected he was only spinning straw into straw. Some of what he did was seen by him as *writing*, in the rather noble sense that this word is used in creative-writing classes; some, on the other hand, was viewed by him merely as typing, an act of mechanical dexterity performed with the fingers, but in itself producing nothing more necessarily valuable than waste paper.

One of the "rules" of folk tales, as of espionage tales, is that a knowledge of true names confers power. Rumpelstiltskin's power resides in his hidden name. His name is never guessed, it's overheard: Rumpelstiltskin cannot be named by others until he has named himself.

The other part of Rumpelstiltskin's power lies in his ability as a spinner. He can spin something worthless into something valuable, a talent that is called an "art" by the greedy-hearted king, reminding us of the fact that *art*, *artful*, *artifice*, *artificial*, and *articulate* share a common root. Whenever we find a spinner in a story, we know we are not too far from the sort of language often applied to narration. The Greek Fates spin out the stories of men's lives, and the terminology of cloth-land is frequently interwoven with that used to describe tale telling, as in "spinning a yarn," "embroidering a tale," and "weaving a story."

Spinning, storytelling, and enchantment have been close companions in human speech, a relationship that recognizes that stories are *made* — concocted, articulated, fabricated — but they may also have a quality that is more organic or indeed magical, a growth or flow like the thread flowing out during the act of spinning. These two qualities of writing — the artificial or fabricated and the organic or magical — were qualities that obsessed Cohen in his own view of what he was trying to do. How to get away from mere mechanical facility to true golden flow — that flow often called by writers "finding the voice" — was a problem for him, one that presented itself at the very outset of his career.

In *Typing*, Cohen talks about this problem in relation to the writing of his third published book, the 1972 short-story collection *Columbus and the Fat Lady*. This book was published by the House of Anansi Press, a small but adventurous literary publishing company in which I had become involved in 1971 without knowing how entangling it would be. It was I who edited *Columbus and the Fat Lady*, although I can remember little about the process. In *Typing*, however, I find myself making a cameo appearance: "Atwood was slight and elfin, with a mop of frizzy hair, piercing eyes, a sharp tongue and a manner that was both brusque and friendly." The elfishness, the slightness, the mop of curly hair, the sharp tongue, and the rest of it — this sounds like the Matt Cohen of those days looking in the mirror. But the "Atwood" elf is spoken of as "frightening," despite the brusque friendliness. An elf with a witchy edge, then; a creature of some power.

In the context of Cohen's *Typing* narrative, this "Atwood" seems to be a spirit helper. Such helpers are, in Jungian terms, an aspect of the protagonist's own psyche, and it is this function "Atwood" would appear to serve in Matt Cohen's tale or fable of himself.

For tale or fable it is. *Typing* as a whole is not a tale but a detailed, realistic memoir of a writer's life qua writer. However, pages 125 through 137 have a folk tale–quest quality about them, plot, language, and all. This little section of the book might be called "How the Writer Found His Voice."

It goes as follows. The writer — let us call him C. — starts his account of how he came to write *Columbus and the Fat Lady* by saying that, having made a bit of a splash with his first and second novels, he had begun his third. This novel was to be "a parable-parody about the idea of art as religion and the artist as half-conscious martyr." But it failed to convince him, and so he began to spend more time on short stories.

Then follows a paragraph about the difference in C.'s mind between the novel — a serious art form, a medium for influencing social consciousness — and the short story, which he considered "an opportunity for a vacation," where "antiquated" "rules" might be discarded. "For me," says C., "each individual story is an adventure embarked upon for its own sake": strictures and responsibilities hedge the novel, while the short story is the realm of "freedom and play" — the realm, that is, of fantasy and fabulation, of Otherworld adventures and quests.

In real time, Dennis Lee of the House of Anansi then suggested a book of short stories by C., and C. decided that he could turn some of his "failed artist's parable" into stories, and write more stories "with a few sleep-deprived weeks of frenzied typing." (The nocturnal activity, the spinning out of product, the rapidity, the dexterity requiring "nimble fingers" — this is the writer in Rumpelstiltskin mode.)

Meanwhile, C. was living on a farm in the woods and his marriage was falling apart. In his writing life, he found he was stuck. There follow three interesting paragraphs about the writing/typing he was doing. He could produce the typed yellow pages, he tells us; he could reel them off, ten or fifteen a night. But instead of spinning something worthless into something valuable, he felt he was merely producing heaps of "yellow scrawled-over garbage." His problem was not writer's block, i.e., the inability to write at all. Instead it was quality control: he was turning out "reams of surface." He decided he was involved in a "juggling act," which had concealed meaninglessness behind incomprehensibility. He felt frustrated by "an inability to break through some indefinable barrier."

He considered other occupations, all of them impossible: he had only one talent, lodged in him useless. Then he made an unscheduled visit to the Underworld, in the guise of a Toronto party where he found himself "wandering through a series of chemically fuelled Hieronymus Bosch tableaus." Very stoned, he encountered another sort of supernatural female, a woman talking loudly in a hypnotic manner, and who, to C., appeared as "a powerful and malign female witch who had stolen everyone's soul."

Battered by the "waves of powerfulness" coming out of this woman, he keeled over and passed out on the floor. "But I wasn't losing consciousness," he says, "I was gaining it." The soul-stealing woman is evidently another spirit helper, another anima, another slice of the psyche: a good witch disguised as a bad one, an ambiguous life-and-death Kali. If she stole his soul, she appears to have handed it back with a gift attached, because after this momentous encounter C. discovered that he was writing "with a confidence and freedom that were entirely new to me."

As so often, the Underworld keeps the keys to dreamland — that is, to the treasure of creativity — and hands them over through unexpected messengers at unexpected moments. The benign elf anima can't do the whole task: the hero of the tale has to confront her malign counterpart and face his own annihilation before the unleashing of his psyche is possible. Over the next few months, Cohen says, the stories for *Columbus and the Fat Lady* "emerged in rapid succession," as though they'd been there the whole time, "just waiting to be discovered." "Each of these stories," he says, "seemed to emerge from a deeper place in my unconscious," "more like strangers I'd met in an all-night diner than contrivances that I'd deliberately put together." Finally, after writing steadily for four years, he had "discovered [his] own voice."

But what was this "own voice" saying? Quite a few things, as it turned out. *Columbus and the Fat Lady* contains fifteen stories, or quasi-stories. Few follow the "rules" for the short story that Cohen might have read in the analyses of such things then available. They are not classical short stories at all, although they are narrations. Here is how they go:

1. "The Watchmaker" is a dialogue with a Jewish watchmaker whose family has been obliterated in the Holocaust. This man survived because he was placed with a man who once had an affair with his mother, and who may possibly be his father. He is now in Canada but feels out of place. This story is the seed material for the later "European Jews" trilogy, comprising *The Spanish Doctor*, *Nadine*, and *Emotional Arithmetic*.

2. "The End." A series of absurdist killings triggered by the question, "What is the meaning of life?" in which a student, a professor, and a doctor take turns with a pistol and one another's foreheads.

3. "Our Passion Lit the Night." Strange sexual triangle involving a young male student and a somewhat older couple. The couple use the student to get the wife pregnant, then turf him out.

4. "The Nurse from Outer Space." Aliens pose as people. One is a nurse who writes short stories consisting of her name and phone number on a candy wrapper; the other is a solitary man. They discuss the short story as a form, in which such analysis is presented as ludicrous.

5. "Keeping Fit." Two pages about compulsive running, ending in the death of the runner.

6. "Country Music." An old lady lives near a dump. Talk of her and of various country characters, including the Frank brothers, who will later turn up in Cohen's Salem novels about Ottawa Valley life in decay. This story and "The Watchmaker" come closest perhaps to literary realism.

7. "Janice." A lyrical rendering of a promiscuous lost lover, with the narrator cast as both cuckolder of other men and the odd man out.

8. "The Toy Pilgrim." One of the writer-martyr stories. A slob named Elmer writes stories under the pen name of Harold Noteworth, and rewrites his own boring domestic life in various incredible ways inside his head. No one else finds him noteworthy, partly because he has concealed the secret of his name. He decides to write a play about a man perpetually embarrassed by himself; also a last novel, in which the hero will pass into pure being after having finally connected his past with his present. This novel will be published only after his death; it will be the only one of his works to bear his "own name." Strange as this story is, it grapples with a problem that obsessed Cohen: who is

the hidden writer in him, really? And how to connect the past with the present?

9. "Uncle Philbert and His Big Surprise." This piece is in the form of a saccharine play for children. Uncle Philbert comes to visit, and ends by initiating the boy of the story into "manhood" via a Grand Guignol killing of a stuffed donkey and a blood-drenched feast. (If written by a woman, this would have been called "feminism.")

10. "Straight Poker." A bravura meditation on love, involving three people, an "I," a "she," and a mysterious entity in some sort of invisible communion with the writer, although they have never met.

11. "After Dinner Butterflies." A surreal exercise in marital tedium and pestering, involving some butterflies that materialize out of the husband's previously empty pocket.

12. "The Empty Room." This too is about an author, who has Walter Mitty–like fantasies in a room inhabited by unwritten novels. Meanwhile, in his real life, he is subjected to the banality of marriage. The author thinks of writing a novel about a wastepaper basket. Then he burns down his house, thus freeing himself to rejoin the desert-adventure heroine of his romantic dreams.

13. "Too Bad Galahad" was published earlier as a children's story; there must have been some confused children. This piece consists of a series of fables about Galahad the perfect knight and his search for the Holy Grail, which either can never be found or else is common as dirt. Again the subject is the writer-as-martyr, this time as the hero of a truly ridiculous quest — for success, for fame? — that always defeats him.

14. "Spadina Time." This story begins with an odd poem about loneliness in the city and goes on to describe the life of Erik, another self-fantasizer. Erik is unemployed, lives in a rooming house, and is involved with two women, one a waitress. Considering his problems with space-time, he may have been doing drugs. The Erik character, the rooming house, the waitress, and

much else in this story are the seeds for the last section of *The Disinherited*, the next book Cohen was to write. There's another "Harold," a fat, intrusive fellow roomer and failed painter; this name will reappear in Cohen's later, extraordinary novel *Last Seen*, as the name of the dead brother who keeps turning up in Elvis bars and in the narrator's house.

15. "Columbus and the Fat Lady." Columbus has failed to discover America because he fell out of the boat. Now, through a time warp, he works as a freak in a sideshow, along with a Fat Lady who glories in the fact that her hard-won fat is real. Perhaps a meditation on the nature of truth and reality — is history "true" when it exists only as stories, or indeed only as performance? Is the flesh "real"? What classes of objects merit these words?

Columbus is another storyteller, but he can never finish the story about himself he begins every day as part of his sideshow act, because he always passes out.

This too is a "seminal" story, the seed for the various Old World/New World stories and novels that followed.

These short descriptions fail to convey the flavour of the adroit but eccentric writing in this grab-bag collection; but think of precise physical descriptions (rooming houses, clothing, weather) blended with literary parody à la Woody Allen, with some Theatre of the Absurd thrown in, blended with Kafka and perhaps a little of the George Gissing of *New Grub Street*, and you get a faint idea. "Facility" and "dexterity" come to mind. "Funny," "surreal," "wistful," "savagely satirical," and "brilliantly inventive" also come to mind, or they must have come to my mind when I was writing the jacket copy, because there they are on the cover.

For the purposes of this essay, several things may be pointed out. First, this collection begins with a story about Jewishness, which is precisely where *Typing* begins. Second, a great many of the pieces either contain writers or play riffs on various literary tropes. Third, the stories may have been written with "confidence and freedom," but they are not about confidence and freedom; rather they are about the absence of these qualities. The narrators are lost, uprooted, wandering, failed, absurd, despairing, unconnected, or dying.

Fourth, the collection seeded almost all of what Cohen was subsequently to write. It's a sort of sampler: here's the range, here are the styles, here are the interests, here are the prototypes: all arrived at through fabulation, through the "adventure," the "freedom and play," of the short-story form, all popping out of the unconscious unbidden. This must have been what Cohen meant when he said he had found his "own voice." Fifth, the collection ends with Columbus passing out: a dead faint, as you'll recall, is the key moment in the Tale of C. and of how he found his "own voice."

From the standpoint of the "finding the voice" fable, the collection is arranged exactly backwards: it should begin with the faint — the handing over of the keys, the opening of the door — and end with the first story, the one about the deracinated Jewish watchmaker; because deracination and Jewishness, and the absurdist dilemma created for the writer who partakes of these things, are at the innermost core of the material Cohen's "own voice" delivered to him during his four months of writerly "confidence and freedom."

A writer's own voice is not of course a real voice. It's a way of putting words on the page that is convincing, first to the writer himself and then to at least some readers. Such writing creates the illusion that a "voice" the reader can trust is saying something interesting or moving, and will not feel to the reader like mere ventriloquism, or like trickery, falsehood, or manipulation.

But it is almost a precondition of such a "voice" being "read" that the reader must recognize at least something about it, and know what sort of name may be applied to it.

Any writer is a sort of anti-Rumpelstiltskin, in the way that antimatter shares the characteristics of matter but spins left to right.

Rumpelstiltskin knows his own name, but the writer must discover his. Rumpelstiltskin loses power when he is truly named by others, the writer gains it. In no human endeavour is "naming" more important than it is in the sphere of the arts. As Lewis Carroll pointed out through the White Knight, there's the thing itself, there's the name of the thing, and there's what the name of the thing is called, and all are different; but in the arts these may suffer easy confusion. The adjectives applied to a work by critics influence how readers may read it, and this process always has something to do with how the work is "named" — what box it is seen to fit into.

The criteria considered worthy aims for quality writing are not absolutes, but change over time according to that nebulous gas, the *Zeitgeist*. Holding a mirror up to Nature, delighting and instructing, creating Beauty, analyzing social problems, peering at gender, digging up history, bearing witness to atrocities, giving a voice to the voiceless, rewarding the virtuous and punishing the wicked, experimenting with language — all have been held up as goals toward which good fiction-writing should aspire.

Which of these goals is considered desirable at the moment will influence how a writer's work is received by reviewers, which in turn has an effect on how readers will read it, or fail to. Though such attitudes are not spread homogeneously over all reviewers and critics, there is nonetheless at any given time a certain consensus. Terminology is often key. If a writer can be fitted into a named box that is also a hot box, then "critical discourse" will take place around that writer. If not, there will be silence, as there has largely been on the subject of Cohen's work, especially among academic critics. And if the writer appears to be in the wrong box at the wrong time, there will be trashing, which is what happened to Cohen's "Jewish" novels, in Canada, in the 1980s.

One of my theories about Matt Cohen is the Wrong Box theory. At certain moments the box was right, at least for some readers: experimental fabulation in the late 1960s was reasonably well received among the literati, though not embraced by a wide reading public. *The Disinherited* (rural family falling apart, deracinated young descendant messing up in the city) was a modest hit in the early 1970s, when rural and small-town themes were in. (It is inaccurate to say, as has become the fashion, that these rural motifs were always the "mainstream," the "canon": most of MacLennan and Callaghan, the red-hot Richler of the 1960s, Gwethalyn Graham's huge success *Earth and High Heaven*, Gabrielle Roy's classic *The Tin Flute*, the early Marian Engel novels — all are urban writing, as was most of the *Columbus and the Fat Lady* collection and a great deal of the writing, both poetry and prose, of the late 1960s and early 1970s.)

Cohen's next two novels in the Salem series were well received, though with diminishing fervour. (What, pray tell, was a Jewish writer doing writing about the crumbling WASP rurals of the Ottawa Valley? Those who wrote about "Jewish" writing couldn't fit him in: there was no Yiddish, there were no bagels, and the characters weren't Jews. Neither could those writing about "Canadian," small-town, Sherwood Anderson–like sagas, because what he was doing wasn't exactly realism of that sort. Nobody seemed to understand the affinity between Jews and crumbling rurals — the common threads, which were destroyed culture, demoralization, and rootless and wandering survivors.)

As the 1970s wore on, times got tougher for certain kinds of writers. New boxes were trendy: "nationalism" gave place to "regionalism"; "feminism" was on the upswing. In the 1960s, from the Right Box point of view, it was better to be male than female; as the 1970s wore on, the reverse became truer. The age factor also came into play: the mid-thirties to the late forties is the danger zone for a writer — no longer a sizzling young firebrand, not yet a grizzled veteran, one to whom neither "promising" nor "established" can be applied. White male writers of a certain age (Graeme Gibson, Robert Kroetsch, Rudy Wiebe, and others) all produced interesting writing in this decade, and all were — relatively speaking — overlooked.

As the 1980s set in, with postmodernist critical theory on the boil, those with a foot or a friend in academia were to some extent better placed — convincing verbal boxes could be manufactured into which such writers could be stuffed — but then along came ethnicity and identity politics and "appropriation of voice." The turf wars were on. It was no longer just what was said and how, but who was considered to have the right to say it, that mattered in evaluation. The boxes multiplied, but the ice got very thin, and who was allowed into which box became crucial for that fragile thing, the bubble reputation.

Into this fraught atmosphere came *The Spanish Doctor*, and what was a *Canadian* Jew doing writing about fifteenth-century *European* Jews? Wrong Box! In addition, "historical" novels were looked on askance, for those who had forgotten *Kamouraska*; the Jane Urquhart *Away* moment had not yet arrived. (Outside Canada, the box was not wrong, and the novel did well.) Then came *Nadine* — what was a Canadian Jewish *male* writer doing writing about a European *female* Jew? And what was he doing writing about *love*, among boring heterosexuals? (Homosexuals would have been daring.) Didn't "love" mean "trashy commercial romance," written only to make money? Looking at this novel again today, this response is very hard to fathom. Only those who have never read any real trashy commercial romances could make such a call.

At the very end of his career, Cohen regained some critical altitude and won the Governor General's Award for *Elizabeth and After*, a novel that continues the string of his fictions that deal with decaying rural life. But it was hard to escape the impression that a lot of wordfolk still didn't know quite what to make of the man.

Consider the case of *Last Seen*, Cohen's penultimate novel. This is a quirky book indeed. In it, a man called Harold dies in excruciatingly described agony and then reappears to his angry and grieving brother in a club frequented by Elvis Presley look-alikes. The brother fears dead-alive Harold, argues with him, makes jokes about him, and longs for his manifestations, which occur at unpredictable intervals until they both end up at Harold's grave, where Harold literally peels off his own mortality.

The juxtaposition of the bizarre image, the dreamlike progression of events, the closely observed realistic detail, and the deeply painful emotional state recall much of the early writing in *Columbus and the Fat Lady*. This time round, Cohen brings it all together: *Last Seen* is a work of considerable power and strange enchantment. But it's not a reassuring book. It isn't familiar, it isn't cozy, and for those attempting to pin the taxonomic tail on the elusive donkey, it's a somewhat outrageous puzzlement. To quote Alice Munro's story "The Dance of the Happy Shades," "what kind of a party is this?"

So what would have been the right box, for Cohen? Into what box might his oeuvre now be placed to allow critical discourse to take place around it? In *Typing*, Cohen made a stab at naming this box himself by putting into it the writers with whom he felt — at least toward the end of his life — a strong affinity. They include Franz Kafka, Walter Benjamin, and especially Joseph Roth; three Jews out of place or in flight, the two writers of fiction both fabulists of a sort. They also include the Leonard Cohen of *Beautiful Losers* (a wildly fabulist novel if ever there was one) and Mavis Gallant, which may seem an odd choice until you consider that she too is uprooted, or, in Cohen's words, "incredibly alienated." As for the already existing boxes — the "Canadian" ones, or at least those Cohen recognized — he felt he simply didn't fit into them. He considered himself to be an oddity, a singularity. Like Elmer/Harold Noteworth in "The Toy Pilgrim," he was a writer with a name, that is, an essential writerly self, that was not recognized by others.

There's another possible box, a "Canadian" one — because, despite the still-expressed belief that Canadian realist domestic writing is the only recognized form, there is a strong tradition of fabulism in Canada. This box would contain Howard O'Hagan's *Tay John*, James Reaney's "The Bully" and "The Box Social," the work of

Larry Garber, Leonard Cohen's *Beautiful Losers* again, Sheila Watson's *The Double Hook*, some of Timothy Findley, Marian Engel's *Bear*, Jane Urquhart's *The Whirlpool*, Graeme Gibson's *Communion*, and the work of Barbara Gowdy and André Alexis and Eden Robinson and Steven Hayward, among others. Perhaps even Michael Ondaatje's *In the Skin of a Lion* and Anne Michaels's *Fugitive Pieces* are more comfortable in such a box than in the box of straight literary realism.

This is the box of the romancers, the fabulists, the yarn spinners; and perhaps it's the frame — or one of the main frames — within which Cohen should have been viewed all along.

39

INTRODUCTION

DOCTOR GLAS
BY HJALMAR SÖDERBERG

Now I sit at my open window, writing — for whom? Not for any friend or mistress. Scarcely for myself even. I do not read today what I wrote yesterday; nor shall I read this tomorrow. I write simply so my hand can move, my thoughts move of their own accord. I write to kill a sleepless hour. Why can't I sleep? After all, I've committed no crime.

DOCTOR GLAS was first published in Sweden in 1905, when it caused a scandal, largely because of its handling of those two perennially scandalous items, sex and death. I first read it in the form of a tattered paperback sent to me by Swedish friends — a reissue of a 1963 translation, published to coincide with the film based on it. On the back of my copy are various well-deserved encomiums from newspaper reviews: "a masterpiece," "the most remarkable book of the year," "a book of rare quality developed with true skill." Nevertheless, *Doctor Glas* has long been out of print in this English version. It's a pleasure to welcome it back.

The uproar around *Doctor Glas* stemmed from the perception that it was advocating abortion and euthanasia, and was perhaps even rationalizing murder. Its protagonist is a doctor, and he has some strong things to say about the hypocrisy of his own society concerning these matters. But Hjalmar Söderberg, its author — already a successful novelist, playwright, and short-story writer — may have been somewhat taken aback by this, because *Doctor Glas* is not a polemic, not a work of advocacy. Instead it is an elegant, vigorous, and tightly knit psychological study of a complex individual who finds himself at a dangerous but compelling open doorway and can't decide whether or not to go through it, or why he should.

The novel's protagonist, Doctor Tyko Gabriel Glas, is a thirtyish medical man whose journal we read over his shoulder as he composes it. His voice is immediately convincing: intelligent, wistful, opinionated, dissatisfied, by turns rational and irrational, and unnervingly modern. We follow him through his memories, his desires, his opinions of the mores of his social world, his lyrical praises or splenetic denunciations of the weather, his prevarications, his self-denunciations, his boredom, and his yearning. Glas is a romantic idealist turned solitary and sad, and afflicted with *fin de siècle* malaise — a compound of fastidious aestheticism, longing for the unobtainable, skepticism concerning the established systems of morality, and disgust with the actual. He would like only beautiful things to exist, but has the sordid forced on him by the nature of his profession. As he himself says, he's the last person on earth who should have been a doctor: it brings him into too much contact with the more unpleasant aspects of human carnality.

What he wants above all is action, a feat to perform which might fit the hero he hopes he may carry around inside him. In romances, such deeds often involve a knight, a troll, and a captive maiden who must be rescued, and this is the sort of situation that fate serves up to Doctor Glas. The troll is a flesh-creepingly loathsome and morally repulsive pastor called Gregorius, whom Glas hates even before he finds he has good reason for his hatred. The maiden in captivity is his young and beautiful wife, Helga, who confides to

Doctor Glas that she has married Gregorius out of mistaken religious notions, and can no longer stand his sexual attentions. Divorce is impossible: a "respectable" clergyman convinced of his own righteousness, as the Reverend Gregorius is, would never consent to it. Mrs. Gregorius will be enslaved to this toadstool-faced goblin forever unless Doctor Glas will help her.

Doctor Glas has now been given a chance to prove himself. But will he discover that he is a brave knight, an ordinarily timorous nobody, or just as much of a troll as Gregorius, only a murderous one? He contains within himself the possibilities of all three. His name, too, is threefold. *Tyko* refers to the great Danish astronomer Tycho Brahe, who kept his eyes on the stars, far away from the earthiness of the earth — as Doctor Glas so often does throughout the novel. *Gabriel* is the name of the Angel of the Annunciation, proclaimer of the Holy Birth, who is also credited with being the Destroying Angel, sent to wipe out Sodom and Sennacherib, and thought to be the angel of the Last Judgement as well. Thus it's a good name for a medical practitioner, who holds the keys to life and death, but it's also a good name for Doctor Glas, who must decide whether or not to take judgement into his own hands.

And *Glas* is glass: like the diary form itself, it's a reflecting surface, a mirror in which one sees oneself. It's hard and impermeable, but easily shattered; and, from certain angles, it's transparent. This last quality is one of Glas's complaints: he can only fall in love with women who are in love with someone else, because their love makes them radiant; but their love for other men means that Glas himself is invisible to them. So it is with Mrs. Gregorius: she is having an adulterous affair with another man, and can't "see" Doctor Glas. She can only see through him, making of him a means to the end she longs for. As for Doctor Glas's nemesis, it's worth noting that although "Gregorius" is the name of a saint and of a couple of popes, it's also the name of a certain kind of telescope. Like Glas, Gregorius is glassy; he wears glasses, and looking into them, Glas sees the reflection of his own bespectacled self. Perhaps he hates Gregorius so much because the man unconsciously reminds Glas of the father who used to punish him, and whose physicality repelled him as a young boy; or perhaps it's because Gregorius is his ogreish double, the sly, whining, selfish, and self-justifying personification of the lust he can't permit himself to act out.

At first glance the structure of *Doctor Glas* is disarmingly casual, almost random. The device of the diary allows us to follow events as they unfold, but allows us also to listen in on Glas's reactions to them. The workings of the novel are so subtle that the reader doesn't notice at first that it has any: so immediate, even blunt, is the voice that we appear to be reading the uncensored thoughts of a real person. Glas promises candour: he won't set down everything, he says, but he will record nothing that isn't true. "Anyway," he adds, "I can't exorcise my soul's wretchedness — if it is wretched — by telling lies." Chance encounters and trivial conversations alternate with fits of midnight scribbling; jokes and pleasant convivial meals are followed by hours of anguish; night and dreamtime counterpoint the world of purposeful daylight. Unanswered questions punctuate the text — "By the way, why do the clergy always go into church by a back door?" — as do odd moments of hilarity verging on the burlesque, as when Gregorius considers administering the communion wine in the form of pills, to avoid germs. (The pill idea soon recurs in a much more evil form.)

Söderberg had read his Dostoevsky: he too is interested in the disgruntlements of underground men, and in charting impulse and rationalization and motive, and in the fine line that runs between the violent thought and the criminal act. He'd read his ghost-ridden Ibsen and that master of bizarre obsession, Poe. He'd also read his Freud, and he knows how to make use of the semiconscious motif, the groundswells of the unspoken. There are two hints in the text that point us toward the book's methods: Glas's meditation on the nature of the artist, who to him is not an originator but an aeolian harp, who makes music only because the winds of his own time play over him

— thus the discursiveness; and his invocation of Wagner, who used the leitmotif to connect large swaths of disparate music into a unified whole. A tracing of all the red roses — from dead mother to out-of-reach beloved to rejected potential sweetheart — reveals some of these interconnections, as does a survey of all the astronomical images, from moon to stars to sun to the sunny, starry-eyed Mrs. Gregorius. "Truth is like the sun," says Glas's friend Markel, "its value wholly depends upon our being at a correct distance away from it." And so it would be, we suspect, with Mrs. Gregorius: she can be valuable for Glas as an ideal only as long as she is kept at a correct distance.

Doctor Glas is deeply unsettling, in the way certain dreams are — or, no coincidence, certain films by Bergman, who must have read it. The eerie blue northern nights of midsummer combined with an unexplained anxiety, the nameless Kierkegaardian dread that strikes Glas at the most ordinary of moments, the juxtaposition of pale spirituality with an almost comic vulgar sensuality — these are from the same cultural context. The novel launches itself from the ground of naturalism set in place by French writers of the nineteenth century, but goes beyond it. Some of Söderberg's techniques — the mix of styles, the collagelike snippets — anticipate, for instance, *Ulysses*. Some of his images anticipate the Surrealists: the disturbing dreams with their ambiguous female figures, the sinister use of flowers, the glasses with no eyes behind them, the handless watchcase in which Doctor Glas carries around his little cyanide pills. A few decades earlier and this novel would never have been published; a few years later and it would have been dubbed a forerunner of the stream-of-consciousness technique.

    Doctor Glas is one of those marvellous books that appears as fresh and vivid now as on the day it was published. As the English writer William Sansom has said, "In most of its writing and much of the frankness of its thought, it might have been written tomorrow." It occurs on the cusp of the nineteenth and the twentieth centuries, but it opens doors the novel has been opening ever since.

40
NAPOLEON'S TWO BIGGEST MISTAKES

IN MY HIGH-SCHOOL music appreciation class we listened to Tchaikovsky's 1812 Overture. We liked it, because there was stuff we could identify: cannons boomed, bells rang, national anthems resounded, and there was a satisfying uproar at the end.

The English — being English — have since produced a version performed by sheep and chickens. Generals screw up, their fiascos get made into art, and then the art gets made into fiascos. Such is the march of progress. We were told that Tchaikovsky's piece celebrated Napoleon Bonaparte's retreat from Moscow, but we weren't told who Napoleon was or what he was doing in Moscow in the first place. So in case you had a similarly vague musical appreciation experience, here's the deep background.

Napoleon was a brilliant soldier who rose like a bubble during a time of unrest and bloodletting, won many battles, and was thus able — like Julius Caesar — to grab near-absolute power. He got hold of Italy and Austria and Prussia and Spain. He replaced the French Republic with an emperor — himself — thus giving rise to much impressive furniture with eagles and columns on it. He also brought in a legal code, still somewhat admired today.

He had laudable motives, or so his spin-doctoring went: he wanted peace and justice, and European unity. But he thought it would be liberating for other countries to have their stifling religious practices junked and their political systems replaced with one like his. To this end, he scrapped the kings of other countries and crested new kings, who happened to be members of his own family.

Which brings me to Napoleon's two biggest mistakes.

The first was Spain. Napoleon got Spain treacherously. He had an agreement whereby he could march through it on the way to Portugal, which was bothering him by interfering with his sanctions against trading with the British. Once his armies were in Spain, he took the place over, whereupon his forces engaged in their usual practices of priest pestering, church looting, and removing sparkly things and artworks to other locations for safekeeping. Napoleon's big mistake was underestimating the religious feelings of the staunchly Catholic Spanish.

He thought they'd embrace "liberation," but it seems they had a curious attachment to their own beliefs. The British annoyed Napoleon in Spain by winning battles against him, but the real defeat of the French was brought about by widespread guerrilla resistance. Things got very nasty on both sides: the Spaniards cut French throats, the French roasted Spaniards alive, the Spaniards sawed a French general in two.

The Spanish population won — although at enormous cost — because you can kill some of the people all of the time and you can kill all of the people some of the time, but you can't kill all of the people all of the time. When a whole population hates you, and hates you fanatically, it's difficult to rule.

Present leaders take note: Never underestimate the power of religious fervour. Also: Your version of what's good for them may not match theirs.

Napoleon's second big mistake was invading Russia. There's no one clear explanation for this. He didn't need to do it. Russia wasn't attacking him, though it had in the past and might in the future. Maybe he just wanted to add it to his set. In any case, he invaded. When his horse stumbled as he crossed the Dnieper — a bad omen — a voice said from the shadows, "A Roman would have turned back."

Warfare at that time meant forcing your opponent to stand and fight, resulting in victory on one side or the other. But the Russians merely retreated, burning crops as they went and leading Napoleon deeper and deeper into the same huge Russian land mass and awful Russian weather that also defeated Hitler. When Napoleon reached Moscow, he thought maybe he'd "won": but the Russians burned Moscow and retreated again. Napoleon hung around in the cinders, expecting the czar to sue for peace, but no message ever arrived. Thus the retreat, and the 1812 Overture, and the decimation of the Grand Army. As others have learned since, it's very hard to defeat an enemy who never turns up.

The occupation of Japan after the Second World War has been proposed as a model for Iraq. It's not a helpful comparison. First, the religious fervour of the Japanese soldier was attached to the emperor, who thus had the power to order a surrender. Iraq will have no such single authority. Second, Japan is an island: no Russian-style, Afghan-style retreat was possible. Third, Japan had no neighbours that shared its religious views and might aid it. The Japanese had only two choices — death or democracy.

Iraq, on the other hand, has many coreligionist neighbours who will sympathize with it, however repugnant they've previously found Saddam Hussein. A foreign occupation — not immediately, but in the long run — is less likely to resemble Douglas MacArthur in Japan than Napoleon in Spain.

Now you know about the 1812 Overture. That moment — after which Napoleon plummeted and the French Empire dissolved — was the hinge on which the rest of the nineteenth century turned, as the First World War was the hinge for the twentieth.

When a door swings open, you never know what will come through it. And as Napoleon himself believed, the fortunes of war — being notoriously unpredictable, and riddled with variables — are ruled by the Goddess of Chance.

41
LETTER TO AMERICA

DEAR AMERICA:

This is a difficult letter to write, because I'm no longer sure who you are. Some of you may be having the same trouble.

I thought I knew you: we'd become well acquainted over the past fifty-five years. You were the Mickey Mouse and Donald Duck comic books I read in the late 1940s. You were the radio shows — Jack Benny, *Our Miss Brooks*. You were the music I sang and danced to: the Andrews Sisters, Ella Fitzgerald, the Platters, Elvis. You were a ton of fun.

You wrote some of my favourite books. You created Huckleberry Finn, and Hawkeye, and Beth and Jo in *Little Women*, courageous in their different ways. Later, you were my beloved Thoreau, father of environmentalism, witness to individual conscience; and Walt Whitman, singer of the great Republic; and Emily Dickinson, keeper of the private soul. You were Hammett and Chandler, heroic walkers of mean streets; even later, you were the amazing trio, Hemingway, Fitzgerald, and Faulkner, who traced the dark labyrinths of your hidden heart. You were Sinclair Lewis and Arthur Miller, who, with their own American idealism, went after the sham in you, because they thought you could do better.

You were Marlon Brando in *On the Waterfront*, you were Humphrey Bogart in *Key Largo*, you were Lillian Gish in *The Night of the Hunter*. You stood up for freedom, honesty, and justice; you protected the innocent. I believed most of that. I think you did, too. It seemed true at the time.

You put God on the money, though, even then. You had a way of thinking that the things of Caesar were the same as the things of God: that gave you self-confidence. You have always wanted to be a city upon a hill, a light to all nations, and for a while you were. Give me your tired, your poor, you sang, and for a while you meant it.

We've always been close, you and us. History, that old entangler, has twisted us together since the early seventeenth century. Some of us used to be you; some of us want to be you; some of you used to be us. You are not only our neighbours: In many cases — mine, for instance — you are also our blood relations, our colleagues, and our personal friends. But although we've had a ringside seat, we've never understood you completely, up here north of the 49th parallel. We're like Romanized Gauls — look like Romans, dress like Romans, but aren't Romans — peering over the wall at the real Romans. What are they doing? Why? What are they doing now? Why is the haruspex eyeballing the sheep's liver? Why is the soothsayer wholesaling the Bewares?

Perhaps that's been my difficulty in writing you this letter: I'm not sure I know what's really going on. Anyway, you have a huge posse of experienced entrail sifters who do nothing but analyze your every vein and lobe. What can I tell you about yourself that you don't already know?

This might be the reason for my hesitation: embarrassment, brought on by a becoming modesty. But it is more likely to be embarrassment of another sort. When my grandmother — from a New England background — was confronted with an unsavoury topic, she would change the subject and gaze out the window. And that is my own inclination: keep your mouth shut, mind your own business.

But I'll take the plunge, because your business is no longer merely your business. To paraphrase Marley's ghost, who figured it out too late, mankind is your business. And vice versa: when the Jolly Green Giant goes on the rampage, many lesser plants and animals get trampled underfoot. As for us, you're our biggest trading partner: We know perfectly well that if you go down the plughole, we're going with you. We have every reason to wish you well.

I won't go into the reasons why I think your recent Iraqi adventures have been — taking the long view — an ill-advised tactical error. By the time you read this, Baghdad may or may not be a pancake, and many more sheep entrails will have been examined. Let's talk, then, not about what you're doing to other people but about what you're doing to yourselves.

You're gutting the Constitution. Already your home can be entered without your knowledge or permission, you can be snatched away and incarcerated without cause, your mail can be spied on, your private records searched. Why isn't this a recipe for widespread business theft, political intimidation, and fraud? I know you've been told that all this is for your own safety and protection, but think about it for a minute. Anyway, when did you get so scared? You didn't used to be easily frightened.

You're running up a record level of debt. Keep spending at this rate and pretty soon you won't be able to afford any big military adventures. Either that or you'll go the way of the USSR: lots of tanks, but no air conditioning. That will make folks very cross. They'll be even crosser when they can't take a shower because your shortsighted bulldozing of environmental protections has dirtied most of the water and dried up the rest. Then things will get hot and dirty indeed.

You're torching the American economy. How soon before the answer to that will be not to produce anything yourselves but to grab stuff other people produce, at gunboat-diplomacy prices? Is the world going to consist of a few mega-rich King Midases, with the rest being serfs, both inside and outside your country? Will the biggest business sector in the United States be the prison system? Let's hope not.

If you proceed much further down the slippery slope, people around the world will stop admiring the good things about you. They'll decide that your city upon the hill is a slum and your democracy is a sham, and therefore you have no business trying to impose your sullied vision on them. They'll think you've abandoned the rule of law. They'll think you've fouled your own nest.

The British used to have a myth about King Arthur. He wasn't dead, but sleeping in a cave, it was said; and in the country's hour of greatest peril, he would return. You too have great spirits of the past you may call upon: men and women of courage, of conscience, of prescience. Summon them now, to stand with you, to inspire you, to defend the best in you. You need them.

42

WRITING ORYX AND CRAKE

ORYX AND CRAKE was begun in March 2001. I was still on a book tour for my previous novel, *The Blind Assassin*, but by that time I had reached Australia. After I'd finished the book-related events, my spouse and I and two friends travelled north, to Max Davidson's camp in the monsoon rain forest of Arnhem Land. For the most part we were birdwatching, but we also visited several open-sided cave complexes where Aboriginal people had lived continuously, in harmony with their environment, for tens of thousands of years. After that we went to Cassowary House, near Cairns, operated by Philip Gregory, an extraordinary birder; and it was while looking over Philip's balcony at the red-necked crakes scuttling about in the underbrush that *Oryx and Crake* appeared to me almost in its entirety. I began making notes on it that night.

I hadn't planned to begin another novel so soon after the previous one. I'd thought I might take some time off, write a few short pieces, clean out the cellar. But when a story appears to you with such insistence, you can't postpone it.

Of course, nothing comes out of nothing. I'd been thinking about "what if" scenarios almost all my life. I grew up among the scientists — "the boys at the lab" mentioned in the Acknowledgements are the graduate students and post-docs who worked with my father in the late 1930s and early 1940s at his forest-insect research station in northern Quebec, where I spent my early childhood. Several of my close relatives are scientists, and the main topic at the annual family Christmas dinner is likely to be intestinal parasites or sex hormones in mice, or, when that makes the nonscientists too queasy, the nature of the universe. My recreational reading — books I read for fun, magazines I read in airplanes — is likely to be pop science of the Stephen Jay Gould or *Scientific American* type, partly so I'll be able to keep up with the family dialogue and maybe throw a curve or two. ("Supercavitation?") So I'd been clipping small items from the back pages of newspapers for years, and noting with alarm that trends derided ten years ago as paranoid fantasies had become possibilities, then actualities. The rules of biology are as inexorable as those of physics: run out of food and water and you die. No animal can exhaust its resource base and hope to survive. Human civilizations are subject to the same law. I continued to write away at *Oryx and Crake* during the summer of 2001. We had some other travels planned, and I wrote several chapters of this book on a boat in the Arctic, where I could see for myself how quickly the glaciers were receding. I had the whole book mapped out and had reached the end of Part 7 when I was due to go to New York for the paperback publication of *The Blind Assassin*.

I was sitting in the Toronto airport, daydreaming about Part 8. In ten minutes my flight would be called. An old friend of mine came over and said, "We're not flying." "What do you mean?" I said. "Come and look at the television," he replied. It was September 11.

I stopped writing for a number of weeks. It's deeply unsettling when you're writing about a fictional catastrophe and then a real one happens. I thought maybe I should turn to gardening books — something more cheerful. But then I started writing again, because what use would gardening books be in a world without gardens, and without books? And that was the vision that was preoccupying me.

Like *The Handmaid's Tale*, *Oryx and Crake* is a speculative fiction, not a science fiction proper. It contains no intergalactic space travel, no teleportation, no Martians. As with *The Handmaid's Tale*, it invents nothing we haven't already invented or started to invent. Every novel begins with a *what if*, and then sets forth its axioms. The *what if* of *Oryx and Crake* is simply, *What if we continue down the road we're already on? How slippery is the slope? What are our saving graces? Who's got the will to stop us?*

"Perfect storms" occur when a number of different forces coincide. So it is with the storms of human history. As novelist Alistair MacLeod has said, writers write about what worries them, and the world of *Oryx and Crake* is what worries me right now. It's not a question of our inventions — all human inventions are merely tools — but of what might be done with them; for no matter how high the tech, *Homo sapiens sapiens* remains at heart what he's been for tens of thousands of years — the same emotions, the same preoccupations. To quote poet George Meredith,

> . . . In tragic life, God wot,
> No villain need be! Passions spin the plot:
> We are betrayed by what is false within.

43

GEORGE ORWELL: SOME PERSONAL CONNECTIONS

I GREW UP WITH George Orwell. I was born in 1939, and *Animal Farm* was published in 1945. Thus I was able to read it at the age of nine. It was lying around the house, and I mistook it for a book about talking animals, sort of like *Wind in the Willows*. I knew nothing about the kind of politics in the book — the child's version of politics then, just after the war, consisted of the simple notion that Hitler was bad but dead. So I gobbled up the adventures of Napoleon and Snowball, the smart, greedy, upwardly mobile pigs, and Squealer the spin doctor, and Boxer the noble but thick-witted horse, and the easily led, slogan-chanting sheep, without making any connection with historical events.

To say that I was horrified by this book would be an understatement. The fate of the farm animals was so grim, the pigs were so mean and mendacious and treacherous, the sheep were so stupid. Children have a keen sense of injustice, and this was the thing that upset me the most: the pigs were so *unjust*. I cried my eyes out when Boxer the horse had an accident and was carted off to be made into dog food, instead of being given the quiet corner of the pasture he'd been promised.

The whole experience was deeply disturbing to me, but I am forever grateful to George Orwell for alerting me early to the danger flags

I've tried to watch out for since. In the world of *Animal Farm*, most speechifying and public palaver is bullshit and instigated lying, and though many characters are good-hearted and mean well, they can be frightened into closing their eyes to what's really going on. The pigs browbeat the others with ideology, then twist that ideology to suit their own purposes: their language games were evident to me even at that age. As Orwell taught, it isn't the labels — Christianity, Socialism, Islam, Democracy, Two Legs Bad, Four Legs Good, the works — that are definitive, but the acts done in their names.

I could see, too, how easily those who have toppled an oppressive power take on its trappings and habits. Jean-Jacques Rousseau was right to warn us that democracy is the hardest form of government to maintain; Orwell knew that in the marrow of his bones, because he's seen it in action. How quickly the precept "All Animals Are Equal" is changed into "All Animals Are Equal, but Some Are More Equal Than Others." What oily concern the pigs show for the welfare of the other animals, a concern that disguises their contempt for those they are manipulating. With what alacrity do they put on the once-despised uniforms of the tyrannous humans they have overthrown, and learn to use their whips. How self-righteously they justify their actions, helped by the verbal web spinning of Squealer, their nimble-tongued press agent, until all power is in their trotters, and pretence is no longer necessary, and they rule by naked force. A *revolution* often means only that: a revolving, a turn of the wheel of fortune, by which those who were at the bottom mount to the top, and assume the choice positions, crushing the former power holders beneath them. We should beware of all those who plaster the landscape with large portraits of themselves, like the evil pig, Napoleon.

Animal Farm is one of the most spectacular Emperor-Has-No-Clothes books of the twentieth century, and it got George Orwell into trouble accordingly. People who run counter to the current popular wisdom, who point out the uncomfortably obvious, are likely to be strenuously baa-ed at by herds of angry sheep. I didn't have all that figured out at the age of nine, of course — not in any conscious way. But we learn the patterns of stories before we learn their meanings, and *Animal Farm* has a very clear pattern.

Then along came *Nineteen Eighty-four*, which was published in 1949. Thus I read it in paperback a couple of years later, when I was in high school. Then I read it again, and again: it was right up there among my favourite books, along with *Wuthering Heights*. At the same time, I absorbed its two companions, Arthur Koestler's *Darkness at Noon* and Aldous Huxley's *Brave New World*. I was keen on all three of them, but I understood *Darkness at Noon* to be a tragedy about events that had already happened, and *Brave New World* to be a satirical comedy, with events that were unlikely to unfold in exactly that way. ("Orgy-porgy," indeed.) *Nineteen Eighty-four* struck me as more realistic, probably because Winston Smith was more like me — a skinny person who got tired a lot and was subjected to physical education under chilly conditions — this was a feature of my school — and who was silently at odds with the ideas and the manner of life proposed for him. (This may be one of the reasons *Nineteen Eighty-four* is best read when you are an adolescent: most adolescents feel like that.) I sympathized particularly with Winston Smith's desire to write his forbidden thoughts down in a deliciously tempting secret blank book: I had not yet started to write myself, but I could see the attractions of it. I could also see the dangers, because it's this scribbling of his — along with illicit sex, another item with considerable allure for a teenager of the 1950s — that gets Winston into such a mess.

Animal Farm charts the progress of an idealistic movement of liberation toward a totalitarian dictatorship headed by a despotic tyrant; *Nineteen Eighty-four* describes what it's like to live entirely within such a system. Its hero, Winston Smith, has only fragmentary memories of what life was like before the present dreadful regime set in: he's an orphan, a child of the collectivity. His father died in the war that has ushered in the repression, and his mother has disappeared, leaving him with only the reproachful glance she gave him as he betrayed her over a chocolate bar — a small betrayal that acts both as the key to Winston's character and as a precursor to the many other betrayals in the book.

The government of Airstrip One, Winston's "country," is brutal. The constant surveillance, the impossibility of speaking frankly to anyone, the looming, ominous figure of Big Brother, the regime's need for enemies and wars — fictitious though both may be — which are used to terrify the people and unite them in hatred, the mind-numbing slogans, the distortions of language, the destruction of what has really happened by stuffing any record of it down the Memory Hole — these made a deep impression on me. Let me restate that: They frightened the stuffing out of me. Orwell was writing a satire about Stalin's Soviet Union, a place about which I knew very little at the age of fourteen, but he did it so well that I could imagine such things happening anywhere.

There is no love interest in *Animal Farm*, but there is one in *Nineteen Eighty-four*. Winston finds a soulmate in Julia, outwardly a devoted Party fanatic, secretly a girl who enjoys sex and makeup and other spots of decadence. But the two lovers are discovered, and Winston is tortured for thought-crime — inner disloyalty to the regime. He feels that if he can only remain faithful in his heart to Julia, his soul will be saved — a romantic concept, though one we are likely to endorse. But like all absolutist governments and religions, the Party demands that every personal loyalty be sacrificed to it, and replaced with an absolute loyalty to Big Brother. Confronted with his worst fear in the dreaded Room 101, where there's a nasty device involving a cage, full of starving rats, that can be fitted to the eyes, Winston breaks — "Don't do it to me," he pleads, "do it to Julia." (This sentence has become shorthand in our household for the avoidance of onerous duties. Poor Julia — how hard we would make her life if she actually existed. She'd have to be on a lot of panel discussions, for instance.)

After his betrayal of Julia, Winston Smith becomes a handful of malleable goo. He truly believes that two and two make five, and that he loves Big Brother. Our last glimpse of him shows him sitting drink-sodden at an outdoor café, knowing he's a dead man walking and having learned that Julia has betrayed him too, while he listens to a popular refrain: "Under the spreading chestnut tree / I sold you and you sold me . . ."

Orwell has been accused of bitterness and pessimism — of leaving us with a vision of the future in which the individual has no chance, and the brutal, totalitarian boot of the all-controlling Party will grind into the human face, forever. But this view of Orwell is contradicted by the last chapter in the book, an essay on Newspeak — the doublethink language concocted by the regime. By expurgating all words that might be troublesome — "bad" is no longer permitted, but becomes "double-plus-ungood" — and by making other words mean the opposite of what they used to mean — the place where people get tortured is the Ministry of Love, the building where the past is destroyed is the Ministry of Information — the rulers of Airstrip One wish to make it literally impossible for people to think straight. However, the essay on Newspeak is written in standard English, in the third person, and in the past tense, which can only mean that the regime has fallen, and that language and individuality have survived. For whoever has written the essay on Newspeak, the world of *Nineteen Eighty-four* is over. Thus it's my view that Orwell had much more faith in the resilience of the human spirit than he's usually been given credit for.

Orwell became a direct model for me much later in my life — in the real 1984, the year in which I began writing a somewhat different dystopia, *The Handmaid's Tale*. By that time I was forty-four, and I'd learned enough about real despotisms — through the reading of history, through travel, and through my membership in Amnesty International — so that I didn't need to rely on Orwell alone.

The majority of dystopias — Orwell's included — have been written by men, and the point of view has been male. When women have appeared in them, they have been either sexless automatons or rebels who've defied the sex rules of the regime. They've acted as the temptresses of the male protagonists, however welcome this temptation may be to the men themselves. Thus Julia, thus the camiknickers-wearing, orgy-porgy seducer of the Savage in *Brave New World*, thus the subversive femme fatale of Yevgeny Zamyatin's 1924 seminal classic, *We*. I wanted to try a dystopia from the female point of view — the world according to Julia, as it were. However, this does not make *The Handmaid's Tale* a "feminist dystopia," except insofar as giving a woman a voice and an inner life will always be considered "feminist" by those who think women ought not to have these things.

In other respects, the despotism I describe is the same as all real ones and most imagined ones. It has a small powerful group at the top that controls — or tries to control — everyone else, and it gets the lion's share of available goodies. The pigs in *Animal Farm* get the milk and the apples, the elite of *The Handmaid's Tale* get the fertile women. The force that opposes the tyranny in my book is one in which Orwell himself — despite his belief in the need for political organization to combat oppression — always put great store: ordinary human decency, of the kind he praised in his essay on Charles Dickens. The Biblical expression of this quality is probably in the verse, "Inasmuch as ye have done it unto the least of these . . . ye have done it unto me." Tyrants and the powerful believe, with Lenin, that you can't make an omelette without breaking eggs, and that the end justifies the means. Orwell, when push came to shove, would have believed — on the contrary — that the means defines the end. He wrote as if he sided with the John Donne who said, "Any man's death diminishes me." And so say — I would hope — all of us.

At the end of *The Handmaid's Tale*, there's a section that owes much to *Nineteen Eighty-four*. It's the account of a symposium held several hundred years in the future, in which the repressive government described in the novel is now merely a subject for academic analysis. The parallels with Orwell's essay on Newspeak should be evident.

Orwell has been an inspiration to generations of writers in another important respect — his insistence on the clear and exact use of language. "Prose like a window pane," he said, opting for plainsong rather than ornament. Euphemisms and skewed terminology should not obscure the truth. "Acceptable megadeaths" rather than "millions of rotting corpses, but hey, it's not us that's dead;" "untidiness" instead of "massive destruction" — this is the beginning of Newspeak. Fancy verbiage is what confuses Boxer the horse and underpins the chantings of the sheep. To insist on *what is*, in the face of ideological spin, popular consensus, and official denial: Orwell knew this takes honesty, and a lot of guts. The position of odd man out is always an uneasy one, but the moment we look around and find that there are no longer any odd men among our public voices is the moment of most danger — because that's when we'll be in lockstep, ready for the Two Minutes Hate.

The twentieth century could be seen as a race between two versions of man-made hell — the jackbooted state totalitarianism of Orwell's *Nineteen Eighty-four*, and the hedonistic ersatz paradise of *Brave New World*, where absolutely everything is a consumer good and human beings are engineered to be happy. With the fall of the Berlin Wall in 1989, it seemed for a time that *Brave New World* had won — from henceforth, state control would be minimal, and all we'd have to do was go shopping and smile a lot, and wallow in pleasures, popping a pill or two when depression set in.

But with the legendary 9/11 World Trade Center attack in the year 2001, all that changed. Now it appears we face the prospect of two contradictory dystopias at once — open markets, closed minds — because state surveillance is back again with a vengeance. The torturer's dreaded Room 101 has been with us for millennia. The dungeons of Rome, the Inquisition, the Star Chamber, the Bastille, the proceedings of General Pinochet and of the junta in Argentina — all have depended on secrecy and on the abuse of power. Lots of countries have had their versions of it — their ways of silencing troublesome dissent. Democracies have traditionally defined themselves by, among other things — openness and the rule of law. But now it seems that we in the West are tacitly legitimizing the methods of the darker human past, upgraded technologically and sanctified to our own uses, of course. For the sake of freedom, freedom must be renounced. To move us toward the improved world — the utopia we're promised — dystopia must first hold sway. It's a concept worthy of doublethink. It's also, in its ordering of events, strangely Marxist. First the Dictatorship of the Proletariat, in which lots of heads must roll; then the pie-in-the-sky Classless Society, which oddly enough never materializes. Instead we just get pigs with whips.

What would George Orwell have to say about it? I often ask myself.

Quite a lot.

44

ARGUING AGAINST ICE CREAM

ENOUGH: STAYING HUMAN IN AN ENGINEERED AGE
BY BILL MCKIBBEN

1

ENOUGH, BY BILL McKIBBEN, is a passionate, succinct, chilling, closely argued, sometimes hilarious, touchingly well-intentioned, and essential summary of the future proposed by "science" for the human race. This is the same Bill McKibben who wrote *The End of Nature*, about how *Homo sapiens* has been rearranging the biosphere with the aid of genetically modified plants to suit what it believes is its own interests, and *Long Distance*, about running marathons, as well as essays for *The New Yorker*, the *New York Times*, *The New York Review of Books*, *The Atlantic*, and others.

Bill McKibben appears to be a smart and thoughtful person, but also kindly and optimistic, as far as can be told from his prose. He likes going for walks in the woods, and he seems very fit, and his jacket photo looks like someone you wouldn't want playing against you at bridge because he'd already know what you had in your hand. In other words, he could qualify for membership in a muscular branch of upper-level-IQ geekhood, and cannot be simply dismissed as a dull-normal Luddite too dumb to understand the nifty customized body-and-brain parts soon to be on offer to you and yours.

On offer for a price, of course. Ah yes, the price. The traditional fee for this kind of thing was your soul, but who pays any attention to that tattered theological rag any more, since it can't be located with a brain probe? And hey, the Special Deal is a super package! How could you refuse? It contains so much that human dreams are made of.

Faust wanted the same sort of stuff. Many have wanted it: eternal youth, godlike beauty, hyperintelligence, Charles Atlas strength. Those of us brought up on the back pages of comic books know the appeal. They'll never laugh again when you sit down at the piano because now you'll have X-Men fingers and Mozart's genius; they won't dare to kick sand in your face at the beach because you'll be built like Hercules; you'll never again be refused a date because of your ugly blackheads, which will have been banished, along with many another feature you could do without. Turning to more adult concerns such as death, you won't have to invest in a cement coffin container, because not only will your loved one be safe tonight, he or she will still be alive, and forever! And so will you.

The line forms to the right, and it'll be a long one. (*Enough* mentions a couple of California artists who set up a piece of conceptual art in the form of a boutique called Gene Genies Worldwide, with printed brochures illustrating what you could buy, and were deluged with serious inquiries.) Anyone who thinks there won't be a demand for what's putatively on sale is hallucinating. But along comes Bill McKibben with his sidewalk-preacher's sandwich board, denouncing the whole enterprise and prophesying doom. There will be catcalls of *killjoy* and *spoilsport*, not to mention *troglodyte*, *naysayer*, and *hand-wringer*. Like Prince Charles, who's just come out against nanotechnology on the ground that it could reduce the world to grey goo, McKibben will be told to keep his nose out of it because it's none of his business.

"Mankind was my business," laments Marley's ghost when it's too late for him. And so says Bill McKibben. Mankind is his business. He addresses the greedy little Scrooge in all of us, and points out to that greedy little Scrooge why he should not want more and more, and more, and, just to top it off, more.

More of what? To that in a minute, but first, a digression on the word *more*. Two emblematic uses of *more* spring to mind. The first is of course the echoing *more* pronounced by Oliver Twist when he is being starved in a foundlings' home by venal officials. That *more* is the legitimate response to *not enough*. It's the *more* of real need, and only the hard-hearted and wickedly self-righteous Mr. Bumbles of this world can be outraged by it. The second *more* is in the film *Key Largo*, in the remarkable exchange between the Humphrey Bogart hero character and the Edward G. Robinson evil crook. The crook is asked what he wants, and he doesn't know. Humphrey knows, however. "He wants more," he says. And this is what the crook does want: more, and more than he can possibly use; or rather, more than he can appreciate, dedicated as he is to mere accumulation and mere power. For the alternative to *more*, in McKibben's book, is not *less*, but *enough*. Its epigraph might well be that old folk saying, "Enough is as good as a feast."

The *enough* of the title, seen rightly — McKibben implies — is already a feast. It's us, as we are, with maybe a few allowable improvements. More than that is too much. These tempting *mores* — for there are many of them — grow on the more and more Trees of Knowledge that crowd the modern scientific landscape so thickly you can't see the forest for them. McKibben takes axe in hand and sets out to clear a path. Which apples should be plucked, which left alone? How hard should we think before taking the fateful bite? And why shouldn't we pig out, and what's our motivation if we do? Is it the same old story — we want to be as the gods? If it's *that* story, we've read it, in its many versions. It's never had a happy ending. Not so far.

The items on the smorgasbord of human alteration divide roughly into three. First, genetic alteration, or gene splicing, whereby parents who are five feet tall and bald can give birth to a six-footer with long blond hair who looks like the next-door neighbour. Well, it'll provide some new excuses. ("Honey, we *chose* that! Remember?") Second, nanotechnology, or the development of single-atom-layer gizmos that can replicate themselves and assemble and disassemble matter. Some of these might be sent into our bodies to repair them, like the miniaturized submarine containing the memorable Raquel Welch in the film *Fantastic Voyage*. Third, cybernetics, or the melding of man with machine, like the bionic man. At least we'll all be able to get the lids off jars.

There's a fourth idea that's glanced at — cryogenics, or getting yourself or your budget-version head flash-frozen until such time as the yellow-brick road to immortality has been built; whereupon you'll be unfrozen and restored to youth and health, and, if the head-only option has been chosen, a new body can be grown for you from a few scrapings of your — or somebody else's — DNA. Investing even a small amount of belief in this scheme puts you in the same league as those who happily buy the Brooklyn Bridge from shifty-looking men in overcoats, for the company — yes, it would be a company — in charge of your frozen head would need to be not only perennially solvent — bankruptcy would equal meltdown — but impeccably honest.

Every field of human endeavour attracts its quota of con men and scam artists, but this one would seem to be a natural. What's to stop the operators from banking your money, subjecting you to the initial gelatification, and then, pleading electrical failure, dumping your unpleasantly melting self into the trash, or better — waste not, want not, and the shareholders expect a solid bottom line — recycling you for cat food? The pyramids of the mummified Egyptian kings, thoroughly pillaged once the relatives' backs were turned, stand as a gloss on this kind of thinking, as does London's Highgate Cemetery, a Garden of Eternity parcelled out in pricey lots that became an overgrown thicket once the money stream petered out.

But McKibben's fervent arguments are of a more clean-cut kind: he is not a novelist or a poet, and thus does not descend all the way into the foul rag-and-bone shop of the heart. He assumes a certain amount of sincerity and probity in the less-wacky advocates of these developments, and his appeals are directed to our rational and ethical faculties. We should act, he believes, out of respect for human history and the human race.

He first tackles genetic engineering, already present in soybeans and not so far off for *Homo sapiens* now that we have the luminous green rabbit and the goat/spider. Gene splicing is the modern answer to the eternal urge to make a more perfect model of ourselves. The novel of record is Mary Shelley's *Frankenstein*: we just can't stop tinkering, partly because it's so interesting, and partly because we have a high opinion of our own abilities; but we risk creating monsters.

Gene splicing depends on cloning — McKibben explains how — but is not the same. It involves inserting selected genes — of those other than the parents — into an egg, which is then implanted in the usual way (or will be until the bottled babies of *Brave New World* make their appearance, and we can do away with the womb altogether). If we become genetically enhanced in this way — enhanced by our parents before we're born — the joy and mystery will go out of life, says McKibben, because we won't have to strive for mastery. Our achievements won't be "ours" but will have been programmed into us; we'll never know whether we are really feeling "our" emotions, or whether they — like the false memories embedded in the replicants in the film *Blade Runner* — are off the shelf. We won't be our unique selves, we'll just be the sum totals of market whims. We truly will be the "meat machines" that some scientists already term us. Right now about all our parents can pick for us are our names, but what if they could pick everything about us? (And you thought your mother had bad taste in sofas!)

Worse, we'll be caught in a keep-up-with-the-Joneses competition whereby each new generation of babies will have to have all the latest enhancements — will have to be more intelligent, more beautiful, more disease free, longer-lived, than the generation before. (Babies of the rich, it goes without saying, because there's gold in them thar frills.) Thus each new generation will be *sui generis* — isolated, disconsolate, as out of date as last year's car model before they're even twenty-one, each of them stuck on a lily pad of enhancement a few hops behind the one that follows them. In addition to that, they'll be cut off from history — from their own family tree — because who knows what family trees they'll really be perpetuating? They'll bear little relation to their so-called ancestors. The loneliness and the sense of disconnection could be extreme.

McKibben does not go on to explore the ultimate hell this situation could produce. Imagine the adolescent whining and sulking that will be visited upon the parents that have chosen their children's features out of a catalogue, and — inevitably — will have chosen wrong. "I didn't ask to be born" will be replaced by resentments such as "I didn't ask to have blue eyes," or "I didn't ask to be a math whiz." Burn that gene brochure! If your kid whines about not being enhanced enough, you can just say you couldn't afford it. (The advocates of gene enhancement might respond that since you'll be able to choose your child's temperament as well, naturally you'll pick a type that will never do any adolescent whining or sulking. Pay no attention: these people will not be talking about flesh-and-blood children, but about Stepford Kids.)

Again, McKibben doesn't go all the way down, into the dark realms of envy, cheating, payoffs, and megalomaniac revenge. What's to prevent your enemy from bribing your gene doctor so that your baby turns out like Hannibal the Cannibal?

But what about heritable diseases? you may reasonably ask. Why should any child get stuck with cerebral palsy, or autism, or schizophrenia, or Huntington's chorea, or the many other maladies that genes are heir to? They shouldn't if there's a remedy, and there is.

McKibben points out that these conditions can be eliminated without taking the final step. (After *Enough* was published and before this review was written, a Canadian team cracked the gene for autism. Help is on the way.) Once their genome has been analyzed, parents at risk could be notified of any defects, and could go the in vitro route, with fertilized eggs lacking in the culpable gene chosen for implanting. This "somatic gene therapy" would not involve the addition of anyone else's genes. Plastic surgery, hormones, vitamin pills, and somatic gene therapy are enough, says McKibben; gene splicing is too much.

Next, McKibben delves into nanotechnology, which is also well on the way. The applicable folk tale for nanotechnology is "The Sorcerer's Apprentice" — what if you get the process started, but the self-replicating nanobot escapes, and you can't turn the darn thing off? We might create an assembler that makes food — dirt in one end, potatoes out the other — or something that destroys bioforms hostile to us. But what if such a nanobot goes on the rampage and attacks all bioforms? This is where Prince Charles's apprehension about "grey goo" comes in. It's a real fear, and one discussed by McKibben.

Cybernetics and artificial intelligence also get a look-in, as man-and-machine combinations are occupying some of our better-paid minds. Visions of microchips implanted in your brain dance in their heads — well, we already have pacemakers, so what's the difference? Why shouldn't we baptize artificial intelligence doodads, because they can be made to resemble us so much that maybe they have whatever we think merits baptism? Call it a soul, why not? Maybe we can get enhanced smellability, X-ray vision, Spidey Sense, the works. Artificial orgasms, better than the real thing. *Everything* will be better than the real thing! Why shouldn't we have eyes in the backs of our heads? Why do we only have one mouth that has to perform several functions — talking, eating, whistling? If we had several buccal orifices we'd be able to do all these things at once! (Sign here. You owe it to yourself. Because you deserve it.)

There's been quite a lot of chat about the shortcomings we've had to put up with thanks to Mother Nature, the dirty treacherous cow, and this is the not-so-cleverly-hidden subtext of a lot of brave-new-world thinking. These folks hate Nature, and they hate themselves as part of it, or her. McKibben cites an amazing speech given by Max More (last name chosen by himself) to the Extropian Convention (*extropy*, coined as the opposite to *entropy*). This speech took the form of a dissing of Mother Nature, and said, essentially, thanks for nothing and goodbye. Nature has made so many mistakes, the chief one being death. Why do we have to get old and die? Why is man the one creature that foresees its own death?

As in many religions — and the energy propelling the wilder fringes of this "more" enterprise is religious in essence — there has to be a second birth, one that gets around the indignity of having come out of a body — a female body — and, come to think of it, of having a body yourself. All that guck and blood and cells and death. Why do we have to eat? And, by implication, defecate. So messy. Maybe we can fix our digestive tracts so we just slip out a little pellet, say once a month. Maybe we can be born again, this time out of an artificial head instead of a natural body, and download the contents of our brains into machines, and linger around in cyberspace, as in William Gibson's novels. Though if you've read William Gibson, you'll know the place is a queasy nightmare.

2

All the enhancements McKibben discusses are converging on the biggie, which is none other than the final nose-thumb at Nature — immortality. Immortality doesn't fare so well in myth and story. Either you get it but forget to request eternal youth too, and become a crumbling horror (Tithonus, the Sibyl of Cumae, Swift's Struldbrugs), or you seize the immortality and the vitality, but lose your soul and must live by feeding on the blood of the innocent (Melmoth the Wanderer, vampires, and so forth). The stories are clear: gods are immortal, men die, try to change it and you'll end up worse off.

That doesn't stop us from hankering. McKibben recognizes the impulse: "Objecting even slightly to immortality," he rightly says, "is a little like arguing against ice cream — eternal life has only been humanity's great dream since the moment we became conscious." But unlike all previous generations, ours might be able to achieve it. This would alter us beyond recognition. We'd become a different species — one living in eternal bliss, in the eyes of its proponents, sort of like, well, angels, or superhuman beings anyway. It would certainly mean an end to narrative. If life is endless, why tell stories? No more beginnings and middles, because there will be no more endings. No Shakespeare for us, or Dante, or, well, any art, really. It's all infested with mortality, and reeks of earthiness. Our new angel-selves will no longer need or understand our art. They might have other art, though it would be pretty bloodless.

But once we're well and truly immortal, what would we do all day? Wouldn't we get tired of the endlessness, the monotony, the lack of meaningful event? Wouldn't we get bored? Nope. We'd sit around and contemplate problems, such as: "Where did the universe come from?" "Why is there something rather than nothing?" "What is the meaning of conscious existence?" Is that to be the result of all this admittedly fascinating science — a tedious first-year philosophy seminar? "Not to be impolite," says McKibben, "but for this we trade our humanity?"

That's the good version of the immortal mind. I encountered the bad version in a paperback I received through a high-school book-a-month club. *Donovan's Brain* was its title, and the brain in question was being kept alive in a large fish tank and fed on brain food. The hope of the scientists doing this was that the brain would grow in power and strength, and solve problems such as "Why is there something rather than nothing," and benefit mankind. But Donovan when he had a body was a stock manipulator or the equivalent, and he bent his new-found mind powers in the direction of world domination, zapping people who got in his way. A big brain does not mean a nice brain. This was made clear to me at the age of twelve, and it's made even clearer in *Enough*. There are some very clever people at work on the parts that will go into making up our immortality, and what they're doing is on some levels fascinating — like playing with the biggest toy box you've ever seen — but they are not the people who should be deciding our future. Asking these kinds of scientists what improved human nature should be like is like asking ants what you should have in your backyard. Of course they would say "more ants."

And while we're on the subject, who exactly is "we?" The "we," that is, who are promised all these goodies. "We" will be the "Gen-Rich," the rich in genes. "We" are certainly not the six billion people already on the planet, nor the ten billion projected for the year 2050 — those will be the "GenPoor." "We," when we appear, will be a select few, and since our enhanced genes and our immortality are going to be so expensive, and will not survive — for instance — being squashed flat by tanks, we will have to take steps to protect ourselves. Doubtless "we" will devise almost-impenetrable walls, as in the Zamyatin novel of the same name, or "we" will live in a castle, with "them" — the serfs and peasants, the dimwits, the mortals — roiling around outside. We will talk like James Dewey Watson; we'll say things like "It's not much fun being around dumb people." In fact, we'll behave a lot like the aristocrats of old, convinced of our own divine right. The serfs and peasants will hate us. Not to throw cold water on it, but if the serfs and peasants are true to form, sooner or later they'll get hold of some pitchforks and torches and storm the barricades. So to avoid the peasants, we'll have to go into outer space. Having fun yet?

The agenda of those who visualize themselves as the GenRich — like Past Lifers, Future Lifers never see themselves playing the role of ditchdigger — is being pushed in the name of that magic duo, progress and inevitability, the twins that always make an appearance when quite a few potential shareholders smell megabucks in the air. (Along with them come the usual my-dick-is-bigger adjectives, as McKibben points out — guts and risk-taking and so forth — so if you don't rush out and get your genes spliced and your head frozen, you're some sort of a wuss.) "Progress" has deluded many, but surely its pretensions as a rallying slogan have been exploded by now: progress is not the same as change. As for "inevitability," it's the rapist's argument: the thing is going to happen anyway, so why not just lie back and enjoy it? Resistance is futile. (That was the old advice: now you're told to scream and vomit, thus influencing the outcome. Times change.)

McKibben takes on both of the magic twins, and is particularly moving on "inevitability." We still have choice, he says. Just because a thing has been invented doesn't mean you have to use it. He offers as exempla the atomic bomb, the Japanese samurais' rejection of guns, the Chinese abandonment of advanced sea power, and the Amish, who examine each new technology and accept or reject it according to social and spiritual criteria. We too, he says, can accept or reject according to social and spiritual criteria. We can, and we should. We must decide as ourselves — as who we already are as human beings. We must decide from the fullness of our present humanity, flawed though it may be. As I've said, McKibben is an optimist. I agree with him about what we should do, but I'm not too sure we'll do it.

The fact is — and this is not a line of thought McKibben pursues — that the argument for the perfectibility of mankind rests on a logical fallacy. Thus: Man is by definition imperfect, say those who would perfect him. But those who would perfect him are themselves, by their own definition, imperfect. And imperfect beings cannot make perfect decisions. The decision about what constitutes human perfection would have to be a perfect decision; otherwise the result would be not perfection, but imperfection. As witness the desire for several different mouths.

Perhaps our striving for perfection should take a different, more Blakean form. Perhaps Infinity can be seen in a grain of sand, and Eternity in an hour. Perhaps happiness is not a goal but a road. Perhaps the pursuit of happiness is that happiness. Perhaps we should take a cue from Tennyson, and separate wisdom and knowledge, and admit that wisdom cannot be cloned or manufactured. Perhaps that admission is wisdom. Perhaps enough should be enough for us. Perhaps we should leave well enough alone.

45

FOREWORD: VICTORY GARDENS

A BREATH OF FRESH AIR

BY ELISE HOUGHTON

I

WHEN I WAS SMALL, people had Victory Gardens. This was during the Second World War, and the idea was that if people grew their own vegetables, then the food produced by the farmers would be freed up for use by the army. There was another strong motivator: rationing was in effect for things you were unlikely to be able to grow yourself, such as sugar, butter, milk, tea, cheese, and meat, so the more you could grow, the better you would eat, and the better the soldiers would eat too. Thus, by digging and hoeing and weeding and watering, you too could help win the war.

But people did not live on vegetables and fruit alone. Anything resembling protein or fat was precious. Shortening, margarine, and bacon drippings were cherished; gizzards, livers, feet, and necks were not scorned. Bits and scraps that today would be carelessly tossed into the trash were hoarded and treasured, making their way from their first appearance as, say, a roasted chicken, through various other incarnations as noodle-and-leftovers casseroles, soups and stews, and mystery ingredients in pot pies. A housewife's skill was measured by the number of times she could serve up the same thing without your knowing it.

Careful planning was required; waste was frowned on. This meant that everything, not only from such things as chickens but from the garden, had to be used, and, if necessary, preserved. Home freezing hadn't arrived yet, so canning and preserving were major activities, especially in the late summer, when the garden would produce more than the family could eat. Housewives cooked up vast quantities of tomato sauce, pickles, green beans, strawberries, applesauce — vegetables and fruits of all kinds. These would be eaten in the winter, along with the cabbages and the winter squash and the root vegetables — beets, carrots, turnips, and potatoes — that had been stored in a cool place.

As children growing up in this era, we knew that every seedling was precious. We were part of the system: we weeded and watered, we picked off cabbage worms and tomato worms and potato bugs. We dug peelings and cores and husks back into the soil; we fended off woodchucks; we sprinkled wood ashes. If lucky enough to be near a source of blueberries, we picked them; and we picked peas and beans, and we dug potatoes. I can't claim that all of this was spontaneous labour, joyfully performed: such tasks were chores. But the connection between tending the vegetables and eating the results was clear. Food did not come wrapped in plastic from the supermarket — there were hardly any supermarkets, anyway. It came out of the ground or it grew on a bush or tree, and it needed water and sunlight and proper fertilization.

My mother's generation was brought up strictly: children were expected to finish everything on their plates, whether they liked it or not, and if they failed to do this they were made to sit at the dinner table until they did. Frequently they were told to remember other children who were starving — the Armenians, the Chinese. I used to think this was both harsh — why force a child to eat when it wasn't hungry? — and ridiculous — what good would eating your bread crusts do for the Armenians? But this method doubtless had at its heart an insistence on respect. Many people had laboured to produce the food on the plate, among them the parents, who had either grown it or paid hard-earned cash for it. You could not snub this food. You should show a proper gratitude. Hence the once-widespread practice of saying grace at meals, which has fallen into disuse. Why be grateful for something — now — so easy to come by?

II

In the plot line of life on earth, gardens are a recent twist. They date back to perhaps ten thousand years ago, when the gathering and hunting that had been the prevailing model for 99 percent of human history could no longer sustain societies in the face of diminishing game and wild food supplies.

When the total population of the earth was less than four million people — before, the experts estimate, about ten thousand years ago — the gathering and hunting way of life was still viable. The myth of the Golden Age appears to have some foundation in fact: food was there in the wild, for the taking, and people didn't have to spend much of their time obtaining it. After that point, conditions became harder, as communities had to adapt more labour-intensive stratagems to feed themselves. "Agriculture" is sometimes used to denote any form of cultivation or domestication — of herd animals for meat and milk, of garden crops and fruit trees, of field crops such as wheat and barley. Sometimes a distinction is made between "agriculture," in which large areas are farmed using the plough to break the ground — traditionally a male activity — and "horticulture," in which smaller, individual garden plots are cultivated, traditionally by women. "Horticulture" is thought to have come first, but all agree that there was a long period of transition in which gathering and hunting, horticulture and agriculture, existed side by side.

Many ills have been ascribed to agriculture. In gathering and hunting cultures, food was — as a rule — obtained and eaten as needed. But once agriculture became firmly established — once crops could be harvested and stored, once surpluses could be accumulated, and, not incidentally, transported, exchanged, destroyed, and stolen — social strata became possible, with slaves at the lower end, peasants above them, and a ruling class on top that made no physical effort in order to eat. Armies could march on surplus food supplies; religious hierarchies could tithe; kings could preside; taxes could be levied. Crop monocultures became widespread, with a dependence on only a few kinds of food, resulting not only in malnutrition, but in famine at times of crop failure.

A city dweller's relation to food is — as a system — closer to the gathering-hunting model than to the horticultural-agricultural one. You don't grow the food yourself, or raise it in the form of an animal. Instead you go to the place where the food is — the supermarket, most likely. Someone else has done the killing, in the case of animal food, or the primary picking, in the case of vegetables, but essentially the shopper is a gatherer. His or her skills consist in knowing where the good stuff is and tracking it down if it's rare. The shopping experience is given all the trappings of a walk in a magic forest — soft music plays, the colours of packages are supernaturally bright, food is displayed as if it's there by miracle. All you have to do is reach out your hand, as in the Golden Age. And then pay, of course.

Such a system disguises origins. The food in shops is dirt-free, and as bloodless as possible. Yet everything we eat comes — in one way or another — out of the earth.

III

The first garden I can remember was in northern Quebec, where my father ran a small forest-insect research station. The area was a glacial scrape — a region where the glaciers had removed the topsoil thousands of years ago, scraping down to the granite bedrock. Thousands of years after their retreat, the soil was just a thin layer on top of sand or gravel. My parents used this sandy soil as the basis for their garden. Luckily they had a source of manure, from a lumber camp — in those days, horses were still used in winter to drag the felled trees down to the lake for eventual transport to the mill by water. My parents ferried boatloads of this manure to their fenced-in sandy patch, where they dug it in. From this unpromising ground they raised — among other things — peas, beans, carrots, radishes, lettuce, spinach, Swiss chard, and even the occasional flower. Nasturtiums are what I remember, and the vivid blossoms of the scarlet runner beans, a favourite with hummingbirds. The moral: Almost any patch of dirt can be a garden, with enough elbow grease and horse manure.

That garden occurred in the 1940s, when the war was still going on, horticulture in the form of Victory Gardens was still widely practised, and every morsel of food was treasured.

IV

After the war the postwar boom set in, and attitudes underwent a major change. After a long period of anxiety and hard work and tragedy, people wanted more ease in their lives. Military production switched off, the manufacture of consumer goods switched on. Home appliances proliferated: the outdoor clothesline was replaced by the dryer, the wringer washer by the automatic. Supermarkets sprang up. Prepackaging arrived. Simple-minded abundance was the order of the day.

The period from 1950 to 2000 might be characterized as the Disposable Period. Waste — including preplanned obsolescence — was no longer seen as an evil and a sin. It became a positive thing, because the more you threw out, the more you would consume, and that would drive the economy, and everyone would become more prosperous. Wouldn't they?

This model works fine as long as there's an endless supply of goods funnelling into the In end of the pipe. But it breaks down when the source of supply becomes exhausted. The ultimate source of supply is the biosphere itself. But in the 1950s, that too appeared to be inexhaustible. And so the party continued. What a thrill, to eat only half of your hamburger, then toss the rest!

There was an undeniable emotional charge to throwing stuff out. Scrimping, saving, and hoarding make a person feel poor — think of Scrooge in *A Christmas Carol* — whereas dispensing largesse, whether in the form of a prize goose, as in Scrooge's case, or in the form of filling up your garbage can with junk you no longer want, makes you feel rich. Saving is heavy, discarding is light. Why do we feel this way? Once we were nomads, and nomads don't carry around grand pianos. They don't hoard food; instead they move to where food is. They leave a light footprint, as the green folk say. Well, it's a theory.

But we can't all be nomads any more. There isn't enough space left for that.

V

Many people gave up their gardens after the war. My parents kept on with theirs, because they said fresh food tasted better. (This is actually true.) The age of full-blown pesticides was just arriving, and that may have had something to do with it as well. My father was an early opponent of widespread pesticide use, partly because this was his field of study. According to him, spraying forests to kill infestations of budworm and sawfly simply arrested the infestation, after which the insects would develop a resistance to the poisons used on them and would continue on their rampage. Meanwhile you'd have killed off their natural enemies, which would no longer be around to fight them. The effects of these poisons on human beings was unknown, but could not be discounted. At that time his views were considered quaint.

Thus the second major garden in my life was in Toronto. Again, the soil was unpromising: heavy clay, which was sticky in the rain but would bake to a hard finish during dry spells. The soil was particularly good for growing giant dandelions and huge clumps of couch grass. It took a lot of work to turn it into anything resembling a garden. Kitchen scraps were composted, fall leaves were dug into the ground by the bushel.

By this time I was a teenager, and was expected to do quite a lot of weeding and watering. News for parents: weeding and watering someone else's garden is not quite as engaging as weeding and watering your own. The high points were the time when I shot a marauding woodchuck with my bow (the arrow was a target arrow, not a hunting arrow, so it bounced off) and the other time when I pulled up all of my father's experimental Jerusalem artichokes by mistake.

Once past my teenage years, I gave up gardening for a time. I'd had enough of it. Also I wasn't in a location that permitted it: I was an itinerant student and sometime teacher and market researcher and writer, and I moved fifteen times in ten years. In the early 1970s, however, I found myself on a farm that had a barn with a large supply of well-rotted horse manure, and the temptation was too great to resist. For eight years we grew everything imaginable. To the staples we added corn, kohlrabi, asparagus, currants — red and white — and elderberries. We tried out new methods — potatoes grown in straw, marigolds to catch slugs. We canned, froze, dried; we made sauerkraut, not an experiment I would choose to repeat. We made wine, jams and jellies, beer. We raised our own chickens and ducks and sheep; we buried parsnips in holes in the ground, and carrots in boxes of sand in the root cellar.

It was a lot of work. This is one reason people don't do more home gardening.

The other, of course, is lack of land. The number of pumpkins you can raise on your apartment balcony is finite, and your wheat crop in this location would not be large.

VI

Lack of land. Lack of *arable* land. To that we may add "lack of sea," because the sea's resources are being destroyed as fast as the earth's. Soon we may have to add "lack of fresh water" and even "lack of breathable air." There's no free lunch after all.

As a species, we're suffering from our own success. From a population of four million ten thousand years ago, we've increased to six billion today, and growing. The exponential population explosion that has occurred since 1750 was unprecedented in human history, and it will never be repeated. We must slow our growth rate as a species, or face a series of unimaginable environmental and human catastrophes. Arable land is finite, and much of it is rapidly being paved over, eroded, polluted, or depleted. The same rules apply to us as to other animals: no biological population can outlive the exhaustion of its resource base. It's an easy thing to demonstrate to children. Get them an ant farm, feed the ants, watch the ants increase in number. Then cut off the food supply. End of ants.

For *Homo sapiens*, the major question of the twenty-first century will be, *How will we eat?* Already 80 percent of the world's people exist on the starvation borderline. Will we see a sudden enormous crash, as in the mouse-and-lemming cycle? And if so, what then?

VII

These are alarming thoughts to place in the foreword to a kindly and attractive book on school gardening. Such an admirable demonstration of care and careful planning, so much variety, such a symbol of hope. I don't apologize for these thoughts, however: the world I have just described is the one today's children will be facing unless there are some fairly large changes of direction.

The reasons for encouraging the school gardening movement are many. Gardens are educational, teaching as they do many lessons.

Food grows in the ground, not in supermarkets; air, soil, sun, and water are the four necessary ingredients; composting is a fine notion; front lawns are a water-gobbling waste of space; the individual can be an instrument for positive change; unless you're a geologist, plants are more interesting than gravel; beetles come in many forms; worms are good; nature must be respected; we are part of nature.

All of these are positive concepts, but fifty years ago — even thirty years ago — they would have been viewed as extra, frilly, prissy, goody-goody. Even now, some in our society would place them in this slot: the hard stuff, the right stuff to grind into the minds of children, is how to make a lot of money.

But money's useless when there's nothing to eat. So there's another set of skills to be learned from school gardens: how to grow your own food. Perhaps today's children will need these skills. Perhaps they'll find themselves in some grim collective dedicated to turning golf courses back into market gardens and superhighways into very long grain fields, and front lawns into potato plots. Perhaps the Victory Garden will make a forced comeback due to scarcity.

Or perhaps our species will solve its problems before droughts and famines become endemic.

Then again, perhaps not.

46

CAROL SHIELDS,
WHO DIED LAST WEEK, WROTE BOOKS
THAT WERE FULL OF DELIGHTS

THE BELOVED CANADIAN AUTHOR Carol Shields died on July 16 at her home in Victoria, British Columbia, after a long battle with cancer. She was sixty-eight. The enormous media coverage given to her and the sadness expressed by her many readers paid tribute to the high esteem in which she was held in her own country, but her death made the news all around the world.

Conscious as she was of the vagaries of fame and the element of chance in any fortune, she would have viewed that with a certain irony, but she would also have found it deeply pleasing. She knew about the darkness, but — both as an author and as a person — she held on to the light. "She was just a luminous person, and that would be important and persist even if she hadn't written anything," said her friend and fellow author Alice Munro.

Earlier in her writing career, some critics mistook this quality of light in her for lightness, light-mindedness, on the general principle that comedy — a form that turns on misunderstanding and confusion, but ends in reconciliation, of however tenuous a kind — is less serious than tragedy, and that the personal life is of lesser importance than the public one. Carol Shields knew better. Human life is a mass of statistics only for statisticians: the rest of us live in a world of individuals, and most of them are not prominent. Their joys however are fully joyful, and their griefs are real. It was the extraordinariness of ordinary people that was Shields's forte, reaching its fullest expression in her novels *Swann*, *The Republic of Love*, and especially *The Stone Diaries*. She gave her material the full benefit of her large intelligence, her powers of observation, her humane wit, and her wide reading. Her books are delightful, in the original sense of the word: they are full of delights.

She understood the life of the obscure and the overlooked partly because she had lived it: her study of Jane Austen reveals a deep sympathy with the plight of the woman novelist toiling incognito, appreciated only by an immediate circle but longing for her due. Born in 1935 in the United States, Shields was at the tail end of the postwar generation of North American college-educated women who were convinced by the mores of their time that their destiny was to get married and have five children. This Carol did; she remained a devoted mother and a constant wife throughout her life. Her husband, Don, was a civil engineer. They moved to Canada, beginning with Toronto in the 1960s, a time of poetic ferment in that city. Carol, who was already writing then and had attended some readings, said of that time, "I knew no writers." Undoubtedly she felt relegated to that nebulous category, "just a housewife," like Daisy in *The Stone Diaries* and like Mary Swann, the eponymous poet who is murdered by her husband when her talent begins to show. (Canadian readers would understand the allusion, but British ones who might consider this plot far-fetched will be interested to know that there was a Canadian woman poet murdered in this way: Pat Lowther, whose best-known collection is *The Stone Diary*.)

After obtaining an MA at the University of Ottawa, Shields taught for years at the University of Manitoba, in Winnipeg, where she began publishing in the 1970s. But this was the decade of rampant feminism, in the arts at least. Her early books, including *Others*, *Intersect*, *Small Ceremonies*, and *The Box Garden*, which examined the vagaries of domestic life without torpedoing it, did not make a large stir, although some of their early readers found them both highly accomplished and hilarious. She had her first literary breakthrough — not in terms of quality of writing but in terms of audience size — in Britain rather than in North America, with her 1992 novel *The Republic of Love.*

Her glory book was *The Stone Diaries*, which was shortlisted for the Booker Prize and won the Canadian Governor General's Award, and then, in 1995, the American Pulitzer Prize, a feat her dual citizenship made possible. Her next novel, *Larry's Party*, won the Orange Prize in 1998. To say that she was not thrilled by success would be to do her an injustice. She knew what it was worth. She'd waited a long time for it. She wore her new-found prominence with graciousness and used it with largesse. One of the last instances of her enormous generosity of spirit may not be well known: she supplied a jacket quotation for Valerie Martin's fine but challenging novel, *Property* — a book that went on to win the 2003 Orange Prize. It takes place in the American south during slavery, and none of the characters are "nice," but as Carol remarked in a letter she wrote me, that was the point.

Unless, her last novel, was written in the small space of time she spent in England, after beating cancer the first time and before it came back. It's a hymn to the provisional: the sense of happiness and security as temporary and fragile is stronger than ever. *Unless* was published in 2002 and was shortlisted for just about every major English-language prize. The Munro Doctrine, informally named after Alice Munro, had set in by then — after a certain number of prizes you are shot into the stratosphere, where you circulate in radiant mists, far beyond the ken of juries.

Several months before her death, Carol published — with co-editor Marjorie Anderson — *Dropped Threads 2*, the sequel to the spectacularly successful 2001 anthology *Dropped Threads*. This was a frankly feminist collection, taking "feminist" in its broadest sense:

contributors were asked to write about subjects of concern to women that had been excluded from the conversation so far. Those who had heard Carol Shields interviewed were probably surprised by this strain in her character, and by the angry letters addressed to male pundits dismissive of woman writers in *Unless*, because in conversation she was discreet and allusive. The little frown, the shake of the head, said it all.

Possibly feminism was something she worked into, as she published more widely and came up against more commentators who thought excellent pastry was a facile creation compared with raw meat on skewers, and who in any case could not recognize the thread of blood in her work, though it was always there. The problem of the luminous is that their very luminosity obscures the shadows it depends on for its brilliance.

I last saw Carol Shields at the end of April. Her new house was spacious, filled with light. Outside the windows, the tulips in her much-loved garden were in bloom. Typically for her, she claimed she couldn't quite believe she deserved to live in such a big and beautiful house. She felt so lucky, she said.

Although she was very ill, she didn't seem it. She was as alert, as interested in books of all kinds, and as curious as ever. She'd recently been reading nonfiction works on biology, she told me: something new for her, a new source of amazement and wonder. We did not speak of her illness. She preferred to be treated as a person who was living, not one who was dying.

And live she did, and live she does. For as John Keats remarked, every writer has two souls, an earthly one and one that lives on in the world of writing as a voice in the writing itself. It's this voice, astute, compassionate, observant, and deeply human, that will continue to speak to her readers everywhere.

47

RESISTING THE VEIL

REPORTS FROM A REVOLUTION

Persepolis: The Story of a Childhood
By Marjane Satrapi, translated by Mattias Ripa and Blake Ferris

Reading Lolita in Tehran: A Memoir in Books
By Azar Nafisi

The Bathhouse
By Farnoosh Moshiri

Shah of Shahs
By Ryszard Kapuściński, translated by William R. Brand and
Katarzyna Mroczkowska-Brand

The Crisis of Islam: Holy War and Unholy Terror
By Bernard Lewis

The Crusades Through Arab Eyes
By Amin Maalouf, translated by Jon Rothschild

THE LITERARY MAP is like the geological one: it's three-dimensional. Mountains are levelled, rifts open, volcanoes suddenly appear where before there were none. Not so long ago, books by émigrés from the Soviet Union or its satellites were almost guaranteed a hearing in the West. Now, ever since 9/11, a catastrophe that is already a logo, the publishing hot spot has shifted to another incandescent region, the Middle East.

There's scant mystery as to why. Like all sentient animals, we can smell the wind, and the wind brings the news, and the news is what we long for, because we need it. Spilled blood is a compelling scent. A wag once commented that what was really required for a country to produce a world-class literature was a powerful navy, which might be revised to "a strategically significant war."

It's a high price for the people of such countries to pay. That's part of the news.

What did we think we knew about that part of the world, before the ground opened so spectacularly beneath our feet? We had such gauzy ideas. Children of my generation were likely to have been given an *Arabian Nights*, illustrated by Maxfield Parrish. Skies in these fabled lands were bluer than blue, gardens were lush, veiled princesses radiant, slave girls resourceful, bandits malevolent, genies obliging. It was all colourful and romantic and, finally, undependable, like Rudolph Valentino playing a sheik.

At school we might have learned something about the Crusades and Richard the Lion-Heart. We might have come across *The Rubáiyát of Omar Khayyám*: In the 1920s, 1930s, and 1940s, every literate household in North America was likely to have a copy. But then the moving finger wrote, and it was time for the Cold War, and our minds were on other things, and harem pants became merely a fashion statement. Apart from the occasional article in *National Geographic* — the wonders of the Pearl Mosque, the gorgeousness of old carpets — we heard little from these places, and what little we had once known, we forgot. It would be wise for us to remember now. How did things get this bad? We need to learn.

All of which is prelude to three recent books by Iranian women writers. A second prelude would come in handy, because all three of these books were written in a context — that of Iranian history — which itself exists within the history of the wider Muslim world. Although included in the well-known "axis of evil" trio and thus a potential target for another preemptive U.S. war, Iran is not the same as Iraq — a country hammered together during the horse-trading that went on after the Great War — nor is it the equivalent of wild and mountainous Afghanistan. True, all are Muslim, all have oil — an extremely mixed blessing — and all have experienced several decades or more of civil war, repression, invasion, and unbelievable horror. But Iran is — and it prides itself in being — the Persia of old, once the centre of a sophisticated empire, renowned for the beauty of its gardens, the intricacy of its literature, and the refinement of its culture.

In the Muslim world, memories are long, so Amin Maalouf's fascinating 1984 book, *The Crusades Through Arab Eyes*, is useful as a starter. In this period it was the Muslim world that was civilized and inventive — "modern," if you like — and the West that supplied the nasty barbarians, and the most admirable leader was not Richard the Lion-Heart but the Muslim hero, Saladin. (Readers of *Ivanhoe* knew that already, plus some peculiar quasi-factoids about the Knights Templar and their rapist proclivities.)

According to Maalouf, the events of the Crusades still deeply colour Muslim thinking. After the Crusades, he writes, "progress was the embodiment of 'the other'. Modernism became alien. Should cultural and religious identity be affirmed by rejecting this modernism, which the West symbolized? Or, on the contrary, should the road of modernization be embarked upon with resolution, thus risking loss of identity. . . . Even today we can observe a lurching alternation between phases of forced Westernization and phases of extremist, strongly xenophobic traditionalism."

For a broad perspective on the most recent phase of the Islamist quarrel with the West, Bernard Lewis's *The Crisis of Islam: Holy War and Unholy Terror* is indispensable. Lewis, a renowned Islamic scholar, explains in some detail how the West, and America in particular, got transformed into the Great Satan by the Islamists, and how very helpful that transformation has been for them. All political leaders bent on suppressing their own people need a Great Satan, or an axis of evil, or something of the sort, so that resistance to the leader can be portrayed as not only futile but heretical.

Perhaps the most necessary background book is Ryszard Kapuściński's artful and hair-raising 1982 classic, *Shah of Shahs*. Kapuściński wrote it during the first years of the Iranian Revolution. It's a report from the inside of the boiling cauldron — what it felt like to live through those blood-spattered years — but it's also a long backward look. We're reminded of how the late Shah's brutal father was elevated to power by the British, who lusted after oil; of how Mossadegh became prime minister, brought in democracy for two years, and nationalized the country's only oil company; of how he was overthrown by the second Pahlavi Shah, supported by the West; of this Shah's reign of terror, with Savak, his secret police agency, let loose to assassinate and torture. Only against this background does the familiar outcome — the return of the ascetic and fanatical Ayatollah Khomeini, the struggle between modernizing leftish elements and religious extremists, the ascent of the punitive mullahs — make any kind of sense.

"These" — says one of Kapuściński's informants — "are the grim and brutal histories we hoard in our national memory. Tyrants won the throne by force, climbing toward it over corpses. . . . The issue of succession was often settled in distant capitals, and the new pretender to the crown would enter Teheran with the British and Russian envoys supporting his elbows on either side. People treated such Shahs as usurpers and occupiers, and when one knows about that tradition one can understand how the mullahs managed to spark off so many uprisings against them."

Kapuściński watches as the mobs who demonstrated against the despotic Shah turn and rend one another, allow the desire for vengeance to possess them, and become despots in their turn. For a writer from Poland, then still under Soviet control, it was a familiar state of affairs. "[Those] who have brought down a dictator often act, in spite of themselves, like his heirs, perpetuating the attitudes and thought patterns of the epoch they themselves have destroyed," he comments. Toward the end of his grim account, he reflects, "A person, an individual being, . . . is riches without end, he is a world in which we can always discover something new. A crowd, on the other hand, reduces the individuality of the person; a man in a crowd limits himself to a few forms of elementary behaviour. The forms through which a crowd can express its yearnings are extraordinarily meagre and continually repeat themselves: the demonstration, the strike, the rally, the barricades. That is why you can write a novel about a man, but about a crowd — never." Which goes a long way toward explaining why despotisms have always aimed to suppress literature: they love the crowd and hate the individual, and literature is, above all, singular.

That's the background. Now for the foreground: three singular books by Iranian writers, all women. Iran has produced many writers — the level of literary culture there is relatively high, as it has been for centuries — and increasingly, many of these writers have been women. The Iranian experience since 1979 has been of special interest to women — not only Iranian women but women everywhere. Iranian women, by the second third of the twentieth century, had made a good deal of progress; they could acquire education, hold jobs, lead individual lives. Then they were shoved backwards, forced into the veil, deprived of most of their autonomy. Their fate reminds all women of the fragility of their so-called rights and freedoms, for, under the rule of the Iranian mullahs, the female body itself was transformed into a highly charged symbol, a vehicle for projections and religious fantasies. For human beings possessing such bodies, the outcome has rarely been happy.

Persepolis: The Story of a Childhood, by Marjane Satrapi, is a drawn autobiography, like Art Spiegelman's *Maus*. There's a short introduction: her book, the author hopes, will be a tribute to the majority of Iranians who are not involved in "fundamentalism, fanaticism, and terrorism." We then launch into the book proper, which begins with a picture of an ominous eye surrounded by black, and the chapter title: "The Veil."

This is the motif that dominates the narrative: Satrapi was ten in 1980, when the veil became mandatory at her school. But her family was "modern" — leftish and intellectual — and had been involved in protests against the Shah and his bloodbaths. Not only that, her grandfather had once been the Prince of Persia, whose father had been overthrown by the first Reza Pahlavi, an illiterate army officer.

Through Satrapi's charming, sometimes humorous, and often melancholy drawings, we meet her whole family, and follow its members from one gruesome national and personal trauma to the next. The most heartbreaking one concerns Satrapi's beloved uncle, imprisoned under the Shah, but executed by the Islamic Revolution. Her book is less a call to arms than a testament: this is what it was like for one family to live through the dark times. Like so many creative people from Iran, Satrapi finally leaves for the West. Otherwise, we assume, her book could never have been published.

And so it is with Azar Nafisi, author of the engaging *Reading Lolita in Tehran: A Memoir in Books*. This book is also an autobiography of sorts, and covers the same time span as *Persepolis*. Nafisi, too, began as an anti-Shah leftist, a member of student protest groups during her college years in the United States. Her real passion was Western literature, however, and she returned to Iran to teach it just as the Shah's regime was falling.

She, too, resisted the veil and the suppression of women it symbolized to her — under the Shah, for instance, the legal age for marriage was eighteen, but under the mullahs it went down to eight-and-a-half lunar years. (She tells of an interesting ruling by the Ayatollah Khomeini concerning chickens you've had sex with, a practice permitted so men would not vent their urges in illegal ways, on women. Are you allowed to eat such chickens? No, said the Ayatollah: Neither you nor your next-door neighbour may eat the chicken, but the family two doors down is allowed to do so. One envisages a lively local street traffic in chickens. This incident is emblematic of the weirdness of matters sexual in Iran at this time, a weirdness encountered in all three of these books.)

Finally, badgered both by the authorities and the fanatics among her students, Nafisi quit the university and set up a private reading group in her own home. Her adventures with Western literature in the Islamic Republic are essential for anyone who wants to know what life is like for women under this regime, but they also show Western literature itself in a different light. Jane Austen, for one, will never seem the same after Nafisi's spirited defence of her work. Austen's novels — and socially realistic novels in general, as distinct from other fictional prose forms such as romances — are democratic in essence, she believes, because all the characters are allowed to speak in their own voices, as they are, for themselves. Under a regime where only one voice is considered legitimate and the usual way to read literature is as an allegory, Jane Austen is transformed — oddly, for Western readers — into an agent for radical dissent.

Both *Persepolis* and *Reading Lolita* mention the obsession of the mullahs with sex, and both refer to one of the more hideous practices of the revolutionary guards: if a woman to be executed was a virgin, she was "married" in a bogus ceremony, then raped by one of the guards, because virgins go to heaven and the guards wanted to prevent that. In Farnoosh Moshiri's novel *The Bathhouse*, this motif moves from the sidelines to centre stage, for the bathhouse of the title is a holding pen for female political prisoners. The narrator of this spare and courageous novel ends up in the bathhouse as many did — through being related to someone who was politically involved — and is subjected to a number of grisly experiences, narrowly avoiding execution at the Wall of the Almighty.

Her escape, like her arrest, is a fluke: the revolutionary guards aren't what you'd call methodical. There's a large component of sadism and opportunism among them, not to mention superstition and borderline lunacy: it's a firm belief among the bathhouse officials that if you can see the Great Leader's face in the full moon, you've been blessed and are therefore saved. Many of the tormentors are women, including ex-prisoners who claim to have been "converted" and are terrified that they will be tortured again if they don't participate.

Those familiar with Holocaust literature will find themselves right at home, for as with crowds, so with tortures: the range of expression is limited. As Sartre pointed out in his introduction to *The Question*, which examines French behaviour in Algiers, the lesson most frequently learned by those who have been brutalized is how to do the same to others.

A clear consensus emerges from all three of these books: the claims of the Iranian regime to purity of religion are nominal. The hijacking of religion by those bent on power grabs is an age-old theme and by no means limited to the Muslim world, but it must be a source of great sadness to the majority of Muslims to see how their faith has been twisted and misused. The Prophets warned against the conversion of false idols into gods, but here we see the conversion of God into a false idol.

It's also true of any society that if you hand people a licence to be vicious and tell them that the exercise of this viciousness is in a good cause — better, the cause of God — that licence will be used to the full. The most frightening thing about such regimes is the emotional deadening and the sheer meanness they bring out in otherwise unremarkable people. A man may be "riches without end . . . a world in which we can always discover something new," but such worlds range all the way from heaven to hell. Unfortunately, although we continue to dream of heaven, we aren't very good at creating it. We're so much better at hell.

48

INTRODUCTION

THE COMPLETE STORIES, VOLUME 4
BY MORLEY CALLAGHAN

MORLEY CALLAGHAN, long considered the most important Canadian story writer of his generation — which he was — has also long been a literary misfit; people never knew quite what to make of him. Doubtless this was how he liked it: he took pleasure in baffling expectation. He's important, he's very important, they say; but why? Even the American critic Edmund Wilson, lavish in his praise of Callaghan in his 1964 book *O Canada*, spends a lot of time scratching his head. Callaghan's effects, he says, are so subtle, so modulated, yet so simple, that it's hard to describe them. And so it has often gone.

For those Canadian writers who began in the early 1960s, cutting their teeth on beatniks and postwar French existentialists and the Theatre of the Absurd, Callaghan was neither fish nor fowl. He wrote of a time before our time, but not so long before that we had no memories of it. In some ways the world he depicted overlapped with our own age — we knew about the squalor of rooming houses, and grubby Depression-scarred lives lived on the financial margins, and the fear of unwanted pregnancy — but in those instances it represented parts of our lives we wanted to change, or hoped we had escaped. Such things held no glamour for us.

The esthetics of Callaghan's minimalist style, devoid of fancy words and metaphors — a style he hoped to render "transparent as glass"[1] — had excellent antecedents in the English tradition, from Addison's efforts to divest the eighteenth-century English stage of bombast and superfluous rhetoric, to Wordsworth's attempt, in *Lyrical Ballads*, to get back to the poetic basics, to Orwell's prose like a windowpane, intended to give us an unimpeded view of real life, like so many raw steaks in a butcher's display case. All such purifiers see their efforts as a sort of excavation: a fraudulent accumulation of grotty old barnacles called "the literary" or "the academic" must be scraped away in order to get to the deep-down freshness and newness of the actual — to truth, to honesty, or, in Callaghan's words, to "the object as it really was."[2]

However, if you're a writer, all this must be done through language, which is — how can the purifier get around it? — man-made, and therefore artificial. But if you must have speech, then make it plain speech; if words, then short words. Awkwardness is to be preferred to an overly carved and varnished elegance; and if elegance, then the elegance of a Shaker chair. These tendencies too can turn mannerist. Taken too far, you'd end up with a literature of monosyllables that would read like a *Dick and Jane* primer, but Callaghan avoided this trap.

Style in every art swings like a pendulum from the plain to the ornamented and back again, with *nature* and *artifice* being the polarizing catchphrases; but we whippersnappers in the early 1960s hadn't thought much about that. To us, the hard-boiled school — decades old by the time we came across it — seemed an almost comic affectation, like talking out of the side of the mouth in gangster films. The young are cruel, and they are most cruel to the quasi-parental generation preceding them, as Callaghan himself was cruel to the aesthetes of the turn of the century — "show-off writers,"[3] he termed them, fixated on demonstrating their own cleverness. It's a necessary cruelty, I suppose, or we would all be replicants.

Callaghan's legend — as opposed to the milieu depicted in his work — did have glamour for us, however. He'd been our age in the 1920s, and had written through the Great Depression and the War — eras that were now so far away that they were already furnishing the costumes for fancy-dress parties. In Paris, still thought of as the proper destination for an artist of any kind, he'd consorted with Hemingway and Fitzgerald — writers we'd studied in school, and who for that reason alone had an aura of semidivinity, while at the same time being ridiculously hoary. Unlike those two, however, he'd become neither a drunk nor a suicide, and was said to be living in Toronto — Toronto! — an unromantic, second-rate city in which no real writer — surely — would live by choice. Why wasn't he stowed away in Paris or New York, where we wouldn't have to bother about him? Why did he stick around, like a burr?

What was it about Callaghan that made us uncomfortable? For one thing, he was doing something thought to be impossible: he was making a living in Canada, as a writer, albeit through sales in the United States and in England. That was a challenge, since it was a truism among us that you'd have to leave the country to get any-where. We were — of course — provincials, who believed that the Great Good Place was somewhere else; and he was a nonprovincial who understood the provincial — having once partaken of it — and who had chosen this very provinciality as his material. (He was a student of — among others — Flaubert and de Maupassant, who had done the same.) We youngsters weren't the only folk made ner-vous by this. As Edmund Wilson said in 1960,

> The reviewer . . . is now wondering whether the primary rea-son for the current underestimation of Morley Callaghan may not be a general incapacity — apparently shared by his compa-triots — for believing that a writer whose work may be mentioned without absurdity in association with Chekhov's and Turgenev's can possibly be functioning in Toronto.[4]

Northrop Frye was another to put his finger on the Canadian uneasiness with Callaghan. After having stated that by 1929 Callaghan had established himself as perhaps the best short-story writer in Canada, he later said,

> Morley Callaghan's books, I think I am right in saying, were sometimes banned by the public library in Toronto — I forget what the rationalization was, but the real reason could only have been that if a Canadian were to do anything so ethically dubious as write, he should at least write like a proper colonial and not like someone who had lived in the Paris of Joyce and Gertrude Stein.[5]

Not surprisingly, Callaghan — who was nothing if not a scrapper — kicked against the pricks. He took the piss out of what he saw as the back-scratching mediocre sham literati in Canada, calling them — among other things — "local medicine men feasting and having a big cultural pow-wow,"[6] and homegrown critics took the piss out of him for it, and he took the piss out of them back. One of these fracases took place live on television, after Callaghan had been praised by Edmund Wilson, and then predictably denounced for it by a two-bit academic, live on a talk show. Callaghan, no stranger to rancorous debate, did not take this sitting down. It was an object lesson in self-respect to the young, and one we needed; for at that time, in Canada, to be a writer was to be thought next door to a junk-bond salesman: shifty, not above pinching the silver, to be sneered at and viewed with suspicion.

Self-respect. Respect. Respectability. These are key concepts in Callaghan's work: in fact, *respect* is the last word in the last story in this collection. Almost every Callaghan character desires to have and to earn "respect," the admiration of others. "Self-respect" — that quality of inner integrity, the ability to hold up your head when you look in the mirror — is also highly valued. "Respectability" is ambiguous. You need it to get and hold a job, which connects you with money — the ability to earn a living, to show a girl a good time, and to buy coveted objects — often articles of clothing, for people were judged very much by their wardrobes in those days. Money is never out of the picture, because, for Callaghan's characters, it doesn't grow on trees. But "respectability" is also a negative. It's the lack of joie de vivre, the absence of passion and energy; it's conformity; it's hypocrisy; it's mediocrity; it's a dingy grey stifling fog. It's also next door to self-righteousness, and self-righteousness was not a quality Callaghan admired, although it occupied him greatly as a subject.

Callaghan has frequently been compared with Fitzgerald and Hemingway, yet the concerns of the three are very different. In a Western shoot-out saga, Fitzgerald would have been interested in the cattle barons hiring the gunmen, Hemingway in the gunmen themselves; but Callaghan, though he might have paid some attention to both of the other groups, would have focused on the jittery townsfolk crouching behind the dry-goods counter. Fitzgerald was drawn to rich people, Hemingway to adventurous people, but Callaghan to people — men, usually — who might long to be rich and adventurous but who cannot actualize their longings, either because life has not provided them with the scope or because their own makeup defeats them. Their sense of their own worth is tenuous, as is their sense of their own bravery: both can stand or fall on an accident, an incident, a misunderstanding, an added pressure brought to bear. We identify with such characters because we've known people like them, but also because, given a change in circumstances, we could so easily find ourselves in their shoes.

As a story writer, Callaghan has been likened with many: Chekhov and Turgenev, Sherwood Anderson, Katherine Mansfield, de Maupassant, the Joyce of *Dubliners*, even O. Henry. His specialties were the small and thwarted life and the brief but exactly sketched state of emotion. Typically, his characters live in rooming houses or cramped apartments; they're unemployed, or in danger of losing their jobs or modest businesses. They borrow money they can't repay, or they get drunk and blow it, or they skirt the edge of minor criminality. If they are women, their husbands may have run off, or — and Callaghan's sense of gender interaction is exact for his times — they may be resented and even physically abused for having jobs when their men do not. If they are children or young people, adults let them down. If they are dogs, they are unfortunate.

Most of them indulge in irrational hopes and yearn for better things, but it's not likely they'll get them. They see themselves reflected in the eyes of others and the reflection does not please them, unless they are puffed up by a soon-to-be-deflated vainglory. Desiring to be looked up to, they more often feel belittled or small: size does matter. Occasionally someone will score points — the boy in "The New Kid" gains status through combat, the umpire in "Mother's Day at the Ball Park" is cheered by the crowd — confusingly for him — because he's punched a mother-insulting heckler. Amid the malice and the disappointment and the rage and the bitterness in these lives there are moments of generosity and joy, however unfounded; but such states of grace, we know, are temporary.

In literature, irony is a mode in which the reader guesses more accurately about the character's fate than he does himself, and in this sense Callaghan is a profoundly ironic writer. Life is not only a struggle, it's a puzzle. Another puzzle is why Callaghan, in *That Summer in Paris*, would claim to applaud the art he admires — his example is Matisse — as "a gay celebration of things as they were."[7] "Why couldn't all people have the eyes and heart that would give them this happy acceptance of reality?" he continues. Happiness and gaiety and acceptance of things as they are may have belonged to the author of Callaghan's stories, but they are not frequently found among his characters. Perhaps the stories are, in part, an attempt by Callaghan to answer his own question — to provide a "because" to go with the "why" — with the lamentable scarcity of the right kinds of hearts and eyes.

The next four words in the curious passage quoted above are "The word made flesh." The context might lead us to believe that this is an endorsement of a philosophy of immanence, of the divine *isness* of things — "The appleness of apples. Yet just apples," as Callaghan had just said of Cézanne. Yet they are also a signpost pointing toward Callaghan the Christian writer.[8]

This side of Callaghan is not obtrusive or doctrinaire, and yet it's there — the ground beneath the house, not always seen, but necessary. It's more obvious in the novels, and avoidable in "The Man with the Coat," the last short fiction Callaghan ever wrote — a transitional form, termed a novel in the 1955 issue of *Maclean's* magazine in which it appeared, but really a novella. Callaghan expanded it and changed the plot, and this version later appeared as *The Many Coloured Coat*.

"The Man with the Coat" is an adroitly constructed piece in which several characters take turns sneering at and belittling one another. Scorn is handed from character to character, like the hot object in a game of Pass the Package, until the sequence of blame leads to a tragic consequence. The motion is not circular but spiral: its end is not its beginning. It's possible that this story was written as an attempt to work out a problem: how to write a tragedy in the age of the common man. Arthur Miller's *Death of a Salesman*, for instance, is pathetic rather than tragic in its effect, because the salesman can't fall from a high place, having never achieved one. The true tragic hero must plummet like a falling star, and his descent must be due in part to a weakness or flaw in his own character. Or so went the theory. Callaghan was widely read, and perfectly aware of the requirements. As he was a Christian writer, the flaw needed to be a flaw in Christian terms: more a sin than a flaw.

The story begins with a trial, and ends with one. The description of the physical ambiance — the smell of wet wool, the annoying *whoosh* of galoshes, every little thing — is spot-on, as is usual in Callaghan. Harry Lane, the hero, starts out as a sort of Timon of

Athens before his reversal of fortune, or a Hamlet before the black-suit phase: he's the observed of all observers. He's a celebrated war hero, handsome, well-off, easygoing, generous, careless in a lily-of-the-field way, admired by all, and with a top-of-the-line girlfriend. The initial event in the plot is driven, like the acts of Cassius in *Julius Caesar*, by envy: a bank manager named Scotty uses Harry as the cat's paw in a fraudulent transaction, hoping to profit by it himself. But he gets caught, and is put on trial, and then kills himself, and Harry — undeservedly — has the moral guilt pinned on him. People look down on him. They expect him to feel small. They no longer respect him. For a Callaghan protagonist, this is awful.

Struggling to regain the esteem of his society, Harry passes the parcel of scorn to Scotty's friend, a tailor and ex-pugilist named Mike Kon. The vehicle is a coat with a faulty lining, made by Kon, interpreted by Harry as a gesture of disrespect toward himself. By spreading its story and wearing it everywhere, Harry makes Kon appear dishonest and a fool. (Kon passes on the scorn in his turn, and so does Molly, the upper-class girl with the cold heart who has thrown Harry over due to his disgrace.) But neither Harry nor Kon can resolve the conflict between them, because both suffer from the sin of pride. Both demand "justice."

The plot develops in rounds, like the boxing match that signals the climax of the action. In the course of vindicating themselves, defending their self-respect, and standing up for their honour, the characters wallop one another both verbally and physically, and are walloped in turn. There are three arbiters, or umpires, who stand outside the ring. One is the owner of the prestigious bar where all gather, or want to. He's the social arbiter: he decides, literally, who's in and who's out. The second is Mike Kon's father, an old man who's suffered a stroke. He's the spiritual arbiter. He can't talk, but he can write, and he delivers himself of a shakily printed oracle that probably says *Judge not*. (The rest of the phrase, not supplied by the old man, is, . . . *lest ye be judged*. And so it is: all who judge are indeed judged in their turn.)

The third arbiter is Annie Laurie, a woman of large heart and easy morals, who unfortunately — like mermaids — has a jinx on her. The Annie Laurie in the song of that name gives promises true, and Callaghan's Annie also tells the truth, because — having no respectability — she has nothing to lose. She's got those coveted Callaghan qualities, honesty and the ability to show the object as it really is, and the reader trusts her. But the Annie Laurie in the song is a creature for whom men would lie down and die, and Callaghan's Annie Laurie also has this effect on men who stay too long with her: they end up prone and breathless.

Are we intended to see her as a sort of femme fatale? I think not: she's connected with truth, not with poisonous wiles. Possibly one way of understanding her place in this story is to refer back to *Everyman*, that other simply written and episodic Christian tale of a man's progress toward the grave. Most of Everyman's companions — Kin, Good Fellowship, and the like — desert him when times get tough, as Harry's pals do. The one left at the end is female, and her name is Knowledge. It could be that Annie Laurie is no fatal woman, but instead a kindly psychopomp, a tender conductress of the soul, a helpful companion on Harry's fated journey. She does try to warn him away from the paths of pride: she's got the kind of knowledge he needs. But he won't listen.

It is Annie who is present when Harry is killed, and Annie who testifies at the trial. Like many a prophetess, she isn't much believed; in her case, because of her dubious sexual reputation. It's Mike Kon, Harry's erstwhile enemy and slayer, who — exonerated by the same legal system that earlier caused Harry so much grief — ends up as the shield bearer, the Horatio figure, the teller of dead Harry's story. He has learned what it is to judge and to be judged, and has opted for the hidden alternative to justice, which is mercy. It's a conclusion both deeply ironic and oddly compassionate.

Which, underneath everything else, would seem to be the appleness of apples at the very bottom of the Callaghan barrel. Irony and compassion. The Callaghanness of Callaghan. Yet just Callaghan. The object as it really is.

1–3. From *That Summer in Paris*, as reprinted in *Canadian Novelists and the Novel*, ed. Douglas Daymond and Leslie Monkman, Borealis Press, Ottawa, 1981, pages 143–146.

4. Edmund Wilson, *O Canada: An American's Notes on Canadian Culture*, Farrar, Strauss and Giroux, New York, 1964, some essays 1960, page 21.

5. *Northrop Frye on Canada*, edited by Jean O'Grady and David Staines, University of Toronto Press, 2003, page 549.

6. From "The Plight of Canadian Fiction" (1938), reprinted in Daymond and Monkman, page 150.

7. Daymond and Monkman, page 146.

8. Right after this, Callaghan makes a dismissive remark about St. Paul. Christians often see themselves as having to choose between the road of St. Paul, which leads to Rome, and that of Christ, which leads to Calvary. Not much doubt about which Callaghan preferred.

HE SPRINGS ETERNAL

HOPE DIES LAST:
KEEPING THE FAITH IN DIFFICULT TIMES
BY STUDS TERKEL

IF STUDS TERKEL were Japanese, he'd be a Sacred Treasure. As John Kenneth Galbraith has said of him, "Studs Terkel is more than a writer, he is a national resource." *Hope Dies Last* is the latest in the series of American oral histories he's been publishing since *Division Street, America* appeared in 1967. In the thirty-six years between then and now, he's covered, in separate books, the Great Depression, the Second World War, race relations, working, the American Dream, and ageing. For each book, he interviewed an amazing variety of people — where does he meet some of these folks, anyway? — and the entire oeuvre has an exhaustiveness and monumentality that will make it necessary reading for future social historians of the American twentieth century.

The arrangement of subjects begins to look less serendipitous than schematic. Books about youth and middle age — initiation, ordeal, and daily life in action — were followed by books about contemplation and stock taking. The second-to-last was entitled *Death: Will the Circle Be Unbroken?* (2001), which carried us into the unknown: Will there be an afterlife? (The general consensus: maybe, maybe not.) The series now resembles a planned cycle, like the cycles of mystery plays put on in medieval towns. You'd think *Death* would have ended it, but with the addition of *Hope Dies Last*, the pattern is now similar to that of Armistice Day ceremonies, where taps, the sundown signal, is followed by reveille, the wake-up call, symbolizing the Resurrection. Death and hope are paired as well on many Christian tombstones, which bear the words *In Spe*. No coincidence then that Terkel kicks off his book with an upward-tending sentiment: "Hope has never trickled down. It has always sprung up." First the dead body, then the young green leaves of grass.

It's very Terkelesque — by now, the man requires an adjective of his own — that after death should come hope, for Terkel's optimism has seldom failed him. His lifetime of ninety-one years has spanned the boom times of the 1920s, the Depression, the Second World War, the McCarthy red-hunting era, the civil rights movement, the hippie activists of the late 1960s, and on into present times. He grew up in Chicago in the 1920s, eavesdropping on the arguments that went on in the lobby of the workingmen's hotel run by his widowed mother — arguments that pitted old Wobblies from the International Workers of the World against anti-unionists, with ordinary working stiffs who "didn't gave a hoot one way or the other" putting their oars in too. This was the perfect education for a man who was to become the American interviewer par excellence: Terkel became a practised listener. He learned how to take the measure of what he was hearing, and to assess who was saying it.

He spent three dispiriting years at the University of Chicago Law School, then took up acting in radio soap operas to avoid being a lawyer — "I was always typecast as a Chicago gangster," he says. Then he became a disc jockey — classical, jazz, and folk — and, with the advent of television, an unorthodox talk-show host. On *Studs's Place*, he ran a version of the entertaining hotel lobby debates of his youth — improvised, filmed live, scrappy, unpredictable. His kind of TV was known as "TV, Chicago style"; it had its own manner, a rough-and-tumble ambiance with a whiff of Carl Sandburg's famous Chicago poem about it: City of the Big Shoulders, "with lifted head singing so proud to be alive and coarse and strong and cunning," not to mention the fearless, defiant, brawling, dusty-faced, white-teethed laughter to which Sandburg gives pride of place.

Terkel was always a laugher in this sense, though of the puckish kind rather than the brawling, white-teethed variety; and he was never afraid of putting himself on the line. Naturally, he got involved with picket lines and petitions — "I never met a picket line or a petition I didn't like," he says, with daunting Pickwickian geniality. Needless to say, he found himself an object of repeated scrutiny during the McCarthy era. FBI agents used to visit him in solemn twosomes, and though his wife was cool toward them, he himself was "always hospitable. Remember, I was an innkeeper's boy." When an emissary from NBC showed up, demanding that he say he was "duped by the communists," he refused. "Suppose communists come out against cancer. Do we have to come out *for* cancer?" he asked. "That is *not* very funny," said the NBC official, like many a schoolmarm before him.

Terkel was then blacklisted for several years, during which he made a living lecturing to women's clubs about jazz. (He's proud of these women's clubs, for they too were fearless Chicago-style laughers: though warned off him, not one club ever cancelled an engagement.) In the mid-1950s he was finally rescued by Mahalia Jackson, who insisted he be the host of her weekly CBS radio show. When an emissary from the network turned up with a loyalty oath, insisting Studs sign it or else, Mahalia said, ". . . If they fire Studs, . . . go find another Mahalia." "In saying no," says Terkel, Mahalia Jackson "revealed more self-esteem, let alone what our country is all about, than . . . all the sponsors and agencies rolled into one."

Those who have had the pleasurable workout of being interviewed by Studs Terkel during his long-running book program on NPR will agree that it was an interview experience like no other. Unlike some, Studs would always read the book. Then he'd reread it. When you arrived for the interview, there would be Studs, hugging your book, which would look as if he'd been rolling around on the floor with it. It would be underlined in different pens and pencils, cross-referenced, with little bits of coloured paper sticking out all over it. Then he'd start in — "I stayed up all night reading this, I couldn't put it down" — and you'd realize that he knew more about your book than you did yourself. This knowledge was not used to make you look like an idiot but to prop you up. The enthusiasm, the energy, the excitement were put across with a verve that had you reeling out of the place feeling you'd just participated in a rafter-raising musical comedy, in which Studs had given you the role of star tap dancer without your having auditioned for it.

While conducting the interviews for his oral history series, Terkel evidently drew on many of the same skills, though he concerned himself not with books but with people. He has made himself into a conduit through which voices have flowed — familiar voices, powerful voices, but also obscure voices, ordinary voices, voices that otherwise might not have been heard. It's been a huge amount of work, in aid of which he's travelled all over the country. In his later years it can't have been physically easy for him — he recounts with appreciation his trip, while visiting a Chicago tycoon, up a flight of stairs in an electric armchair — and it must also have been hard in other ways: the stories he's recorded have not been without their conflicts and defeats, the lives celebrated have often been tough, and not all of them have had happy endings. Some of those he interviewed for this book were old and ill. Their wives had died, or they'd had a stroke, or they were using a walker, or they were in a wheelchair. The two people to whom the book is dedicated are the lawyer Clifford Durr and his Southern belle wife, Virginia Durr, of Montgomery, Alabama, who spearheaded the civil rights movement there in the 1950s, against fearful odds. Both are dead.

What drove Terkel on? Partly it was the same kind of alert and open curiosity that led him to interviewing in the first place. "I've always wondered what made Virginia and Clifford Durr tick," he muses, without coming up with a definitive theory. But it's more than simple wondering. The answers to such questions, he implies, are in the stories, and he lets his subjects tell these stories for themselves.

It's perhaps helpful to think of Studs Terkel as the inheritor of the same strain of American idealistic romanticism that produced Walt Whitman, and Mark Twain's Huckleberry Finn, and John Dos Passos, and John Steinbeck, and many more. According to this tradition, "democracy" is a serious idea, indeed an article of belief, rather than a snippet of election-year rhetoric or Oscar Wilde's wisecrack about the bludgeoning of the people, by the people, for the people. For those who still keep faith with the early, bright-eyed concept of American democracy, all men really are created equal, and to treat any human being as less than human is a heresy. No coincidence that Terkel quotes Tom Paine, that eighteenth-century gadfly and apologist for the rights of man, and finds his words appropriate in the America of 2003:

> Freedom had been hunted round the globe; reason was considered as rebellion; and the slavery of fear had made men afraid to think. But such is the irresistible nature of truth that all it asks, and all it wants, is the liberty of appearing. . . . In such a situation, man becomes what he ought. He sees his species, not with the inhuman eye of a natural enemy, but as a kindred.

"One's-Self I sing, a simple separate person, / Yet utter the word Democratic, the word En-masse," says Whitman . . .

> One of the Nation of many
> nations, the smallest the same
> and the largest the same. . . .
> Of every hue and caste am I, of
> every rank and religion,

A farmer, mechanic, artist,
gentleman, sailor, quaker,
Prisoner, fancy-man, rowdy,
lawyer, physician, priest.

This could almost be a prospectus for Terkel's life's work: the bringing together of diverse voices until they join in harmony and counterpoint, the goal being a unified whole in which every individual nevertheless remains distinct. "It's . . . like a legion of Davids, with all sorts of slingshots. It's not one slingshot that will do it," says Terkel.

But there are problems with a legion of Davids. An aroused and rightfully annoyed society is not the same thing as a mob on the rampage, but how do you keep the one from turning into the other? And if the Davids win, won't some of them become Goliaths in their turn, as witness the histories of some unions? *E pluribus unum*, says the Great Seal of the United States, but it doesn't say what kind of one is to be made out of the many, or how you keep the country from becoming a de facto dictatorship, ruled by fear, with everybody snooping on everybody else. These are the difficulties faced by a pluralistic, individualistic, market-driven, yet officially democratic society like that of the United States. "The price of liberty is eternal vigilance," said Thomas Jefferson. Terkel might amend this to "The price of liberty is eternal slingshots." But does liberty mean you can do whatever you like as long as you don't get caught? At what point does the liberty of one depend on the serfdom of another? And what Goliaths, exactly, ought the Davids to shoot at with their slingshots? Any Goliaths who forget that liberty entails responsibility. Terkel would probably reply: Walk on people and you're fair game.

The subject of *Hope Dies Last* isn't just any kind of hope, such as "Hope you're feeling better," "Hope for the best," or even "I hope you die." Lots of things have been said about hope; nor has it always had a good press. For some, hope is a phantom, a deluding will-o'-the-wisp, luring men away from reality — presupposed to be grim — and into attractive but deadly swamps. For some, Camus included, it's the dirty trick at the bottom of Pandora's box, the deceptive gizmo that keeps Sisyphus rolling the stone up the hill. "Hope sustains us, to be replaced sooner or later by a walking stick," said the Bulgarian epigrammatist Kouncho Grosev. "There is an abundance of hope, but none for us," said Franz Kafka. "I can't go on, I have to go on, I'll go on," says Beckett in *The Unnameable*.

Terkel knows his Camus and his Beckett and the Greek myths, but does not change course for them. Two of his subjects refer to Emily Dickinson's poem:

> "Hope" is the thing with
> feathers —
> That perches in the soul —
> And sings the tune without the
> words —
> And never stops — at all —
>
> And sweetest — in the Gale — is
> heard —
> And sore must be the storm —
> That could abash the little Bird —
> That kept so many warm. . . .

This is the kind of hope Terkel means, the hope that persists in the face of discouragement. All but a few of the people he interviews in his book have been chosen because they did not cease from mental fight, or let their swords sleep in their hands: they took up their bows of burning gold and their arrows of desire, and let fly.

If there are Biblical echoes here it's not by accident. "Studs . . . you have such a big mouth, you should have been a preacher," Terkel quotes a pal as saying. But he is a sort of preacher. One branch of

Christianity has always led to activism: according to it, all souls are equal before God, the first shall be last and the last shall be first, and you must love your neighbours as yourself and visit them when they are sick and in prison, and if you do bad things unto the least of these, you do them unto God. (There's another branch of Christianity that rests on the verse about those who have getting more, and those who have not being deprived even of what they have, which these folks interpret financially; but that's another story.) A number of the subjects in this book started out along the path of religion: among them are priests, seminarians, Quakers, Methodists, Baptists.

As for hope, it goes hand in hand — Biblically — with faith and charity: you might say faith is the belief, hope is the emotion made possible by it, and charity is the action required. Terkel's hope is not vain hope, but is one with the kindly light that leads amid the encircling gloom: it's hope for something better. The book's title comes from a saying that was current among the Spanish-speaking farm workers organized by Cesar Chavez — "*La esperanza muere última*" — but is cited by others in the book as well. Terkel comments, "It was a metaphor for much of the twentieth century." He quotes Kathy Kelly of the Voices in the Wilderness project: "I'm working toward a world in which it would be easier for people to behave decently."

It's possible to get swept away by what at times resembles an inspirational revival meeting. The spirit moves you; Good Samaritan kindly feelings suffuse you; you feel like rushing out and joining something. Perhaps a caveat is in order: one person's hope-inspired activism is another's pain in the neck. Who's to choose what "a better world" is, and how to best bring it about? There's a point of view that might characterize various well-intentioned activities as misguided obstructionism, illegal interference, subversive undermining of the social order, godless communism, and so on. Should actions be judged by the sincerity of their intentions? Yes, say the Romantics; no, say the historians, they should instead be judged, like wars, by their outcomes. As for good intentions, we know what Hell's paved with. Were the Resistance fighters behind the German lines in the Second World War brave heroes striking a blow for freedom, or were they criminal thugs? Depends on who's doing the labelling.

Hope respects no national boundaries, and it crosses ideological lines at will. Terkel's book dodges this issue, though his inclusion of General Paul Tibbetts — pilot of the *Enola Gay*, the plane that dropped the bomb that wiped out Hiroshima — makes us sit up and blink. To be sure, Tibbetts says he was motivated by hope of a kind — he hoped his action would end the war and "save a lot of lives." American lives, it's understood, for his attitude toward the Japanese civilians who were snuffed out is cavalier: "That's their tough luck for being there." As Lenin famously remarked, you can't make an omelette without breaking eggs, but what kind of omelette is needed will always be a matter of dispute, and there's no long line of candidates anywhere for the position of egg.

That said, *Hope Dies Last* captures the reader, though the choices will not be to everyone's taste. Terkel's main emphasis is on people from the parts of society familiar to him: old lefties, workers in housing projects and among the poor, students who fought on behalf of custodial staff during the sit-in at Harvard in 2001, union activists as well as activists against corruption in unions, civil rights workers, peace workers, teachers in difficult neighbourhoods. No surprise that quite a few of these are from Chicago.

But there are surprises of other kinds. In one section — "Easy Riders" — the interviewees share only the fact that they ride around on bicycles. One is a courier, living in the moment. Another is a doctor who goes

> a half day every week out into Golden Gate Park on my bicycle with medicines. . . . Usually, if you work in a clinic, people come to you. Whereas if you're doing outreach in the park, you go up and offer your services. It's a different kind of playing field.

Another section, "Immigrants," contains a sound engineer of Iraqi origin, two undocumented Guatemalans whose hope consists in the hope of not being found out, and a man of Japanese descent who describes how, as a high-school senior, he was put in a detention camp with his family after Pearl Harbor and has since worked with the movement to redress the harm done to the Japanese. Will American Iraqis one day have their own redress movement? After September 11, Mr. Usama Alshaibi told Terkel,

> I was very worried because the government took three thousand men and put them in detention centers. They weren't officially charged. . . . I wouldn't be surprised right now if they grabbed me and just started asking me a bunch of questions.

The unpleasant surprises include many horror stories — jailings, beatings, murders. Among them are the account of wheelchair-ridden Dierdre Merriman, a recovering alcoholic whose neck was broken by an ex-boyfriend and who now lives in a single room in a large Chicago apartment building and works as a rape victim advocate, and that of Leroy Orange, tortured with electrodes to obtain a confession of murder during a police department reign of terror in Chicago, wrongfully convicted, and finally pardoned by Governor George Ryan in 2003 after a courageous legal campaign.

By no means all of Terkel's subjects are from the bottom crust of the social pie. John Kenneth Galbraith contributes a pithy statement to the section called "Concerning Enronism":

> As things now stand, we allow enormous incompetence and enormous compensation to those who have power. I see that as a great unsolved problem of our time. And since it is all quite legal, I call it the likelihood of innocent fraud. I entered the world of politics at a time when there were Fifth Amendment communists, and

I've reached the age of ninety-four, when there are Fifth Amendment capitalists.

He's followed by Wallace Rasmusson, who worked his way up through the Depression to become the president and CEO of Beatrice Foods, a company worth $7.8 billion when he retired in 1975.

What's happened at Enron and WorldCom — cooking books — is criminal. A great country lasts about four hundred years. We're in the declining-morality period. That is what ruined Rome. . . . Greed. . . . I always said, "In God we trust, everything else we audit."

There are several kinds of activism that might seem obvious to some readers, but that are not much represented in *Hope Dies Last*. The women's movement marks one of the most noteworthy social shifts of the last two centuries, but it is barely present here. There are women interviewed, yes — seventeen out of fifty-eight — and intrepid women at that. One of those mentioned is anonymous — an old white woman who kept a sit-in at a Woolworth's lunch counter in Nashville from becoming a massacre, purely through force of character and through believing that some ways are no way to behave — a case of Miss Manners to the rescue. "I just came in to buy an egg poacher," was her story. She walked

up and down between the students seated and the mob that would come up and put out a cigarette on them, spit on a young woman's neck and all. The students just sat, they didn't protest. This old woman . . . [would] go up and talk to these young white thugs. "How would you feel if that was your sister?" And they would kind of, "Oh, I didn't mean nothing." Then they'd go back in the mob and someone else would take over.

Some of the women are among Terkel's bravest subjects — women like Kathy Kelly, jailed for planting corn on missile silos, and Mollie McGrath, who worked to reform sweatshops and took part in protests against the World Trade Organization — but they are included because they were involved in movements of other kinds. Why is that? Terkel has nothing against women; in fact, so nondiscriminatory is he toward them that he doesn't appear to view them as a special category, or not one needing a movement of their own. Maybe he has the somewhat bashful attitude — so common among men once — of not wanting to butt in on a hen party. Maybe he can't quite believe in oppression by a gender, of a gender, because of gender. There are no gay activists here either.

With Mollie McGrath the antiglobalization movement gets a look-in, but no more than that. The green movement is touched on through Pete Seeger, folk singer to a generation, now busily trying to clean up the Hudson River; also through Frances Moore Lappé. Many will remember Lappé fondly as the author of *Diet for a Small Planet*. How would we ever have known about soy flour without her? *Hope Dies Last* is so filled with quotable quotes you sometimes think you're reading Bartlett's, and Lappé has some ringers. "Hunger is not caused by a lack of food, it's caused by a lack of democracy," she says.

> My daughter, Anna, loves to say, "I used to think that hope was for wimps." Hope is not for wimps; it's for the strong-hearted who can recognize how bad things are and yet not be deterred, not be paralyzed.

> Hope is not something we find, hope is something we become.

> This is the first generation to know that the choices we're making have ultimate consequences. It's a time when you either choose life or you choose death. . . . Going along with the current order means that you're choosing death.

We're just a drop in the bucket. . . . If you have a bucket, those raindrops fill it up very fast. . . . Our work is helping people see that there is a bucket. There are all these people all over the world *who* are creating this bucket of hope.

If we were picking teams — the Hopes versus the Despairs — Lappé would be my first choice for captain of the Hopes. Her outlook is global, she knows where we stand as a species, she's tough as a week-old soy flour biscuit, and she's looking ahead, not back.

And Studs Terkel would be the umpire. No, I'll rethink that: he'd be too biased on the side of the Hope team. He'd have to be the coach. He'd bring to the task many decades of experience, the ability to galvanize, lots of anecdotal lore, and a store of energy to help out during the hard parts. That's what *Hope Dies Last* is, in essence: not just a social document, not just fascinating American history, but a coach's manual, complete with a number of model pep talks that may get you out of your armchair and propel you right into Blake's mental fight. It's all the more impressive that Terkel was putting this book together in the days after September 11 and before the invasion of Iraq, when it might have looked as if he'd be preaching to the sea. Now many will find the words he's collected both inspiring and timely: Representative Dennis Kucinich speaks for many in *Hope Dies Last* when he says,

. . . We're challenged to insist even more strongly on the basic freedoms that we have, because it is through those freedoms that we're vindicated. If we lose those freedoms, we're not America any more.

50

TO BEECHY ISLAND

The tourist is part of the landscape of our times,
as the pilgrim was in the Middle Ages.
— V. S. PRITCHETT, *The Spanish Temper*

A WEEK BEFORE my pilgrimage began, my partner, Graeme Gibson,
and I found a dead crow in the backyard. West Nile Virus, we
thought. We put it in the freezer and called the Humane Society.
They took the frozen crow away, but said they would not be inform-
ing us of the diagnosis as they did not want panic to spread. About
this time it occurred to me that I ought to have put on some DEET
before pruning the rose bushes: there had been a few mosquitoes.

The day before my departure, I noticed some pink blotches
around my waist. I put them down to a Thai spring roll I'd eaten.
Perhaps I had an allergy.

Soon the blotches were more numerous, and spreading ouwards.
I checked my tongue for furriness, my brain for light-headedness, my
neck for stiffness. I did feel peculiar, although no one else seemed to
be noticing. By this time I was on a plane bound for Greenland, and,
then, suddenly — time passes quickly when you're infested with
microbes — I found myself on a Russian arctic-research vessel called

the *Akademic Ioffe*. I was a temporary staff member of an outfit called Adventure Canada, which sublet the Russian research ship from Peregrine, an Australian tour company that leased the boat for Antarctic cruises. On board with me were a mixed bunch: the Russian crew, the Australian folks who ran the "hotel" aspects of the trip, and the Canadians who planned and executed the daily programs for the sake of the hundred or so eager adventurers who had booked passage. My job was to give a couple of talks on northern exploration as shaped by literary and artistic concepts — a job that, in my virus-addled state, I felt ill-equipped to perform.

Soon we were sailing down the long, long Sondreström Fjord — a fjord being, as our on-board geologist explained, a valley originally scooped out by glaciers and subsequently filled by the sea. Then we turned north and skirted the western coast of Greenland, cruising among huge and spectacular icebergs. The sea was blue, the sky was blue, the icebergs were blue as well, or their recently sheared surfaces were: an unearthly blue, inklike, artificial. As we cruised among them in our rubber Zodiacs, thousand-year-old ice fizzed in the water as its compressed air escaped.

We were bound — eventually — for Baffin Bay, then Lancaster Sound, and finally for Beechy Island, where the first three members of the doomed 1847 Franklin expedition were buried. Was I fated to join them? I wondered, as the mountains rose to the right, and the dazzling ice-filled sea stretched out to the left, and the sunsets went on for hours. Was my head about to explode, for reasons that would appear mysterious to those observing? Was history poised to repeat itself, and would I perish of unknown causes, to be followed shortly by the entire passenger list and crew, just as in the Franklin expedition? I shared these thoughts with no one, although I felt it might be fitting to make a few illegible but poignant notes, to be discovered later, in a tin can or plastic pill container, like the garbled scrap that survived the Franklin debacle: *Oh, the dire sad.*

But the subject is pilgrimages, or a pilgrimage. I was supposed to be writing about one — this one, the one I was on. But in my blotchy state — the blotches had now reached my wrists, and possibly my brain — I couldn't quite focus on the general idea. What was a pilgrimage? Had I ever made one before? Could what I was doing now be considered one? And if so, in what sense?

I'd made some literary pilgrimages in my youth, of a sort. I'd thrown up beside the road in Wordsworth country; I'd inspected the Brontë manse and marvelled at the tiny size of its famous inhabitants; I'd been to Dr. Johnson's house in London, and to the House of the Seven Gables, in Salem, Massachusetts; but did such visits count? All of them had been accidents: I happened to be passing by. How much of the essence of a pilgrimage resides in the intention, rather than in the journey as such?

The dictionary provides some flexibility: a pilgrim can mean simply a wanderer, a sojourner; or it can mean one who travels to a sacred place as an act of religious devotion. Motion is involved, relics not necessarily. But the motion has to be protracted — a stroll to the corner store for a loaf of bread wouldn't qualify. It also has to be — surely — non-commercial in nature. Marco Polo, although a magnificent traveller, was not a pilgrim. Also, a pilgrimage was supposed to be good for you: good for your health (Temples of Asclepius, Lourdes, the heart of Brother André, with its trail of abandoned crutches), or good for the state of your soul (purchase an indulgence, get time off in Purgatory; become a Pilgrim Father, found the righteous New Jerusalem, somewhere in the Boston area).

Needless to say, not all pilgrimages work out as advertised. Consider the Crusades.

When I thought of pilgrims, however, I thought first of literature. Most of the pilgrims I'd known had been encountered there.

There's Chaucer, of course: his Canterbury pilgrims are a sociable batch, making their trip together because it's spring, and they've got wanderlust, and they want to have fun. Whatever religious gloss they may put upon it, what they really enjoy is travelling in a merry company, and observing one another's wardrobes and foibles, and telling tales.

There's the seventeenth-century variety of pilgrim, exemplified by those in Bunyan's *The Pilgrim's Progress*. For these hardy Protestants, the pilgrim's journey took him not to a shrine but through this mortal vale of tears and spiritual battles toward his goal, the heavenly home to be gained after his death.

The eighteenth century went on grand tours and sentimental journeys rather than pilgrimages, but with the Romantic age the pilgrimage was back. Consider Lord Byron's long poem, *Childe Harold's Pilgrimage*. Its hero is a wastrel, though filled with restless longing for he knows not what. But the sacred places he visits are not churches; they are sublime landscapes, with many a cliff and chasm, and the poem ends with a panegyric to the immensity of the sea, which contains the frequently-quoted stanza,

> Roll on, thou deep and dark blue ocean — roll!
> Ten thousand fleets sweep over thee in vain;
> Man marks the earth with ruin — his control
> Stops with the shore; — upon the watery plain
> The wrecks are all thy deed, nor doth remain
> A shadow of man's ravage, save his own,
> When for a moment, like a drop of rain
> He sinks into thy depths with bubbling groan,
> Without a grave, unknell'd, uncoffin'd, and unknown.

Putting all these varieties of pilgrimages together, what do we get? At first glance, nothing very consistent. However, there are a few links. For instance, a pilgrim — it seems — is never first on the ground. Someone else has always been there before him, and has come to an unfortunate (though heroic or saintly) end. It is in honour of these forerunners that the pilgrim takes up his staff. Chaucer's jolly company is headed to Canterbury, scene of the murder of Thomas à Becket. Bunyan's pilgrims are following in the footsteps of the crucified Christ; and even Byron's *Childe Harold* ends with the contemplation of a myriad tragic shipwrecks and drownings. A dead body, it seems, usually precedes the live pilgrim.

The journey I undertook had elements of all three sorts of pilgrimages. I sojourned with a merry company, and told tales, and listened to them as well. I observed sublime landscapes, and sublime seascapes too, and meditated on dead sailors and drowned vessels.

As for spiritual battles, although I myself did not engage in any, those who'd given the route its haunted notoriety had most certainly engaged in them. We were taking the same sea road travelled by Franklin and his crew when they set out to discover the Northwest Passage in 1845 and were never seen again; between their hopeful departure and the discovery of their silverware and gnawed bones, much anguish must have occurred.

But Franklin himself was not the direct object of my pilgrimage. My immediate agenda concerned a friend of mine, fellow poet Gwendolyn MacEwen. In the early 1960s, when she was in her early twenties, she'd written a remarkable verse drama for radio about the Franklin expedition, named after Franklin's two ships: the *Terror* and the *Erebus*. I'd heard this play when it was first broadcast, and had been very impressed by it — all the more so because Gwen had never been to the Arctic and had never visited the Franklin expedition's three poignant graves. She had sailed these seas in imagination only, and had died in her mid-forties, without ever glimpsing an iceberg.

My pilgrimage — if it can be called that — was undertaken for her. I would go where she'd been unable to go, stand where she had never stood, see what she had seen only with the mind's eye.

A sentimental gesture, but then, pilgrimages are sentimental by nature.

The voyage proceeded. Elements of the Chaucerian pilgrimage man-ifested themselves at mealtimes, with merry tales, and jests involving Viking outfits and kilts and false beards, and, on one memorable occasion, fur sunglasses and fur jockstraps. The Protestant-style soul-searching spiritual journey was an individual matter, as such things are: there was a lot of journal keeping aboard ship. Ruminations of the human state and the state of nature were frequent: anxiety not over the life to come but over the near future, for it was evident even to an untrained eye that the glaciers are receding at a rapid pace.

The Byronic version of the pilgrimage was experienced on the bridge or (with mittens) out on deck, as the (where are the adjectives? "Spectacular," "grand" and "sublime" hardly do it) indescribable scenery drifted past. "Look at that iceberg/cliff/rockface," people would say, entranced. "It looks just like a Lawren Harris painting." And yes, it did, only better, and so did that one, and the amazing one over there, purple and green and pink in the sunset, and then indigo and an unearthly yellow colour . . . You found yourself just standing, with eyes and mouth open, for hours.

By the time of my first talk on board ship, the original pink blotches were fading, but more had appeared. (Considerately, they stopped at the neckline.) The disorganization of my discourse was probably set down to the scrambled state in which "creative" people are thought to exist on a daily basis. I considered explaining about my curious dis-ease, but then people might have thought they were on a plague ship and jumped overboard, or got themselves airlifted. Anyway, I was still walking and talking. It's just that I didn't appear to myself to be entirely responsible for what was coming out of my mouth. "Was that all right?" I asked Graeme. But he had been up on the bridge, watch-ing fulmars.

What did I say? I think I began by remarking to my audience that Voltaire would have considered them all mad. To pay money for a voyage, not to some centre of civilization where the proper study of mankind would be man, or even to some well-tended chateau with symmetrical plantings surrounding it, but to an icy waste with very large amounts of rock, water, and sand in it — this would have seemed to Voltaire the height of folly. Men did not risk their lives in such places unless there was a reason — money to be made, for instance. What changed between Voltaire and us — or between Voltaire and, for instance, Sir Edmund Hilary uselessly climbing Mount Everest, and Scott uselessly freezing himself in the Antarctic? A changed world view. Burke's idea of the Sublime became a Romantic yardstick, and the sublime could not be the Sublime without danger. The history of arctic exploration in the nineteenth century was seen through this glass, and those who went north and described and painted these landscapes did so with the Romantic hero looking over their shoulders.

Franklin's expedition — I think I said — occurred at a sort of hinge in time — the moment when such risky explorations ceased to be undertaken in hope of gain — no one deeply believed, by 1847, that the Northwest Passage would be the key to China and would make Britain very, very rich — and began to be undertaken in the spirit of heroic enterprise, as a sort of barrel trip over Niagara Falls. What was being defied by derring-do explorers and potential martyrs was not pagans, but Nature herself. "They forged the last link with their lives," reads the inscription on Franklin's memorial in Westminster Abbey — an inscription for which Lady Jane Franklin, the widow, worked long and hard, as she worked to ensure that Franklin was seen as a hero in the Christian Romantic mode. But the last link of what? Of an idea. For as Ken McGoogan so ably demonstrates in his book, *Fatal Passage* — a book I was reading as I was ferried blotchily across Baffin Bay — Franklin didn't really find the Northwest Passage. He found a body of water that was always choked with ice, instead, and which ought not to have counted.

After he died, and after his ships had been locked in the ice for three years, his men set out overland, cooking and eating one another as they went. When the first news of these culinary activities reached England, brought by the intrepid explorer John Rae, Lady Franklin was most distressed: for if Franklin had indulged in cannibalism, he would not be a hero, but only a sort of chef. (John Rae, we now know, was right about the cannibalism, though Franklin himself had undoubtedly died before it got underway.)

Some time during this admittedly rambling talk, I read from Gwendolyn's verse drama, in which she suggests that Franklin created the Northwest Passage by an act of imagination and will:

Ah, Franklin!
To follow you, one does not need geography.
At least not totally, but more of that
Instrumental knowledge the bones have,
Their limits, their measurings.
The eye creates the horizon,
The ear invents the wind,
The hand reaching out from a parka sleeve
By touch demands that the touched thing be.

A fitting motif for pilgrimages: for what inspires them if not a purely imaginative link between place and spirit?

Having crossed Baffin Bay, we travelled through Lancaster Sound, and finally along the wild, and — again, adjectives fail — oddly Egyptian-looking sandstone cliffs of Devon Island. Devon is the largest uninhabited island in the world. Was it here we saw two polar bears eating a dead walrus, while groups of seal swam in the little harbour? I find I have recorded the event and the date — September 1 — but not the exact location. There were several sites from the Thule people — those who preceded the present Inuit — and our on-ship archaeologist explained them to us. The huge whale ribs that once acted as roof beams were still there.

The sun shone, the breezes blew. Although it was autumn, several small arctic flowers were still in bloom. Pakak Innuksuk and Akoo Peters, Inuit culture resource people, drum-danced and sang. At such moments the Arctic is intensely alive. It seems a benign landscape, mild and hazy and welcoming, a place of many delights.

The next day it was colder and the wind was up. We reached the westernmost end of Devon Island and dropped anchor in the harbour of Beechy Island, a small knob at the western end of Devon. Franklin's two ships, the *Terror* and the *Erebus*, spent their first winter there, protected from the crush of ice. The shore, once the edge of a warmer sea where marine life thrived, is now fossil-strewn, barren, windswept. Many have visited since Franklin's day; many have posed for the camera beside the three graves there; many have pondered.

Some years ago the three bodies were disinterred, in an attempt to learn more about the expedition. The scientists engaged in this venture — as recorded in John Geiger's book, *Frozen in Time* — discovered that high levels of lead poisoning from tinned food must have made a substantial contribution to the disaster. The tin cans themselves can still be seen on the beach: lead as thick as candle drippings closes their seams. The dangers of eating lead were not well understood then, and the symptoms mimicked scurvy. Lead attacks the immune system, and causes disorientation and lapses in judgement. The supplies that were supposed to keep the expedition members alive were in fact killing them.

We disembarked from the *Akademic Ioffe* in Zodiacs and walked along the beach. I was blotch-free by this time; nevertheless I felt quite weightless. After visiting the graves — the markers are replicas now, as the originals suffered from the pilgrim's urge to chip off a piece of the action — Graeme and I sat on the shingle near an old coal depot where ships used to leave supplies for other ships until polar bears tore the storage building apart. We ate a piece of chocolate, hoarded by me for this occasion, and toasted Gwen in water from our water bottles, and Graeme sang "The Ballad of Lord Franklin," the words swallowed up by the wind. Farther along the beach, some bag-piping was underway, so faint we could scarcely hear it.

Inchoate thoughts about spaces, emptiness, gaps; jumping crevasses, I wrote in my notebook. *Words travelling across.*

The next day we were beset by drifting pack ice, just like Franklin. It was astonishing how quickly the ice moved, and with what strength. We had to go seventy miles around to get away from it.

Pilgrims have traditionally brought something back with them from their journeys. Sometimes it was a cockleshell to show they'd been to Jerusalem, or an expensive splinter claiming to be a piece of the true cross, or the alleged finger-bone of a saint. Modern-day pilgrims, dis-guised as tourists, bring photos of themselves sticking out their tongues in front of the Eiffel Tower, or postcards, or purchased mementoes — coffee spoons with the crests of cities on them, base-ball caps, ashtrays.

There was no stand selling bits of explorer's finger or T-shirts with *Souvenir of Beechy Island* on them, so I brought back a pebble. It was identical with the millions of other pebbles on the beach — dun-coloured sandstone, no distinguishing features. This pebble travelled with me to Toronto in a makeup kit.

I called my doctor as soon as I arrived, and described my symp-toms. "I think I've had West Nile Virus," I said. "Hard to tell," was his reply. (Worst come to worst, at least I wouldn't have been buried in the permafrost. I'd have been popped into the ship's freezer kept specially for that one purpose, so as not to get the bodies mixed up with the beef stroganoff.)

On a hot, dry day in mid-September, I put the Beechy Island pebble into my pocket, took a serving spoon from the kitchen, and walked over to Gwendolyn MacEwen Park, imagining to myself the rather sardonic poem Gwen might have made, both out of the park and out of the pebble event in which I was about to indulge. Accompanying me was David Young, one of whose plays — *Unimaginable Island* — deals with the unsung heroes of the Scott Antarctic expedition — unsung because they'd had the dubious taste to survive. In order to be a hero — at least in the nineteenth and early twentieth centuries — it was almost mandatory to be dead.

When we got to the park, David looked the other way while I dug a dusty hole with my spoon and inserted the pebble. So now, somewhere in the heart of darkest Toronto, its exact location known only to me, there's a tiny piece of geology brought all the way from Beechy Island. The only link between the two places is an act of the imagination, or perhaps two acts — Franklin's imagining of the Northwest Passage, and the twenty-two-year-old Gwendolyn MacEwen's imagining of Franklin.

> So I've followed you here
> Like a dozen others, looking for relics
> of your ships, your men.
> Here to this awful monastery,
> where you, where Crozier died,
> and all the men with you died,
> Seeking a passage from imagination to reality. . . .

51

MORTIFICATION

MORTIFICATIONS NEVER END. There is always a never-before-experienced one waiting just around the corner. As Scarlett O'Hara might have said, "Tomorrow is another mortification." Such anticipations give us hope: God isn't finished with us yet, because these things are sent to try us. I've never been entirely sure what that meant. Where there is blushing, there is life? Something like that.

While waiting for the mortifications yet to come, when I'll have dentures and they'll shoot out of my mouth on some august public occasion, or else I will topple off the podium or be sick on my presenter, I'll tell you of three mortifications past.

EARLY PERIOD

Long, long ago, when I was only twenty-nine and my first novel had just been published, I was living in Edmonton, Alberta, Canada. It was 1969. The women's movement had begun, in New York City, but it had not yet reached Edmonton, Alberta. It was November. It was freezing cold. I was freezing cold, and I went about wearing a second-hand fur coat — muskrat, I think — that I'd bought at the Salvation Army for $25. I also had a fur hat I'd made out of a rabbit shruggie — a shruggie was a sort of fur bolero — by deleting the arms and sewing up the armholes.

My publisher arranged my first-ever book signing. I was very excited. Once I'd peeled off the muskrats and rabbits, there I would be, inside the Hudson's Bay Company Department Store, where it was cozily warm — this in itself was exciting — with lines of eager, smiling readers waiting to purchase my book and have me scribble on it.

The signing was at a table set up in the Men's Sock and Underwear Department. I don't know what the thinking was behind this. There I sat, at lunch hour, smiling away, surrounded by piles of a novel called *The Edible Woman*. Men in overcoats and galoshes and toe rubbers and scarves and earmuffs passed by my table, intent on the purchase of boxer shorts. They looked at me, then at the title of my novel. Subdued panic broke out. There was the sound of a muffled stampede as dozens of galoshes and toe rubbers shuffled rapidly in the other direction.

I sold two copies.

Middle period

By this time I'd achieved a spoonful or two of notoriety, enough so that my U.S. publisher could arrange to get me onto an American TV talk show. It was an afternoon show, which in those days — could it have been the late 1970s? — meant variety. It was the sort of show at which they played pop music, and then you were supposed to sashay through a bead curtain, carrying your trained koala bear, or Japanese flower arrangement, or book.

I waited behind the bead curtain. There was an act on before me. It was a group from the Colostomy Association, who were talking about their colostomies, and about how to use the colostomy bag.

I knew I was doomed. No book could ever be that riveting. W. C. Fields vowed never to share the stage with a child or a dog;

I can add to that, "Never follow the Colostomy Association." (Or any other thing having to do with frightening bodily items, such as the port-wine-stain removal technique that once preceded me in Australia.) The problem is, you lose all interest in yourself and your so-called "work" — "What did you say your name was? And tell us the plot of your book, just in a couple of sentences, please" — so immersed are you in picturing the gruesome intricacies of . . . but never mind.

Modern period

Recently I was on a TV show in Mexico. By this time I was famous, insofar as writers are, although perhaps not quite so famous in Mexico as in other places. This was the kind of show where they put make-up on you, and I had eyelashes that stood out like little black shelves.

The interviewer was a very smart man who had lived — as it turned out — only a few blocks from my house, in Toronto, when he'd been a student and I'd been elsewhere, being mortified at my first book signing in Edmonton. We went merrily along through the interview, chatting about world affairs and such, until he hit me with the F-question. The do-you-consider-yourself-a-feminist question. I lobbed the ball briskly back over the net ("Women are human beings, don't you agree?"), but then he blindsided me. It was the eyelashes: they were so thick I didn't see it coming.

"Do you consider yourself *feminine?*" he said.

Nice Canadian middle-aged women go all strange when asked this by Mexican talk-show hosts somewhat younger than themselves, or at least I did. "What, at my age?" I blurted. Meaning: *I used to get asked this in 1969 as part of being mortified in Edmonton, and after thirty-four years I shouldn't have to keep on dealing with it!* But with eyelashes like that, what could I expect?

"Sure, why not?" he said.

I refrained from telling him why not. I did not say: *Geez, Louise, I'm sixty-three and you still expect me to wear pink, with frills?* I did not say: *feminine, or feline, pal? Grr, meow.* I did not say: *This is a frivolous question.*

Whacking my eyelashes together, I said, "You really shouldn't be asking *me*. You should be asking the men in my life." (Implying there were hordes of them.) "Just as I would ask the women in *your* life if you are masculine. They'd tell me the truth."

Time for the commercial.

A couple of days later, still brooding on this theme, I said, in public, "My boyfriends got bald and fat and then they died." Then I said, "That would make a good title for a short story." Then I regretted having said both.

Some mortifications are, after all, self-inflicted.

My THANKS TO all who have contributed to this book. To Phoebe Larmore, my agent of a quarter of a century; to Martha Sharpe and Adrienne Leahey of Anansi, who so charmingly twisted my arm; to Adrienne again, for helping to pull the book together; to Gene Goldberg, who is twenty-five in his soul, and rides a motorcycle; to Jen Osti, my assistant, to Surya Bhattacharya, who helped to track things down, and to Coleen Quinn, who kept me in running order. There are many, many editors with whom I've worked over the years: thank you to all.

And to Graeme Gibson, who has so often and so wisely said, "I wouldn't write that if I were you"; and to Jess Gibson, constant reader, who is sometimes able to correct my slang.

Lastly, to the four Irish women on the train from Galway to Dublin, overheard by me while they were discussing my books. "The last ones have been rather long," they said. Right after this I became violently ill and spent the rest of the trip locked in the washroom — some of us are sensitive to criticism, or maybe it was the injudicious carrot juice — but I would like these commentators to know that I took their remarks to heart. Some of the pieces in this book are quite short. So I've tried.

ACKNOWLEDGEMENTS

We would like to acknowledge the following sources of the work contained in this volume:

1. Dennis Revisited. *Descant*, No. 39 (Winter 1982), pp. 13–15.

2. Wondering What It's Like to Be a Woman. Review of *The Witches of Eastwick* by John Updike. *New York Times Book Review*, 13 May 1984, pp. 1, 40.

3. The Sorcerer as Apprentice. Review of *Difficult Loves* by Italo Calvino. *New York Times Book Review*, 1 October 1984, p. 13.

4. Margaret Atwood Remembers Marian Engel. *Saturday Night*, Vol. 100, No. 8 (August 1985), pp. 38–40.

5. Introduction to *Roughing It in the Bush, Or, Life in Canada* by Susanna Moodie. (London: Virago, 1986), pp. vii–xiv.

6. True North. *Saturday Night*, Vol. 102, No. 1 (January 1987), pp. 141–44, 146, 148.

7. Haunted by Their Nightmares. Review of *Beloved* by Toni Morrison. *New York Times Book Review*, 13 September 1987, pp. 1, 49–50.

8. Afterword to *A Jest of God* by Margaret Laurence. (Toronto: M&S, 1988), pp. 211–15.

9. Preface to *The Canadian Green Consumer Guide*, eds. Pollution Probe Foundation, Warner Troyer, and Glenys Moss. (Toronto: M&S, 1989), pp. 2–3.

10. Great Aunts. From *Family Portraits: Remembrances by Twenty Distinguished Writers*, ed. Carolyn Anthony. (New York: Doubleday, 1989).

11. Introduction: Reading Blind. Introduction to *The Best American Short Stories, 1989*, eds. Margaret Atwood and Shannon Ravenel. (New York: Houghton, 1989), pp. xi–xxiii.

12. The Public Woman as Honorary Man. Review of *The Warrior Queens* by Antonia Fraser. *Los Angeles Times Book Review*, 2 April 1989, p. 3.

13. Writing Utopia. Unpublished speech, 1989.

14. A Double-Bladed Knife: Subversive Laughter in Two Stories by Thomas King. From *Native Writers and Canadian Writing*, ed. W. H. New. (Vancouver: UBC Press, 1990), pp. 243–50.

15. Nine Beginnings. From *The Writer on Her Work, Volume 2*, ed. Janet Sternburg. (New York: Norton, 1990, 2000), pp. 150–56.

16. A Slave to His Own Liberation. Review of *The General in His Labyrinth* by Gabriel García Márquez. *New York Times Book Review*, 16 September 1990, pp. 1, 30.

17. Afterword to *Anne of Green Gables* by Lucy Maud Montgomery. (Toronto, M&S, 1992), pp. 331–36.

18. Introduction: The Early Years. Introduction to *The Poetry of Gwendolyn MacEwen: The Early Years*, eds. Margaret Atwood and Barry Callaghan. (Toronto: Exile Editions, 1993) pp. vii–xii.

19. Why I Love *Night of the Hunter*. Review of *The Night of the Hunter*, dir. Charles Laughton (1955). *The Guardian*, 19 March 1999, p. 12.

20. Spotty-handed Villainesses: Problems of Female Bad Behaviour in the Creation of Literature. An address delivered in the Cheltenham Lecture Series, University of Gloucester, 8 October 1993.

21. The Grunge Look. From *Writing Away: The PEN Canada Travel Anthology*, ed. Constance Rooke. (Toronto: M&S, 1994), pp. 1–11.

22. Not So Grimm: The Staying Power of Fairy Tales. Review of *From the Beast to the Blonde: On Fairy Tales and Their Tellers* by Marina Warner. *Los Angeles Times Book Review*, 29 October 1995, p. 1.

23. A Rich Dessert from a Saucy Carter. Review of *Burning Your Boats: The Collected Short Stories* by Angela Carter. *Globe and Mail*, 6 April 1996, p. C18.

24. Review of *An Experiment in Love* by Hilary Mantel. *New York Times Book Review*, 2 June 1996, p. 11.

25. In Search of *Alias Grace*: On Writing Canadian Historical Fiction. An address given at Bronfman Lecture Series (Ottawa: November 1996),

Smithsonian Institute (Washington: 11 December 1996), Chicago Library Foundations (6 January 1997), Oberlin College Friends of the Library (8 February 1997), City Arts & Lectures (San Francisco: 5 March 1997). Reprinted in *American Historical Review*, Vol. 103, No. 5 (December 1998), p. 1503 (1).

26. Masterpiece Theatre. Review of *Trickster Makes This World: Mischief, Myth and Art* and *The Gift: Imagination and the Erotic Life of Property* by Lewis Hyde. *Los Angeles Times Book Review*, 25 January 1998, p. 7.

27. The Awkward Sublime. *BorderCrossings*, Vol. 19, No. 4 (November 2000), pp. 46–51.

28. Mordecai Richler: 1931–2001: Diogenes of Montreal. *Globe and Mail*, 4 July 2001, pp. R1, R7.

29. Introduction to *She* by H. Rider Haggard. (New York: Random House, 2002), pp. xvii–xxiv.

30. When Afghanistan Was at Peace. *New York Times Magazine*, 28 October 2001, p. 82.

31. Mystery Man. Review of: *The Selected Letters of Dashiell Hammett, 1921–1960*, eds. Richard Layman and Julie Rivett; *Dashiell Hammett: A Daughter Remembers* by Jo Hammett; and *Dashiell Hammett: Crime Stories & Other Writings*, ed. Steven Marcus. *New York Review of Books*, Vol. 49, No. 2 (14 February 2002), pp. 19–21.

32. Of Myths and Men. Review of *Atanarjuat: The Fast Runner*, dir. Zacharias Kunuk (2001). *Globe and Mail*, 13 April 2002, p. R10.

33. Cops and Robbers. Review of *Tishomingo Blues* by Elmore Leonard. *New York Review of Books*, Vol. 49, No. 9 (23 May 2002), pp. 21–23.

34. Tiff and the Animals. An address delivered on the occasion of the Timothy Findley Memorial Evening, University of Toronto, 29 September 2002.

35. The Indelible Woman. *The Guardian*, 7 September 2002.

36. The Queen of Quinkdom. Review of *The Birthday of the World and Other Stories* by Ursula K. Le Guin. *New York Review of Books*, Vol. 49, No. 14 (26 September 2002).

37. Introduction to *Ground Works: Avant-Garde for Thee*, ed. Christian Bök. (Toronto: Anansi, 2002), pp. ix–xv.

38. The Wrong Box: Matt Cohen, Fabulism and Critical Taxonomy. From *Uncommon Ground: A Celebration of Matt Cohen*, eds. Graeme Gibson, Wayne Grady, Dennis Lee, and Priscila Uppal. (Toronto: Knopf, 2002), pp. 66–82.

39. Introduction to *Doctor Glas* by Hjalmar Söderberg, trans. Paul Britten Austin. (New York: Anchor, 2002), pp. 5–10.

40. Napoleon's Two Biggest Mistakes. From "Bonaparte to Bush: You'll Be Sorry." *Globe and Mail*, 1 March 2003, p. A17.

41. Letter to America. *The Nation*, 14 April 2003, pp. 22–23.

42. Writing *Oryx and Crake*. Book-of-the-Month Club/Bookspan (January 2003).

43. George Orwell: Some Personal Connections. An address broadcast on BBC Radio 3 on 13 June 2003. Reprinted as "Orwell and Me," *The Guardian*, 16 June 2003.

44. Arguing Against Ice Cream. Review of *Enough: Staying Human in an Engineered Age* by Bill McKibben. *New York Review of Books*, 12 June 2003, pp. 6, 8, 10.

45. Victory Gardens. Foreword to *A Breath of Fresh Air: Celebrating Nature and School Gardens* by Elise Houghton. (Toronto: Sumach Press, 2003), pp. 13–19.

46. Carol Shields, Who Died Last Week, Wrote Books That Were Full of Delights. From "Lives & Letters: Carol Shields." *The Guardian*, 26 July 2003, p. 28.

47. Resisting the Veil: Reports from a Revolution. Review of: *Persepolis: The Story of a Childhood* by Marjane Satrapi; *Reading Lolita in Tehran: A Memoir in Books* by Azar Nafisi; *The Bathhouse* by Farnoosh Moshiri; *Shah of Shahs* by Ryszard Kapuściński; *The Crisis of Islam: Holy War and Unholy Terror* by Bernard Lewis; and *The Crusades Through Arab Eyes* by Amin Maalouf. *The Walrus*, Vol. 1, No. 1 (October 2003), pp. 86–89.

48. Introduction to *The Complete Stories, Volume 4* by Morley Callaghan. (Toronto: Exile Editions, 2003), pp. ix–xix.

49. He Springs Eternal. Review of *Hope Dies Last: Keeping the Faith in Difficult Times* by Studs Terkel. *New York Review of Books*, 6 November 2003, pp. 78–80.

50. To Beechy Island. From *Solo: Writers on Pilgrimage*, ed. Katherine Govier. (Toronto: M&S, 2004), pp. 201–16.

51. Mortification. From *Mortification: Writers' Stories of Their Public Shame*, ed. Robin Robertson. (London: Fourth Estate, 2003), pp. 1–4.

INDEX

Achebe, Chinua: *Anthills of the Savannah*, 87–88

Afghanistan, 9, 242–44, 366; chador, 243–44

Agee, James, 153; *The African Queen* (film), 153; *A Death in the Family*, 153; *Let Us Now Praise Famous Men*, 153; *The Night of the Hunter* (film), 152–56

Alias Grace (novel): Grace Marks, 211, 212, 213–14, 215; James McDermott, 211, 212, 214, 215; Kinnear, Thomas, 211, 213; *Life in the Clearings versus the Bush* (Moodie), 211; Nancy Montgomery, 211, 212, 214, 215; Susanna Moodie, 210–11, 212, 213, 215; writing of, 210–11, 212–15

Alone of All Her Sex (Warner), 183

American dream, the, 273, 382

American vernacular in literature, 251–52. *See also Tishomingo Blues*

Anansi: *See* House of Anansi Press

Anderson, Marjorie: *Dropped Threads* and *Dropped Threads 2*, 362–63

Anderson, Sherwood, 252, 300, 311, 376

Anderson-Dargatz, Gail: *The Cure for Death by Lightning*, 207

Animal Farm (Orwell), 331–33, 334, 336

Anne of Green Gables (L. M. Montgomery), 141, 295; *Anne* "phenomenon," 141–42; child/adult relationships in, 145–46; Nature, as motif in, 142; theme, orphan as heroine, 142–43

Anthology: See CBC (Canadian Broadcasting Corporation)

Apprenticeship of Duddy Kravitz, The (Richler), 233

"appropriation of voice," 86, 312

Arabian Nights, 183, 243; Maxfield Parrish, illustrator, 365

Atanarjuat: The Fast Runner, 259–62. *See also* Homer; Camera d'Or (Cannes), 259; Genie Awards, 259; Pakak Innuksuk, 262; Toronto International Film Festival, 261; Zacharias Kunuk, director, 259

Atwood, Margaret: ancestors, 77–80, 107; Aunt J., 72, 73–75, 76, 77, 80, 81, 82, 83–84; Aunt K., 76, 77, 78–79, 80, 81, 82, 83–84; birth of, 197; cameo appearance in *Typing* by Matt Cohen, 303; childhood visits to Nova Scotia, 79–80; early years in Ottawa, 197–98; as editor at House of Anansi Press, 297; first trip to Europe (1964), 173–74, 175–82; first writers' conference (Montreal, 1958), 72, 73–75; gardening, 280, 356–57, 395; as graduate student, Harvard Department of English Literature, 35, 65, 66; Graeme Gibson, partner, 32, 242–43, 311, 395, 403–4; Great-Aunt Winnie, first woman to receive MA from Dalhousie University, 79; as instigator for *Ground Works*, 293; Jess, daughter, 158–59, 242–43; living in West Berlin, 102; mother (Margaret Killam Atwood), 72, 76, 77, 78–79, 144; Perry Miller, Harvard professor, 107; pilgrimage to Beechy Island, 395–96, 399–401, 402–404; on reviewing the work of others, 3–4; Second Cousin Lindsay, English professor at Dalhousie University, 73; Shakesbeat Latweed, 14; teaching Canadian literature in Alabama, 44; trip to Afghanistan (1978), 242–44; at Victoria College, University of Toronto, 13–14; works of: *See Alias Grace; The Blind Assassin; Cat's Eye; The Circle Game; Good Bones; The Handmaid's Tale; The Journals of Susanna Moodie; Lady Oracle; Morning in the Burned House; Murder in the Dark; Oryx and Crake; Power Politics; The Robber Bride; Second Words; Survival: A Thematic Guide to Canadian Literature; Wilderness Tips*

Austen, Jane, 35, 107, 361, 370; *Pride and Prejudice*, 160

Barclay, Byrna, 30
Barney's Version (Richler), 233
Bear (Engel), 26, 28, 44, 314
beatniks/Beat Generation, 83, 148, 175, 298, 372
Beckett, Samuel: *Krapp's Last Tape*, 201; *The Unnameable*, 388; *Waiting For Godot*, 294
Be Cool (Leonard), 263
Beechy Island, 395, 396, 403, 404, 405
Bellamy, Edward: *Looking Backward*, 104, 283
Beloved (Morrison), 59–64, 170; American slavery experience as paradigm, 59, 61–62; supernatural elements in, 60, 63; theme, black *vs.* white, 62–63
Berlin Wall, the, 5, 9, 11, 337
Best American Short Stories, 1989, The: choosing entries for, 85–87, 91–92, 93–98; "reading blind," 86–87; Shannon Ravenel, series editor, 86
Bettelheim, Bruno: *The Uses of Enchantment*, 184
birdwatching, 328. See also *Oryx and Crake*
Birthday of the World and Other Stories, The (Le Guin), 281, 285, 287, 289–92; Ekumen, 284–86
bissett, bill, 15, 149; *nobody owns th earth*, 15
Blind Assassin, The (novel), 116–17; Booker Prize, 117
Bluest Eye, The (Morrison), 87
Bonaparte, Napoleon, 140, 320–23; Iraq, U.S. invasion of, 322; Napoleonic Wars, 36; Tchaikovsky's 1812 Overture, 320, 322
Bowering, George, 297; *Burning Waters*, 207; *The Gangs of Kosmos*, 15
Boyd, Blanche McCrary: "The Black Hand Girl," 96
Bradbury, Ray: *Fahrenheit 451*, 284; *The Martian Chronicles*, 284
Breath of Fresh Air, A (Houghton), foreword to, 351–59. See also Victory Gardens
Brown, Larry: "Kubuku Rides (This Is It)", 96
Buckler, Ernest: *The Mountain and the Valley*, 81–82
Burning Your Boats: The Collected Short Stories (Carter), 188, 189–90
Butler, Samuel: *Erewhon*, 104, 283

Callaghan, Morley, 295, 296, 311, 372–81, 381; comparison with Hemingway and Fitzgerald, and others, 376; *The Complete Stories*, Volume 4, introduction to, 372–81; making a living in Canada as a writer, 374–75; short stories, 377, 378
Calvino, Italo: *Difficult Loves*, 23–25
Camus, Albert, 278, 388
Canada, Upper and Lower: *See also Alias Grace, Roughing It in the Bush*; early history, 36–37; immigrants to, 36–37; literature of, 40–41
Canada House (London), 174, 175
Canadian Authors Association, 73
Canadian Green Consumer Guide, The, preface to, 70–71. See also environmental issues
Canadian literary magazines, 296, 297; *Acta Victoriana*, 14
Canadian writers in the '40s, '50s, and '60s, hurdles facing, 295–96
Cariboo Horses, The (Purdy), 224
Carter, Angela, 300; *Burning Your Boats: The Collected Short Stories*, 188, 189–90
Cat's Eye (novel), 9, 10–11
cbc (Canadian Broadcasting Corporation), 30, 149, 204, 212, 217; *Anthology*, 149, 296; Bob Weaver (former producer of *Anthology*), 30
Centaur, The (Updike), 17
Chandler, Raymond, 91, 246, 252, 324; *The Simple Art of Murder*, 91, 246
Circle Game, The (poetry volume), 14; Governor General's Award for Poetry, 14
civil rights movement, the, 298, 383, 390; Clifford and Virginia Durr (activists), 385–86
Clemens, Samuel: *See* Twain, Mark
Cohen, Leonard, 148, 150, 313, 314; *Beautiful Losers*, 313, 314; *Let Us Compare Mythologies*, 150
Cohen, Matt, 300; author as Rumpelstiltskin, 301–2, 304, 309–10; fabulism *vs.* literary realism, 300–302, 303–4, 309, 312–14; literary realism in writing, 300, 306, 314
Columbus and the Fat Lady (Matt Cohen), 302, 303, 305, 313; the fifteen stories that comprise, 305–308

Company of Wolves, The (Carter), 188
Complete Stories, The, Volume 4 (Callaghan), introduction to, 372–81
Conrad, Joseph: *Heart of Darkness*, 240
Contact Press, 224, 297
Cooper, James Fenimore, 203, 251; *Leatherstocking Tales*, 124, 251
Cuba Libre (Leonard), 263
Cunningham, Michael: "White Angel," 94

Dain Case, The (Hammett), 248
Davies, Robertson, 197, 207; *Murther and Walking Spirits*, 207
Death: Will the Circle Be Unbroken? (Terkel), 382–83
DeMarinis, Rick: "The Flowers of Boredom," 94
Dickens, Charles, 174, 202, 233, 278; *A Christmas Carol*: Marley's ghost, 326, 340; Scrooge, 202, 340–41, 356
Dickinson, Emily, 18, 41, 160, 324, 388
Difficult Loves (Calvino), 23–25
Disinherited, The (Matt Cohen), 308
Diviners, The (Laurence), 67, 206
Division Street America (Terkel), 382
Doctor Glas (Söderberg), 315–19
Doerr, Harriet: "Edie: A Life," 96
Douglass, Frederick, 221–22
Dropped Threads and *Dropped Threads 2* (Shields, Anderson, ed.), 362–63
Dystopias, 335–36, 337; Utopias *vs.* Dystopias, 103–106

Edible Woman, The (novel), 407
Eliot, T. S., 41, 72, 174, 222
Elizabeth and After (Matt Cohen), 312; Governor General's Award for Fiction, 312
End of Nature, The (McKibben), 339
Engel, Marian, 26–33, 44, 206, 298, 311; Governor General's Award for Fiction, 31; Writers' Union of Canada, 32
Enough: Staying Human in an Engineered Age (McKibben), 339, 340, 343–46, 347, 349; cybernetics, 342, 345; genetic engineering, 343–45; immortality, 346–48; Mother Nature, 346; nanotechnology, 345
environmental issues. *See also Enough: Staying Human in an Engineered Age*; "horror stories of the north"; Victory

Gardens; acid rain, 49–50; conservation, salvaging, and rationing as solutions, 70–71; disappearance of arable land, 358; pesticide use, 356; "Reduce. Reuse. Recycle.", 71; space junk, 57; "the Disposable Period," 355–56; U.S. lack of environmental protections, 326
"European Jews" trilogy, *The Spanish Doctor, Nadine, Emotional Arithmetic* (Matt Cohen), 305, 312

Experiment in Love, An (Mantel), 191–94, 195; theme, mother as controller, 192–94

fabulism *vs.* literary realism, 300–302, 303–304, 309, 312–14
Faulkner, William, 252, 257, 258, 278, 324; *Sanctuary*, 257
female leaders, 99–101. *See also She*; Wonder Woman
feminists, feminism, and feminist principles, 41, 144, 158, 160, 165, 166–67, 168, 170, 174, 180, 188, 288, 307, 311, 336, 361, 362, 363, 408. *See also* women's movement, the; fairy tales attacked by feminists, 184; Mother Goose as feminist heroine, 184
Findley, Timothy, 28, 207, 275–77, 314; Peter Rabbit, 275–77; Writers' Union of Canada, 28
Fire-Dwellers, The (Laurence), 67
First World War, 83, 109, 280, 322, 366
Fisherman of the Inland Sea, A (Le Guin), 290
Fitzgerald, F. Scott, 324, 374, 376
Franklin (Sir John) expedition, 206, 233, 396, 399, 401–402, 403–404, 405. *See also Terror and Erebus*; Beechy Island, 395, 396, 403, 404, 405
Fraser, Antonia, 99–101
From the Beast to the Blonde: On Fairy Tales and Their Tellers (Warner), 183, 185–87; Mother Goose as feminist heroine, 184, 185
Frye, Northrop, 375; *Anatomy of Criticism*, 150; *The Secular Scripture: A Study of the Structure of Romance*, 239–40

Gallant, Mavis, 298, 313; "The Concert Party," 97
García Márquez, Gabriel, 137, 138–40

General in His Labyrinth, The (García Márquez), 137, 138–40; Simon Bolívar (The Liberator), 137–40

Get Shorty (Leonard), 263

Gibson, Graeme, 32, 242–43, 311, 395, 403–4; *Communion*, 314; *Perpetual Motion*, 207

Gift, The: Imagination and the Erotic Life of Property (Hyde), 218–20, 223

Gilman, Charlotte Perkins: *Herland*, 289

Glass Key, The (Hammett), 248

Glitz (Leonard), 263

Glover, Douglas: "Why I Decide to Kill Myself and Other Jokes," 96

Good Bones (short stories), 116

Governor General's Award, 14, 31, 65, 66, 312, 362

Govier, Katherine: *Angel Walk*, 207

Gowdy, Barbara, 314; "Disneyland," 94

Great Depression, the, 75, 154, 203, 233, 265, 295–96, 297, 372, 374, 382, 383

Greene, Graham, 46, 94, 175–176, 176, 200, 263; *The Lawless Roads*, 94; *The Ministry of Fear*, 200

Grimm's Fairy Tales, 185, 274

Ground Works (Bök, ed.), 293, 297, 299. *See also* Beckett, Samuel; Ondaatje, Michael; "experimental fiction," 293–95, 298, 299; genesis in Canada, 295, 298

Grubb, Davis: *The Night of the Hunter* (novel), 153, 265

Haggard, H. Rider, 150, 167, 229, 234–35, 237, 238, 239–40, 282; *She*, 150, 167, 229, 234–36, 237–40, 282

Hammett, Dashiell, 245–57, 258–59, 324; American vernacular in literature, 251–52; *Black Mask*, 248, 250; Jo Hammett, daughter, 247–48, 249, 255, 257, 258; Josephine Dolan, wife, 247, 249, 250; Lillian Hellman, 246, 248, 249, 250, 256; Mary Hammett, daughter, 247–48, 250; McCarthy Red Scare, 246, 249; *The Thin Man*, 253, 255

Hammett, Jo: *See also* Hammett, Dashiell; *Dashiell Hammett: A Daughter Remembers*, 247–48, 249, 255–56, 257, 258

Handmaid's Tale, The (novel), 4, 9, 10, 11, 102, 106, 107, 110, 111, 244, 330, 335, 336. *See also* Afghanistan; *Nineteen Eighty-four*; Orwell, George; as speculative fiction, 103; as theocracy, 108; Utopias *vs.* Dystopias, 103–106

Hawthorne, Nathaniel, 153, 170; *The Scarlet Letter*, 170, 210

Hébert, Anne: *Kamouraska*, 206, 312

Hellman, Lillian, 248, 249, 250, 256; *Pentimento*, 246

Hemingway, Ernest, 189, 278, 324, 374, 376; *The Sun Also Rises*, 252

Hiassen, Carl, 252; *Skin Tight*, 258

Hoban, Russell: *Riddley Walker*, 284

Hogan, Linda: "Aunt Moon's Young Man," 96

Homer, 260, 261; House of Atreus, 260; *The Iliad*, 260

Honeyman Festival, The (Engel), 27, 31

Hope Dies Last: Keeping the Faith in Difficult Times (Terkel), 382, 383, 385, 387, 388, 389, 390–94; Cesar Chavez, 389; Clifford and Virginia Durr (civil rights activists), 385–86; Dennis Kucinich, 394; Frances Moore Lappé, 393–94; General Paul Tibbetts (pilot of the *Enola Gay*), 390

"horror stories of the north," 55–56

House of Anansi Press, 302; Dennis Lee as editor, 14–15, 304; Margaret Atwood as editor, 297

Hudson, W. H.: *A Crystal Age*, 104, 105, 289

Huxley, Aldous: *Brave New World*, 104, 283, 333, 336, 337, 343

Hyde, Lewis, 218, 219, 220, 221, 222, 223, 274

If on a Winter's Night a Traveler (Calvino), 23

Innuksuk, Pakak, 262, 403

Invisible Cities (Calvino), 23

Iran, 366

Iraq, 366; American Iraqis, 391; U.S. invasion of (2003), 322, 326, 366, 394. *See also* Bonaparte, Napoleon

Italian Folk Tales (Calvino), 23

Jameson, Anna: *Winter Studies and Summer Rambles in Canada*, 40

Jefferson, Thomas, 387

Jest of God, A (Laurence), 65, 66, 67–68, 69; Rachel Cameron, 66–69

"Joe the Painter and the Deer Island Massacre" (King), 121–24, 125; as parody of Fenimore Cooper's *Leatherstocking Tales*, 124

Journals of Susanna Moodie, The (poetry volume), 35, 206, 210. See also *Alias Grace*

Joyce, James, 87; *Dubliners*, 376; *A Portrait of the Artist as a Young Man*, 222; *Ulysses*, 319

Kafka, Franz, 313, 388

Kapuściński, Ryszard: *Shah of Shahs*, 367–68

King, Thomas, 121, 125, 129

Kinnear, Thomas: See *Alias Grace*

Koestler, Arthur: *Darkness at Noon*, 106, 333

Lady Macbeth, 158, 167, 169

Lady Oracle (novel), 15

Langton, Anne: *A Gentlewoman in Upper Canada*, 40

Lappé, Frances Moore: *Diet for a Small Planet*, 393–94

Larry's Party (Shields), 362; Orange Prize, 362

Last of the Crazy People, The (Findley), 276

Last Seen (Matt Cohen), 301, 308, 312–13

Laurence, Margaret, 65, 66, 67, 68, 196, 206, 298

Layman, Richard, ed.: *The Selected Letters of Dashiell Hammett, 1921–1960*, 247, 249–50

Le Carré, John, 264

Lee, Dennis, 10, 13–16, 304; "Dennis-as-editor," 15–16; House of Anansi Press, 14–15; Shakesbeat Latweed, 14; *Alligator Pie*, 16

LeFanu, Sheridan: *Carmilla*, 239

Left Hand of Darkness, The (Le Guin), 285

Le Guin, Ursula K., 281, 284, 285–87; awards, 284

Leonard, Elmore, 252, 263, 264–66, 267–68, 271, 273; demotic stylings of, 263

Lessing, Doris: *The Golden Notebook*, 179

Lethem, Jonathan: *Motherless Brooklyn*, 252

Lewis, Bernard: *The Crisis of Islam: Holy War and Unholy Terror*, 366–67

Lewis, C. S., 240, 282

Life in the Clearings versus the Bush (Moodie), 35, 36, 210

literary critics and criticism, 162

Long Distance (McKibben), 339

Longfellow, Henry Wadsworth, 256, 258. See also Hammett, Dashiell; *Giles Corey of the Salem Farms*, 256–57, 258; "The Children's Hour," 256

Louie, David Wong: "Displacement," 96

Maalouf, Amin: *The Crusades Through Arab Eyes*, 366

MacDonald, Anne-Marie: *Fall on Your Knees*, 207

MacDonald, Wilson, 74

MacEwen, Gwendolyn, 147, 148, 149–51, 206, 399, 402, 405; Franklin expedition, 150, 206, 233, 396, 399, 401–402, 403–404, 405; Gwendolyn MacEwen Park (Toronto), 404–5

Mackenzie, William Lyon, 198, 214. See also *Alias Grace*

MacLennan, Hugh, 311

Macpherson, Jay, 148, 149

Mad Trapper of Rat River, 53

Maladicta (scholarly journal devoted to foul language), 264

Maltese Falcon, The (Hammett), 248–49, 253

Mantel, Hilary, 191, 195

Many Coloured Coat, The (Callaghan), 378–81

Marcus, Steven: See also Hammett, Dashiell; *Dashiell Hammett: Crime Stories and Other Writings*, 247, 251, 253

Marias, Javier: *All Souls*, 201–202

Marks, Grace: See *Alias Grace*

Marlatt, Daphne: *Ana Historic*, 207

McCarthy Red Scare, 246, 249, 257, 297, 383, 384

McDermott, James: See *Alias Grace*

McKibben, Bill, 339, 340–41, 343, 344, 345, 346, 347, 349

McLuhan, Marshall, 150, 162

Medea (Euripides), 167, 169–70

Michaels, Anne: *Fugitive Pieces*, 207, 314

Middle Eastern literature, 364–66

Miller, Arthur, 324; *The Crucible*, 257; *Death of a Salesman*, 273–74, 378

Montgomery, Lucy Maud, 143–46, 295. See also *Anne of Green Gables*

Montgomery, Nancy: See *Alias Grace*

Monuments and Maidens (Warner), 183

Moodie, Susanna, 34–39, 40, 41, 210–11, 212, 213, 215. See also Traill, Catharine Parr

Moore, Brian: *Blackrobe*, 207

Morning in the Burned House (poetry volume), 116

More, Sir Thomas, 103; *Utopia*, 104, 282

Morris, William: *News From Nowhere*, 104, 283

Morrison, Toni, 59, 62, 63, 64, 87, 170; *Sula*, 167

Moshiri, Farnoosh: *The Bathhouse*, 370–71

Mother Nature, 346; Wordsworth's Mother Nature, 18, 238

motifs: confrontation with a harsh and vast geography, 40, 50–52, 298; illusion *vs.* reality, 268; Nature, 38, 53, 120, 142, 310

Mukherjee, Bharati: "The Management of Grief," 96

Munro, Alice, 27, 97–98, 207, 298, 313, 360, 362; "A Wilderness Station," 207; "Meneseteung," 97–98, 207; the "Munro Doctrine," 362; "The Dance of the Happy Shades," 313

Murder in the Dark (short stories), 116

Muskoka, 43, 46

Nafisi, Azar: *Reading Lolita in Tehran: A Memoir in Books*, 369–70

nationalism, Canadian cultural, 298, 311

Native writing, emergence of humour in, 120–21. *See also* King, Thomas

Nature: as motif in literature, 38, 53, 120, 142, 310

Newby, Eric: *A Short Walk in the Hindu Kush*, 39–40

Nichol, bp, 149

Night of the Hunter, The (film), 152–56, 325. *See also* Grubb, Davis; Charles Laughton, director, 152–53, 154; James Agee, screenwriter, 153; Lillian Gish, 153, 325; Robert Mitchum, 153, 154; Shelley Winters, 152, 153; theme, struggle between evil and innocence, 154, 155

9/11: *See* September 11

Nineteen Eighty-four (Orwell), 104, 105, 106, 201, 283, 333–35, 336, 337. *See also* *Handmaid's Tale, The*; dystopias, 335–36

No Clouds of Glory (Engel), 26

Not Wanted on the Voyage (Findley), 275

"old days," the, 54–55

Ondaatje, Michael, 15, 207, 294, 297, 314; *The Collected Works of Billy the Kid*, 15, 294; *The English Patient*, 207; *In the Skin of a Lion*, 207, 314

"One Good Story, That One" (King), 121, 125–28

Orwell, George, 331–33, 334, 335, 336, 337, 338, 373. *See also* *Handmaid's Tale, The*; "prose like a window pane," 189, 337, 373

Oryx and Crake (novel), 229; birdwatching, 328; September 11, 229, 329; as speculative fiction, 330; writing of, 328–330

Pagan Babies (Leonard), 263

Paine, Tom, 386

Phillips, Dale Ray: "What Men Love For," 95

Piano Man's Daughter, The (Findley), 207

Piercey, Marge: *Woman on the Edge of Time*, 104, 289

pilgrimages in literature, 402; *The Canterbury Tales* (Geoffrey Chaucer), 397–98, 399, 400; *Childe Harold's Pilgrimage* (Lord Byron), 398, 399, 400; *The Pilgrim's Progress* (John Bunyan), 398, 399

Pilgrim (Findley), 276

Planet of Exile (Le Guin), 284

Poems for All the Annettes (Purdy), 224

Poetry of Gwendolyn MacEwen, The (MacEwen), 147, 151

Power Politics (poetry volume), 15

publishing, Canadian: Canadian Authors Association, 73; early paperback book industry, 203, 295; Giller Prize, 233; Governor General's Awards, 14, 31, 65, 66, 312, 362; Writers' Union of Canada, 28, 32

publishing presses, small Canadian, 297. *See also* Contact Press; House of Anansi Press

Purdy, Al, 206, 224–225

Puritans and Puritanism, American, 17, 20, 41, 107, 108, 109, 110, 153, 155, 210

"reading blind," 86–87

Reaney, James, 148, 150, 206, 295, 313; *Alphabet* (magazine), 150; *A Suit of Nettles*, 295; "The Box Social," 313; "The Bully," 313

Rebellion of 1837, 198, 205, 214. *See also* *Alias Grace*

Red Harvest (Hammett), 248
Republic of Love, The (Shields), 361
Richards, Mark: "Strays," 95
Richler, Mordecai, 3, 229, 232–33, 311;
    Giller Prize, 233
Robber Bride, The (novel), 116
Robinson, Arthur: "The Boy on the
    Train," 95
Rocannon's World (Le Guin), 284
Roche, Mazo de la, 203, 295
Room of One's Own (Engel), 27
Roughing It in the Bush (Moodie), 34–35, 39,
    41, 210–11; confrontation with a harsh
    and vast geography, as motif in, 40;
    Nature, as motif in, 38
Rousseau, Jean-Jacques, 140, 332
Roy, Gabrielle: *The Tin Flute*, 311
Rubáiyát of Omar Khayyám, The, 365
Rule, Jane, 30, 65

Salem novels, the (Matt Cohen), 306, 311
Salutin, Rick: *The Farmers' Rebellion*, 206
Sandburg, Carl: "Chicago," 383–84
Sarah Bastard's Notebook (Engel), 27
Sartre, Jean-Paul, 43, 297; *The Question*, 371
Satrapi, Marjane: *Persepolis: The Story of a
    Childhood*, 368–69, 370
Schroeder, Andreas, 297
science fiction: as literary label, 281–84,
    288; rearranged human societies in,
    283; reliance on anthropology, 286–87;
    science-fiction fantasy, 281–284; science
    fiction proper, 281, 284; speculative
    fiction, 103, 281, 283
Scott, F. R., 74
Second Words (nonfiction), 1, 2, 4
Second World War, 75, 106, 199, 203, 233,
    249, 295–96, 297, 322, 351, 355, 374,
    383, 390. *See also* Victory Gardens
September 11 (World Trade Center attack),
    5, 229, 261, 329, 337, 391, 394
Sharif, M. T.: "The Letter Writer," 95
She (Haggard), 150, 167, 229, 234–36,
    237–40, 282
Shelley, Mary: *Frankenstein*, 191, 234, 294,
    343; as the first work of science fiction,
    282
Shields, Carol, 207, 360–63; early books,
    361–62; study of Jane Austen, 361
Snow White and the Seven Dwarfs, 167, 169
Söderberg, Hjalmar, 316

Solomon Gursky Was Here (Richler), 233;
    Franklin expedition, 233
space junk, 57
Spadework (Findley), 276
speculative fiction, 281, 283, 330; *Oryx
    and Crake* as, 330
Stoker, Bram: *Dracula*, 163, 230, 234, 239
Stone Angel, The (Laurence), 65, 67, 196
Stone Diaries, The (Shields), 207, 361, 362;
    American Pulitzer Prize, 362; Governor
    General's Award for Fiction, 362
supernatural elements in novels: *Beloved*,
    60, 63
*Survival: A Thematic Guide to Canadian
    Literature* (nonfiction), 15, 119
Swann (Shields), 361
Swift, Jonathan, 283; *Gulliver's Travels*, 282

Tennyson, Alfred, Lord, 200; *Idylls of the
    King*, 238
Terkel, Studs, 382, 383–89, 394; book pro-
    gram on NPR, 384–85; John Kenneth
    Galbraith, 382; Mahalia Jackson, 384;
    McCarthy Red Scare, 384; *Studs's Place*
    (television talk show), 383
Terror and Erebus (MacEwen), 206, 399,
    402, 405
That Summer in Paris (Callaghan), 377–78
themes: black *vs.* white: *See Beloved*;
    Tishomingo Blues; mother as controller:
    See Experiment in Love, An; orphan as
    heroine: *See Anne of Green Gables*; rob-
    ber as folk hero: *See Tishomingo Blues*;
    struggle between good and evil: *See
    Night of the Hunter, The* (film); wicked-
    ness and mischief: *See Witches of
    Eastwick, The*
Thin Man, The (Hammett), 253, 255
Thomson, Tom, 52–53
Thoreau, Henry David, 41, 218; "Civil
    Disobedience," 265; as "father of envi-
    ronmentalism," 324
Tishomingo Blues (Leonard), 263–64, 266–67,
    268–71, 272–73; American Civil War,
    270–72; demotic stylings in, 263; motif,
    illusion *vs.* reality, 268; theme, black *vs.*
    white, 270; theme, robber as folk hero,
    265–66; trickster figure in, 269, 271;
    Tunica, Mississippi, 267–268, 269
Tolkein, J. R. R.: *The Lord of the Rings*,
    240, 282

To the Lighthouse (Woolf), 278–280
Traill, Catharine Parr, 37, 40, 206; *The Canadian Settler's Guide*, 37; *The Young Emigrants; or, Pictures of Canada*, 37
trickster figures and traits, 220–21, 222, 269, 271
Trickster Makes This World: Mischief, Myth and Art (Hyde), 218, 220–23; trickster figures and traits, 220–21, 222
Tunica, Mississippi, 267–68, 269
Twain, Mark, 153, 251, 386; *Huckleberry Finn*, 155, 251, 386; American vernacular in literature, 251; theme, black *vs.* white, 270
Typing: A Life in 26 Keys (Matt Cohen), 301, 302, 303, 308, 313

Unless (Shields), 362, 363
Updike, John, 17, 18, 19–20, 21, 22
Urquhart, Jane: *Away*, 207, 312; *The Whirlpool*, 207, 314
U.S. invasion of Iraq (2003), 322, 326, 366, 394. *See also* Bonaparte, Napoleon

Vanderhaeghe, Guy: *The Englishman's Boy*, 207
Victory Gardens, 71, 355, 356, 359; agriculture and horticulture, 353–54; Second World War, 351, 355, 356
Vietnam War, 19, 21, 174, 298
"voice of the story," 87–90
Voltaire, 400–401
Vonnegut, Kurt: *Slaughterhouse Five*, 283

Warner, Marina, 183, 184, 185, 186–87
Warrior Queens, The (Fraser), 99–101; Boadicea, 99–100; female leaders, 99–101; Margaret Thatcher, 100, 101

Wars, The (Findley), 207, 276
Watson, Sheila: *The Double Hook*, 298, 314
Webb, Phyllis, 148
Wells, H. G., 234; *The Island of Dr. Moreau*, 283; *The Time Machine*, 104, 283; *The War of the Worlds*, 283
Wharton, Edith: *The Custom of the Country*, 171; "The Pelican," 3
Whitman, Walt, 210, 222, 225, 252, 324, 386
Wiebe, Rudy, 311; *The Scorched Wood People*, 206; *The Temptations of Big Bear*, 206
Wilde, Oscar, 117, 275–76, 277, 386
Wilderness Tips (short stories), 115
Wilkinson, Anne, 148
Wilson, Edmund, 374; *O Canada*, 372
Wister, Owen: *Virginian*, 252
Witches of Eastwick, The (Updike), 17–22; as magic realism, 20; theme, wickedness and mischief, 17–19; Vietnam War as backdrop, 19, 21
Wizard of Earthsea, A (Le Guin), 285
women's movement, the, 2, 19, 41, 164, 165, 392, 406. *See also* feminists, feminism, and feminist principles
Wonder Woman, 236
Woolf, Virginia, 278–79
Wordsworth, William: *See also* Mother Nature; *Lyrical Ballads*, 373
World War I: *See* First World War
World War II: *See* Second World War
Writers' Union of Canada, 28, 32
Wyndham, John, 283; "Consider Her Ways," 289

Young, David, 31, 45; *Unimaginable Island*, 405
You Went Away (Findley), 207